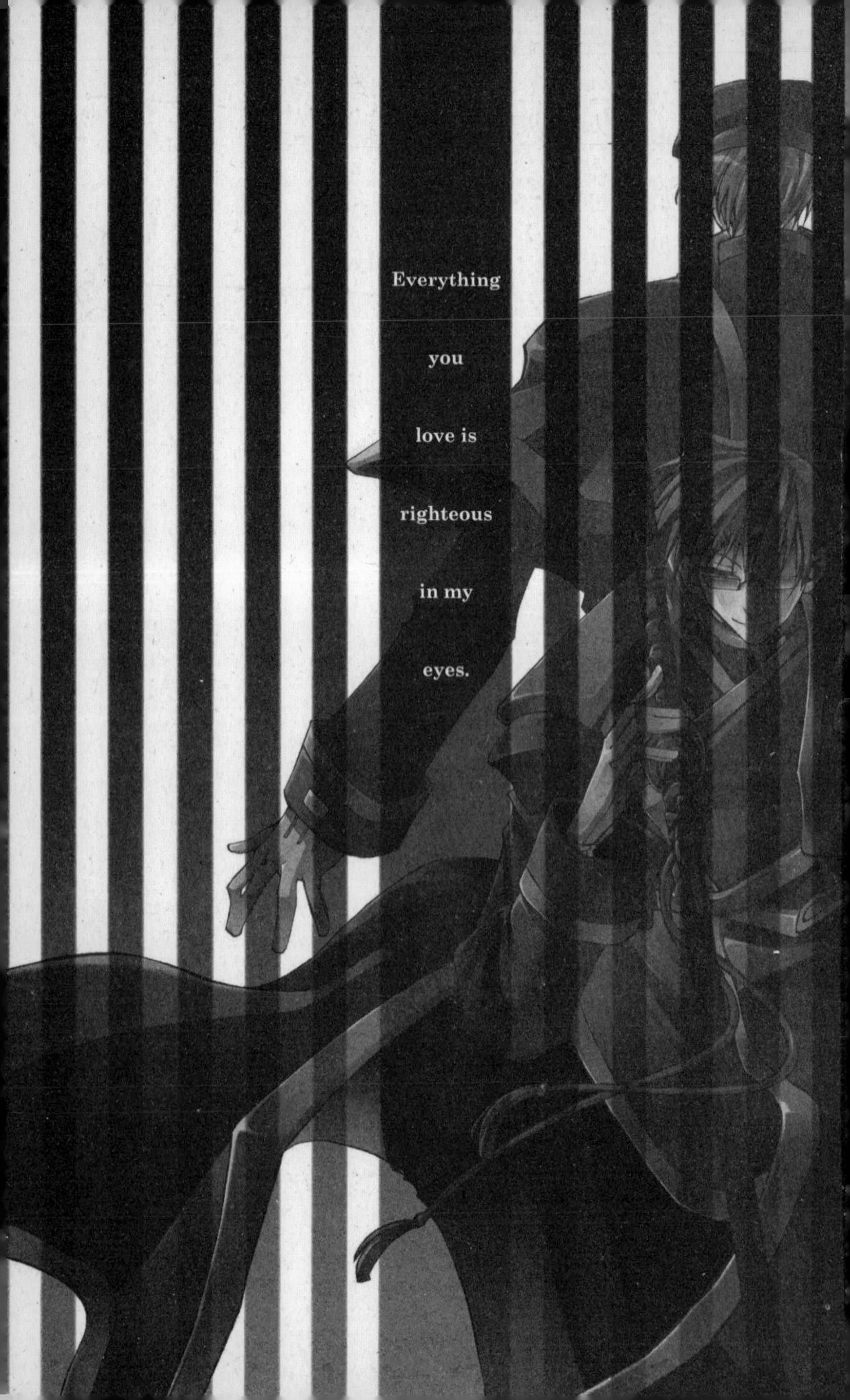
Everything you love is righteous in my eyes.

G H O S T

no Ichihara Presents

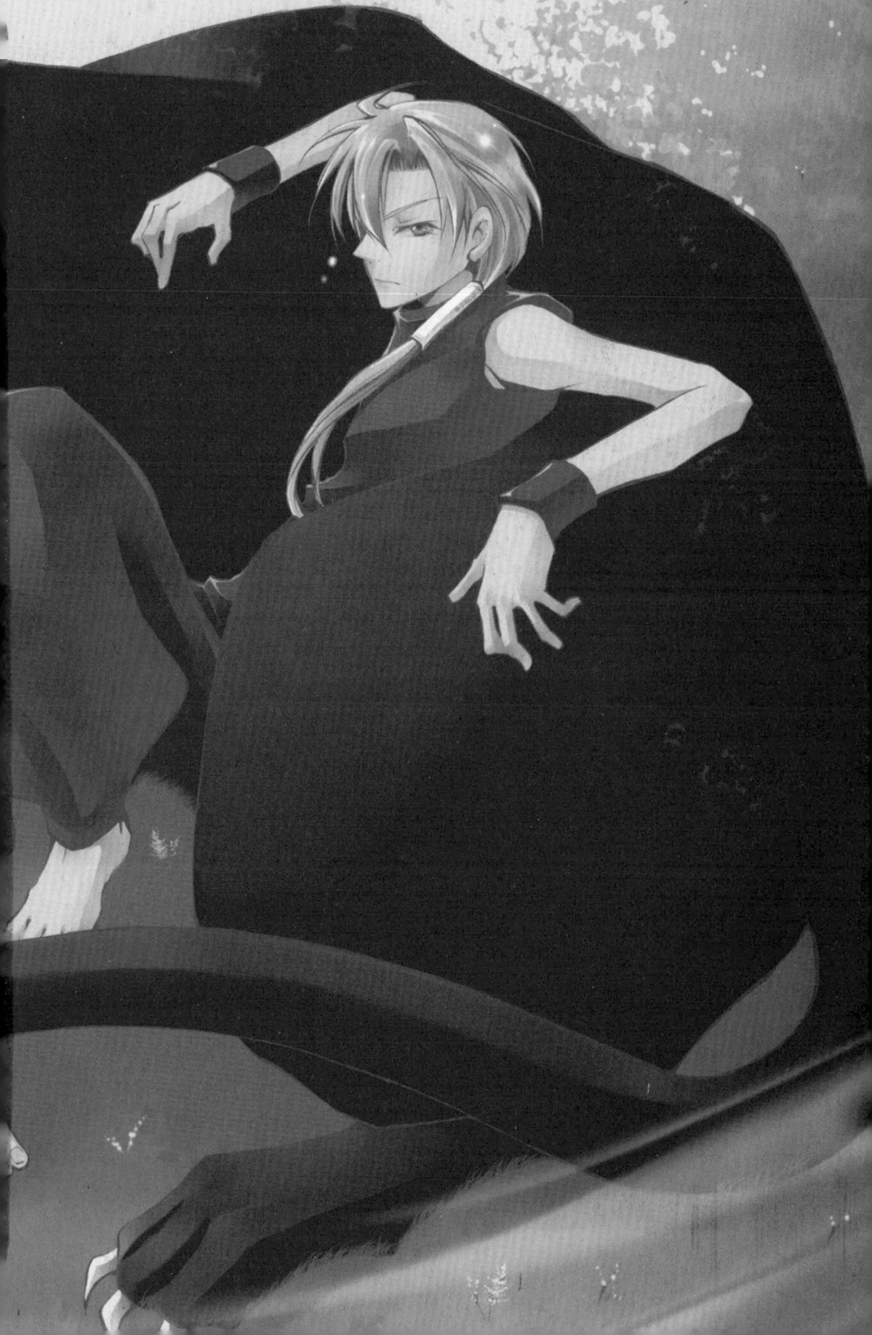

SEVEN

Yuki Amemiya & Yuki

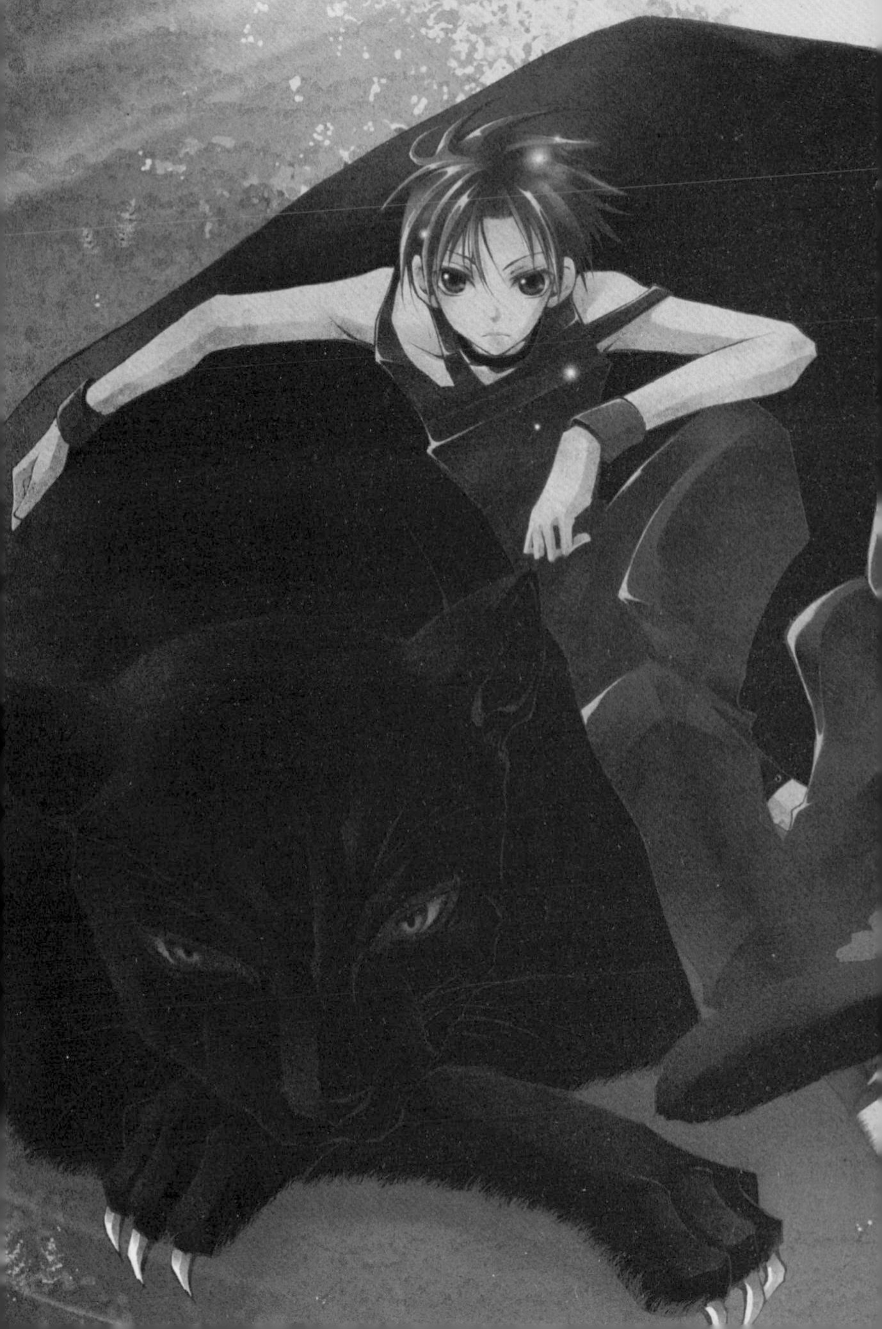

CONTENTS

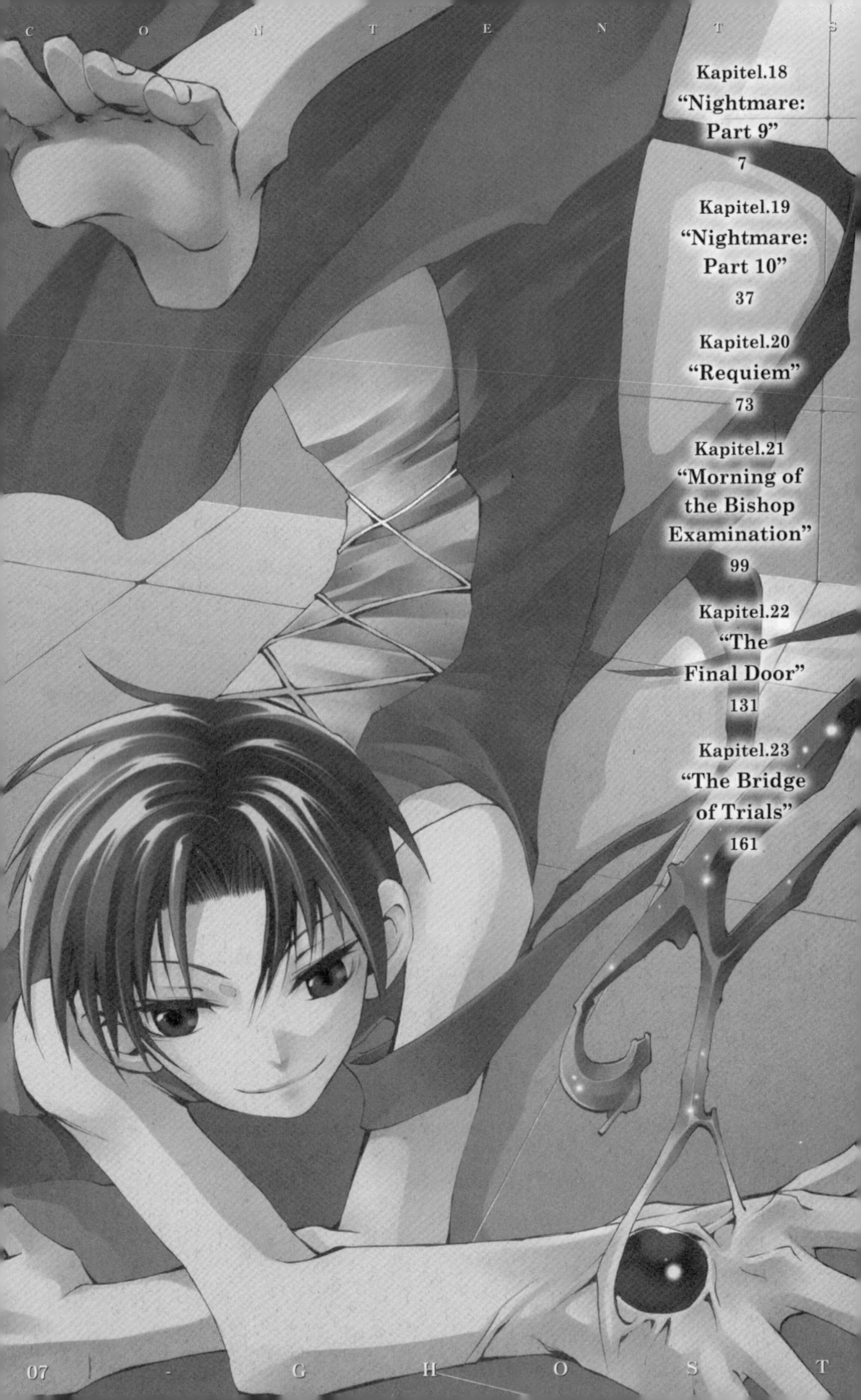

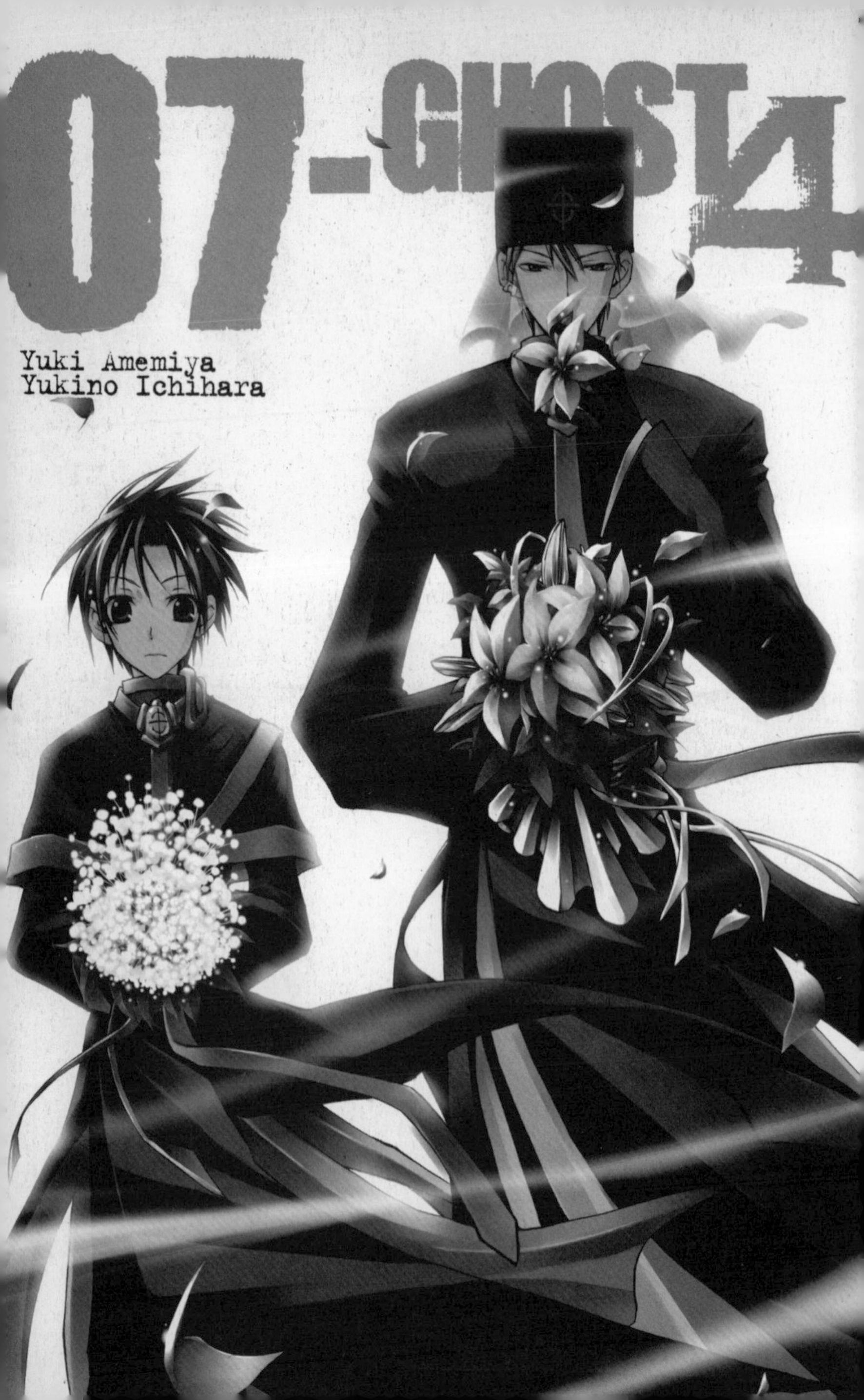
07-GHOST 4
Yuki Amemiya
Yukino Ichihara

Characters

One thousand years ago, two equally powerful nations coexisted. One was the Barsburg Empire, protected by the Eye of Rafael. The other was the Raggs Kingdom, protected by the Eye of Mikael. Now that the Raggs Kingdom has been destroyed, things have changed...

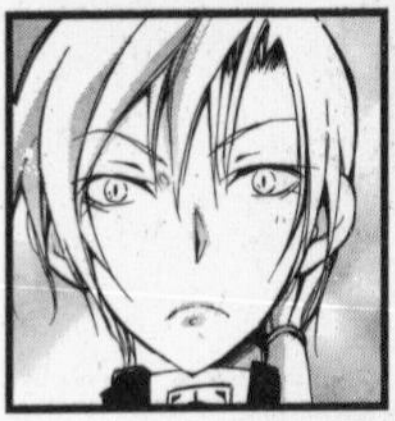

Hakuren

A bishop examinee from the prestigious Oak family. He's Teito's roommate and an ardent admirer of Frau.

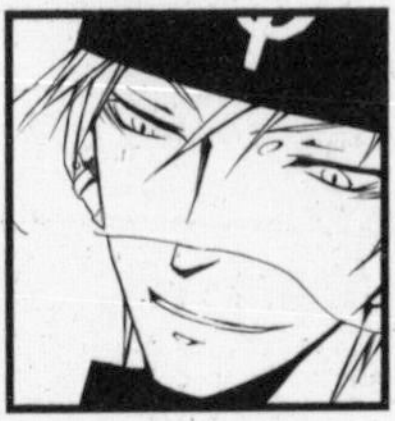

Frau

Bishop who saved Teito when he was fleeing from the academy. He is Zehel of the Seven Ghosts.

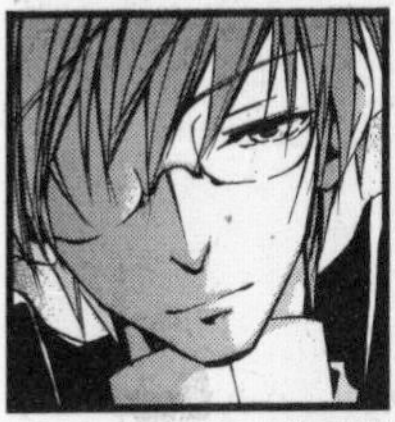

Castor

Bishop who can manipulate puppets. Along with Frau, he shelters Teito and is one of the Seven Ghosts.

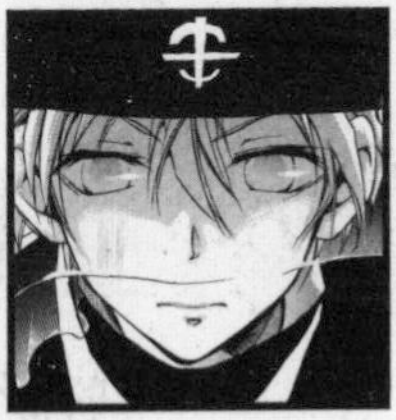

Labrador

Quiet bishop with the power of prophecy. One of the Seven Ghosts.

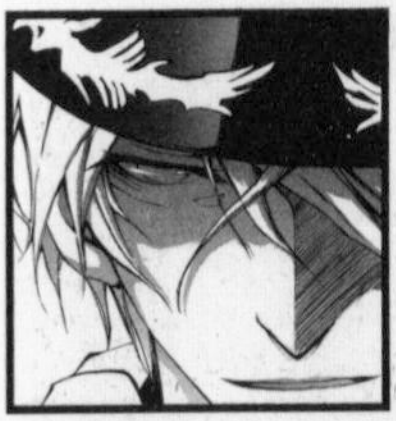

Ayanami

Imperial Army's Chief of Staff. Seeks the Eye of Mikael, and may be responsible for the king of Raggs' death.

Black Hawks

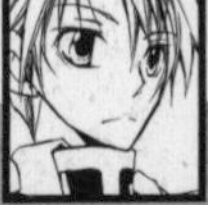

Hyuga's Begleiter: Konatsu

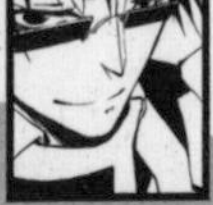

Major Hyuga

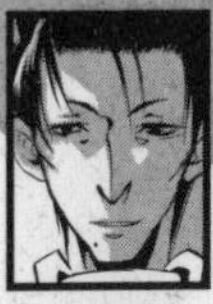

Colonel Katsuragi

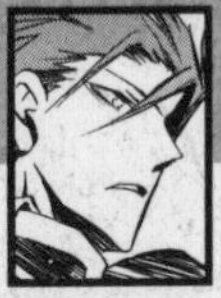

Kuroyuri's Begleiter: Haruse

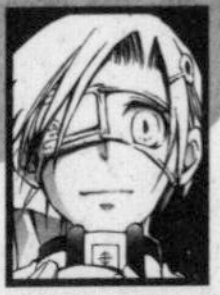

Lieutenant-Colonel Kuroyuri

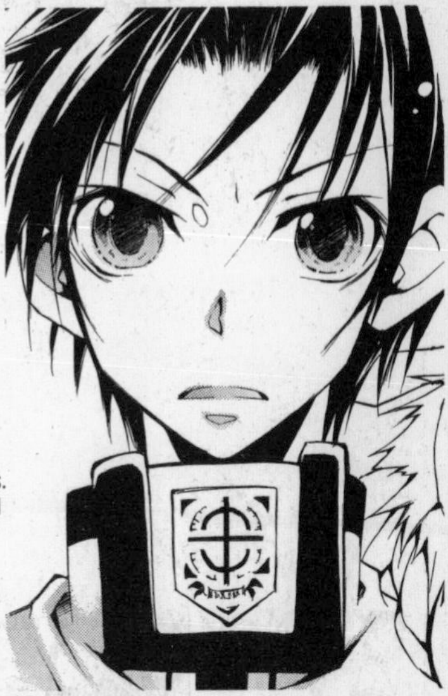

Teito Klein

Born a prince of Raggs, Teito was stripped of his memories and raised as a soldier by the military academy's chairman. He harbors the Eye of Mikael in his right hand. Currently training for the Bishop Examination. A boy of small stature.

Story

Teito is a student at the Barsburg Empire's military academy until the day he discovers that his father was the king of Raggs, the ruler of a kingdom the Barsburg Empire destroyed. Teito receives sanctuary from the Barsburg Church, but loses his best friend Mikage, who Ayanami controlled like a puppet to get at Teito. To avenge Mikage's death, Teito decides to become a bishop to obtain travel privileges to enter District 1 without inspection. Meanwhile, Ayanami's Black Hawks commit murder on church grounds!

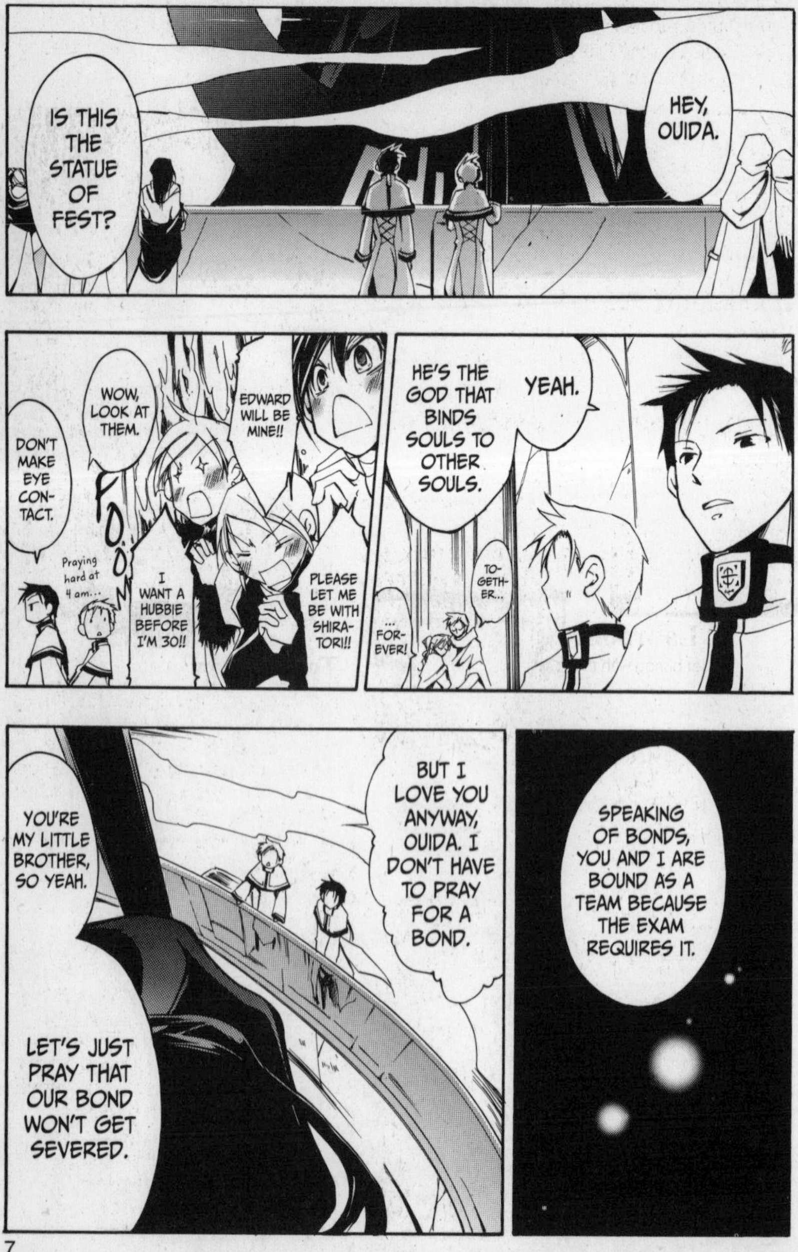
HEY, OUIDA.
IS THIS THE STATUE OF FEST?
YEAH.
HE'S THE GOD THAT BINDS SOULS TO OTHER SOULS.
TO-GETH-ER...
...FOR-EVER!
EDWARD WILL BE MINE!!
WOW, LOOK AT THEM.
DON'T MAKE EYE CON-TACT.
FOOM
PLEASE LET ME BE WITH SHIRA-TORI!!
I WANT A HUBBIE BEFORE I'M 30!!
Praying hard at 4 am...
SPEAKING OF BONDS, YOU AND I ARE BOUND AS A TEAM BECAUSE THE EXAM REQUIRES IT.
BUT I LOVE YOU ANYWAY, OUIDA. I DON'T HAVE TO PRAY FOR A BOND.
YOU'RE MY LITTLE BROTHER, SO YEAH.
LET'S JUST PRAY THAT OUR BOND WON'T GET SEVERED.

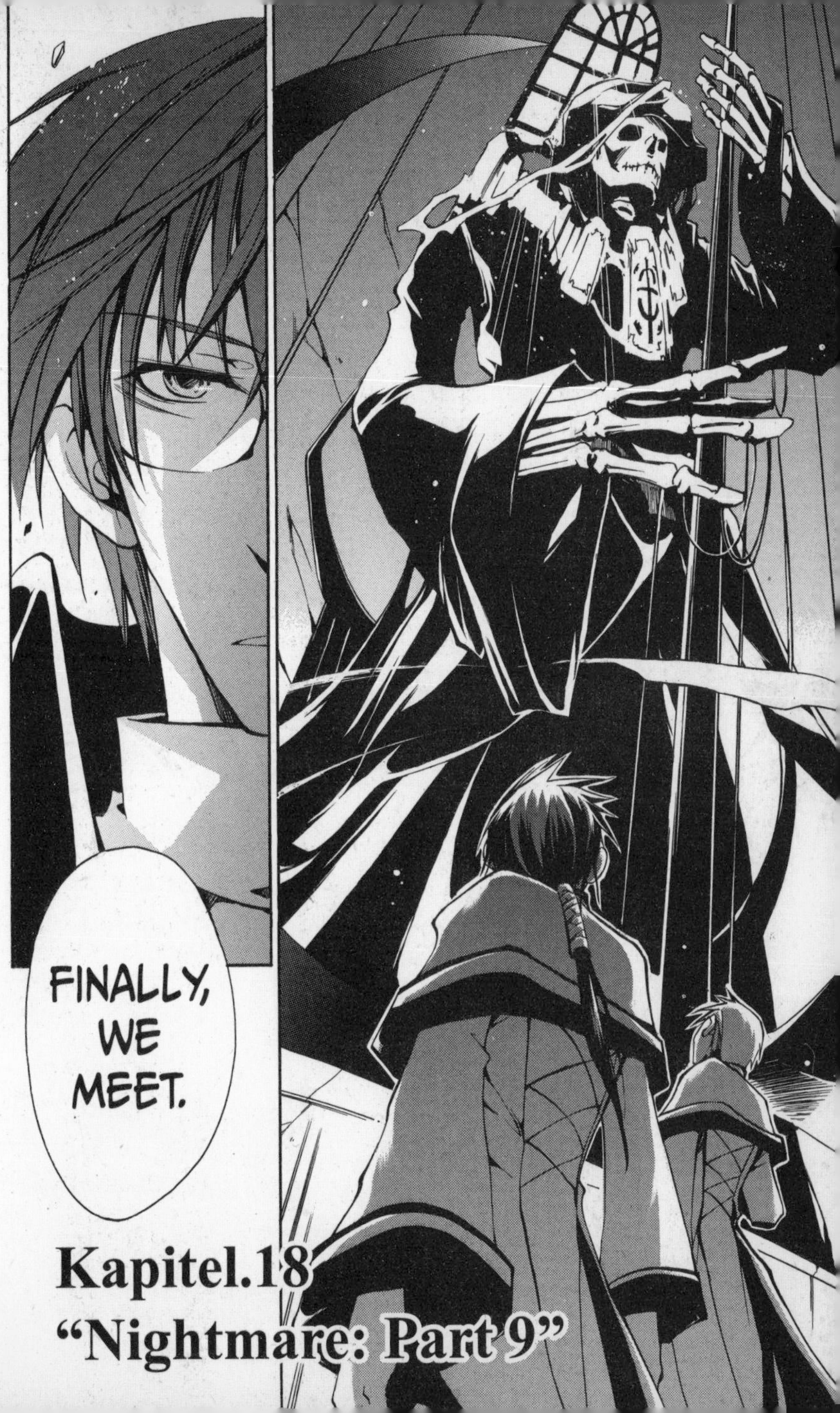
FINALLY, WE MEET.

Kapitel.18
"Nightmare: Part 9"

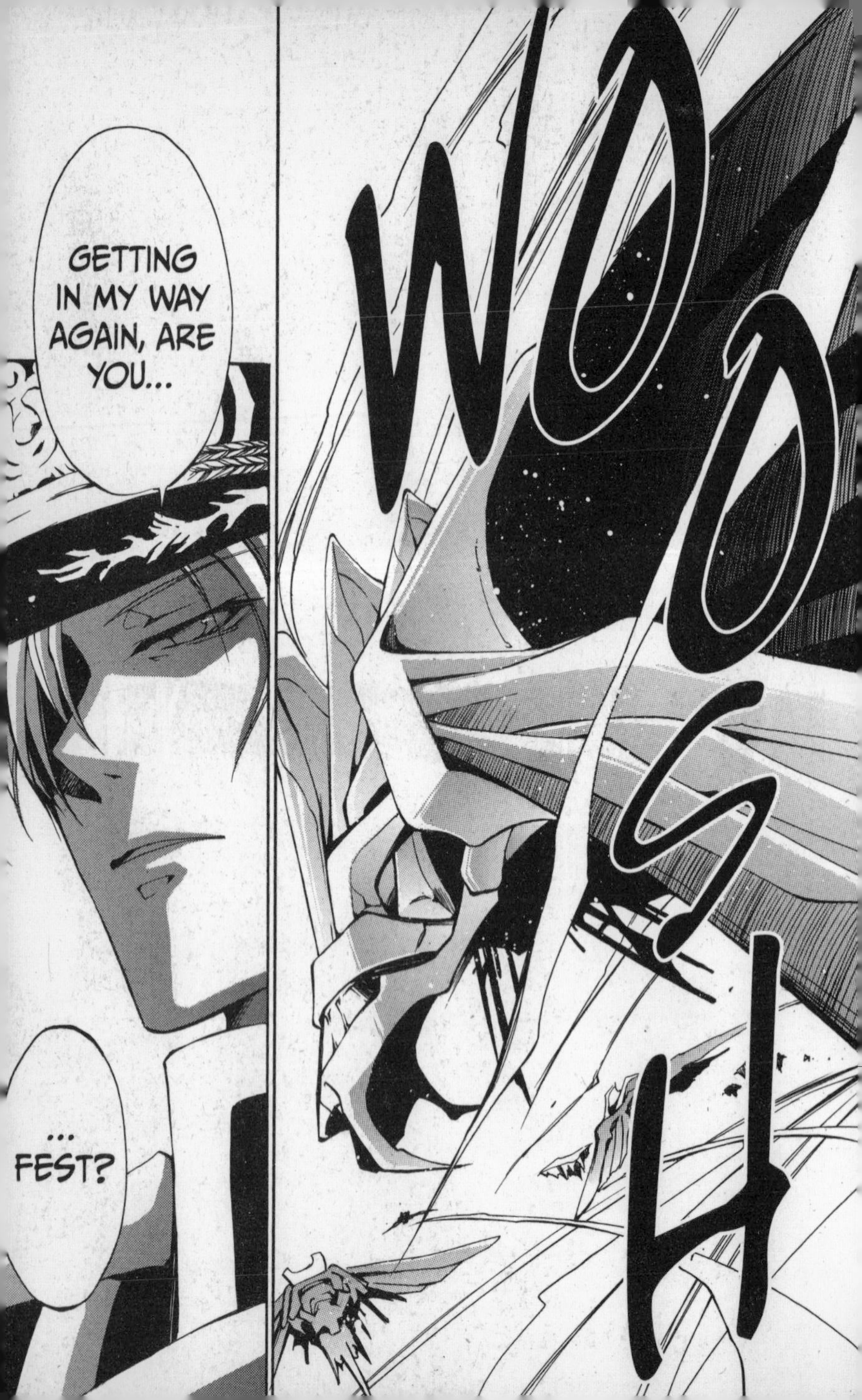
WOOSH
GETTING IN MY WAY AGAIN, ARE YOU...
... FEST?

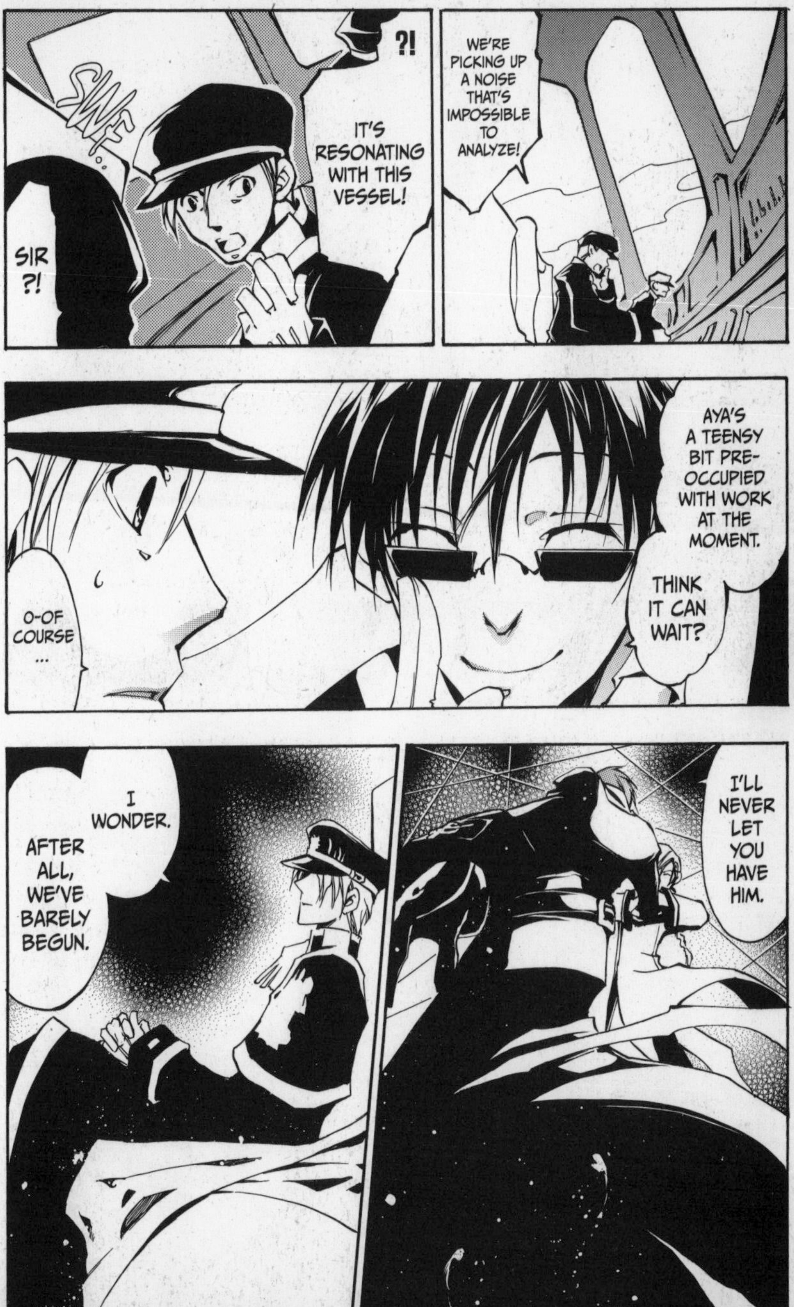
WE'RE PICKING UP A NOISE THAT'S IMPOSSIBLE TO ANALYZE!
?!
IT'S RESONATING WITH THIS VESSEL!
SWF
SIR ?!
AYA'S A TEENSY BIT PRE-OCCUPIED WITH WORK AT THE MOMENT.
THINK IT CAN WAIT?
O-OF COURSE ...
I'LL NEVER LET YOU HAVE HIM.
I WONDER.
AFTER ALL, WE'VE BARELY BEGUN.

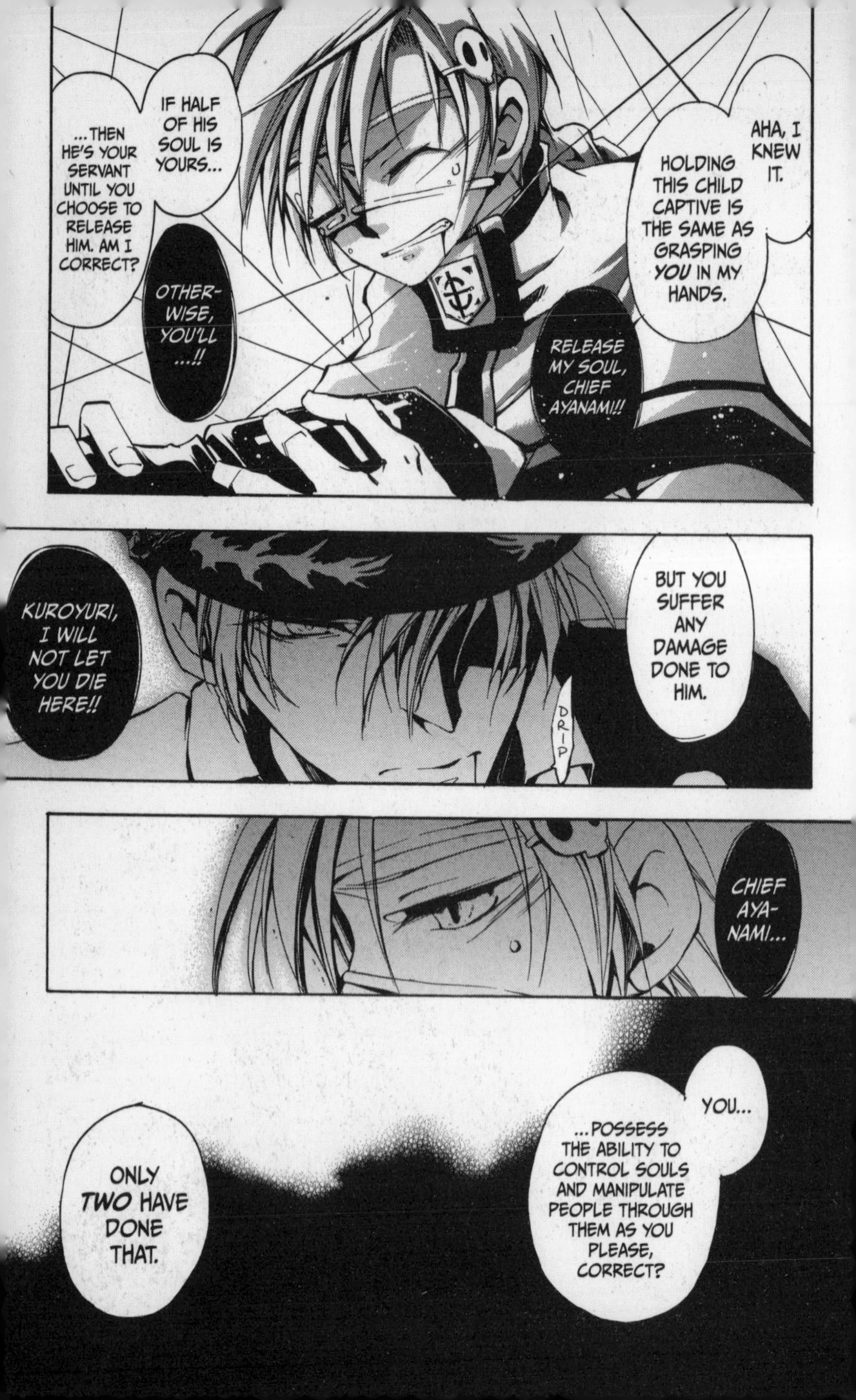
AHA, I KNEW IT.
HOLDING THIS CHILD CAPTIVE IS THE SAME AS GRASPING *YOU* IN MY HANDS.
RELEASE MY SOUL, CHIEF AYANAMI!!
IF HALF OF HIS SOUL IS YOURS...
...THEN HE'S YOUR SERVANT UNTIL YOU CHOOSE TO RELEASE HIM. AM I CORRECT?
OTHER-WISE, YOU'LL ...!!
BUT YOU SUFFER ANY DAMAGE DONE TO HIM.
DRIP
KUROYURI, I WILL NOT LET YOU DIE HERE!!
CHIEF AYA-NAMI...
YOU...
...POSSESS THE ABILITY TO CONTROL SOULS AND MANIPULATE PEOPLE THROUGH THEM AS YOU PLEASE, CORRECT?
ONLY *TWO* HAVE DONE THAT.

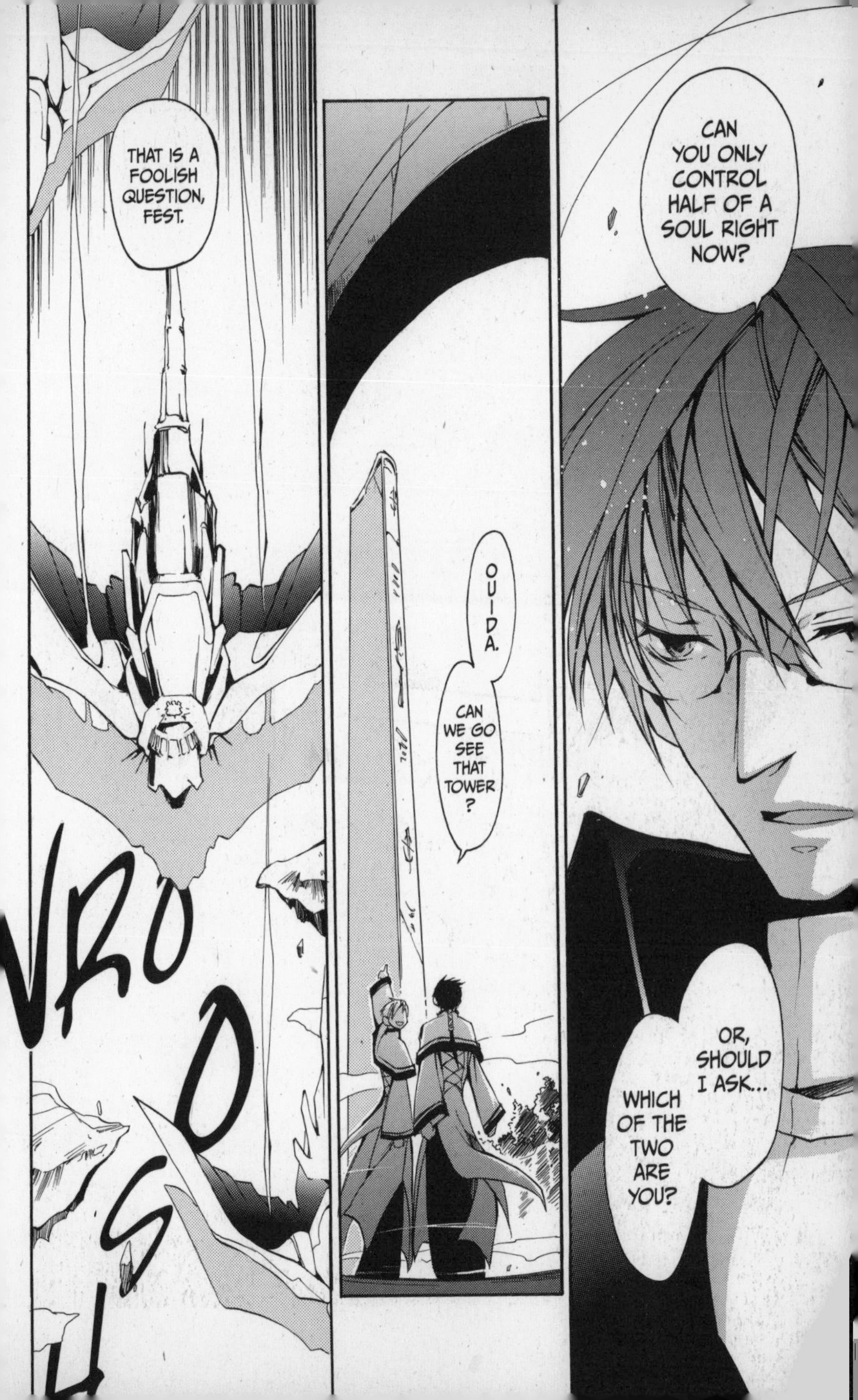
CAN YOU ONLY CONTROL HALF OF A SOUL RIGHT NOW?
OR, SHOULD I ASK...
WHICH OF THE TWO ARE YOU?
OUIDA.
CAN WE GO SEE THAT TOWER?
THAT IS A FOOLISH QUESTION, FEST.

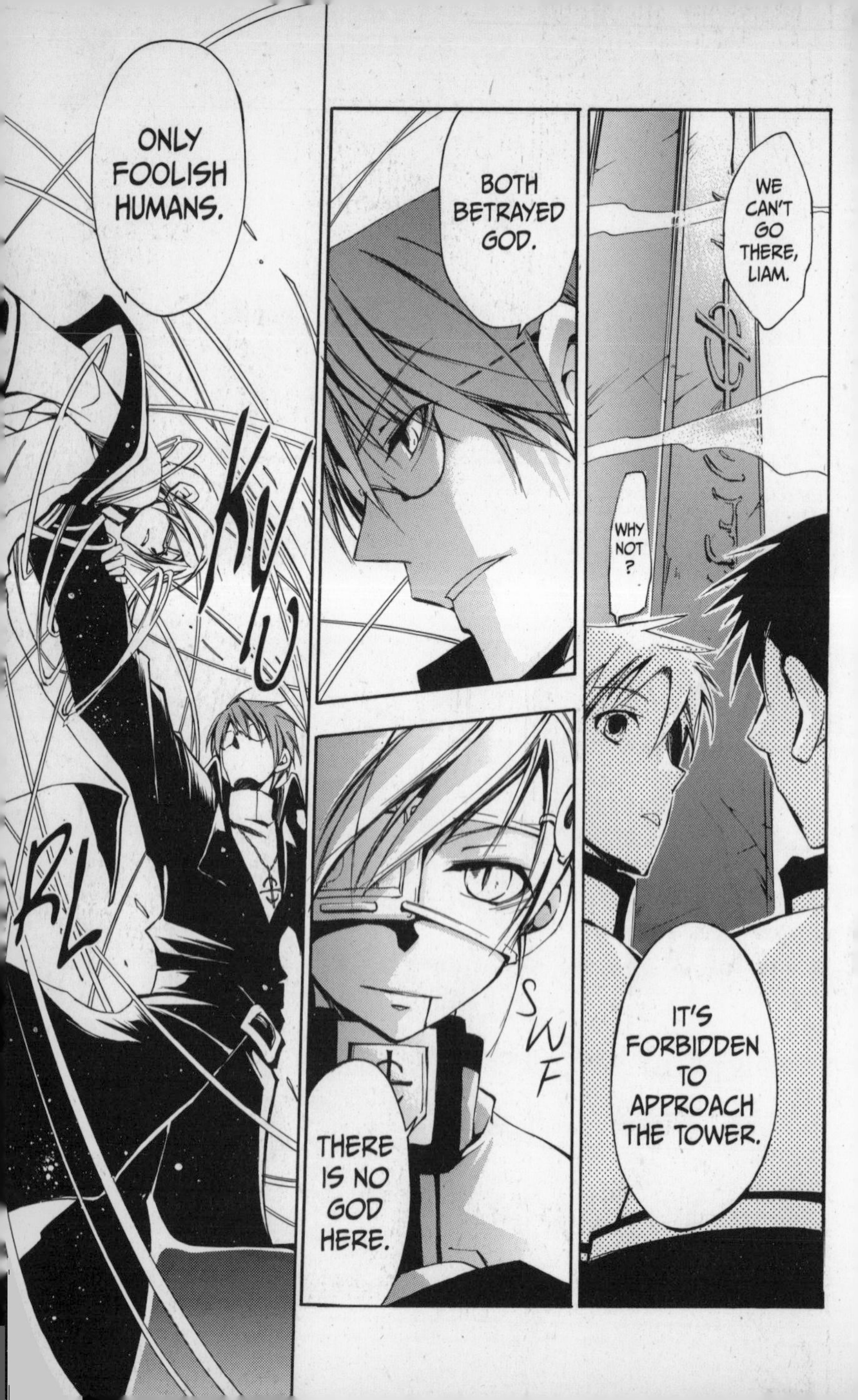
WE CAN'T GO THERE, LIAM.
WHY NOT?
IT'S FORBIDDEN TO APPROACH THE TOWER.
BOTH BETRAYED GOD.
SWF
THERE IS NO GOD HERE.
ONLY FOOLISH HUMANS.
KYU
RL

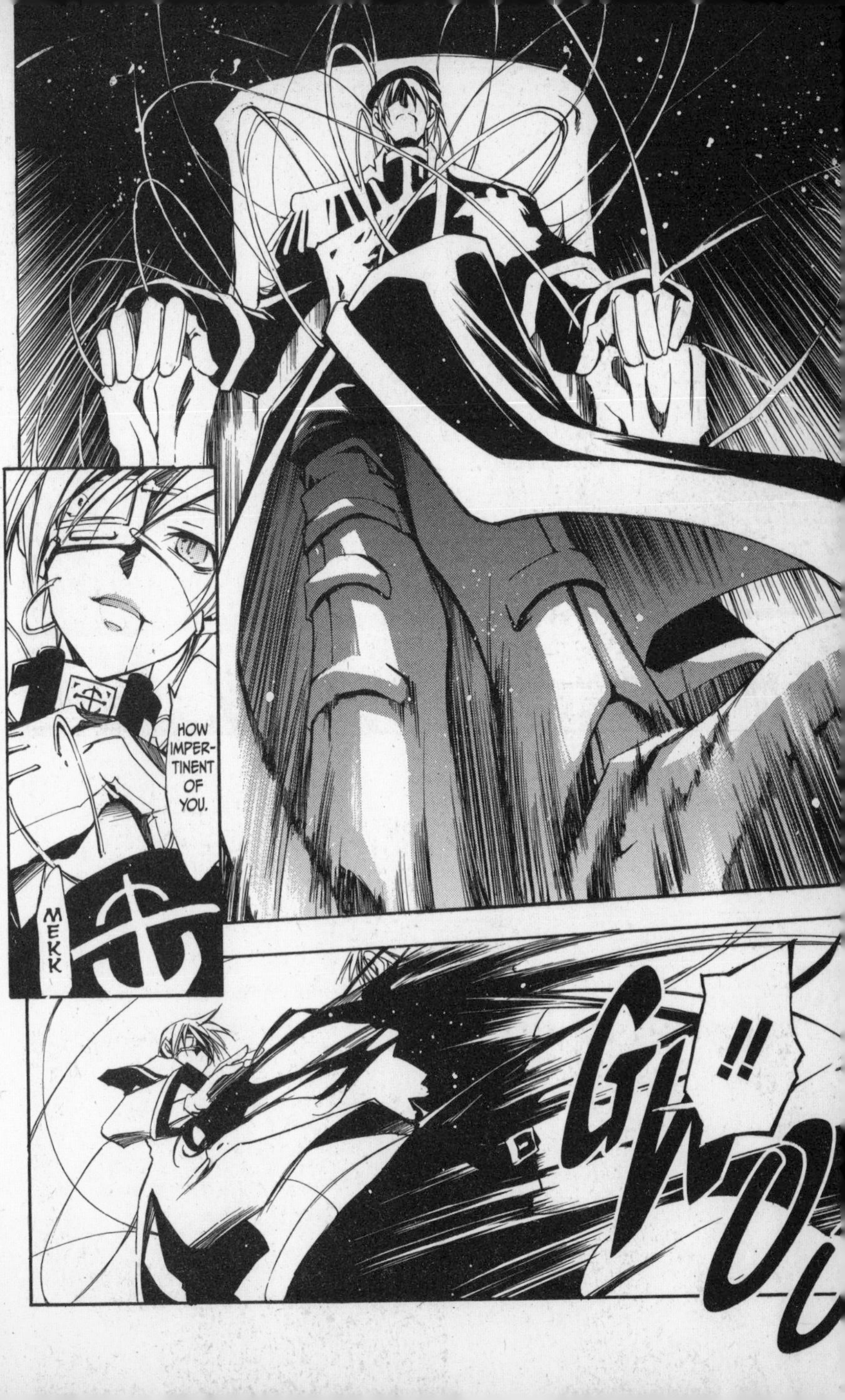
HOW IMPERTINENT OF YOU.
MEKK
!!
GWOO

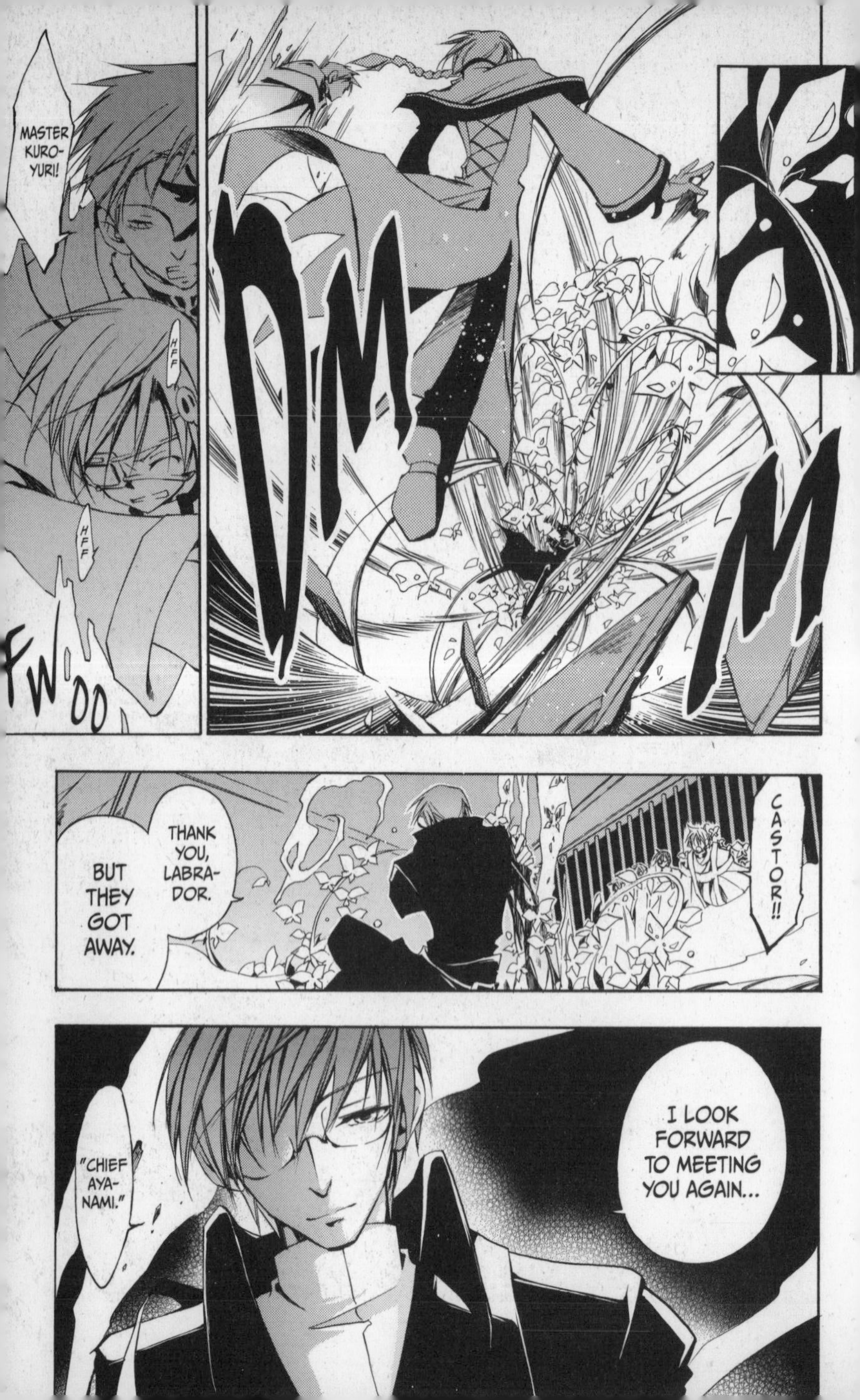
MASTER KURO-YURI!
HFF
HFF
FWOO
CASTOR!!
THANK YOU, LABRADOR.
BUT THEY GOT AWAY.
I LOOK FORWARD TO MEETING YOU AGAIN...
"CHIEF AYANAMI."

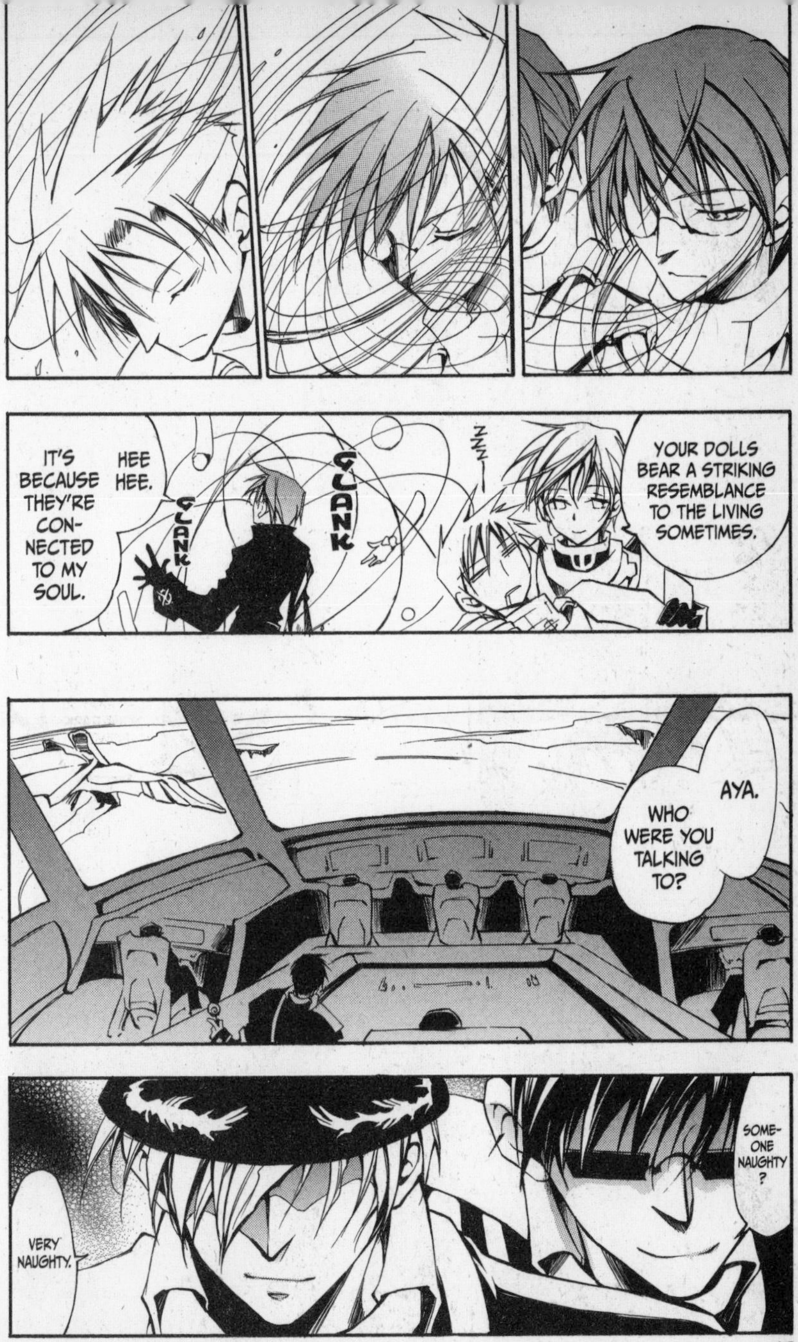
YOUR DOLLS BEAR A STRIKING RESEMBLANCE TO THE LIVING SOMETIMES.
ZZZ
CLANK
CLANK
HEE HEE.
IT'S BECAUSE THEY'RE CON-NECTED TO MY SOUL.
AYA.
WHO WERE YOU TALKING TO?
SOME-ONE NAUGHTY?
VERY NAUGHTY.

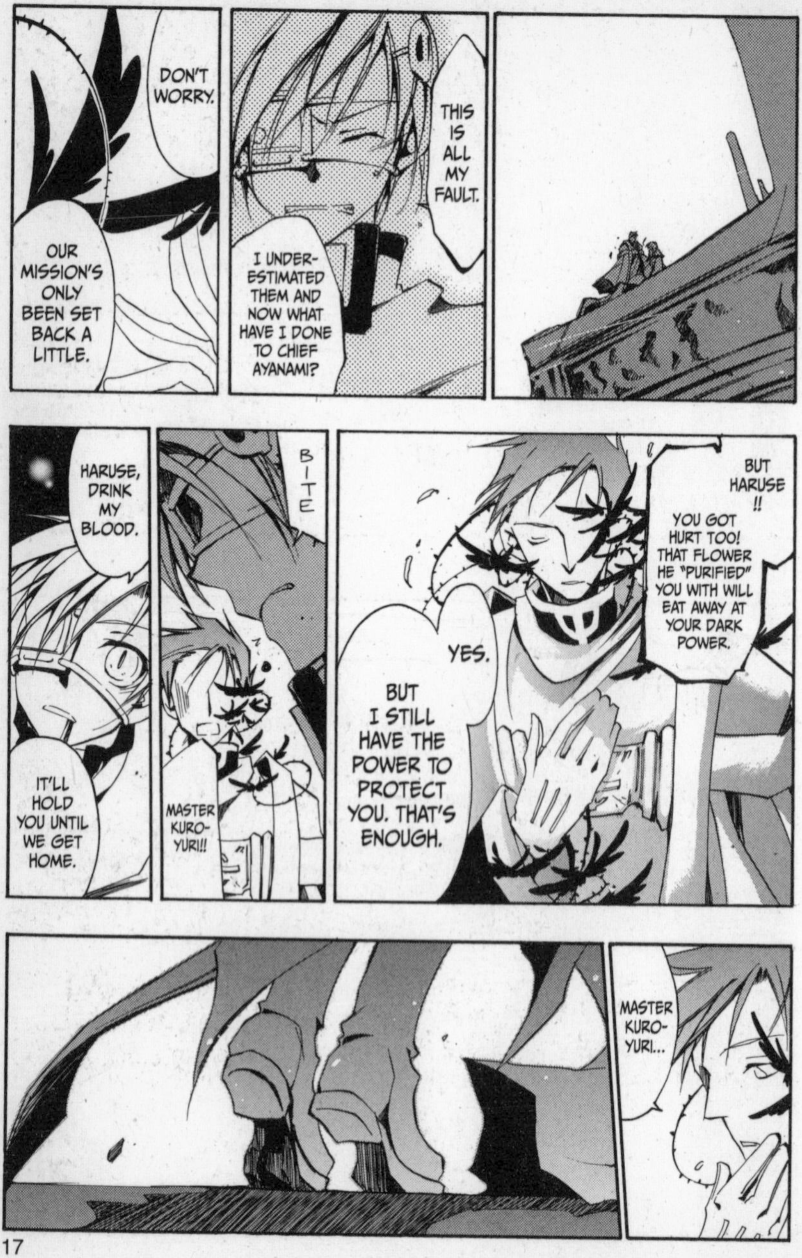
THIS IS ALL MY FAULT.
I UNDER-ESTIMATED THEM AND NOW WHAT HAVE I DONE TO CHIEF AYANAMI?
DON'T WORRY.
OUR MISSION'S ONLY BEEN SET BACK A LITTLE.
BUT HARUSE!!
YOU GOT HURT TOO! THAT FLOWER HE "PURIFIED" YOU WITH WILL EAT AWAY AT YOUR DARK POWER.
YES.
BUT I STILL HAVE THE POWER TO PROTECT YOU. THAT'S ENOUGH.
BITE
MASTER KURO-YURI!!
HARUSE, DRINK MY BLOOD.
IT'LL HOLD YOU UNTIL WE GET HOME.
MASTER KURO-YURI...

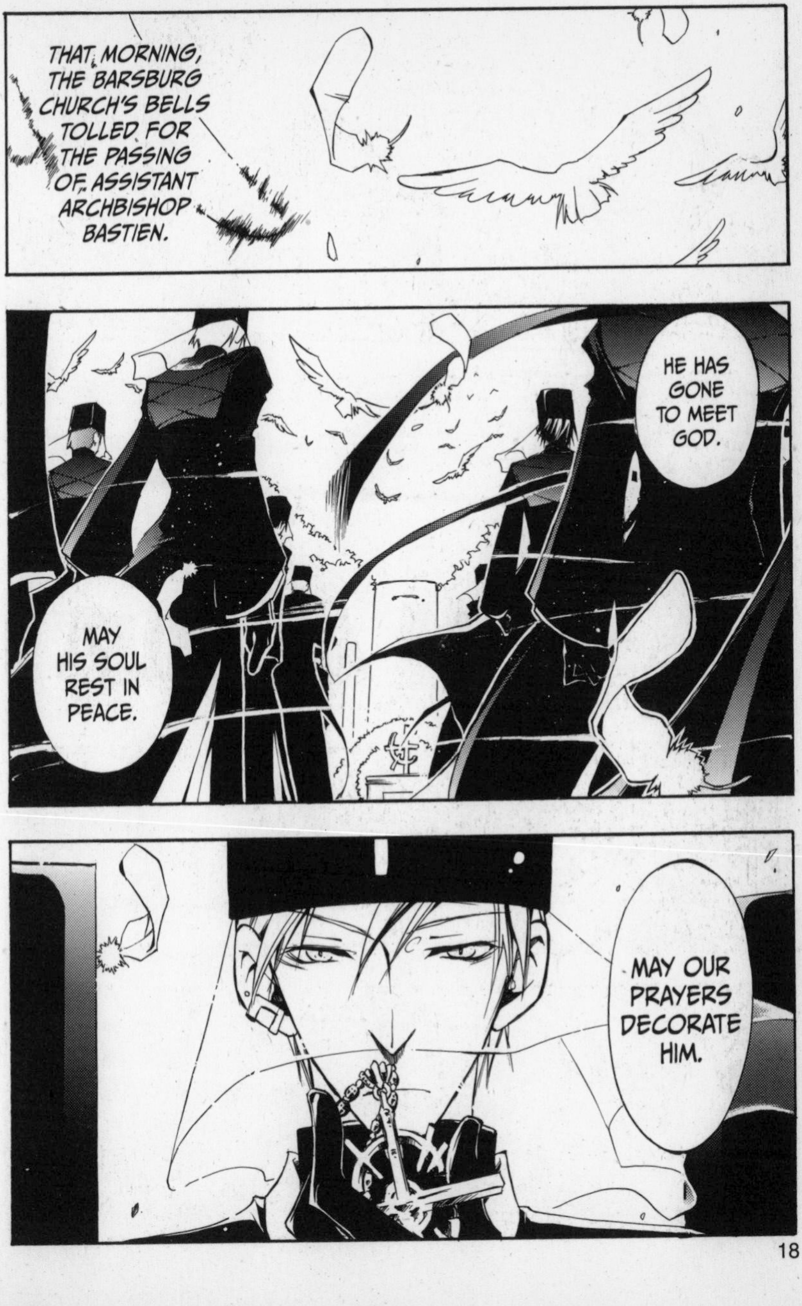
THAT MORNING, THE BARSBURG CHURCH'S BELLS TOLLED FOR THE PASSING OF ASSISTANT ARCHBISHOP BASTIEN.
HE HAS GONE TO MEET GOD.
MAY HIS SOUL REST IN PEACE.
MAY OUR PRAYERS DECORATE HIM.

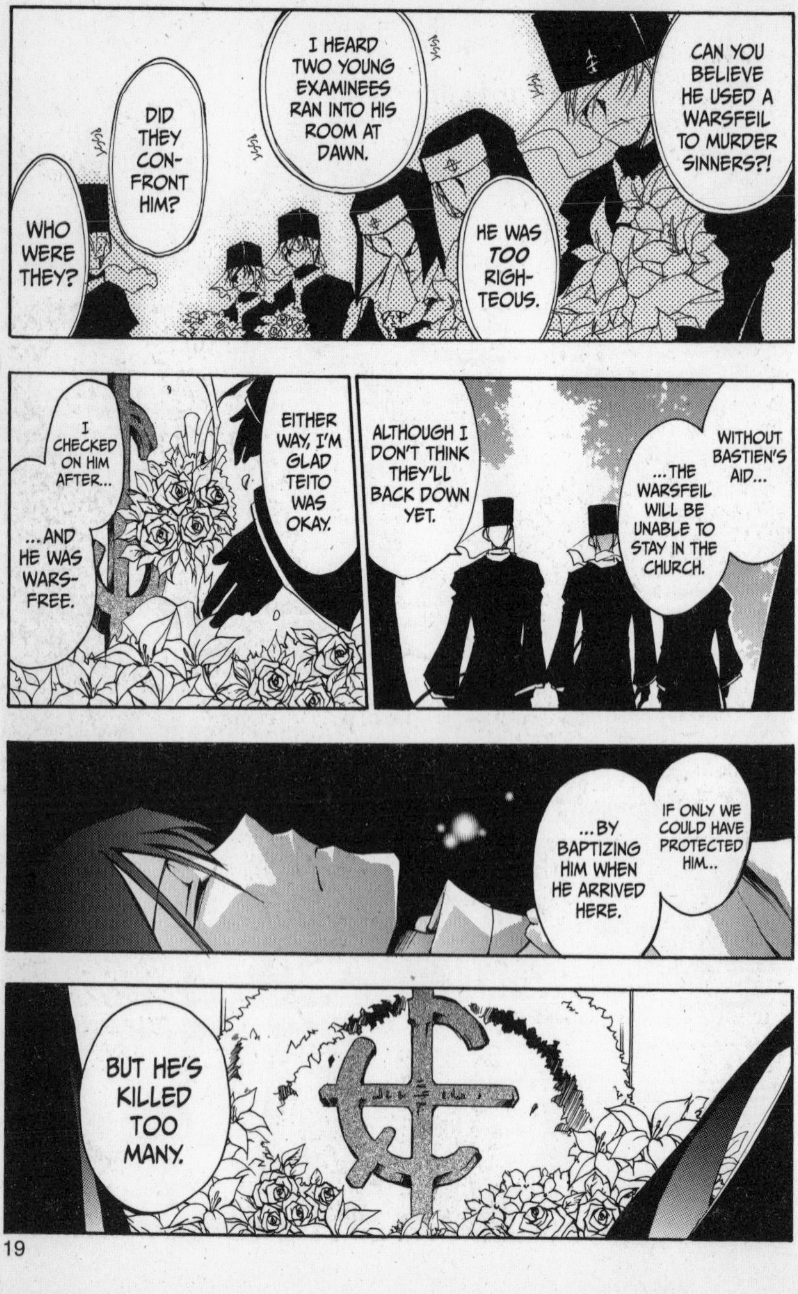
CAN YOU BELIEVE HE USED A WARSFEIL TO MURDER SINNERS?!
I HEARD TWO YOUNG EXAMINEES RAN INTO HIS ROOM AT DAWN.
HE WAS *TOO* RIGHTEOUS.
DID THEY CONFRONT HIM?
WHO WERE THEY?
WITHOUT BASTIEN'S AID...
...THE WARSFEIL WILL BE UNABLE TO STAY IN THE CHURCH.
ALTHOUGH I DON'T THINK THEY'LL BACK DOWN YET.
EITHER WAY, I'M GLAD TEITO WAS OKAY.
I CHECKED ON HIM AFTER...
...AND HE WAS WARS-FREE.
IF ONLY WE COULD HAVE PROTECTED HIM...
...BY BAPTIZING HIM WHEN HE ARRIVED HERE.
BUT HE'S KILLED TOO MANY.

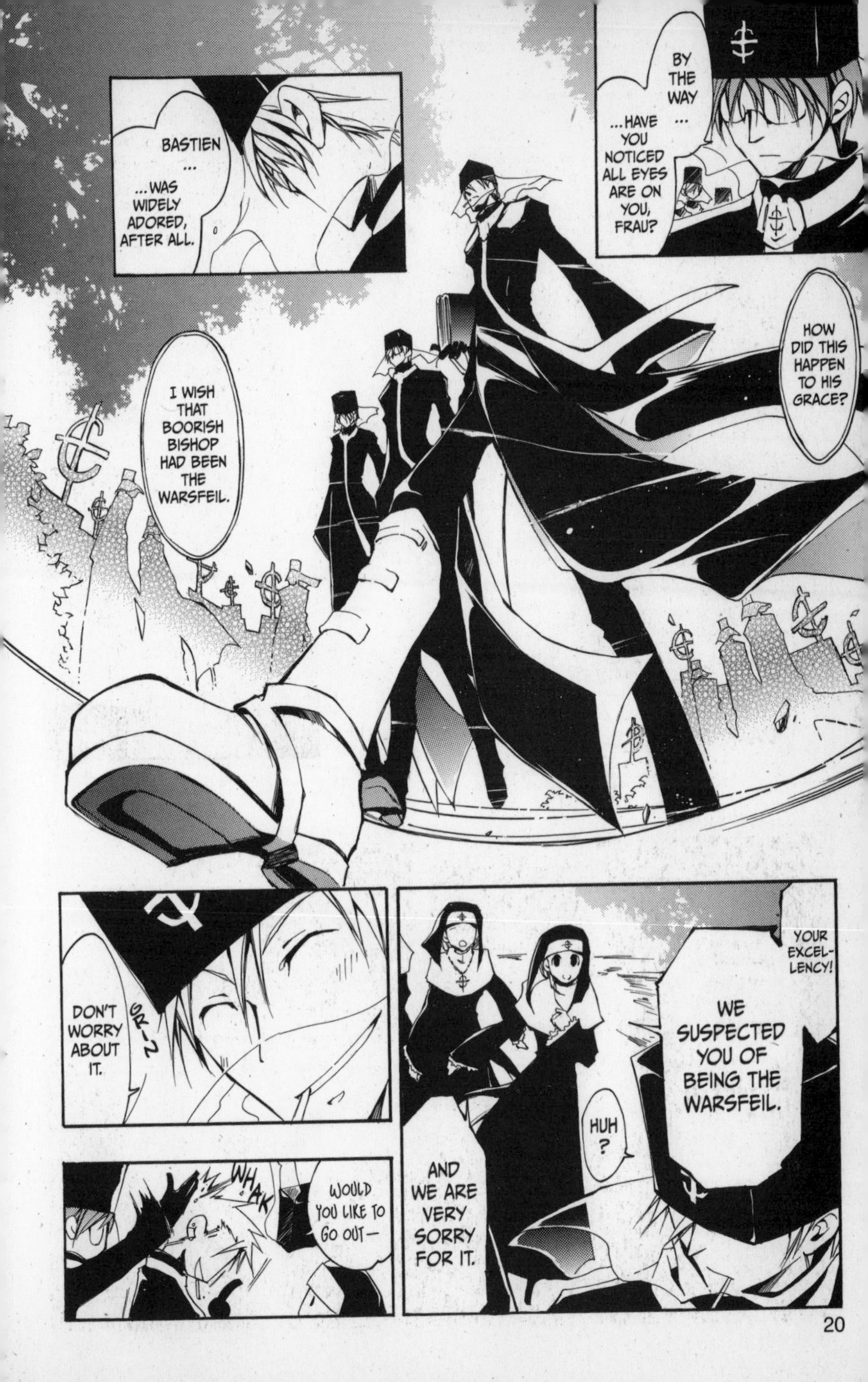
BY THE WAY ...
...HAVE YOU NOTICED ALL EYES ARE ON YOU, FRAU?
BASTIEN ...
...WAS WIDELY ADORED, AFTER ALL.
HOW DID THIS HAPPEN TO HIS GRACE?
I WISH THAT BOORISH BISHOP HAD BEEN THE WARSFEIL.
YOUR EXCEL-LENCY!
WE SUSPECTED YOU OF BEING THE WARSFEIL.
HUH?
AND WE ARE VERY SORRY FOR IT.
GRIN
DON'T WORRY ABOUT IT.
WHAK
WOULD YOU LIKE TO GO OUT—

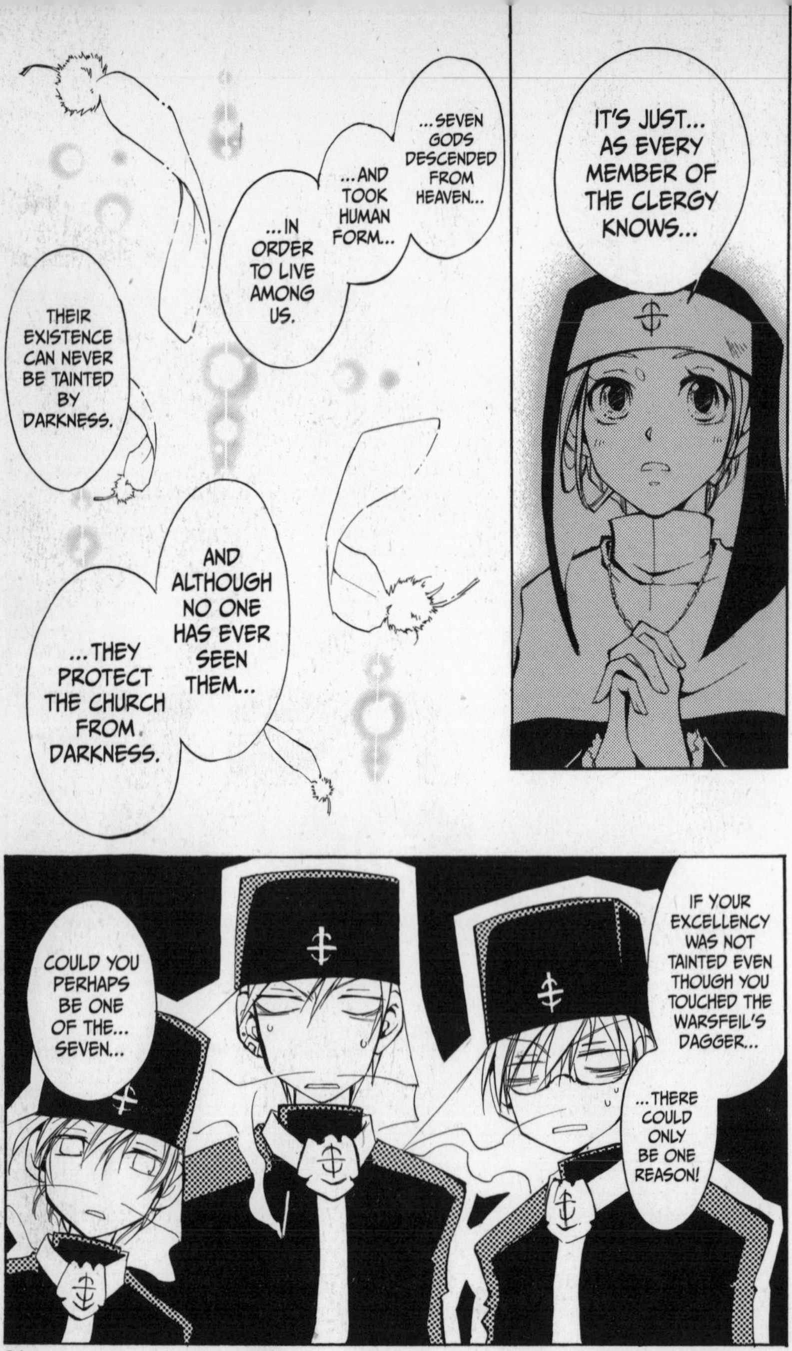
IT'S JUST... AS EVERY MEMBER OF THE CLERGY KNOWS...
...SEVEN GODS DESCENDED FROM HEAVEN...
...AND TOOK HUMAN FORM...
...IN ORDER TO LIVE AMONG US.
THEIR EXISTENCE CAN NEVER BE TAINTED BY DARKNESS.
AND ALTHOUGH NO ONE HAS EVER SEEN THEM...
...THEY PROTECT THE CHURCH FROM DARKNESS.
IF YOUR EXCELLENCY WAS NOT TAINTED EVEN THOUGH YOU TOUCHED THE WARSFEIL'S DAGGER...
...THERE COULD ONLY BE ONE REASON!
COULD YOU PERHAPS BE ONE OF THE... SEVEN...

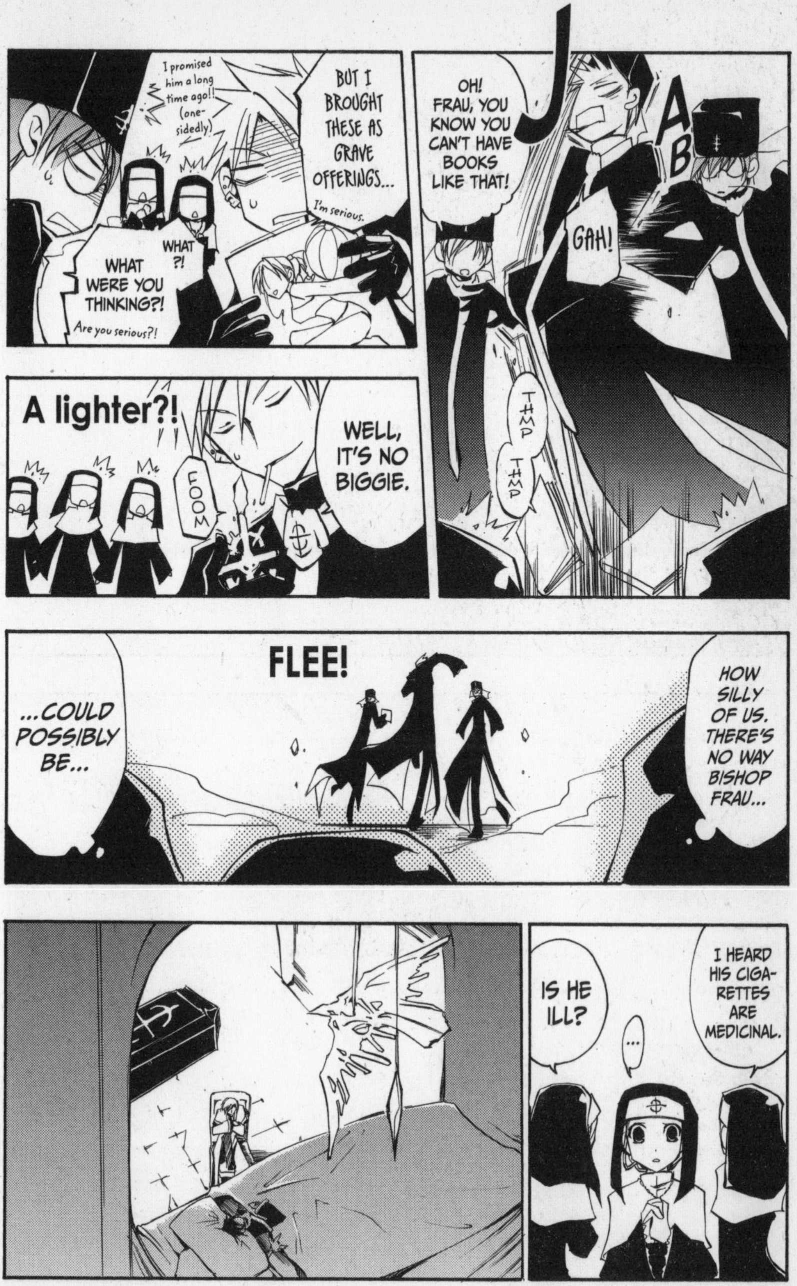
OH! FRAU, YOU KNOW YOU CAN'T HAVE BOOKS LIKE THAT!
JAB
GAH!
THMP
THMP
BUT I BROUGHT THESE AS GRAVE OFFERINGS...
I'm serious.
I promised him a long time ago!! (one-sidedly)
WHAT?!
WHAT WERE YOU THINKING?!
Are you serious?!
WELL, IT'S NO BIGGIE.
FOOM
A lighter?!
HOW SILLY OF US. THERE'S NO WAY BISHOP FRAU...
FLEE!
...COULD POSSIBLY BE...
I HEARD HIS CIGA-RETTES ARE MEDICINAL.
...
IS HE ILL?

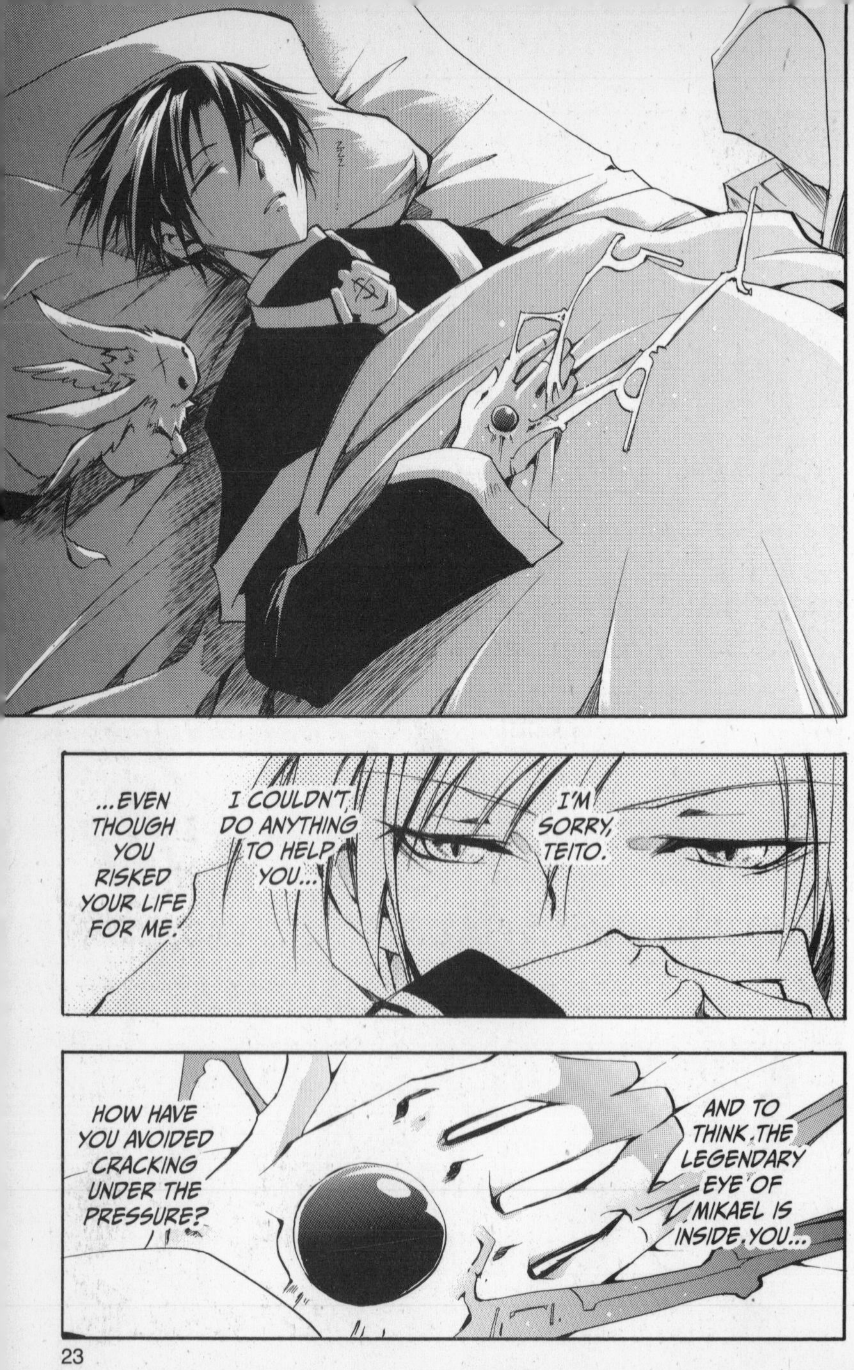
I'M SORRY, TEITO.
I COULDN'T DO ANYTHING TO HELP YOU...
...EVEN THOUGH YOU RISKED YOUR LIFE FOR ME.
AND TO THINK THE LEGENDARY EYE OF MIKAEL IS INSIDE YOU...
HOW HAVE YOU AVOIDED CRACKING UNDER THE PRESSURE?

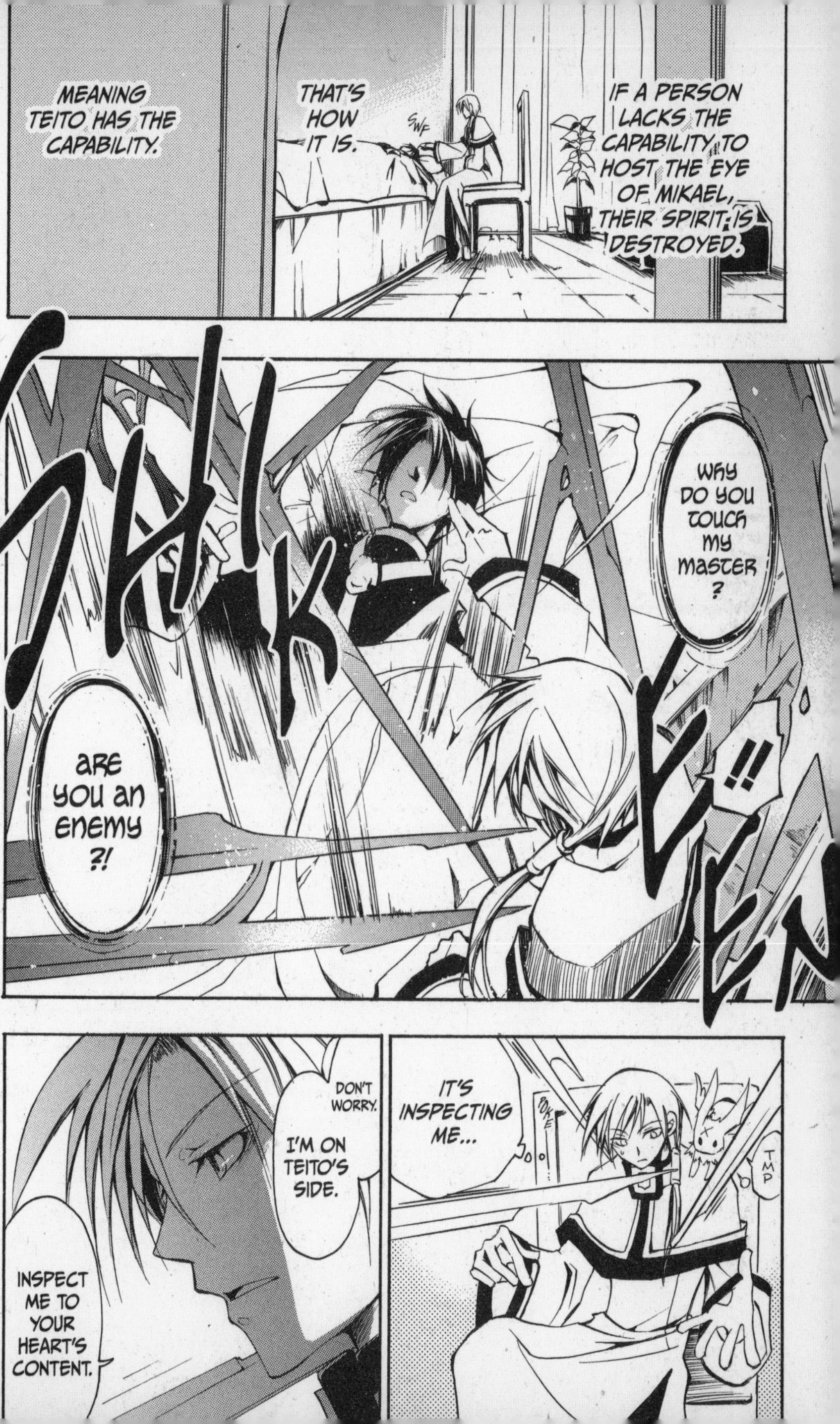
IF A PERSON LACKS THE CAPABILITY TO HOST THE EYE OF MIKAEL, THEIR SPIRIT IS DESTROYED.
SWF
THAT'S HOW IT IS.
MEANING TEITO HAS THE CAPABILITY.
WHY DO YOU TOUCH MY MASTER ?
!!
ARE YOU AN ENEMY ?!
TMP
IT'S INSPECTING ME...
POKE
DON'T WORRY.
I'M ON TEITO'S SIDE.
INSPECT ME TO YOUR HEART'S CONTENT.

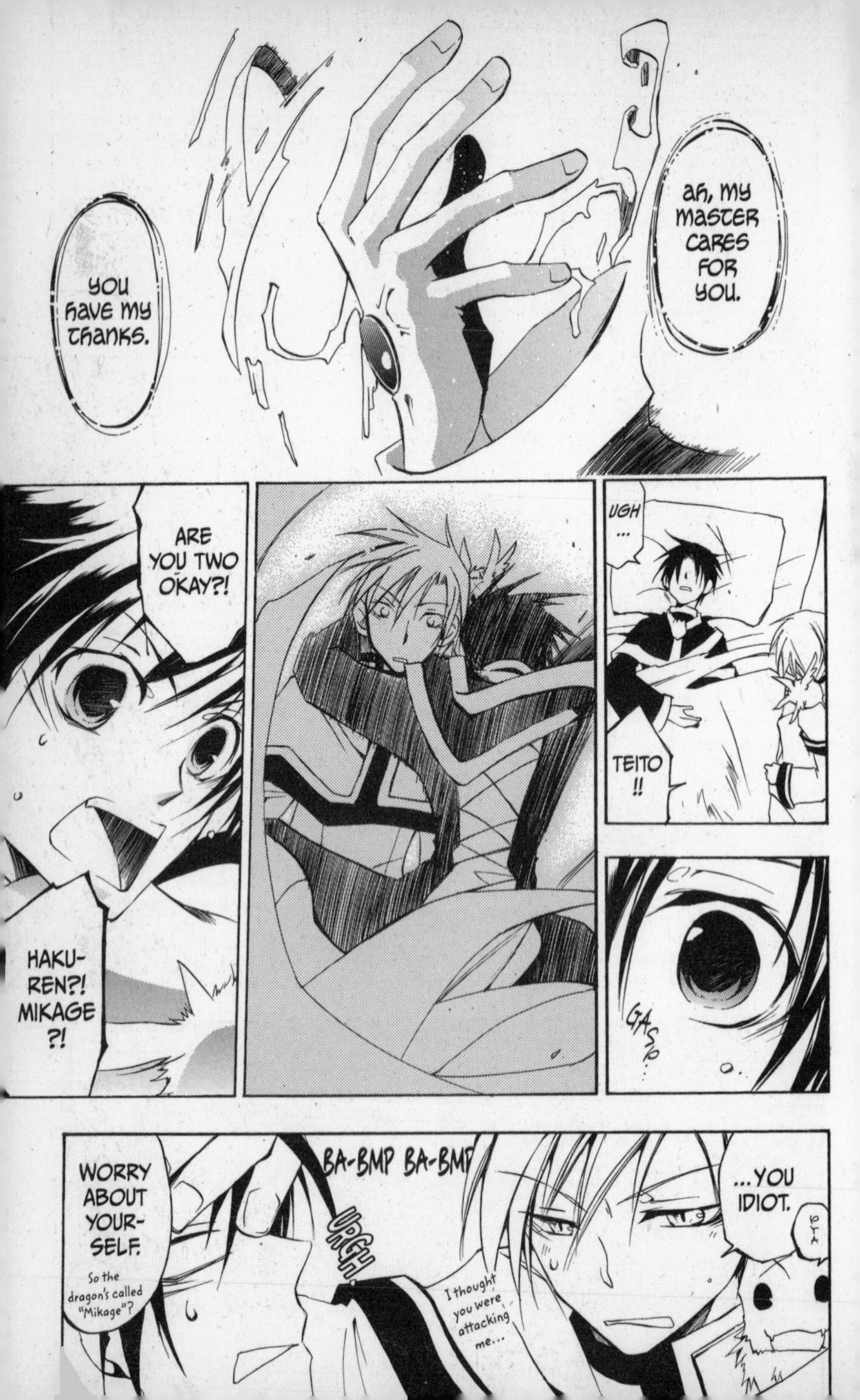
AH, MY MASTER CARES FOR YOU.
YOU HAVE MY THANKS.
UGH ...
TEITO !!
GASP...
ARE YOU TWO OKAY?!
HAKU-REN?! MIKAGE ?!
...YOU IDIOT.
I thought you were attacking me...
BA-BMP BA-BMP
URGH
WORRY ABOUT YOUR-SELF.
So the dragon's called "Mikage"?

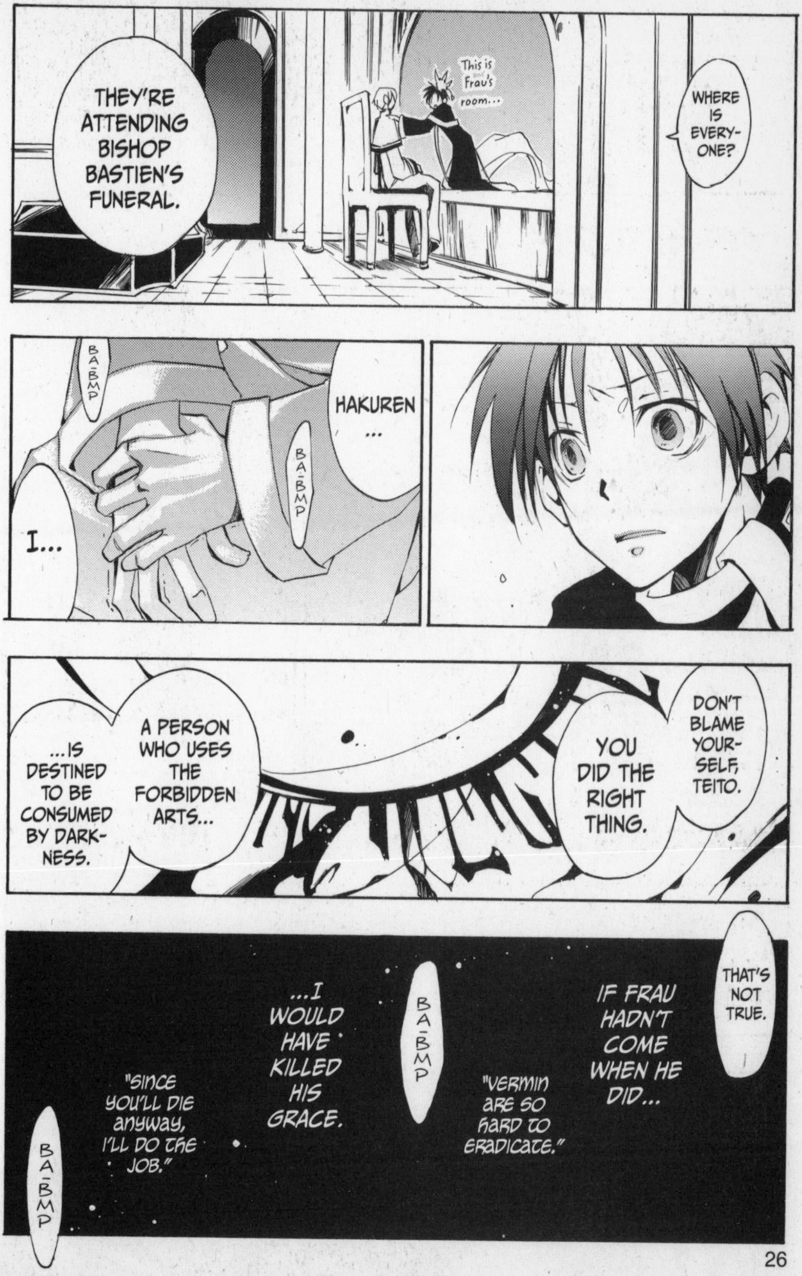
WHERE IS EVERY-ONE?
This is Frau's room...
THEY'RE ATTENDING BISHOP BASTIEN'S FUNERAL.
HAKUREN ...
BA-BMP
BA-BMP
I...
DON'T BLAME YOUR-SELF, TEITO.
YOU DID THE RIGHT THING.
A PERSON WHO USES THE FORBIDDEN ARTS...
...IS DESTINED TO BE CONSUMED BY DARK-NESS.
THAT'S NOT TRUE.
IF FRAU HADN'T COME WHEN HE DID...
"VERMIN ARE SO HARD TO ERADICATE."
BA-BMP
...I WOULD HAVE KILLED HIS GRACE.
"SINCE YOU'LL DIE ANYWAY, I'LL DO THE JOB."
BA-BMP

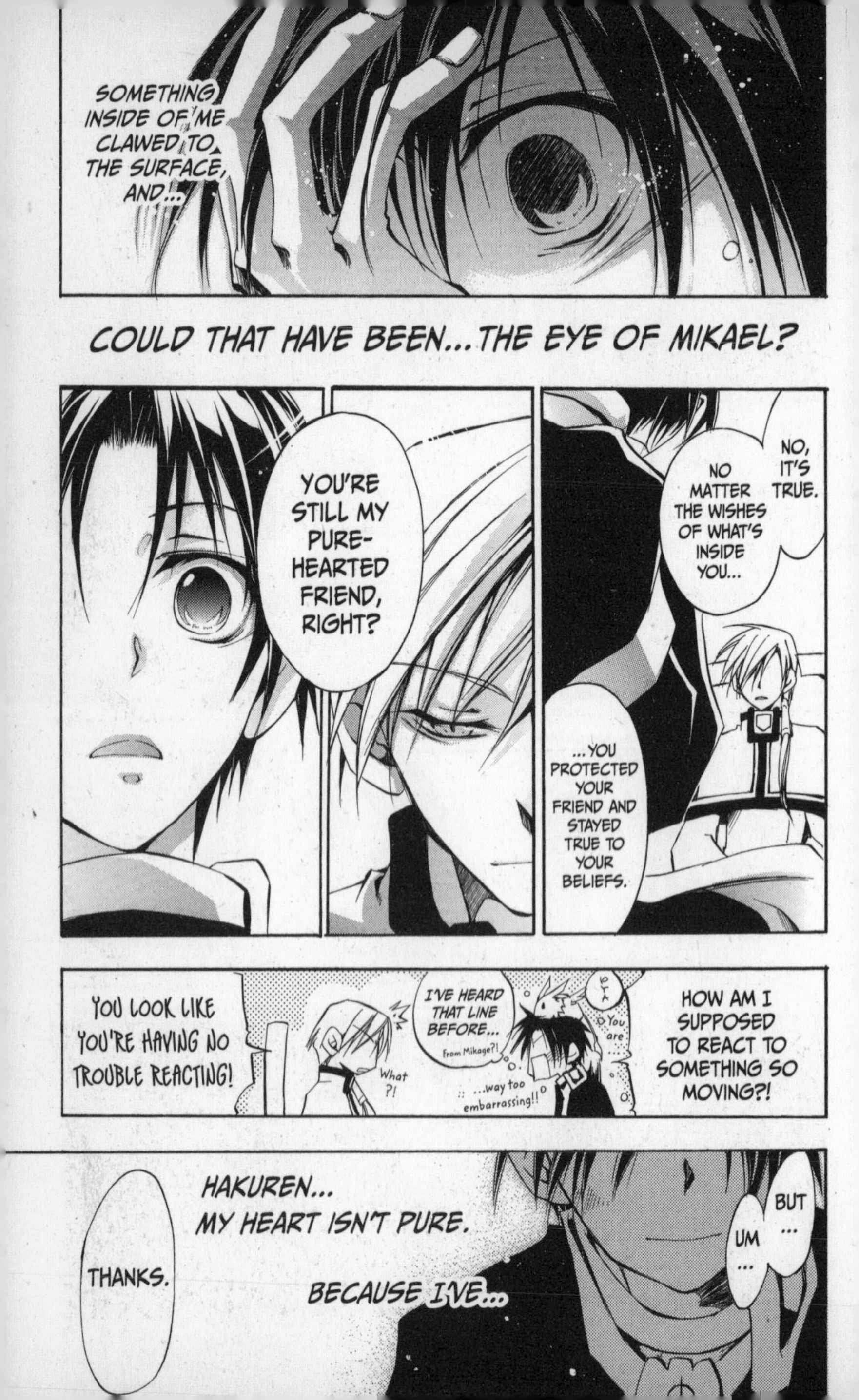
SOMETHING INSIDE OF ME CLAWED TO THE SURFACE, AND...
COULD THAT HAVE BEEN... THE EYE OF MIKAEL?
NO, IT'S TRUE.
NO MATTER THE WISHES OF WHAT'S INSIDE YOU...
...YOU PROTECTED YOUR FRIEND AND STAYED TRUE TO YOUR BELIEFS.
YOU'RE STILL MY PURE-HEARTED FRIEND, RIGHT?
HOW AM I SUPPOSED TO REACT TO SOMETHING SO MOVING?!
You are...
...way too embarrassing!!
I'VE HEARD THAT LINE BEFORE...
From Mikage?!
What?!
YOU LOOK LIKE YOU'RE HAVING NO TROUBLE REACTING!
BUT...
UM...
HAKUREN... MY HEART ISN'T PURE.
BECAUSE I'VE...
THANKS.

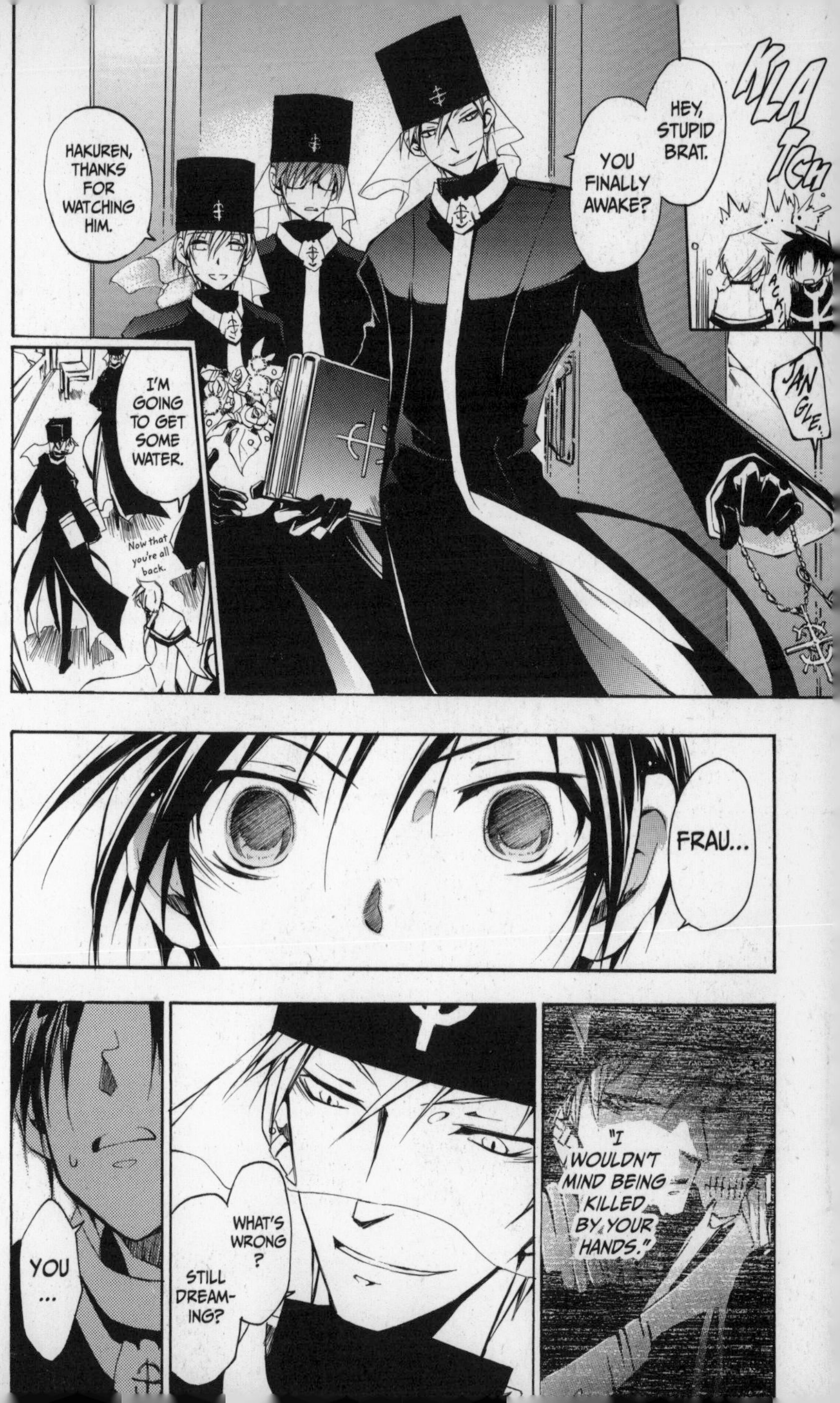
KLATCH
ACK!
HEY, STUPID BRAT.
YOU FINALLY AWAKE?
HAKUREN, THANKS FOR WATCHING HIM.
JANGLE...
I'M GOING TO GET SOME WATER.
Now that you're all back.
FRAU...
"I WOULDN'T MIND BEING KILLED BY YOUR HANDS."
WHAT'S WRONG?
STILL DREAMING?
YOU...

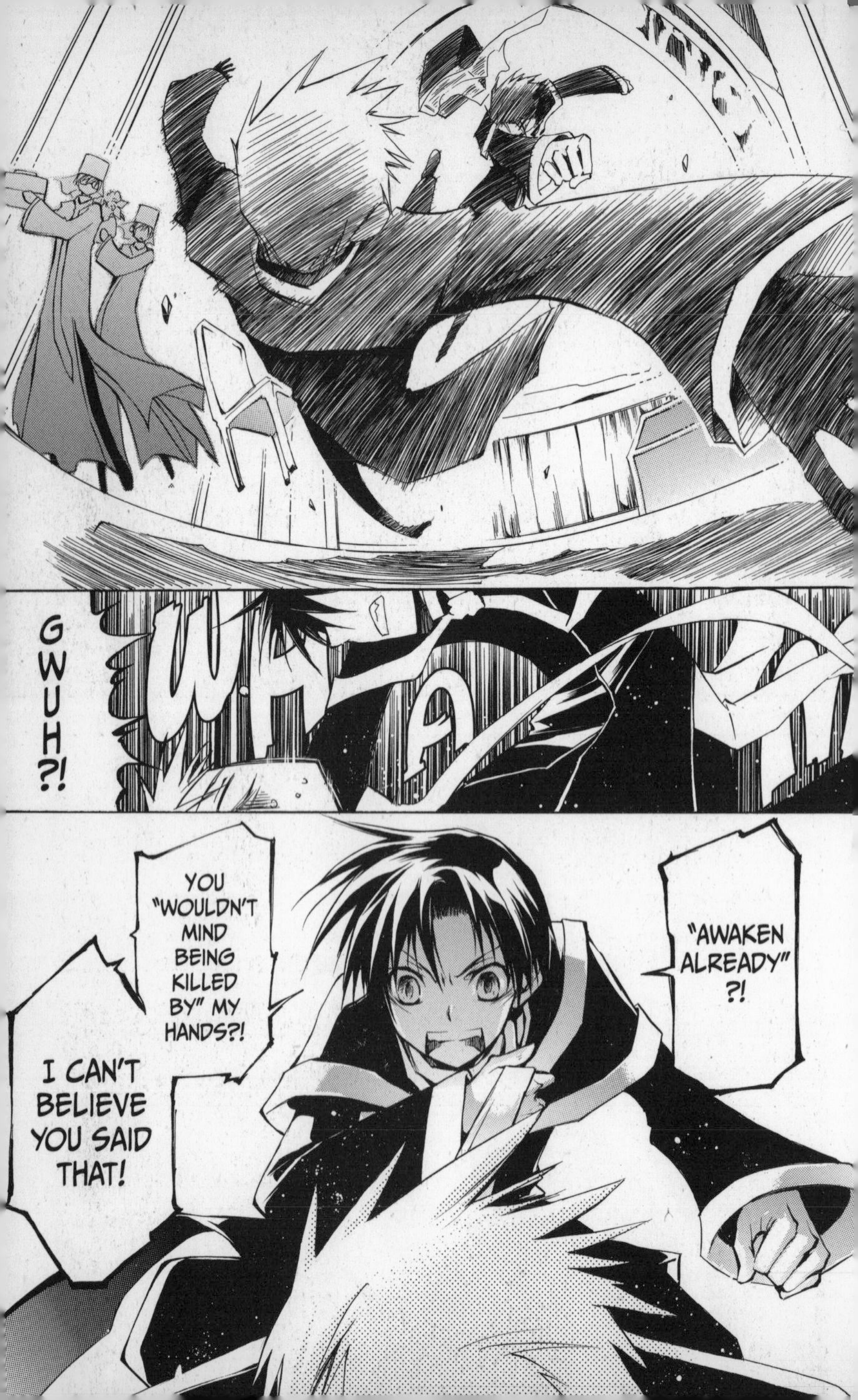
GWUH?!
"AWAKEN ALREADY" ?!
YOU "WOULDN'T MIND BEING KILLED BY" MY HANDS?!
I CAN'T BELIEVE YOU SAID THAT!

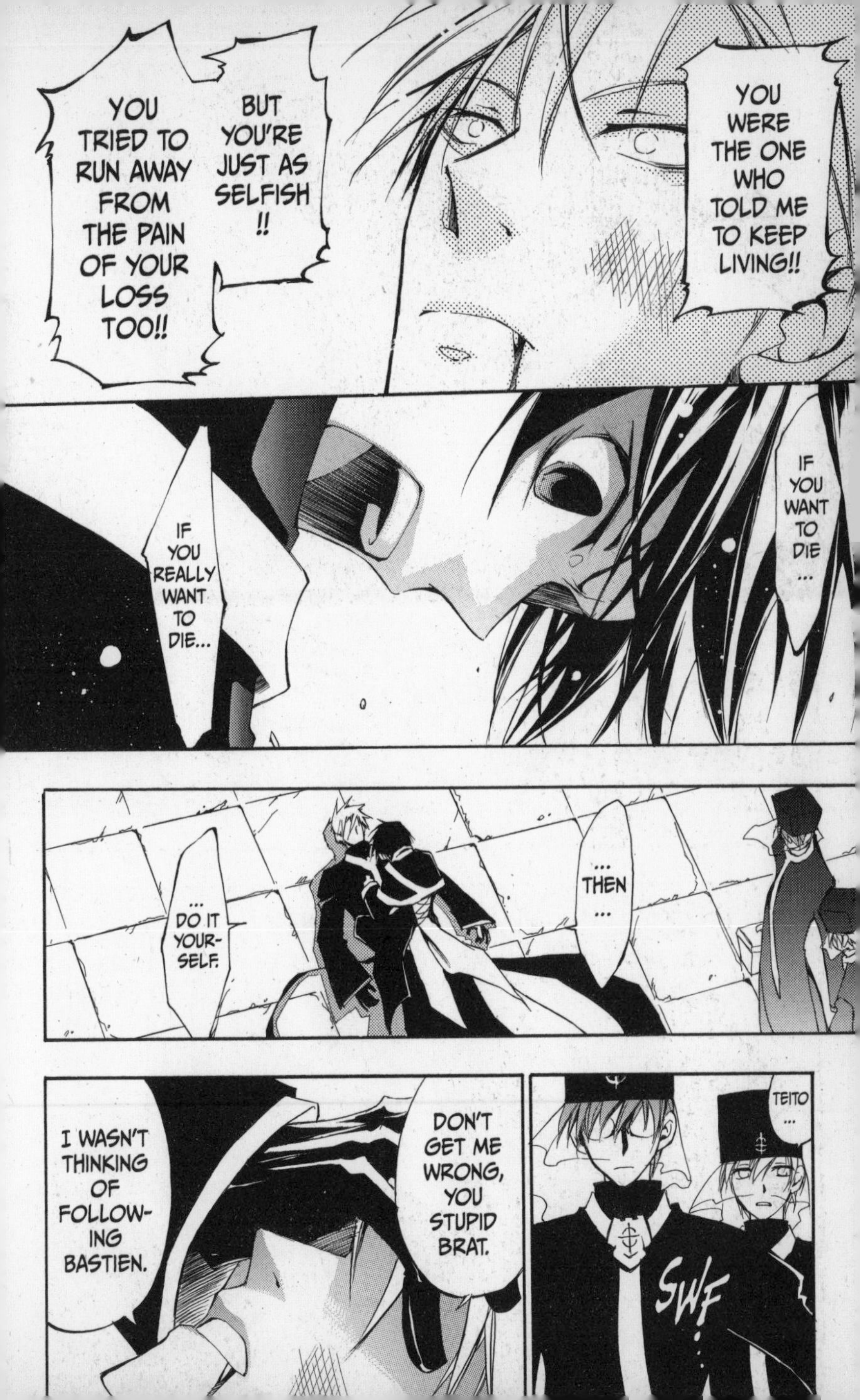
YOU WERE THE ONE WHO TOLD ME TO KEEP LIVING!!
BUT YOU'RE JUST AS SELFISH!!
YOU TRIED TO RUN AWAY FROM THE PAIN OF YOUR LOSS TOO!!
IF YOU WANT TO DIE...
IF YOU REALLY WANT TO DIE...
...THEN...
...DO IT YOUR-SELF.
TEITO...
SWF
DON'T GET ME WRONG, YOU STUPID BRAT.
I WASN'T THINKING OF FOLLOW-ING BASTIEN.

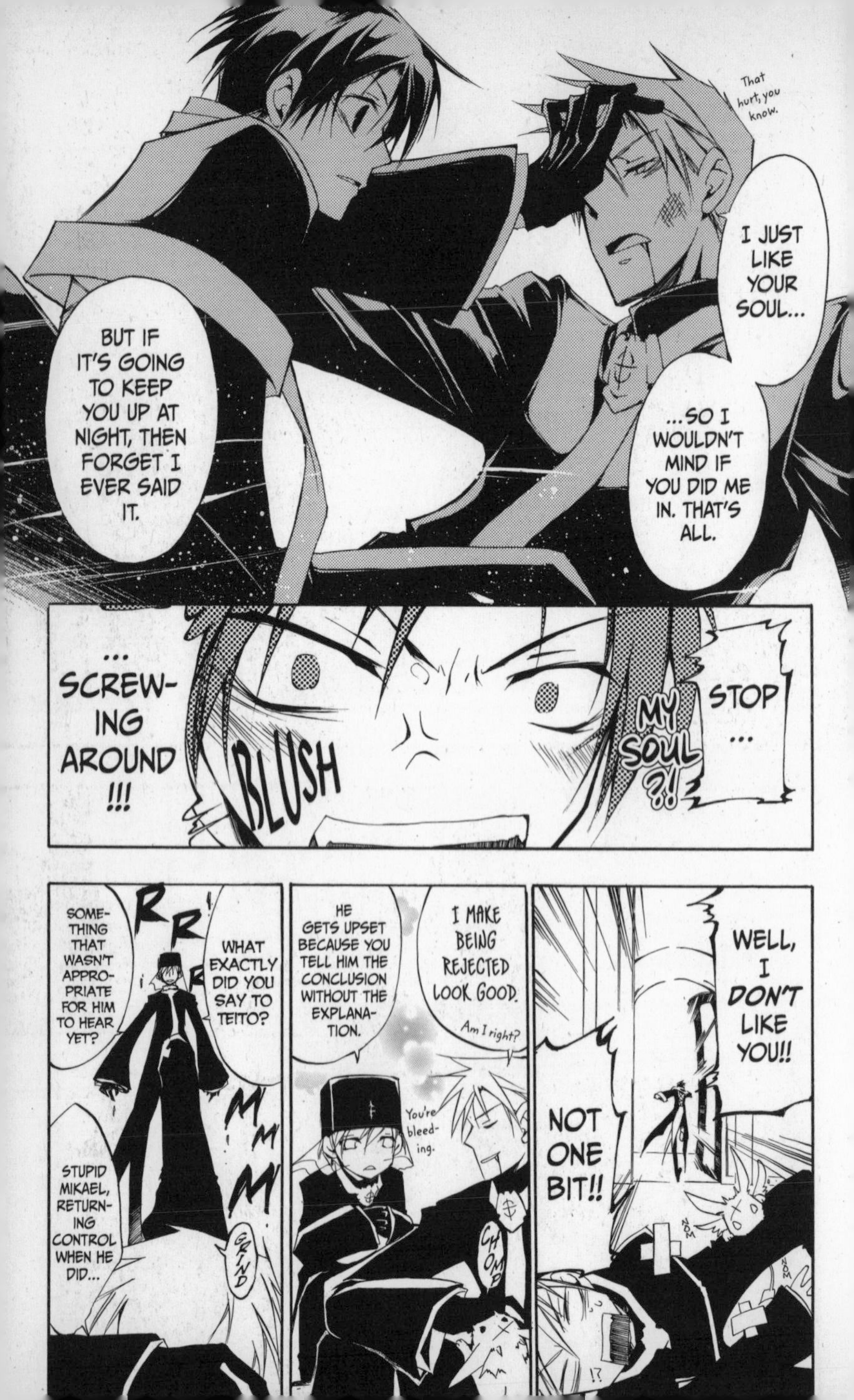
That hurt, you know.
I JUST LIKE YOUR SOUL...
...SO I WOULDN'T MIND IF YOU DID ME IN. THAT'S ALL.
BUT IF IT'S GOING TO KEEP YOU UP AT NIGHT, THEN FORGET I EVER SAID IT.
STOP ...
MY SOUL ?!
BLUSH
... SCREWING AROUND !!!
WELL, I DON'T LIKE YOU!!
NOT ONE BIT!!
NOM
NOM
I MAKE BEING REJECTED LOOK GOOD.
Am I right?
HE GETS UPSET BECAUSE YOU TELL HIM THE CONCLUSION WITHOUT THE EXPLANATION.
You're bleeding.
CHOMP
WHAT EXACTLY DID YOU SAY TO TEITO?
RRR
SOMETHING THAT WASN'T APPROPRIATE FOR HIM TO HEAR YET?
MMM
GRIND
STUPID MIKAEL, RETURNING CONTROL WHEN HE DID...

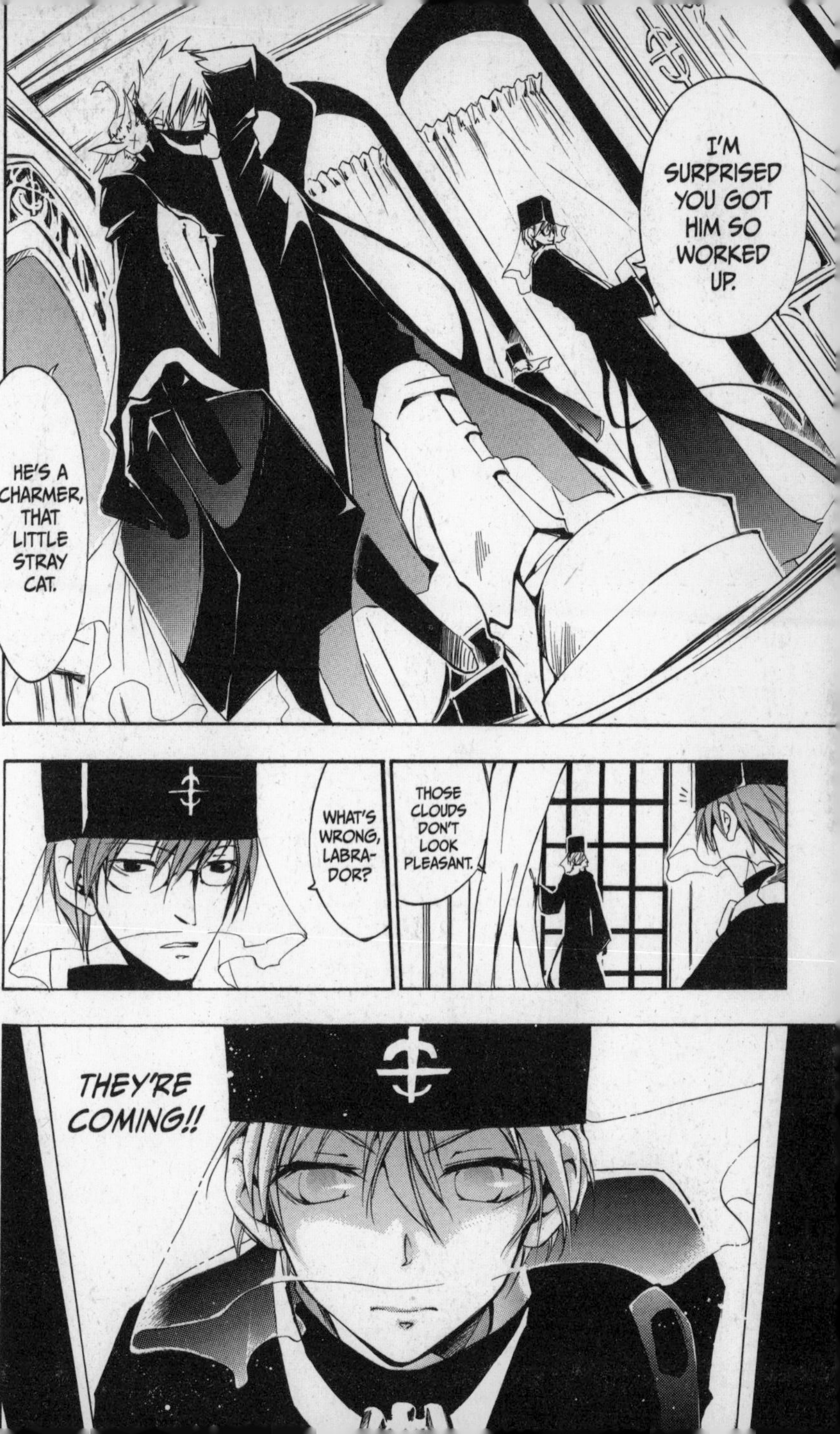
I'M SURPRISED YOU GOT HIM SO WORKED UP.
HE'S A CHARMER, THAT LITTLE STRAY CAT.
THOSE CLOUDS DON'T LOOK PLEASANT.
WHAT'S WRONG, LABRA-DOR?
THEY'RE COMING!!

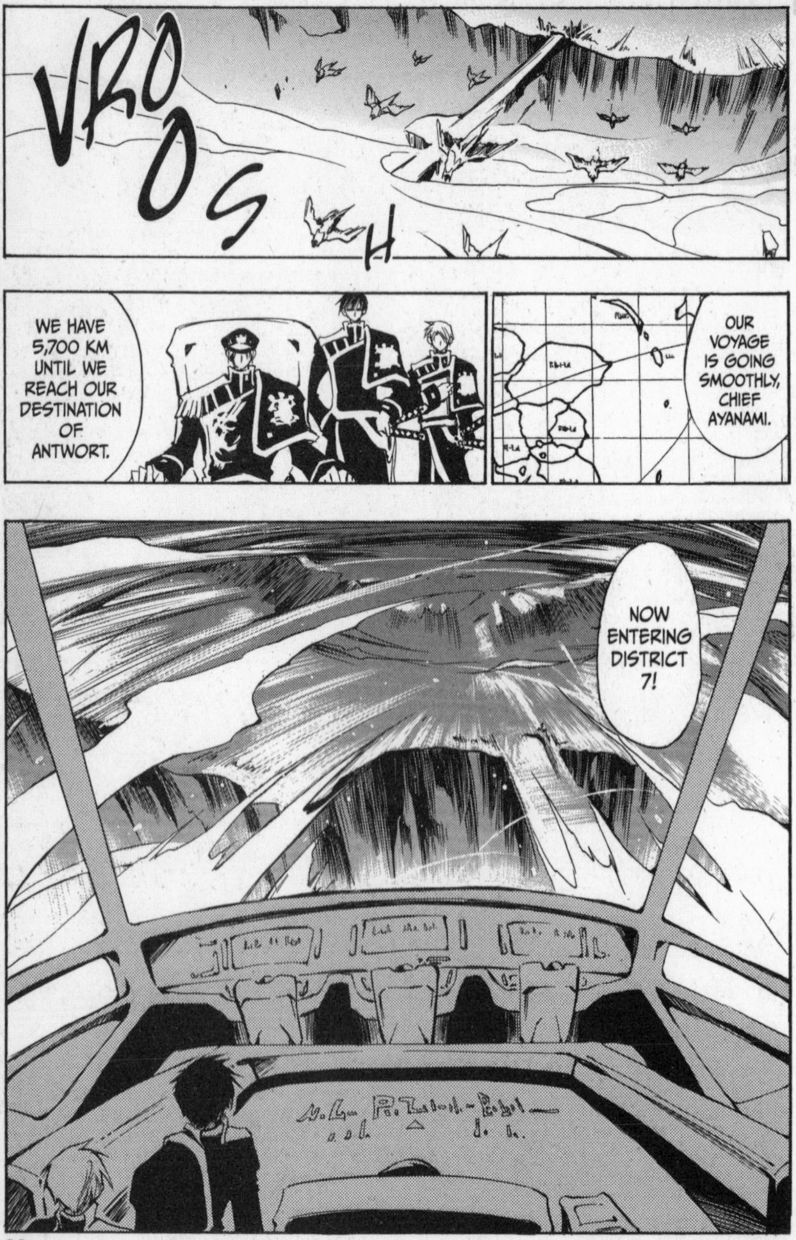
VROOOSH
OUR VOYAGE IS GOING SMOOTHLY, CHIEF AYANAMI.
WE HAVE 5,700 KM UNTIL WE REACH OUR DESTINATION OF ANTWORT.
NOW ENTERING DISTRICT 7!

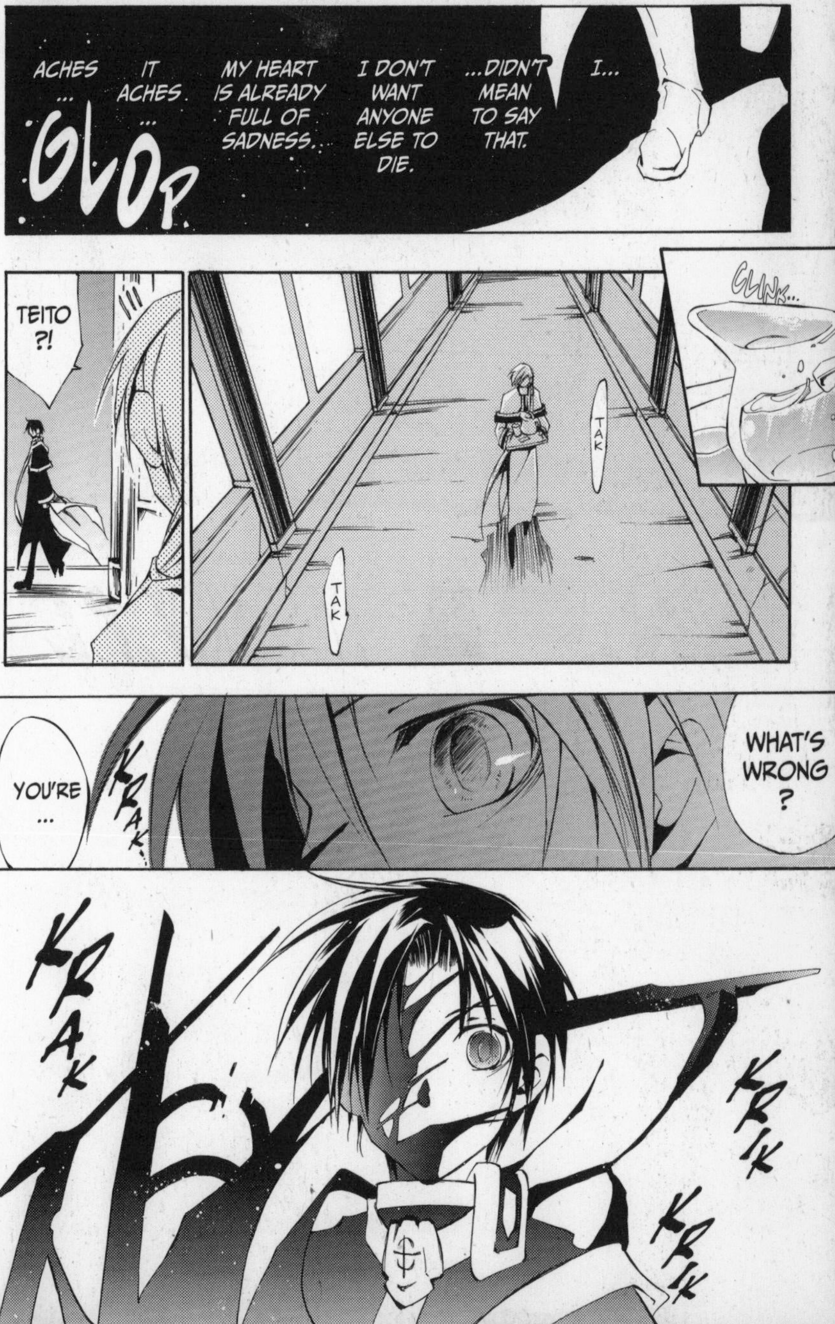
I...
...DIDN'T MEAN TO SAY THAT.
I DON'T WANT ANYONE ELSE TO DIE.
MY HEART IS ALREADY FULL OF SADNESS...
IT ACHES...
ACHES...
GLOP
CLINK...
TAK
TAK
TEITO?!
WHAT'S WRONG?
KRAK...
YOU'RE...
KRIK
KRIK
KRAK

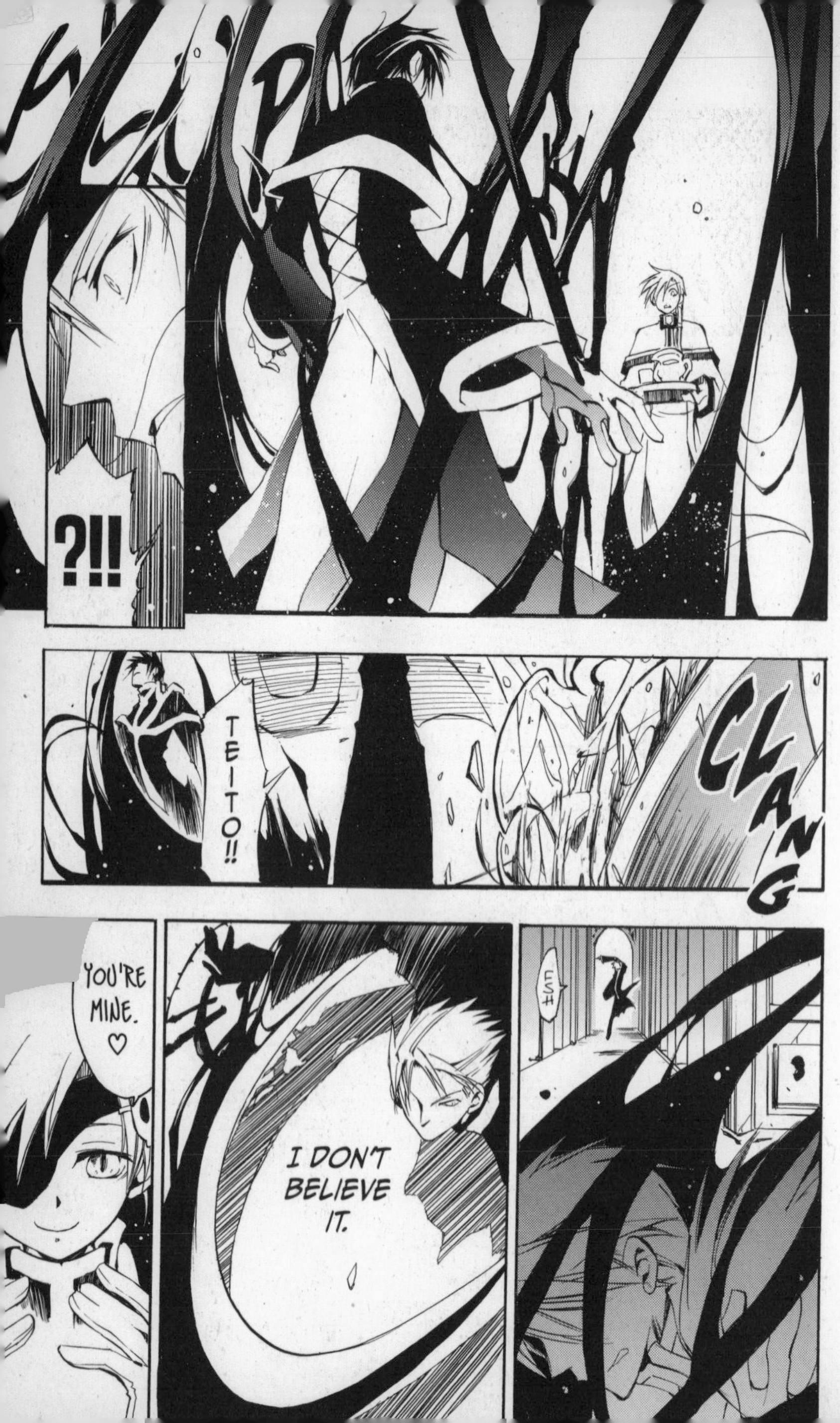
?!!
CLANG
TEITO!!
I DON'T BELIEVE IT.
YOU'RE MINE. ♡

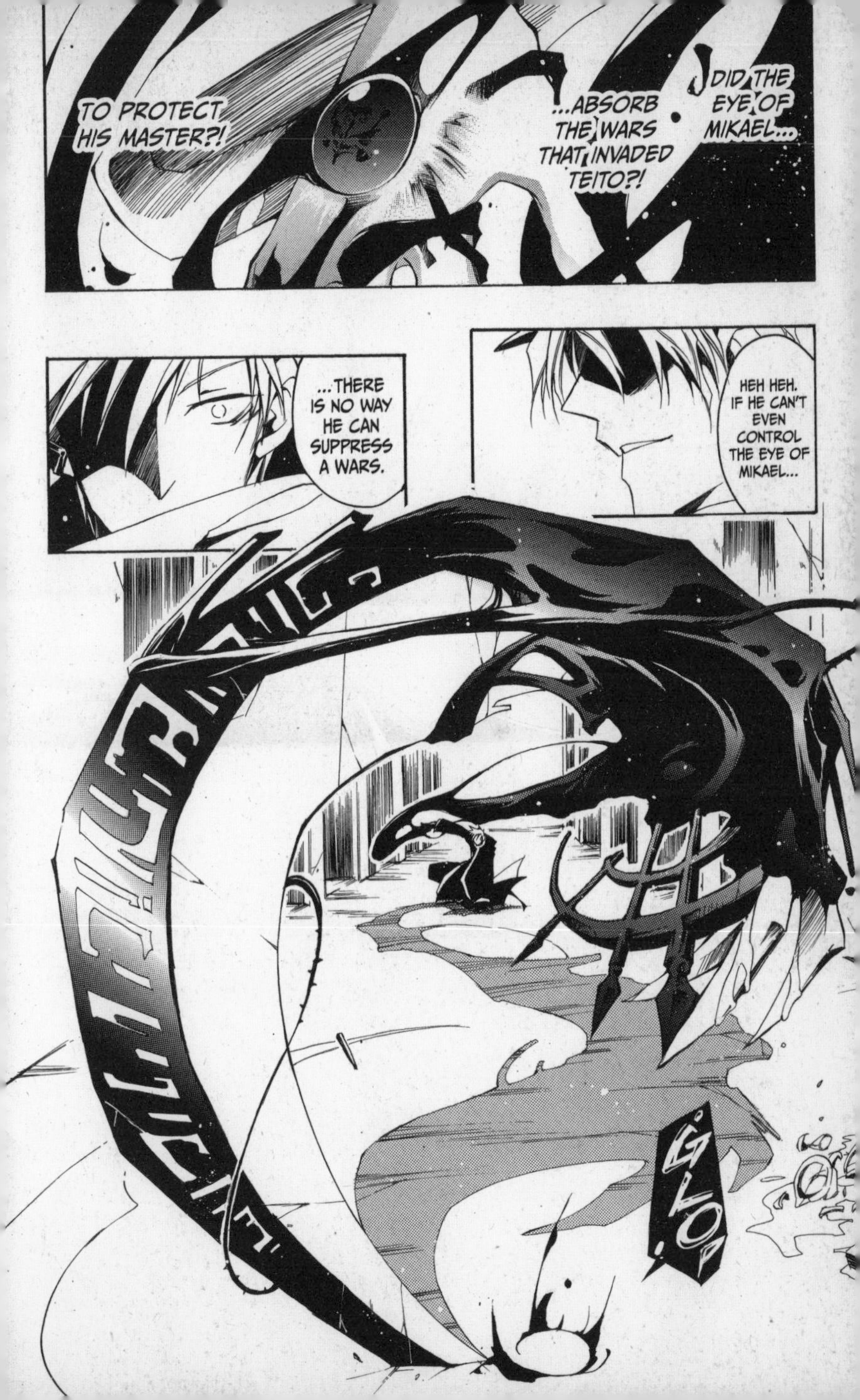
DID THE EYE OF MIKAEL...
...ABSORB THE WARS THAT INVADED TEITO?!
TO PROTECT HIS MASTER?!
HEH HEH. IF HE CAN'T EVEN CONTROL THE EYE OF MIKAEL...
...THERE IS NO WAY HE CAN SUPPRESS A WARS.
GLOP

Kapitel.19 “Nightmare: Part 10”

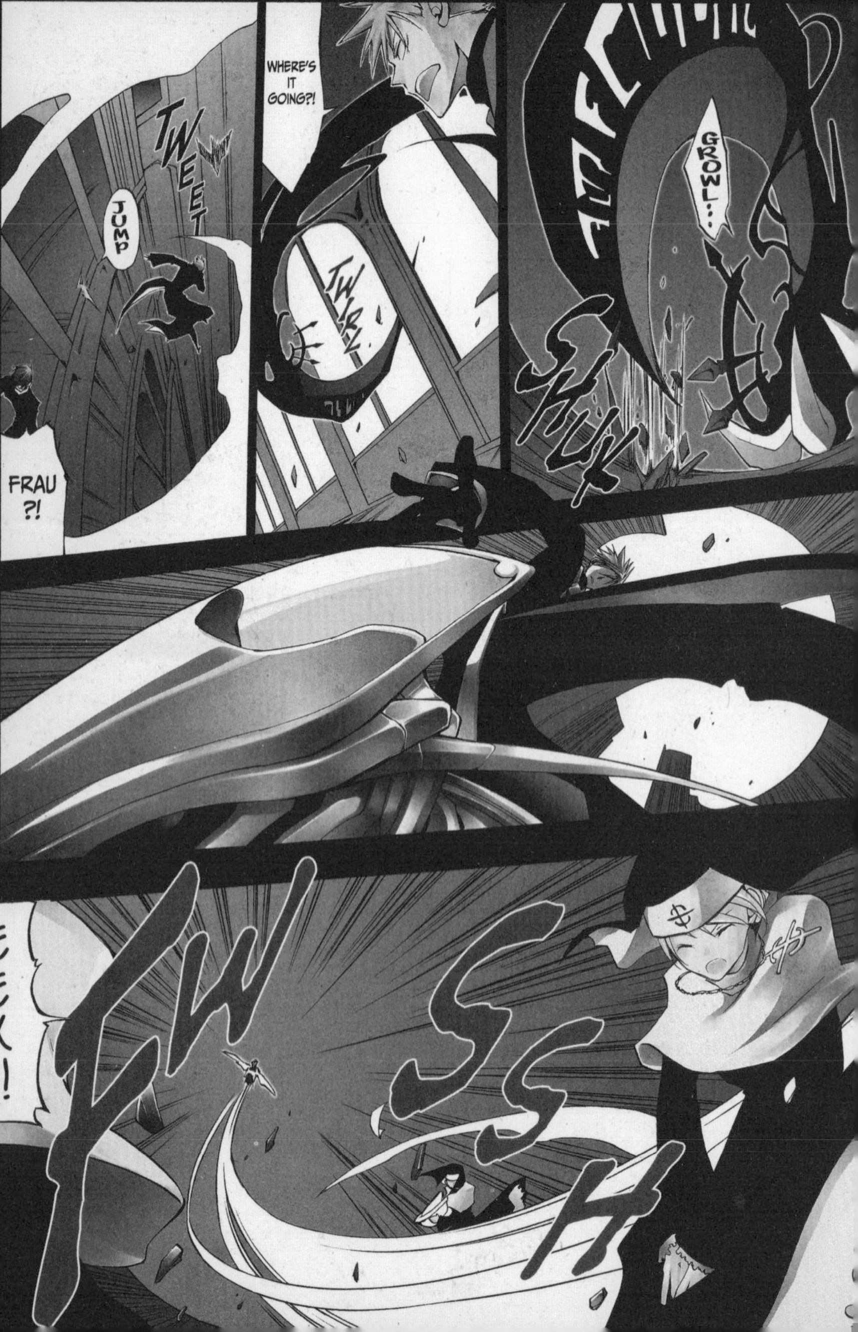
GROWL...
SHUNK
WHERE'S IT GOING?!
TWIRL
TWEET
JUMP
FRAU ?!
FWSSH
EEK!!

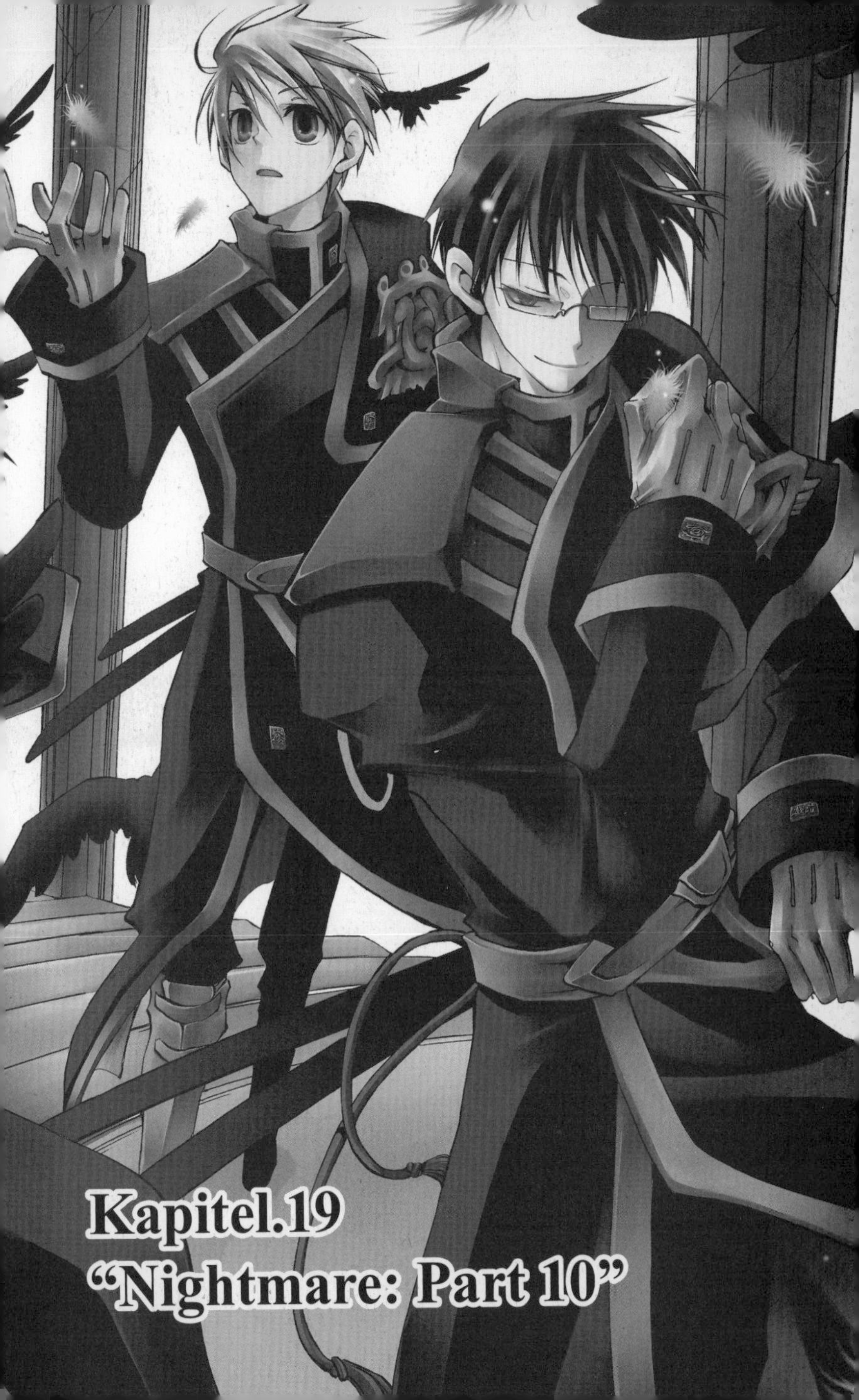

Kapitel.19
"Nightmare: Part 10"

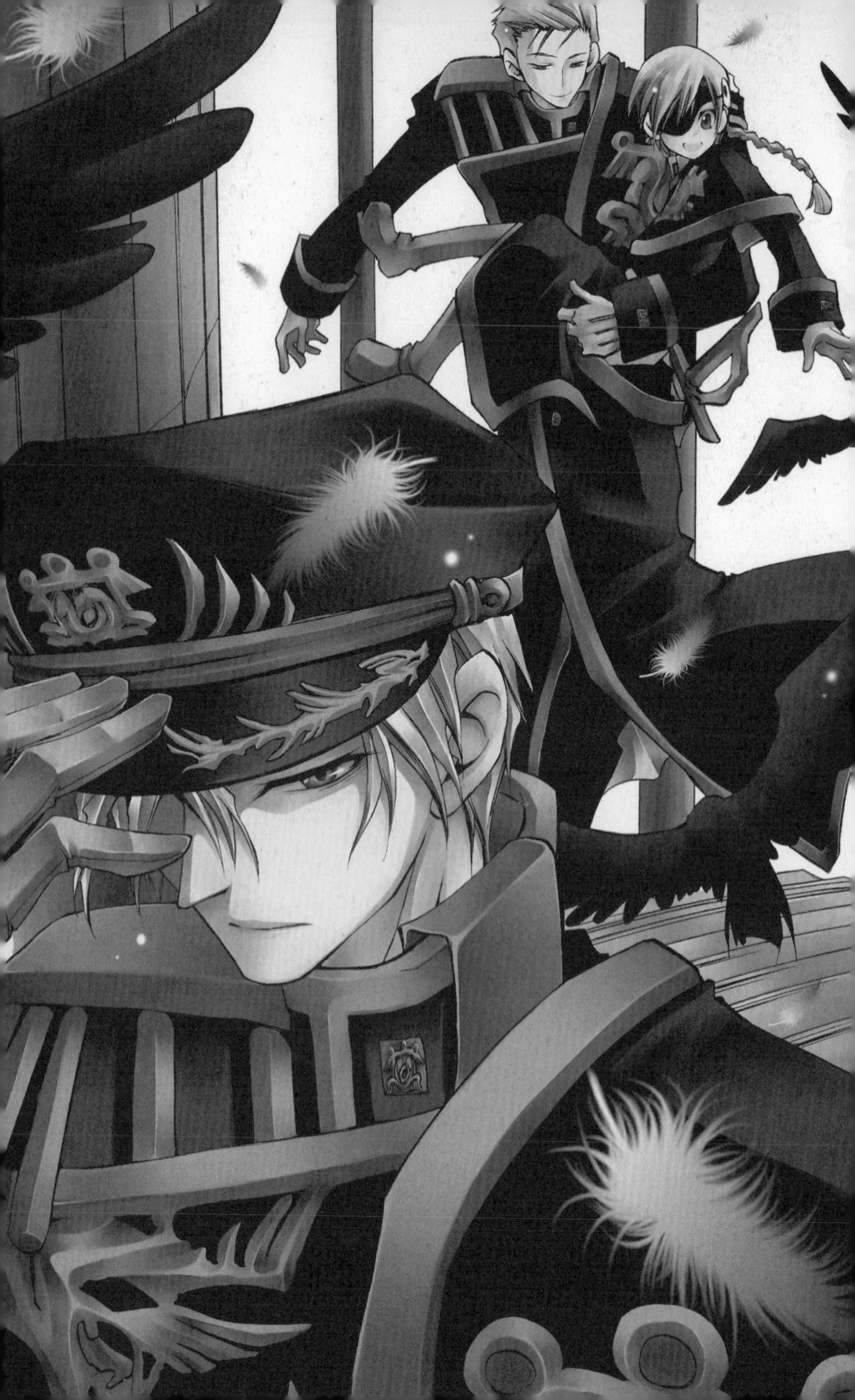

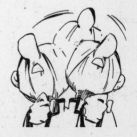

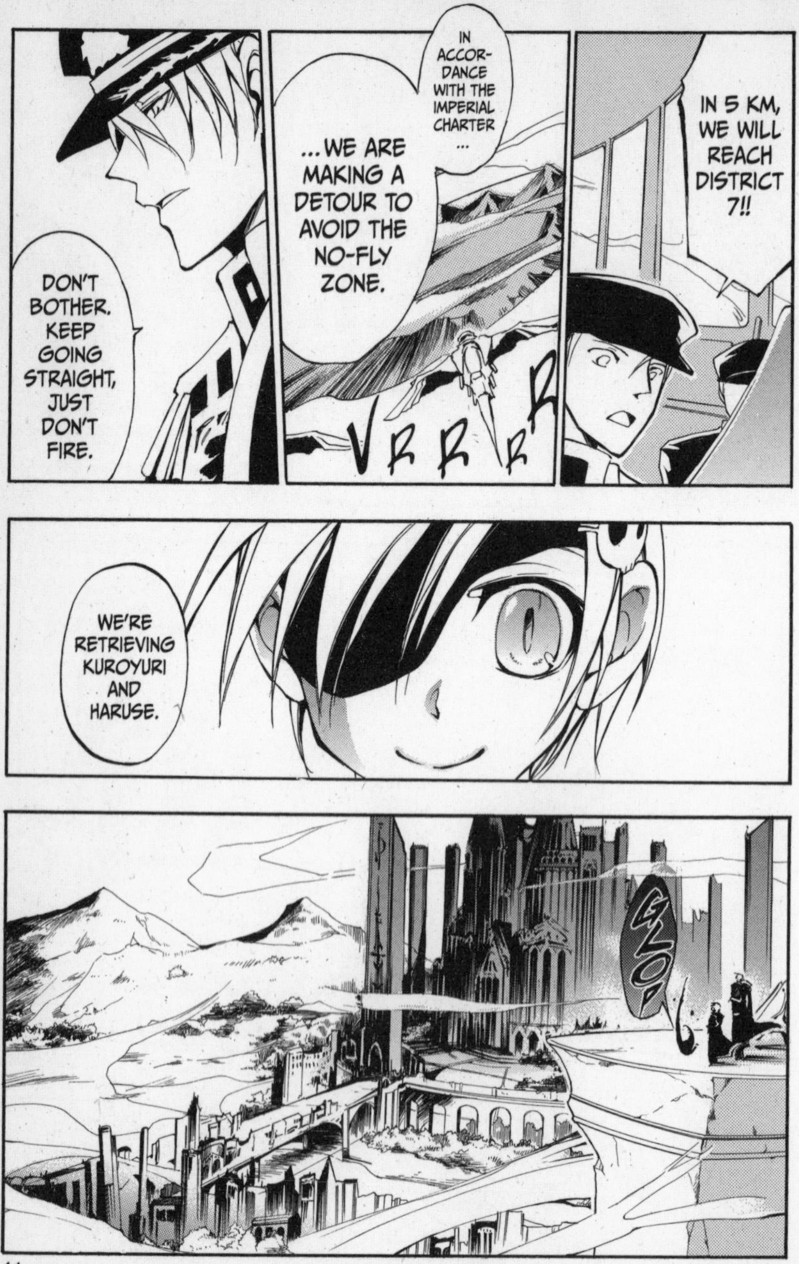
IN 5 KM, WE WILL REACH DISTRICT 7!!
IN ACCORDANCE WITH THE IMPERIAL CHARTER...
...WE ARE MAKING A DETOUR TO AVOID THE NO-FLY ZONE.
VRRRR
DON'T BOTHER. KEEP GOING STRAIGHT, JUST DON'T FIRE.
WE'RE RETRIEVING KUROYURI AND HARUSE.
GLOP

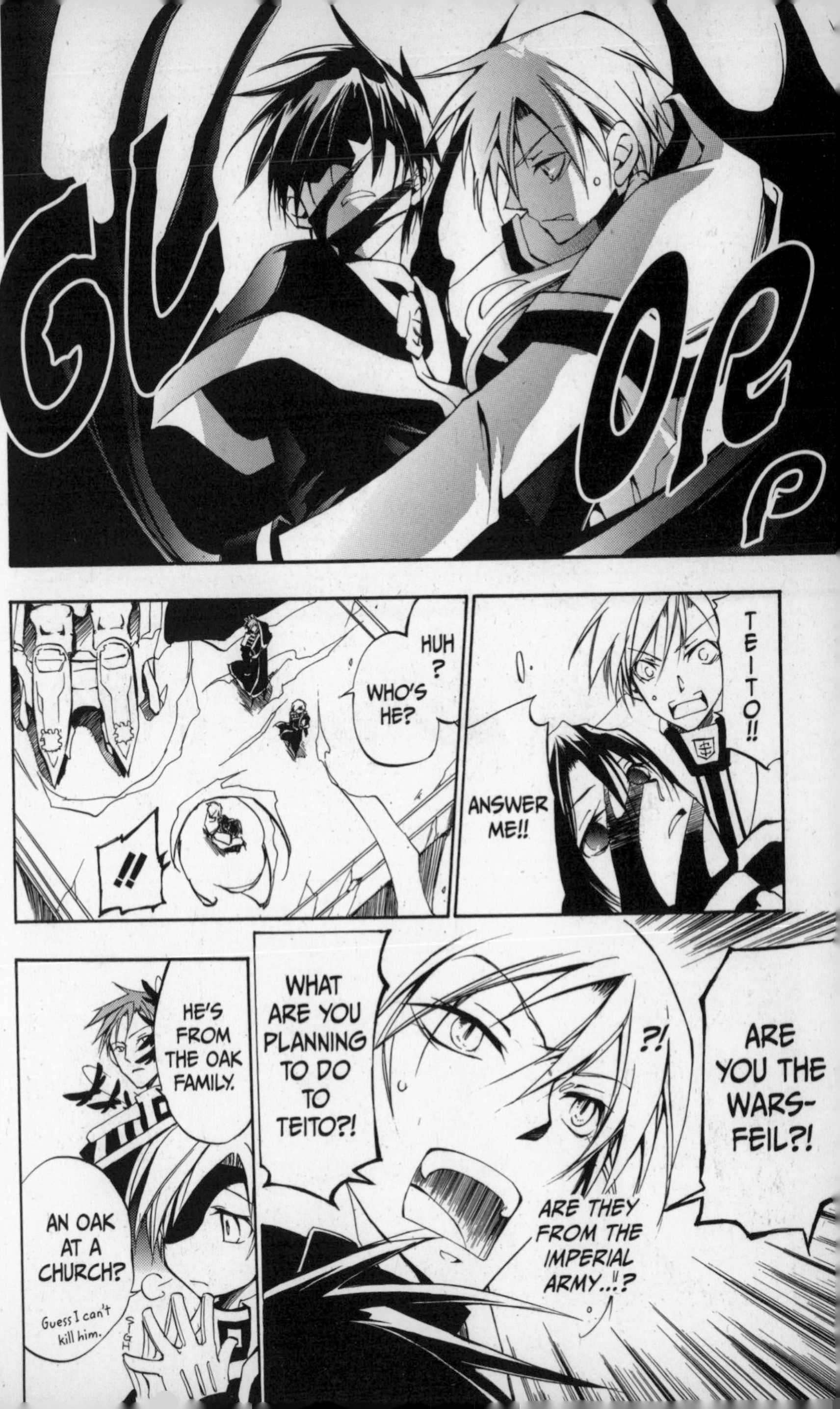
TEITO!!
ANSWER ME!!
HUH? WHO'S HE?
!!
ARE YOU THE WARS-FEIL?!
?!
WHAT ARE YOU PLANNING TO DO TO TEITO?!
ARE THEY FROM THE IMPERIAL ARMY...!?
HE'S FROM THE OAK FAMILY.
AN OAK AT A CHURCH?
Guess I can't kill him.
SIGH

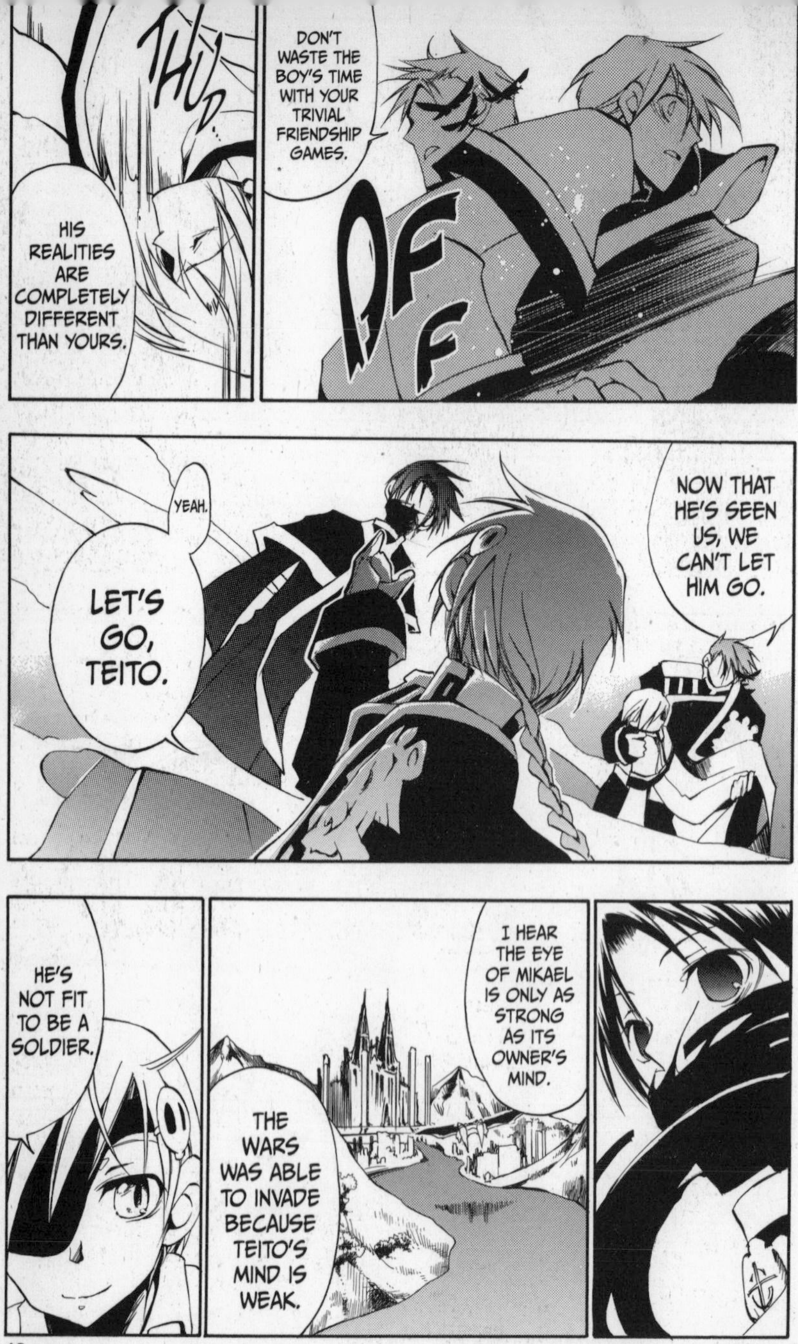
DON'T WASTE THE BOY'S TIME WITH YOUR TRIVIAL FRIENDSHIP GAMES.
THUD...
HIS REALITIES ARE COMPLETELY DIFFERENT THAN YOURS.
NOW THAT HE'S SEEN US, WE CAN'T LET HIM GO.
YEAH.
LET'S GO, TEITO.
I HEAR THE EYE OF MIKAEL IS ONLY AS STRONG AS ITS OWNER'S MIND.
THE WARS WAS ABLE TO INVADE BECAUSE TEITO'S MIND IS WEAK.
HE'S NOT FIT TO BE A SOLDIER.

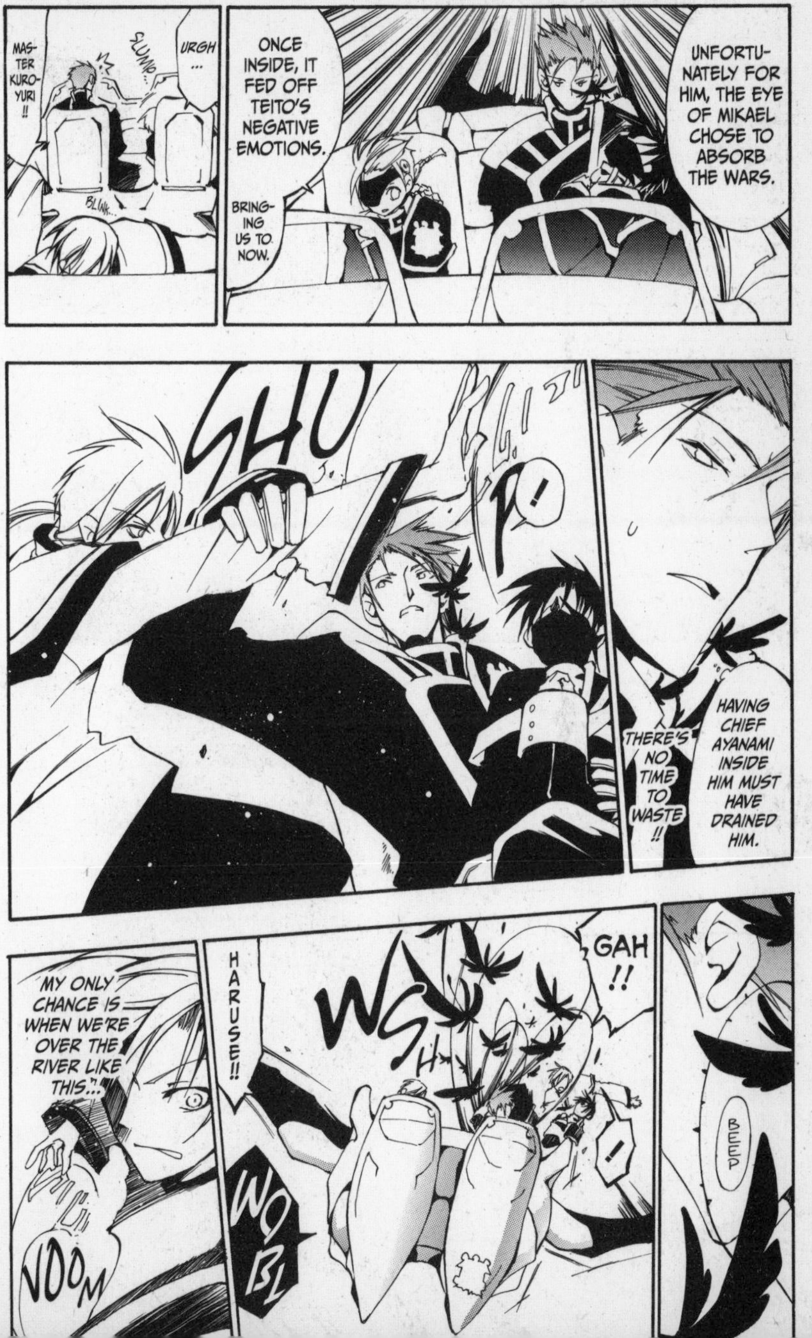
UNFORTUNATELY FOR HIM, THE EYE OF MIKAEL CHOSE TO ABSORB THE WARS.
ONCE INSIDE, IT FED OFF TEITO'S NEGATIVE EMOTIONS.
BRINGING US TO NOW.
URGH ...
SLUMP...
MASTER KUROYURI !!
BLINK...
HAVING CHIEF AYANAMI INSIDE HIM MUST HAVE DRAINED HIM.
THERE'S NO TIME TO WASTE !!
SHU
P!
BEEP
GAH !!
HARUSE!!
WSH
WOBBL
MY ONLY CHANCE IS WHEN WE'RE OVER THE RIVER LIKE THIS...
VOOM

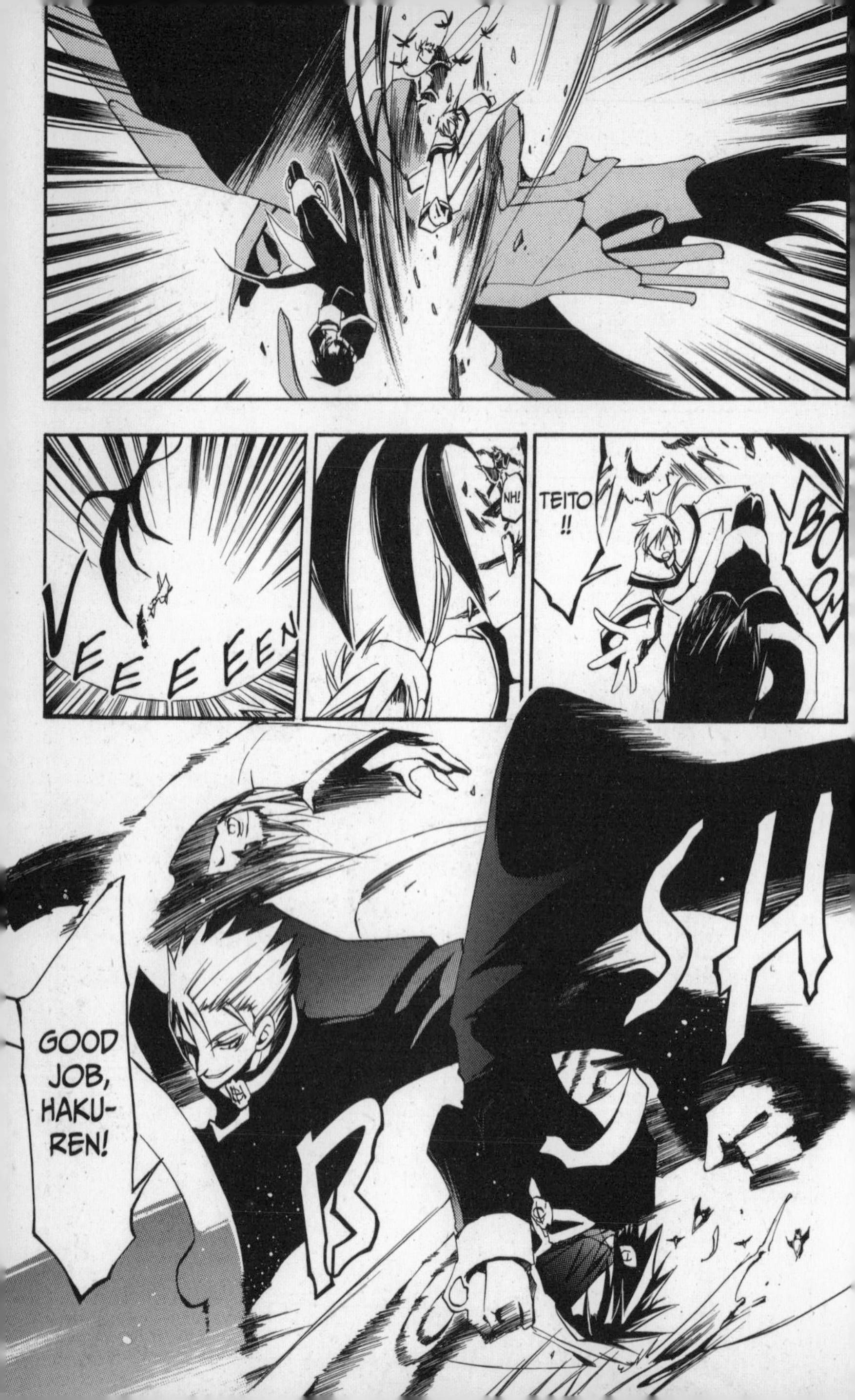
BOOM
TEITO !!
NH!
VEEEEEN
SH
GOOD JOB, HAKU-REN!

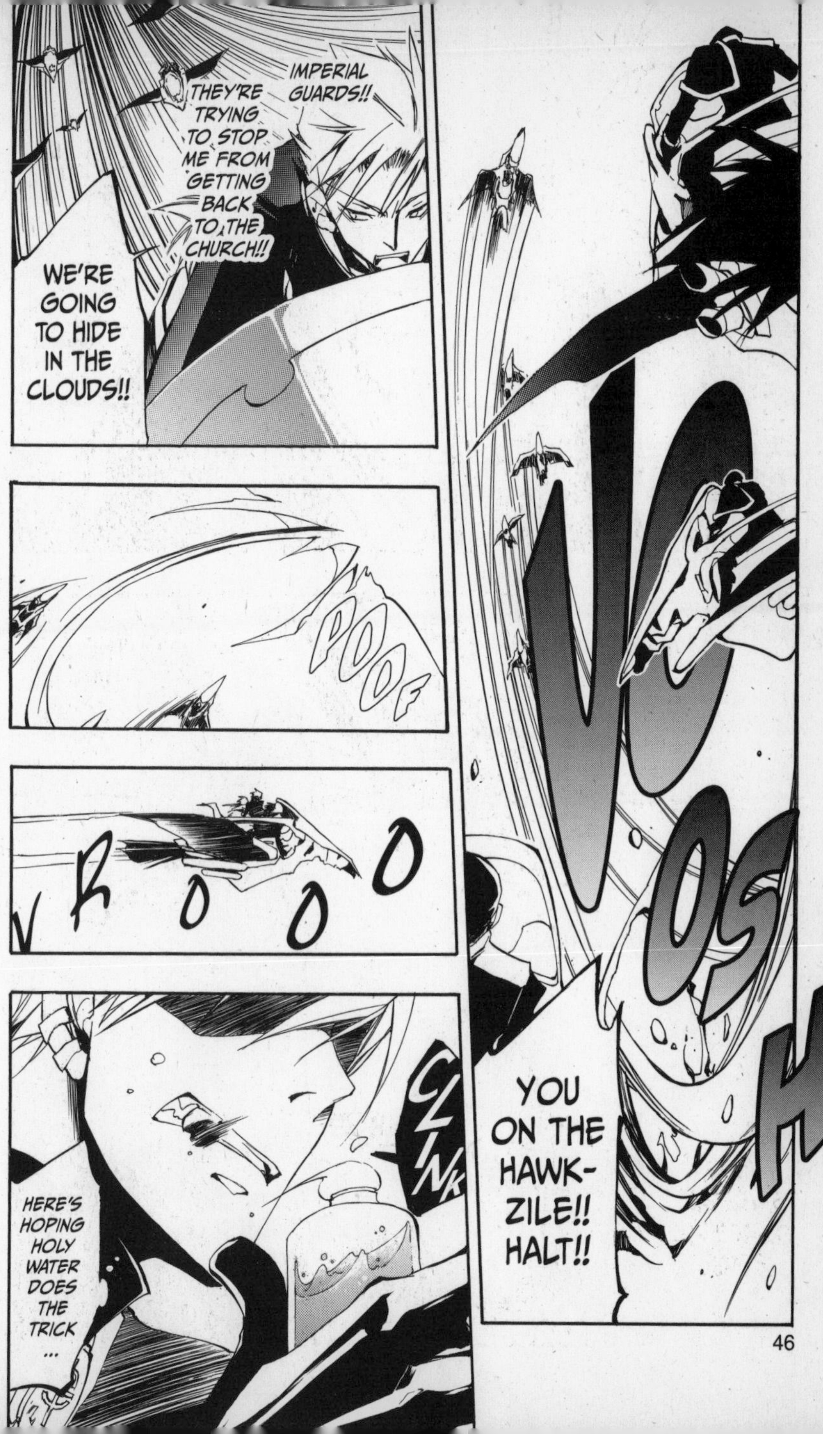
VOOSH
YOU ON THE HAWK-ZILE!! HALT!!
IMPERIAL GUARDS!!
THEY'RE TRYING TO STOP ME FROM GETTING BACK TO THE CHURCH!!
WE'RE GOING TO HIDE IN THE CLOUDS!!
POOF
VROOOO
CLINK
HERE'S HOPING HOLY WATER DOES THE TRICK ...

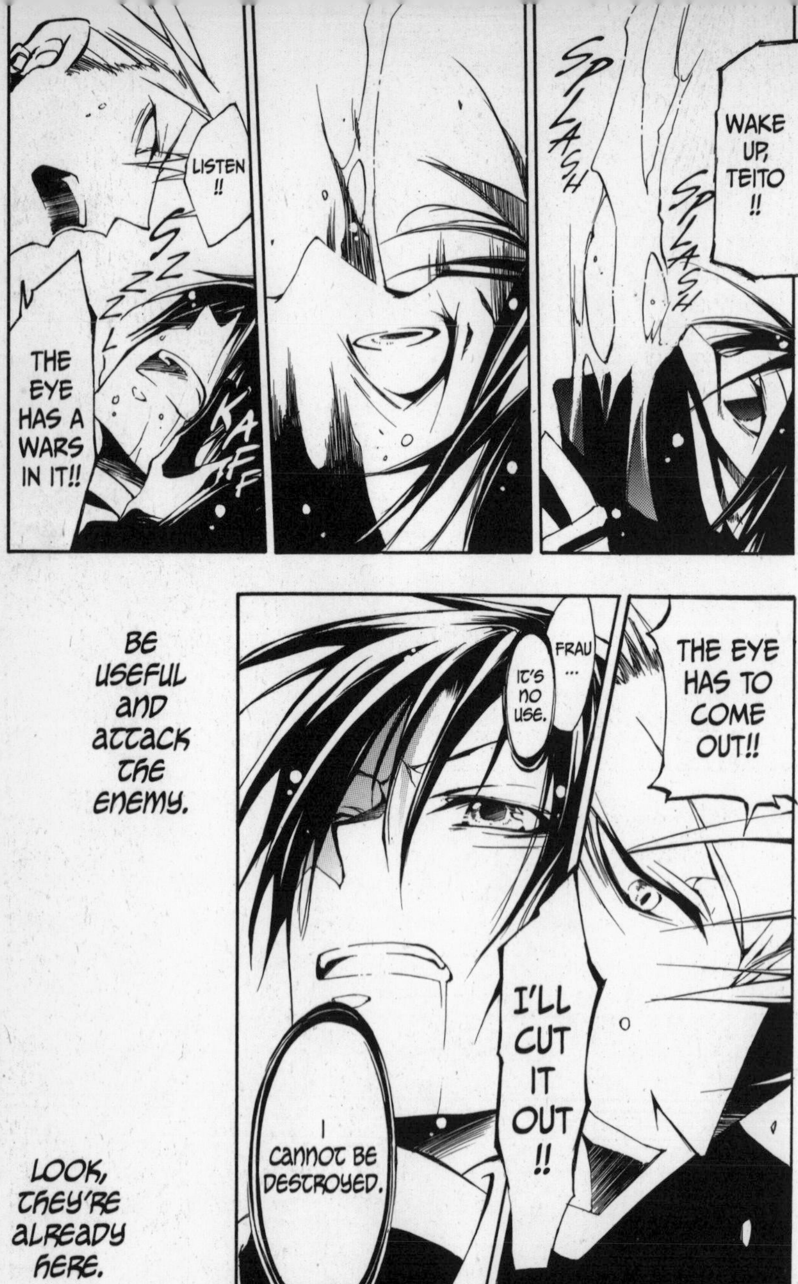

WAKE UP, TEITO!!
SPLASH
SPLASH
LISTEN!!
THE EYE HAS A WARS IN IT!!
KAFF
THE EYE HAS TO COME OUT!!
FRAU...
IT'S NO USE.
I'LL CUT IT OUT!!
I CANNOT BE DESTROYED.
BE USEFUL AND ATTACK THE ENEMY.
LOOK, THEY'RE ALREADY HERE.

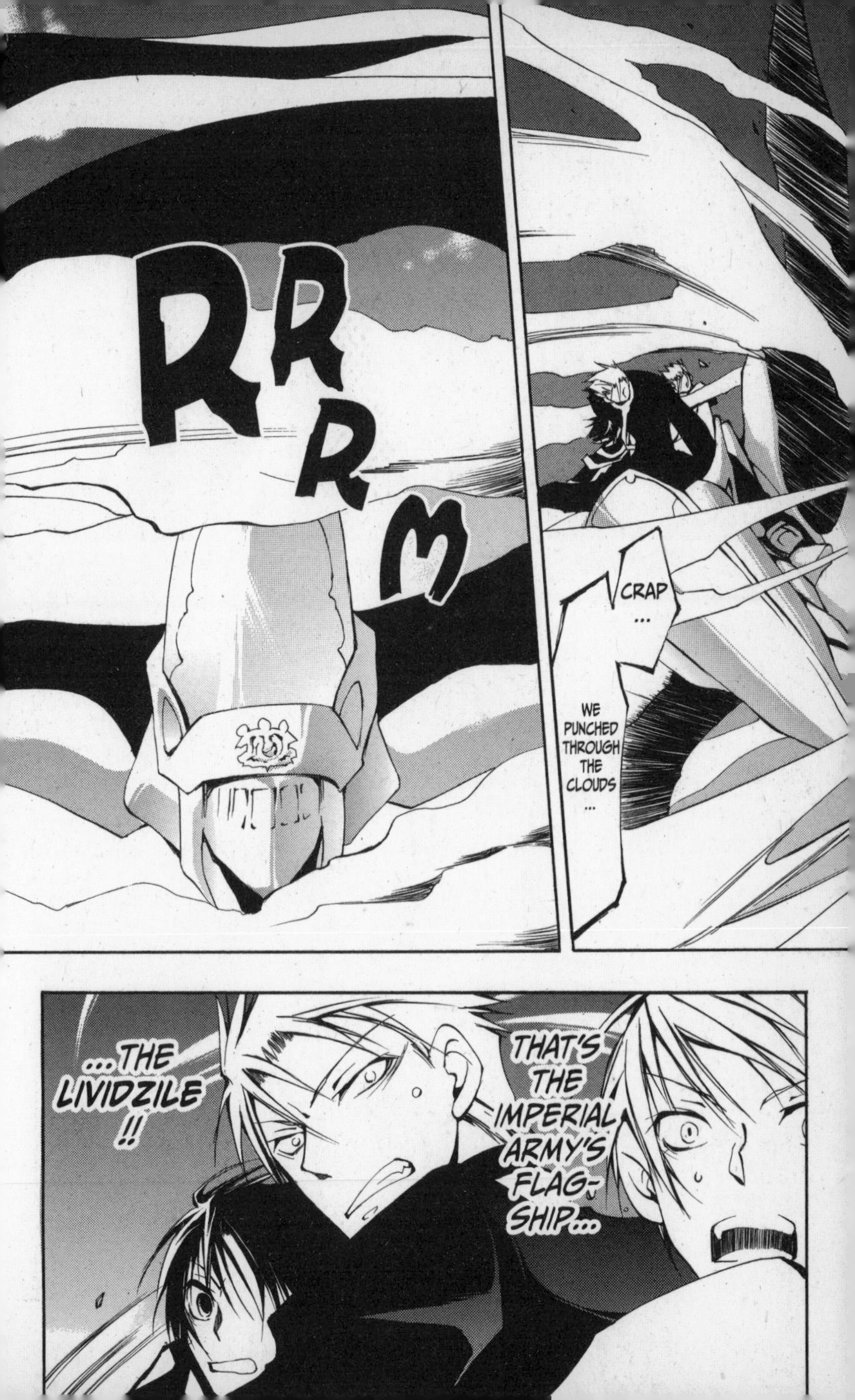
CRAP ...
WE PUNCHED THROUGH THE CLOUDS ...
RRRM
THAT'S THE IMPERIAL ARMY'S FLAG-SHIP...
...THE LIVIDZILE !!

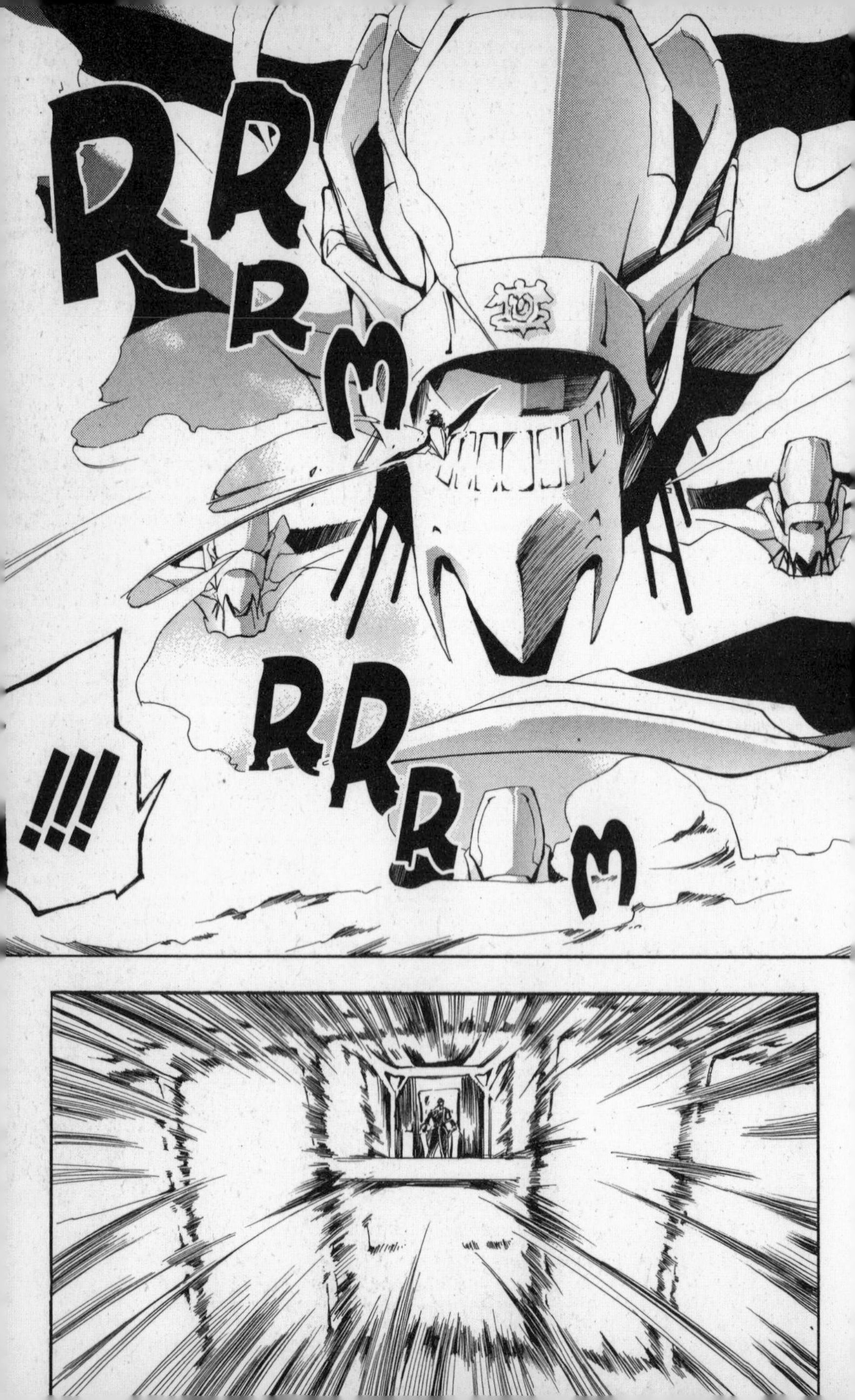
RRRM
RRRM
!!!

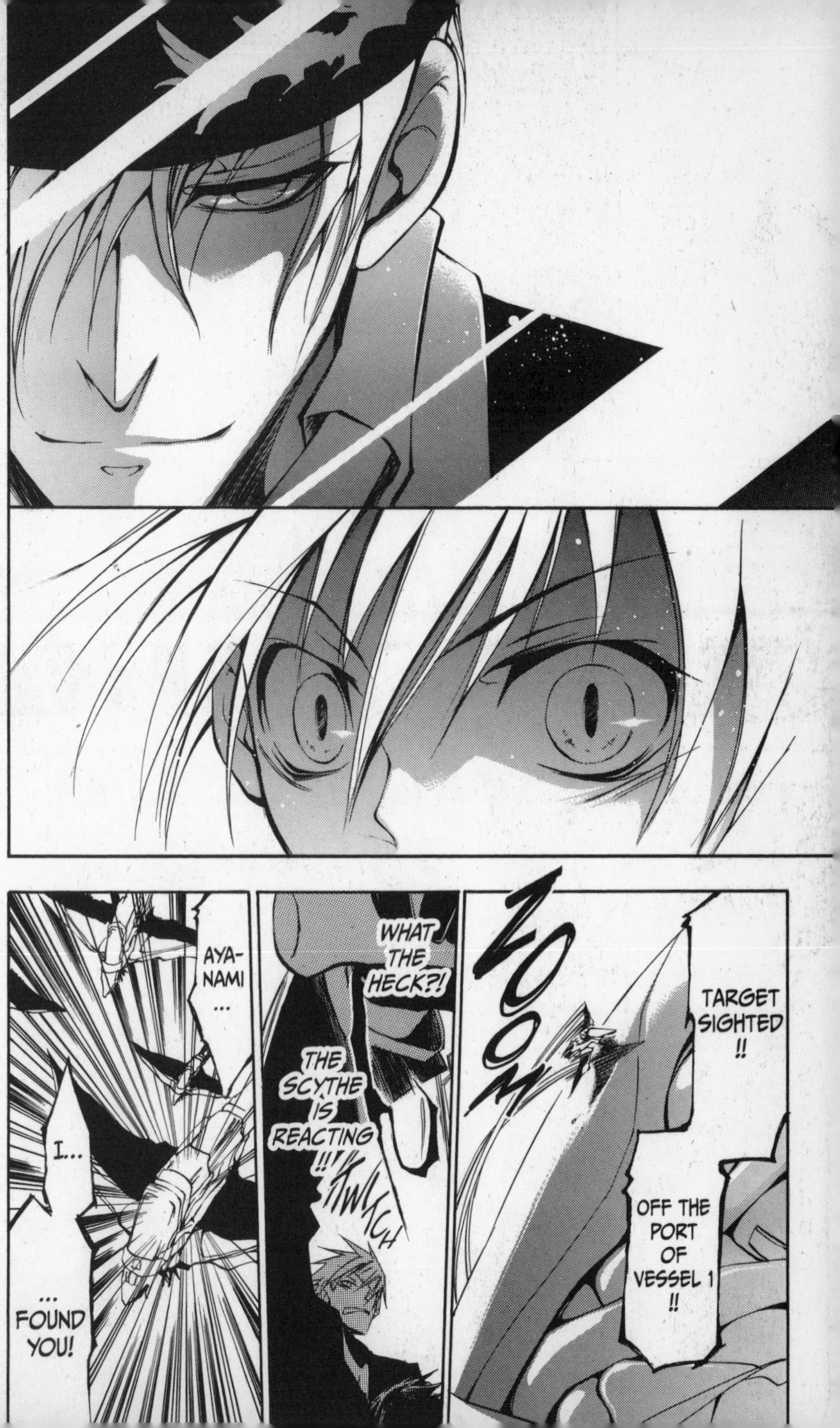
TARGET SIGHTED!!
OFF THE PORT OF VESSEL 1!!
ZOOM
WHAT THE HECK?!
THE SCYTHE IS REACTING!!
AYA-NAMI...
I...
...FOUND YOU!

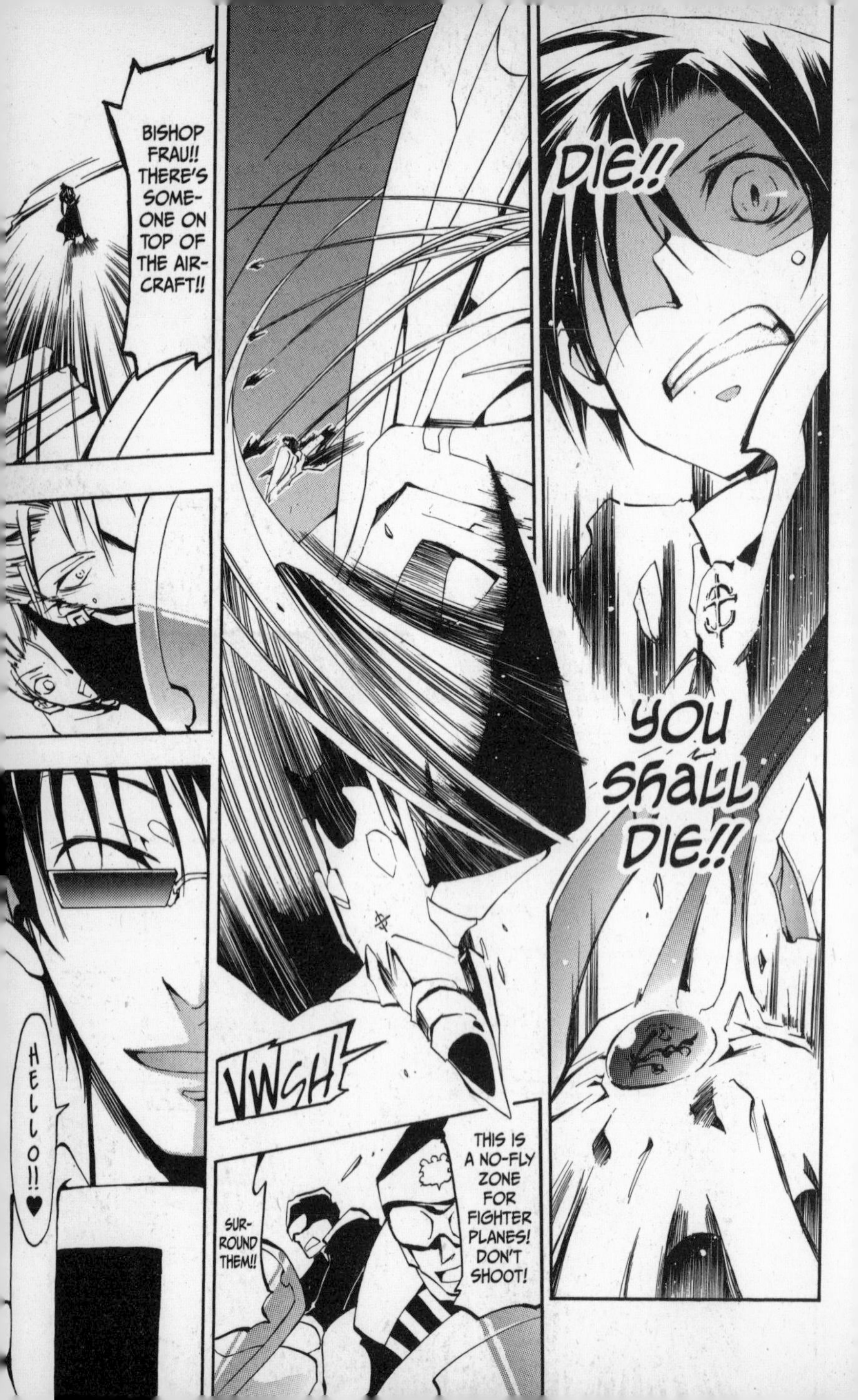
DIE!!
YOU SHALL DIE!!
VWSH
THIS IS A NO-FLY ZONE FOR FIGHTER PLANES! DON'T SHOOT!
SURROUND THEM!!
BISHOP FRAU!! THERE'S SOMEONE ON TOP OF THE AIRCRAFT!!
HELLO!!♥

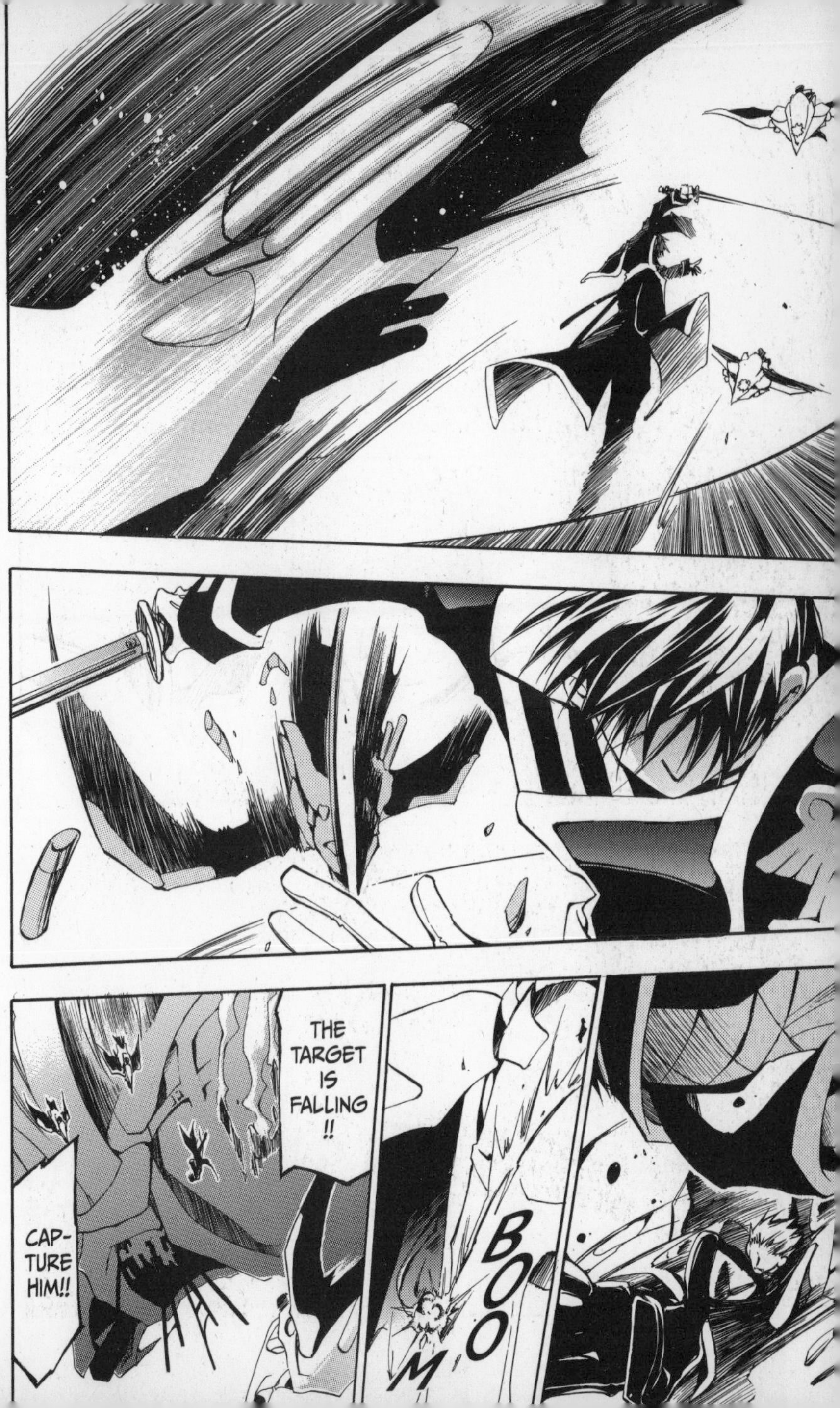
BOOOM
THE TARGET IS FALLING!!
CAP-TURE HIM!!

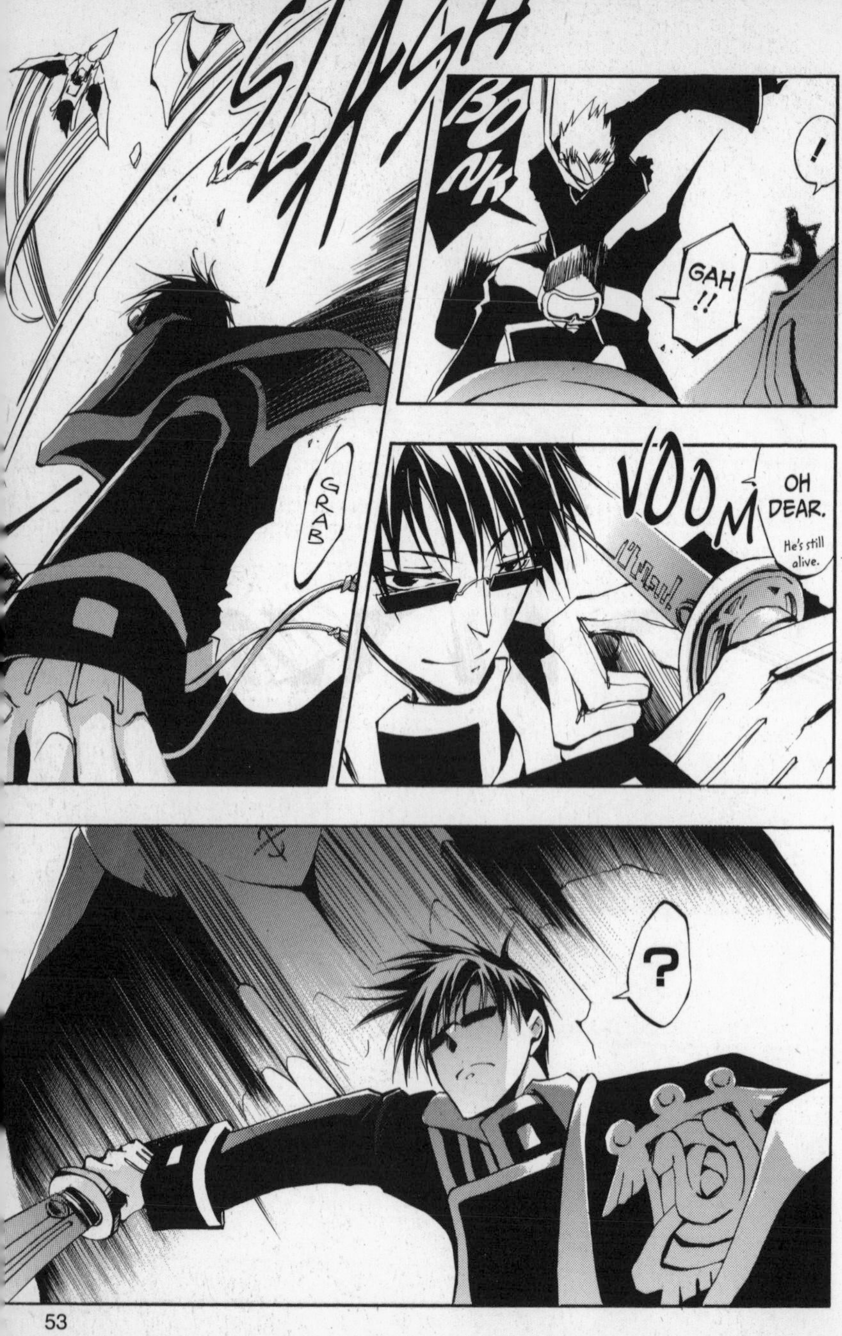
!
BONK
GAH !!
OH DEAR.
He's still alive.
VOOM
GRAB
SLASH
?

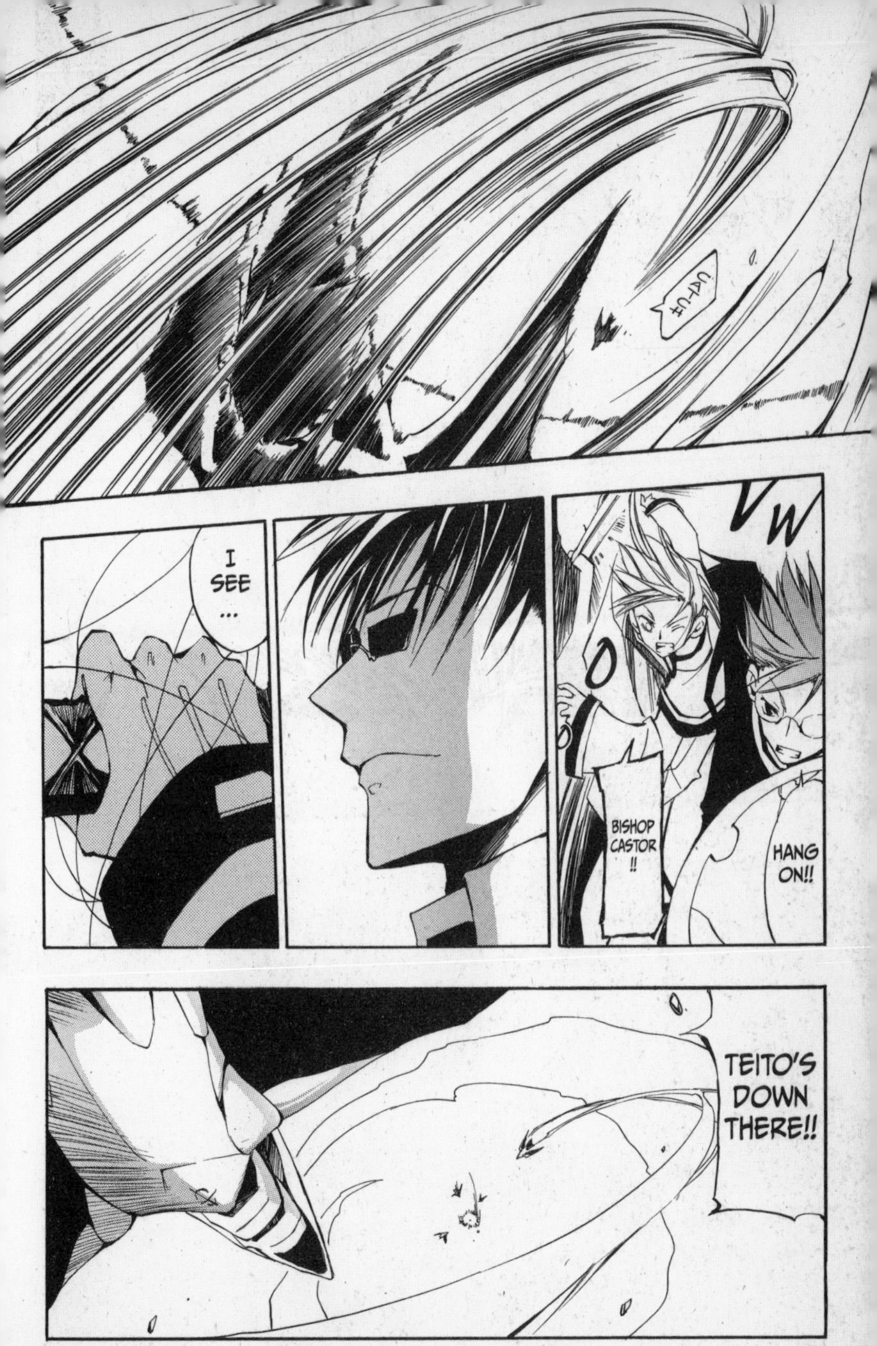
VW
HANG ON!!
BISHOP CASTOR !!
I SEE ...
TEITO'S DOWN THERE!!

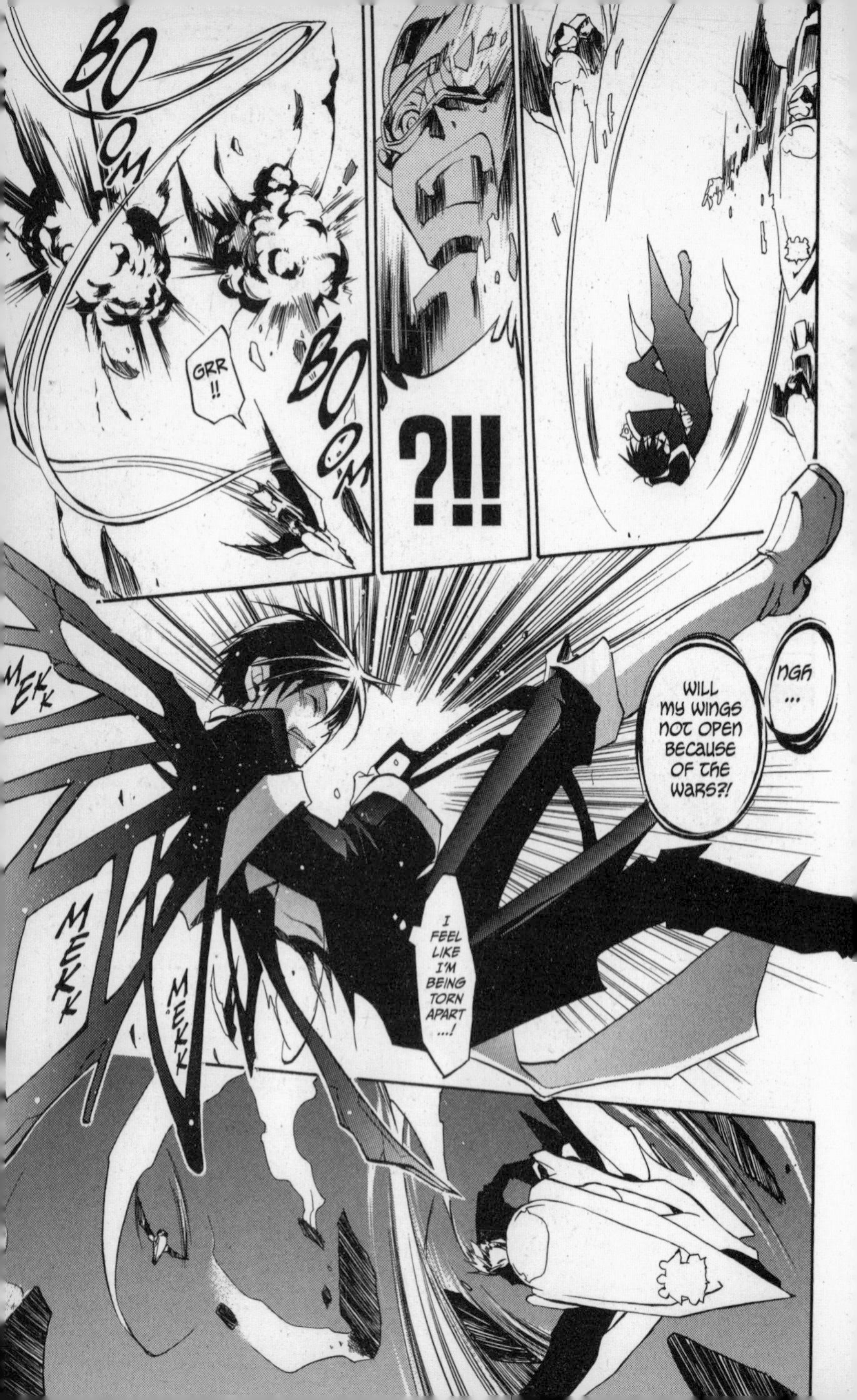
?!!
BOOM
GRR !!
BOOM
NGH ...
WILL MY WINGS NOT OPEN BECAUSE OF THE WARS?!
I FEEL LIKE I'M BEING TORN APART ...!
MEKK
MEKK
MEKK

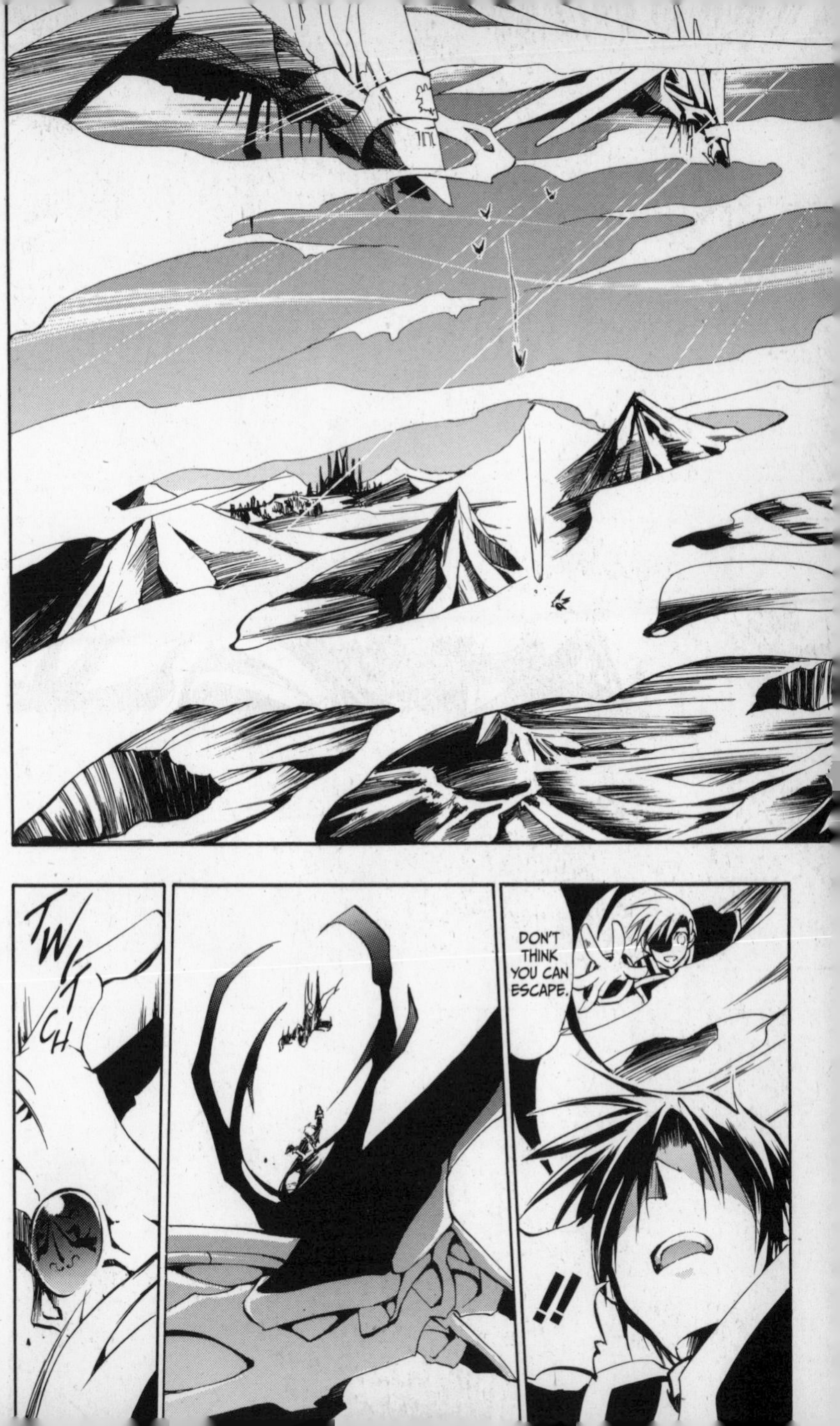
DON'T THINK YOU CAN ESCAPE.
!!
TWITCH

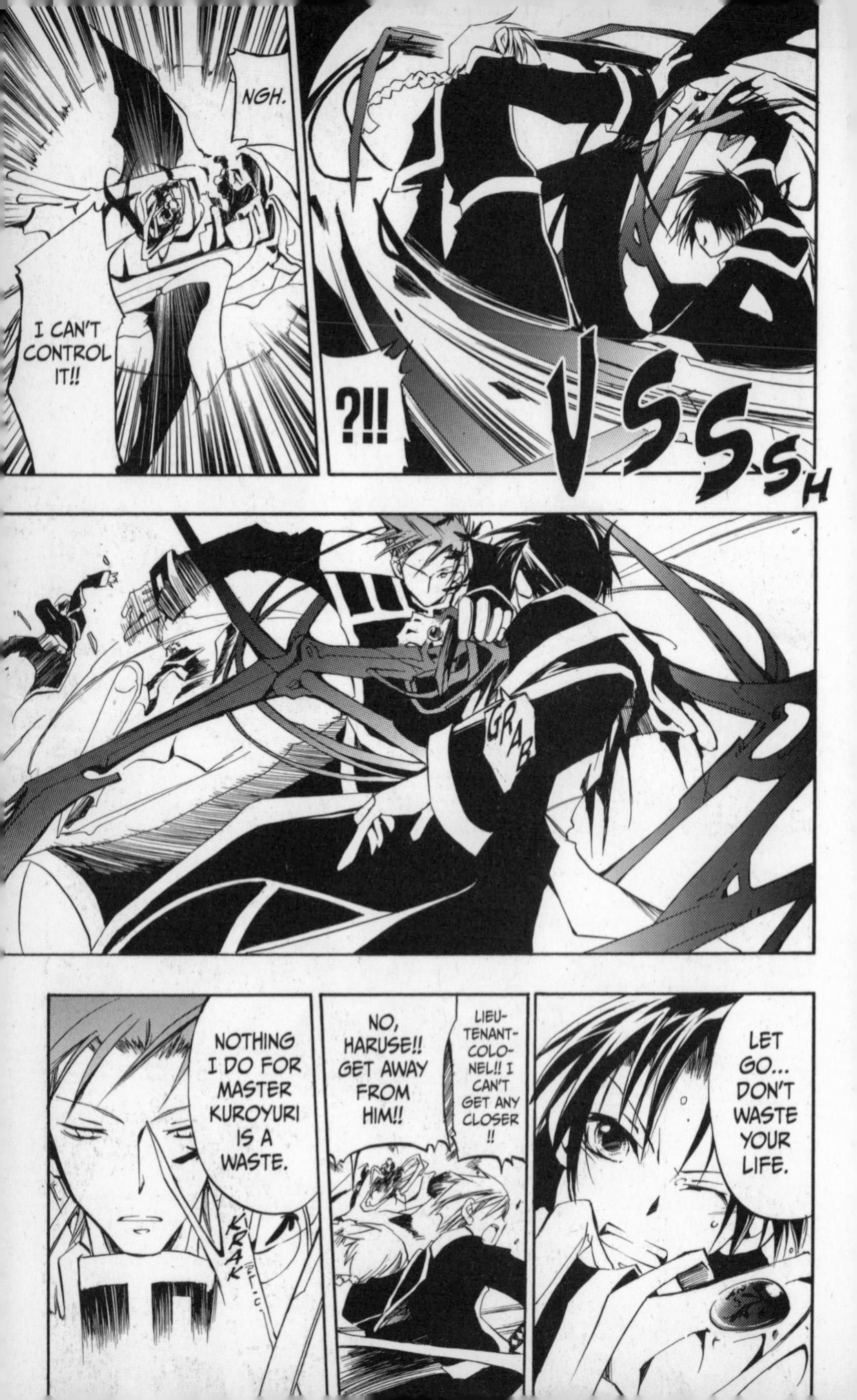
?!!
VSSSH
NGH.
I CAN'T CONTROL IT!!
GRAB
LET GO... DON'T WASTE YOUR LIFE.
LIEU-TENANT-COLO-NEL!! I CAN'T GET ANY CLOSER!!
NO, HARUSE!! GET AWAY FROM HIM!!
NOTHING I DO FOR MASTER KUROYURI IS A WASTE.
KRAK

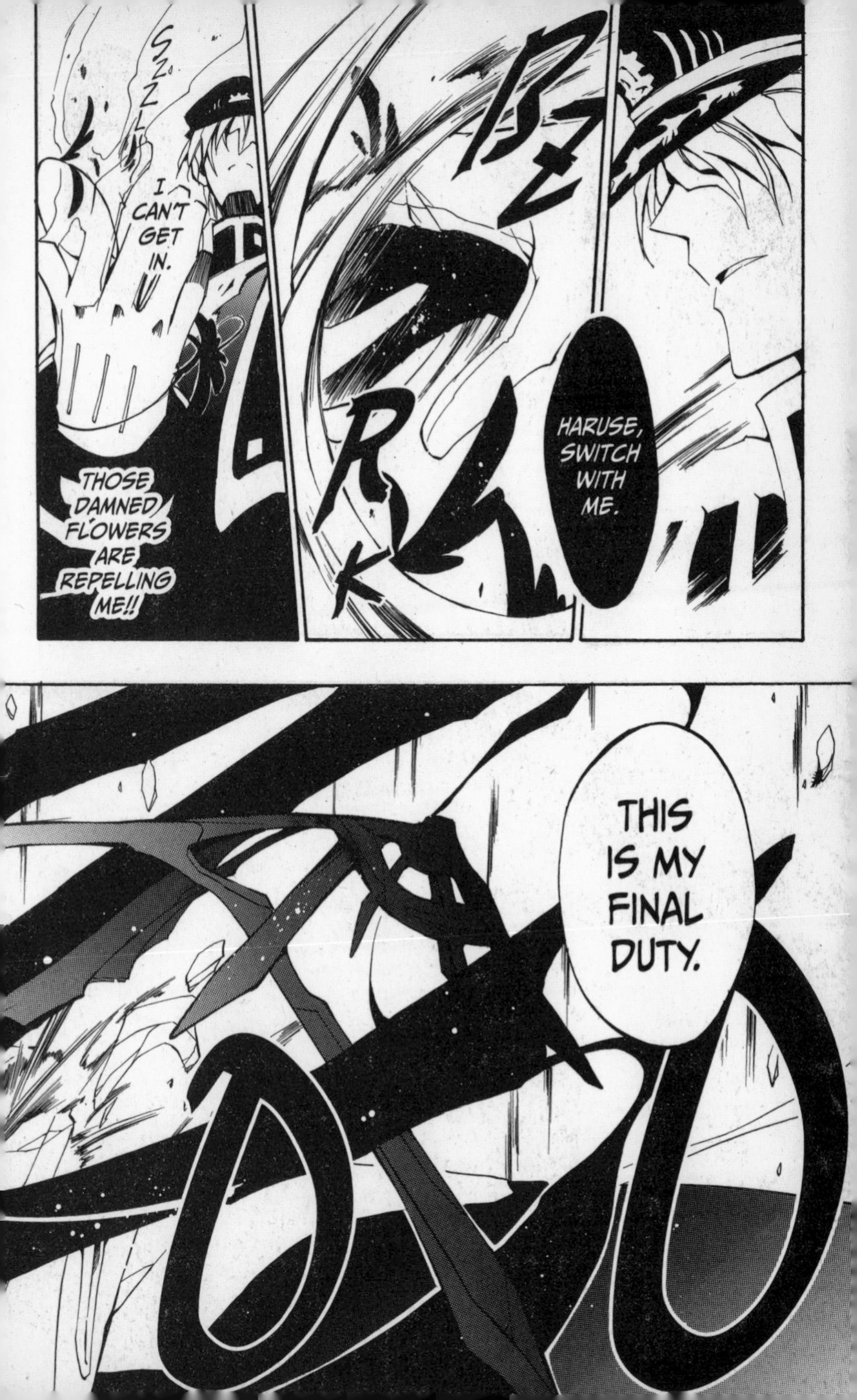
HARUSE, SWITCH WITH ME.
I CAN'T GET IN.
THOSE DAMNED FLOWERS ARE REPELLING ME!!
THIS IS MY FINAL DUTY.

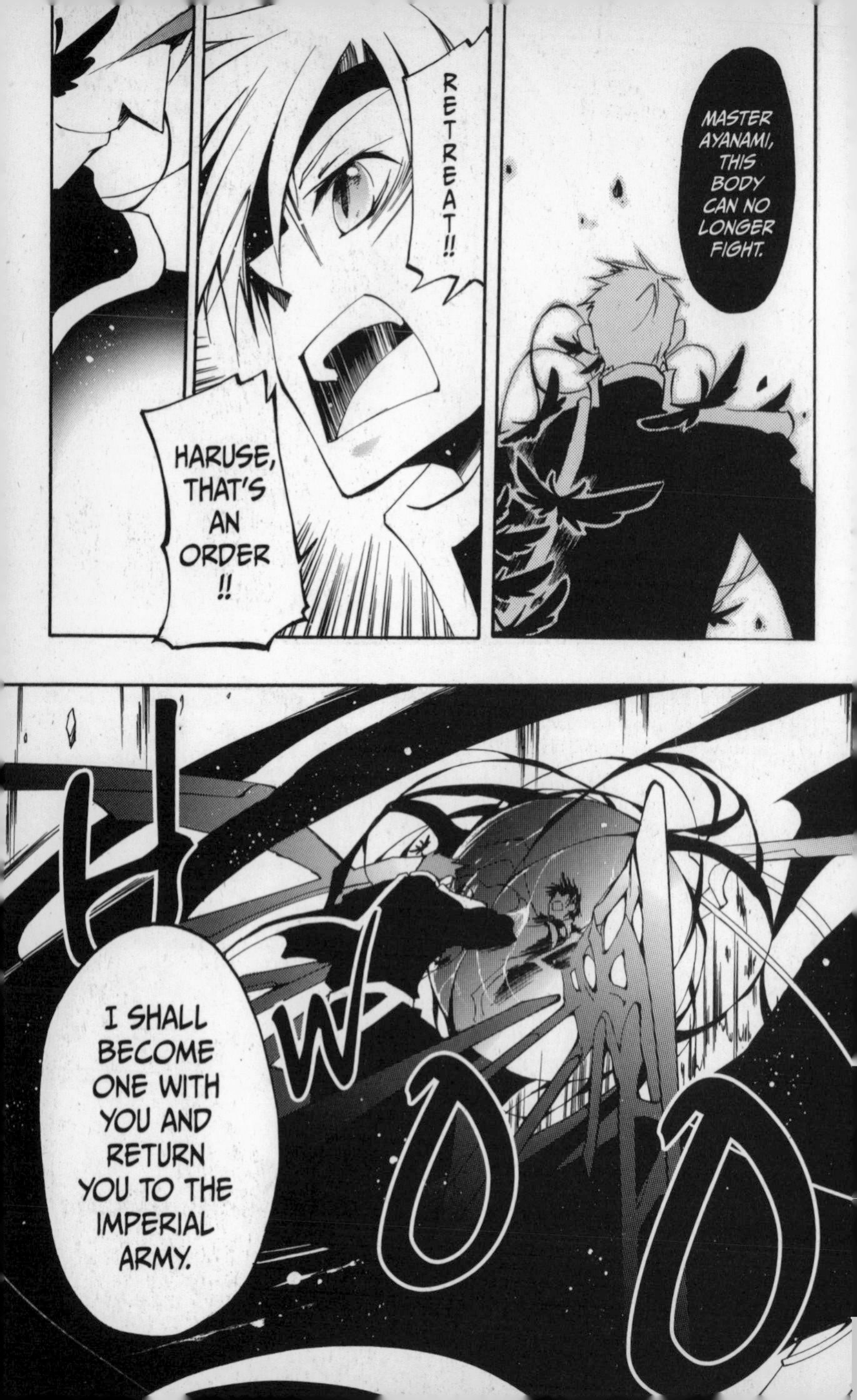
MASTER AYANAMI, THIS BODY CAN NO LONGER FIGHT.
RETREAT!!
HARUSE, THAT'S AN ORDER!!
I SHALL BECOME ONE WITH YOU AND RETURN YOU TO THE IMPERIAL ARMY.

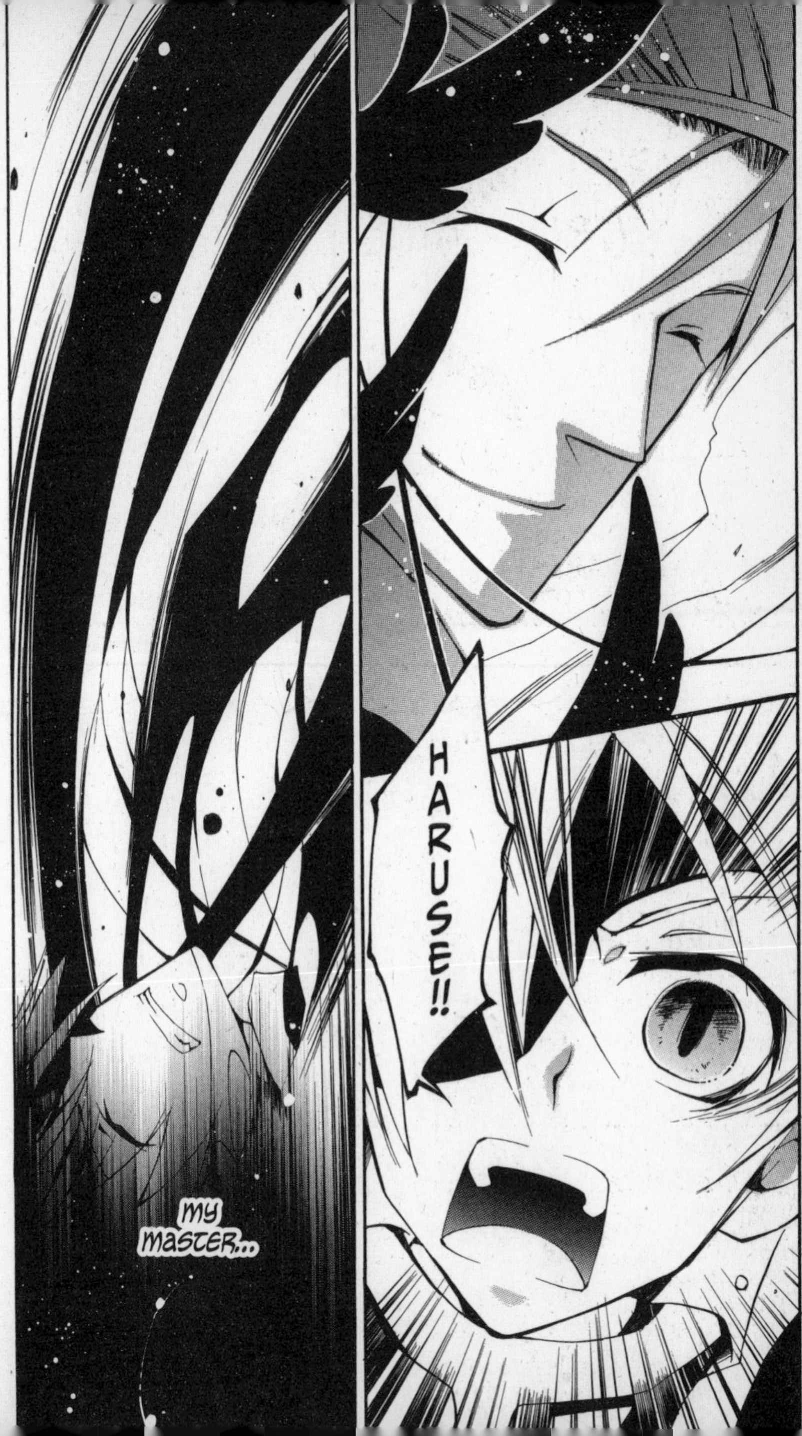
HARUSE!!
my master...

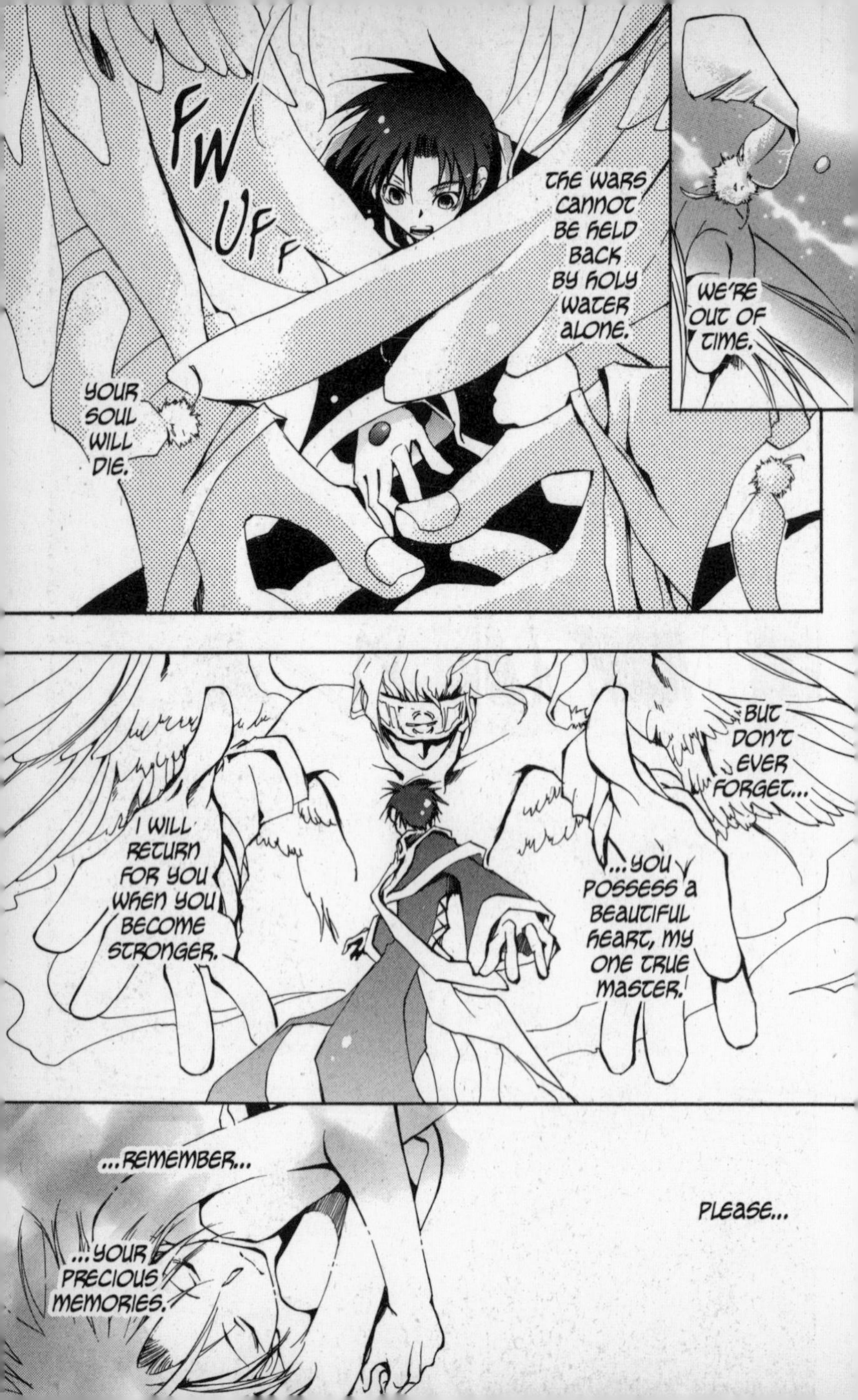
WE'RE OUT OF TIME.
THE WARS CANNOT BE HELD BACK BY HOLY WATER ALONE.
FWUFF
YOUR SOUL WILL DIE.
BUT DON'T EVER FORGET...
...YOU POSSESS A BEAUTIFUL HEART, MY ONE TRUE MASTER.
I WILL RETURN FOR YOU WHEN YOU BECOME STRONGER.
PLEASE...
...REMEMBER...
...YOUR PRECIOUS MEMORIES.

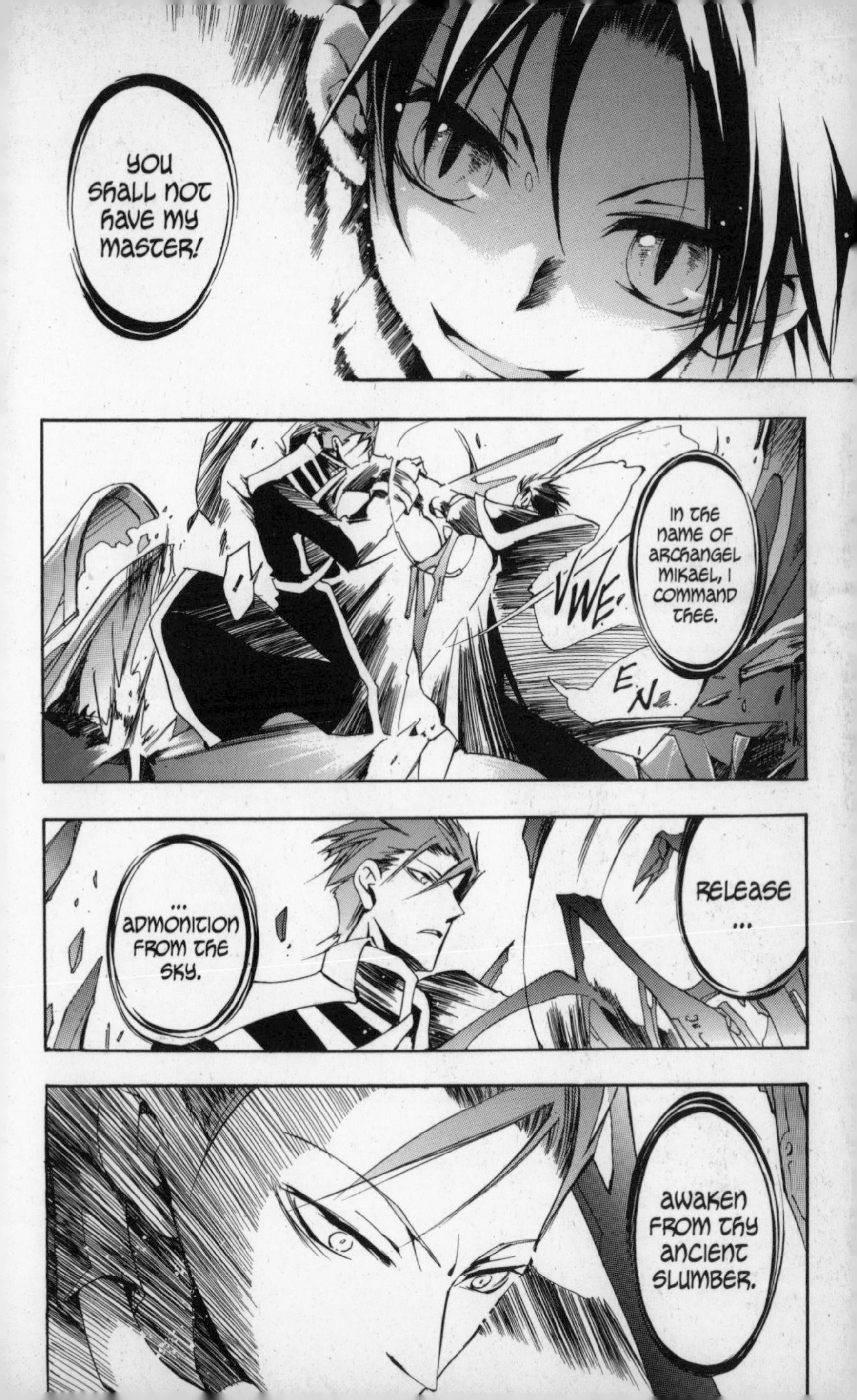
YOU SHALL NOT HAVE MY MASTER!
IN THE NAME OF ARCHANGEL MIKAEL, I COMMAND THEE.
VWE
EN
RELEASE ...
... ADMONITION FROM THE SKY.
AWAKEN FROM THY ANCIENT SLUMBER.

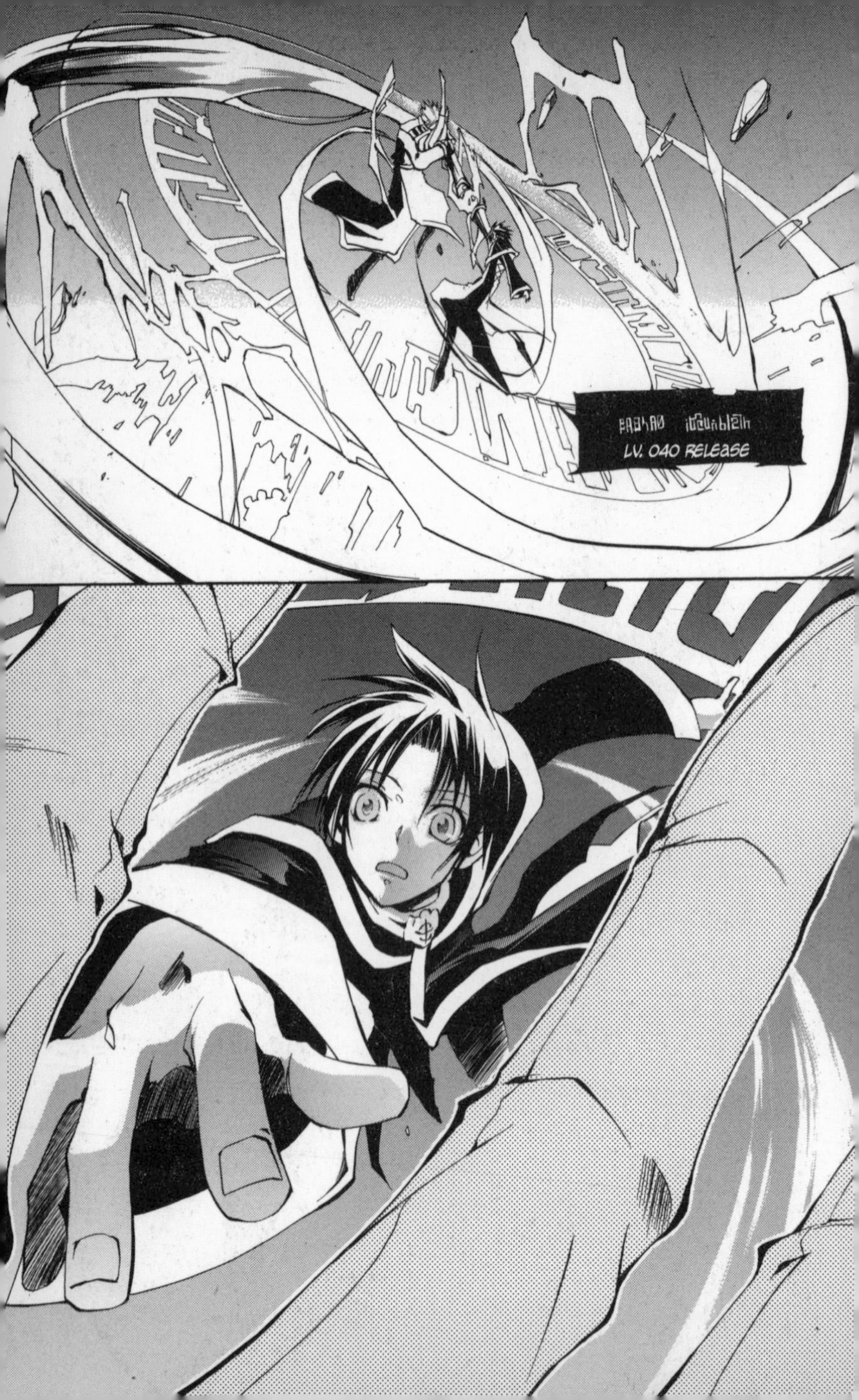
LV. 040 RELEASE

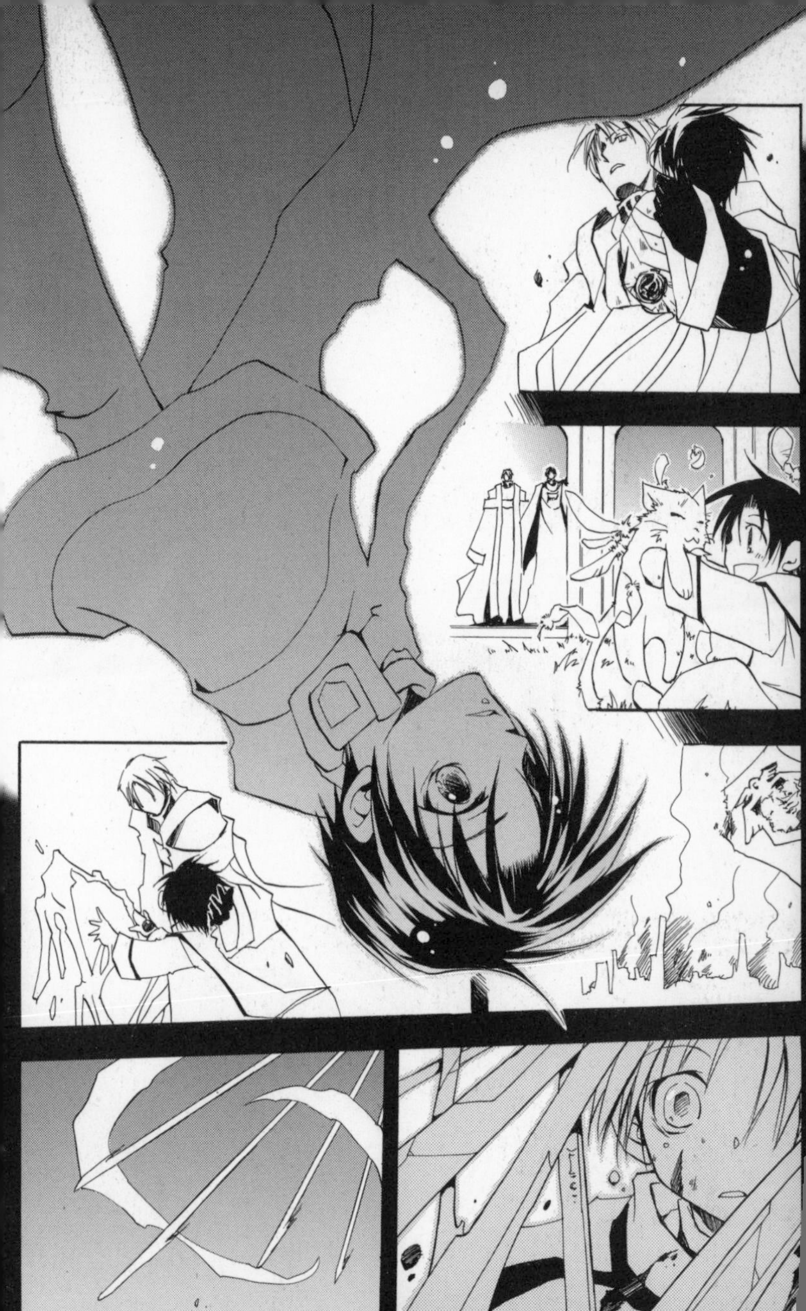

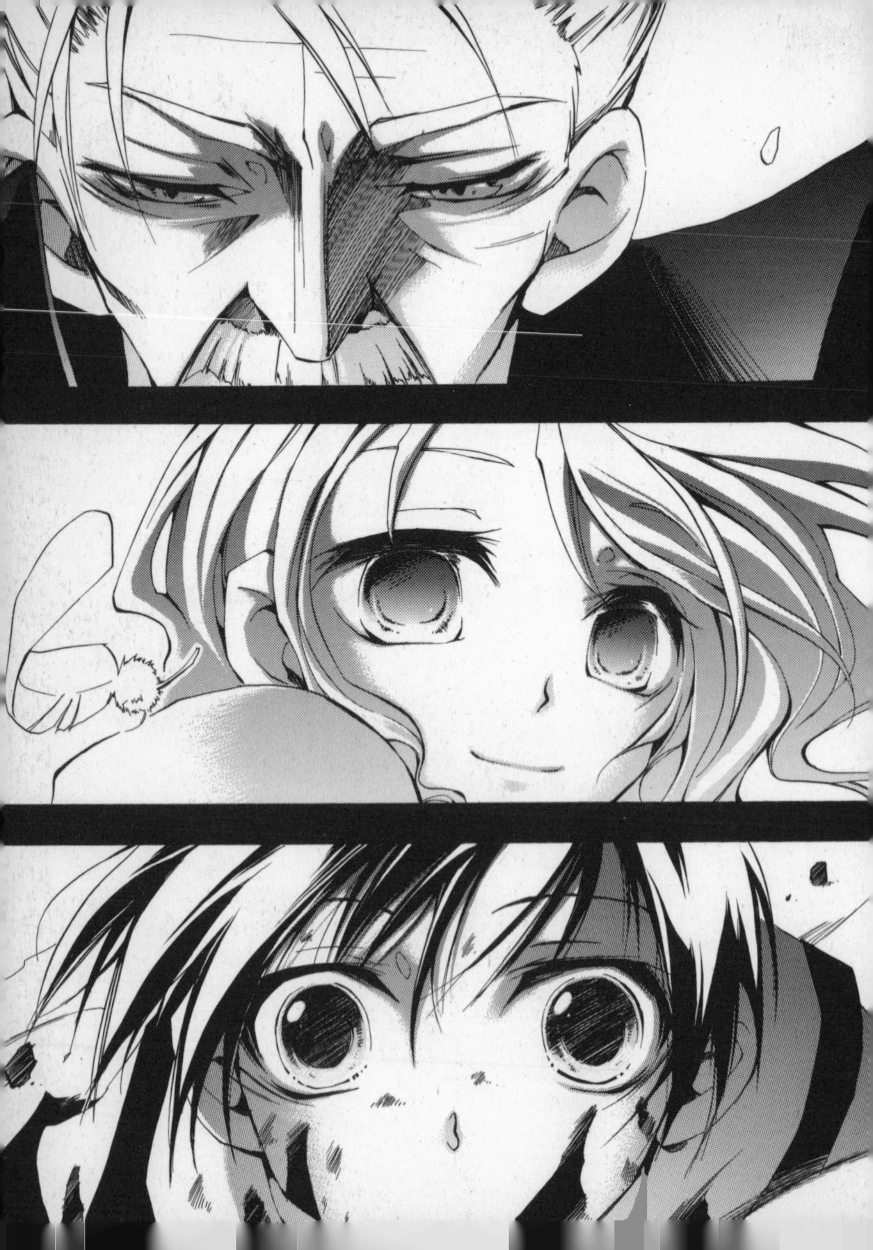

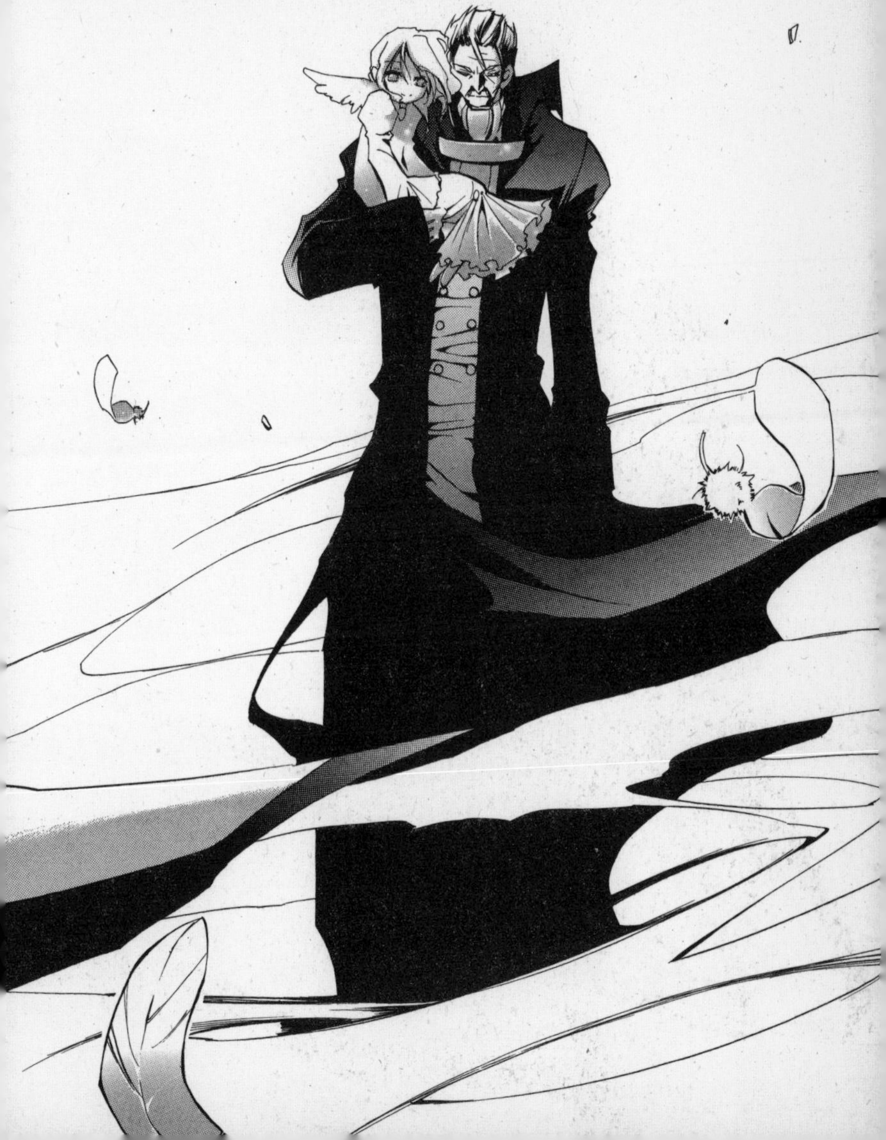

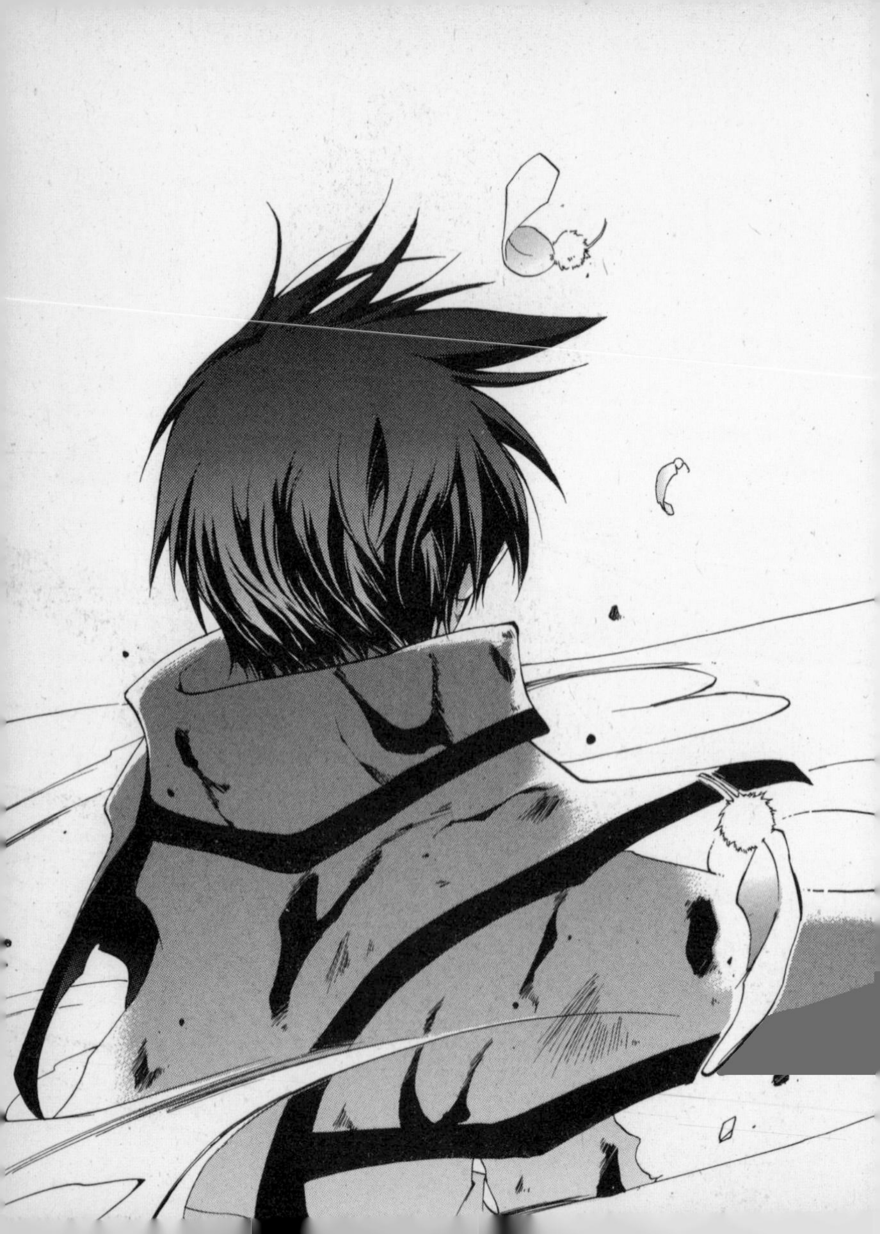

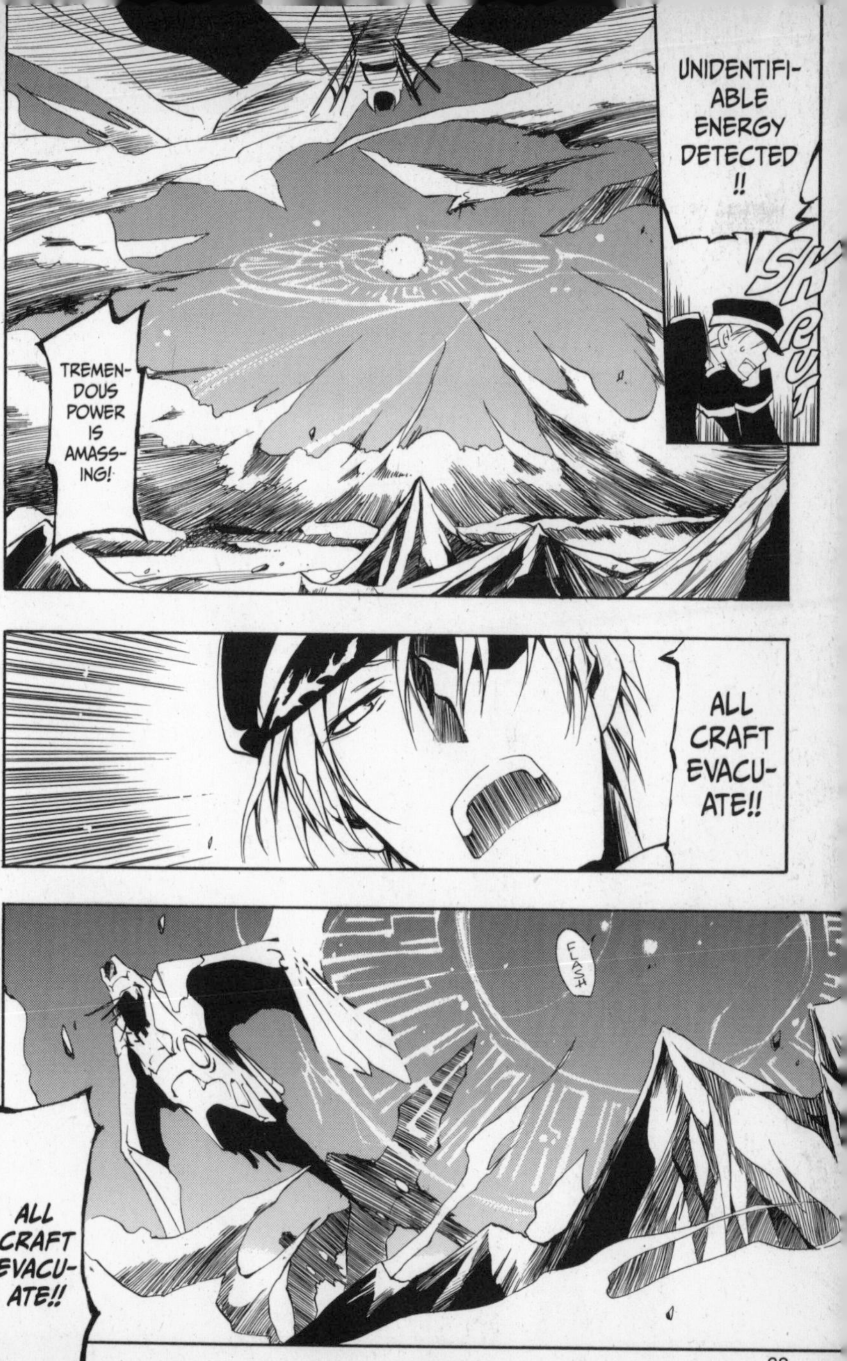

UNIDENTIFIABLE ENERGY DETECTED!!
TREMENDOUS POWER IS AMASSING!
ALL CRAFT EVACUATE!!
FLASH
ALL CRAFT EVACUATE!!

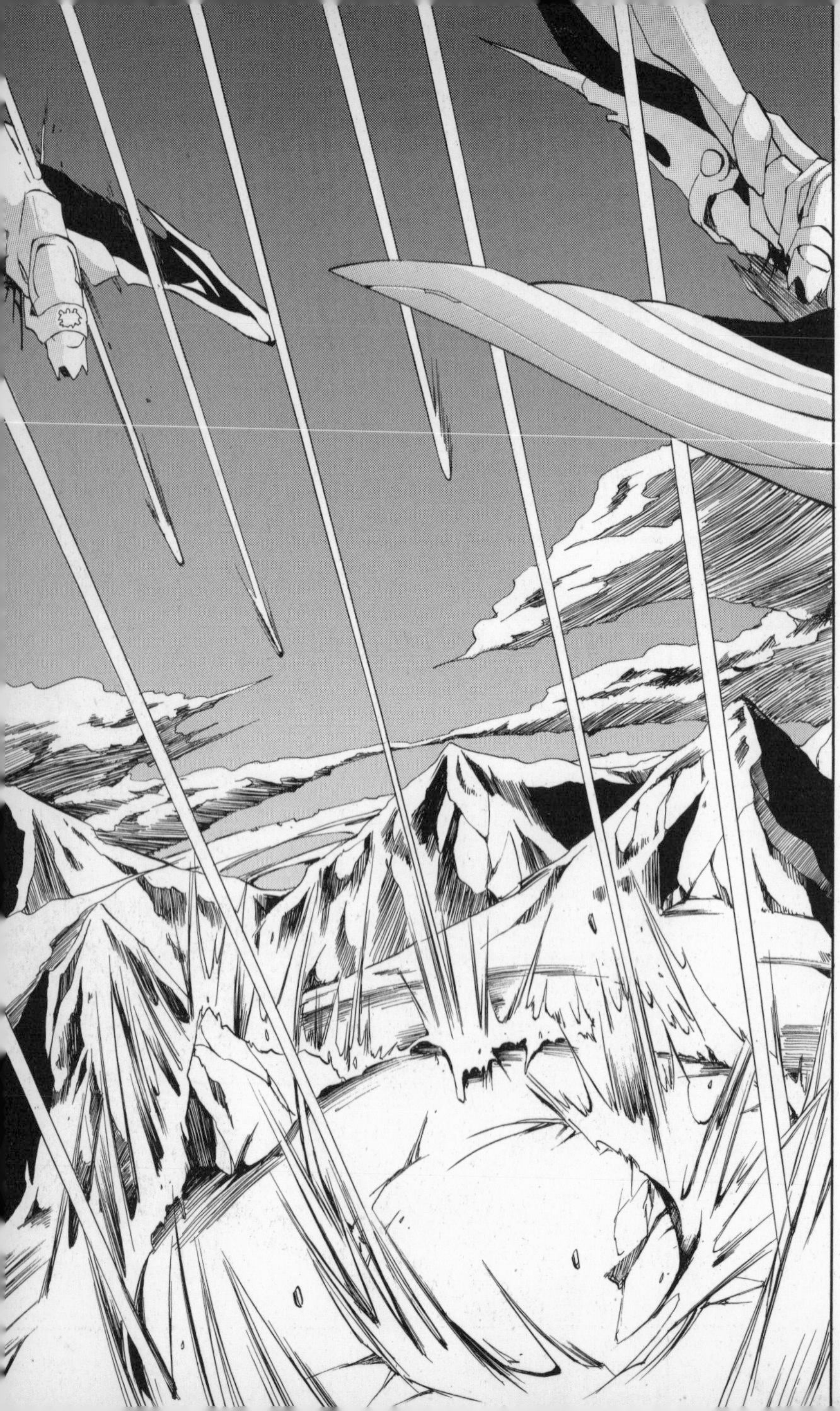

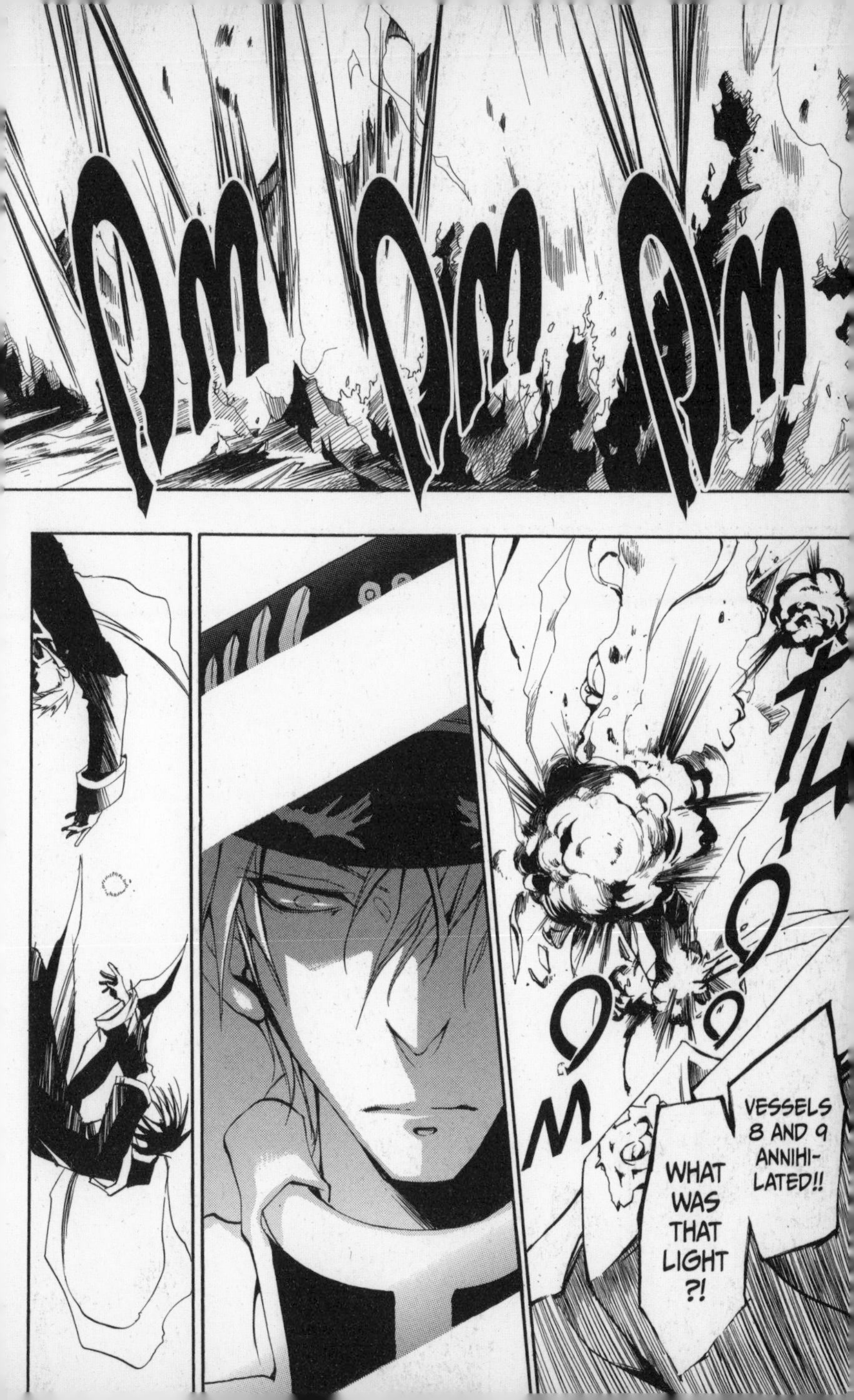
VESSELS 8 AND 9 ANNIHILATED!!
WHAT WAS THAT LIGHT?!

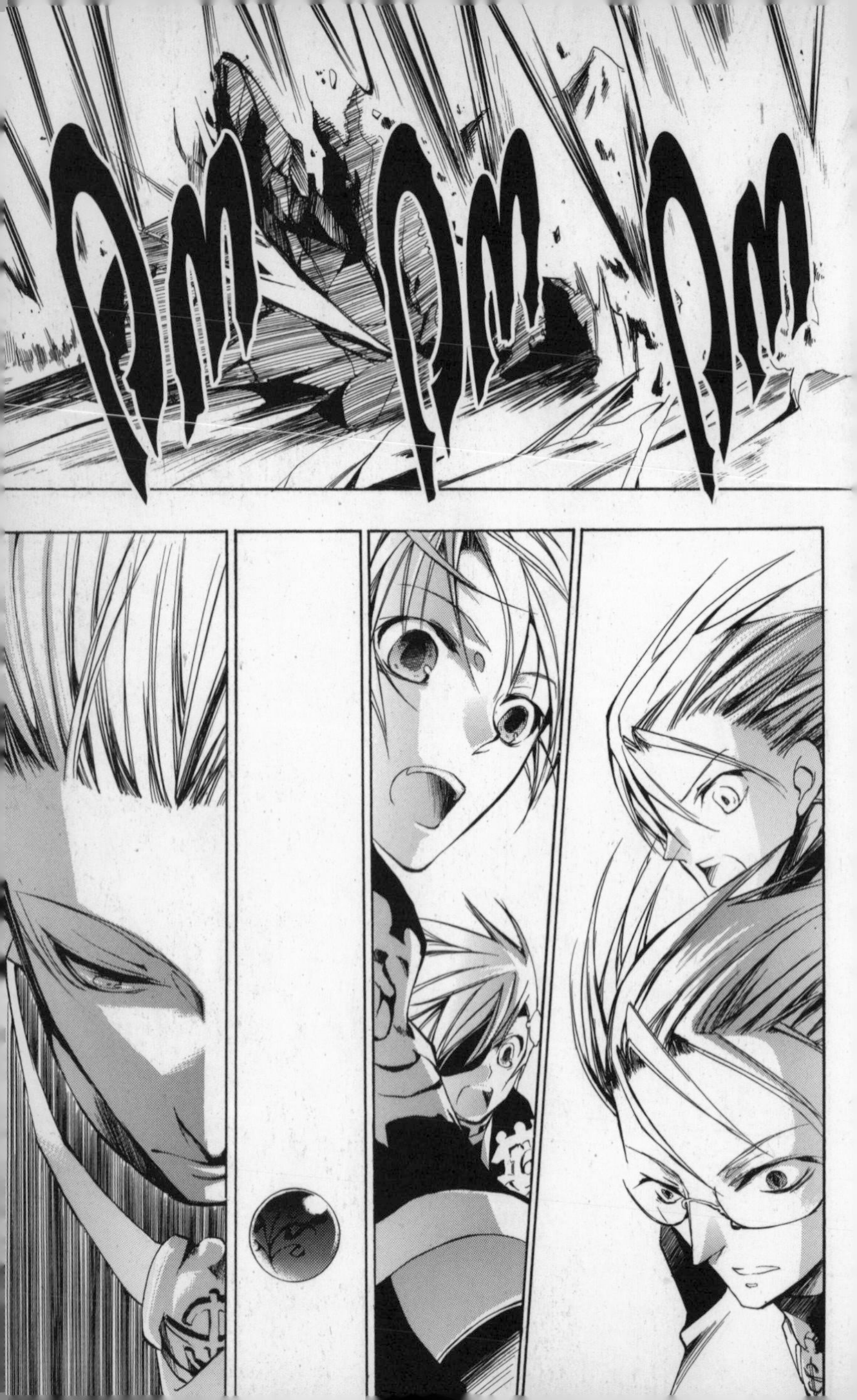

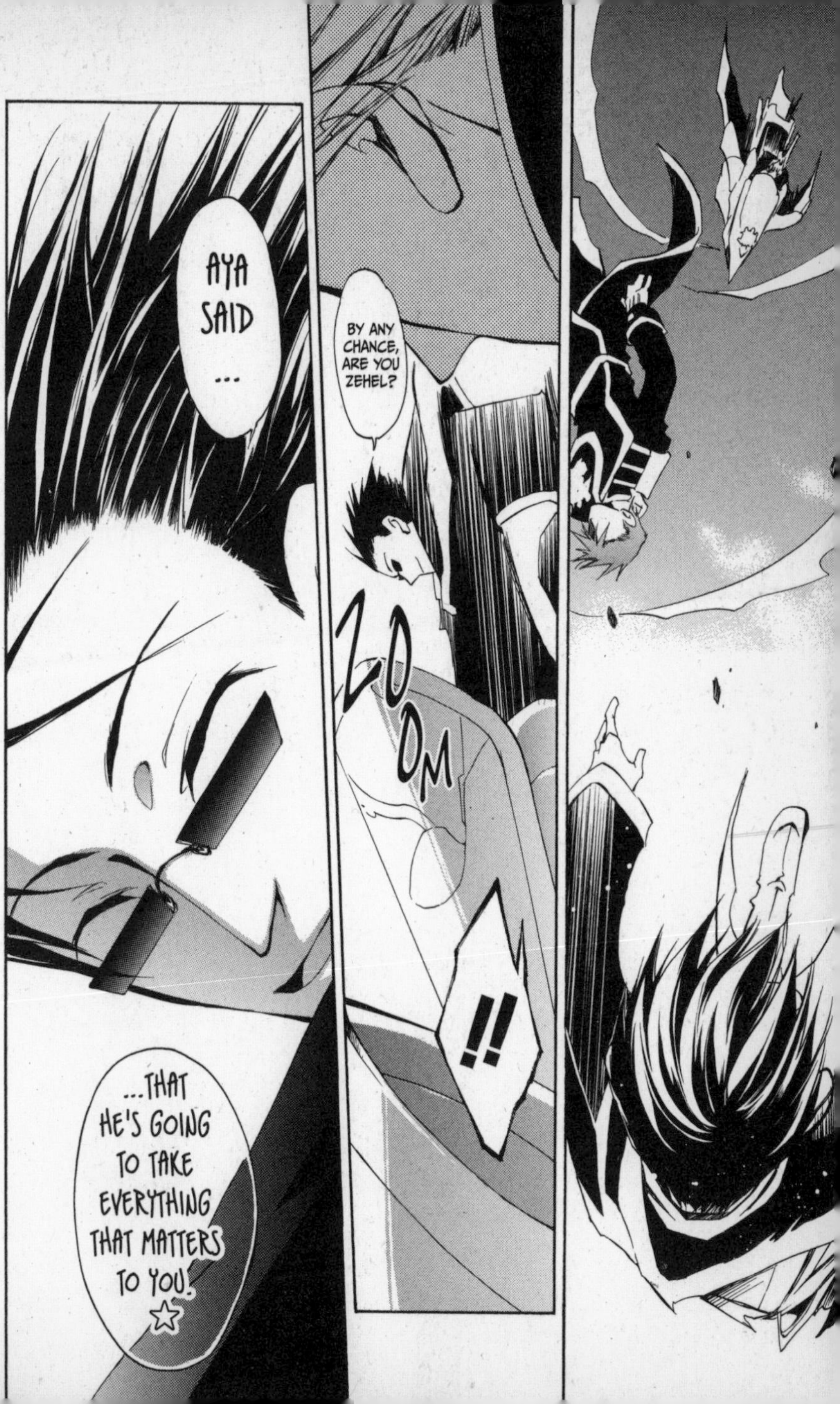
BY ANY CHANCE, ARE YOU ZEHEL?
ZOOM
!!
AYA SAID ...
...THAT HE'S GOING TO TAKE EVERYTHING THAT MATTERS TO YOU. ☆

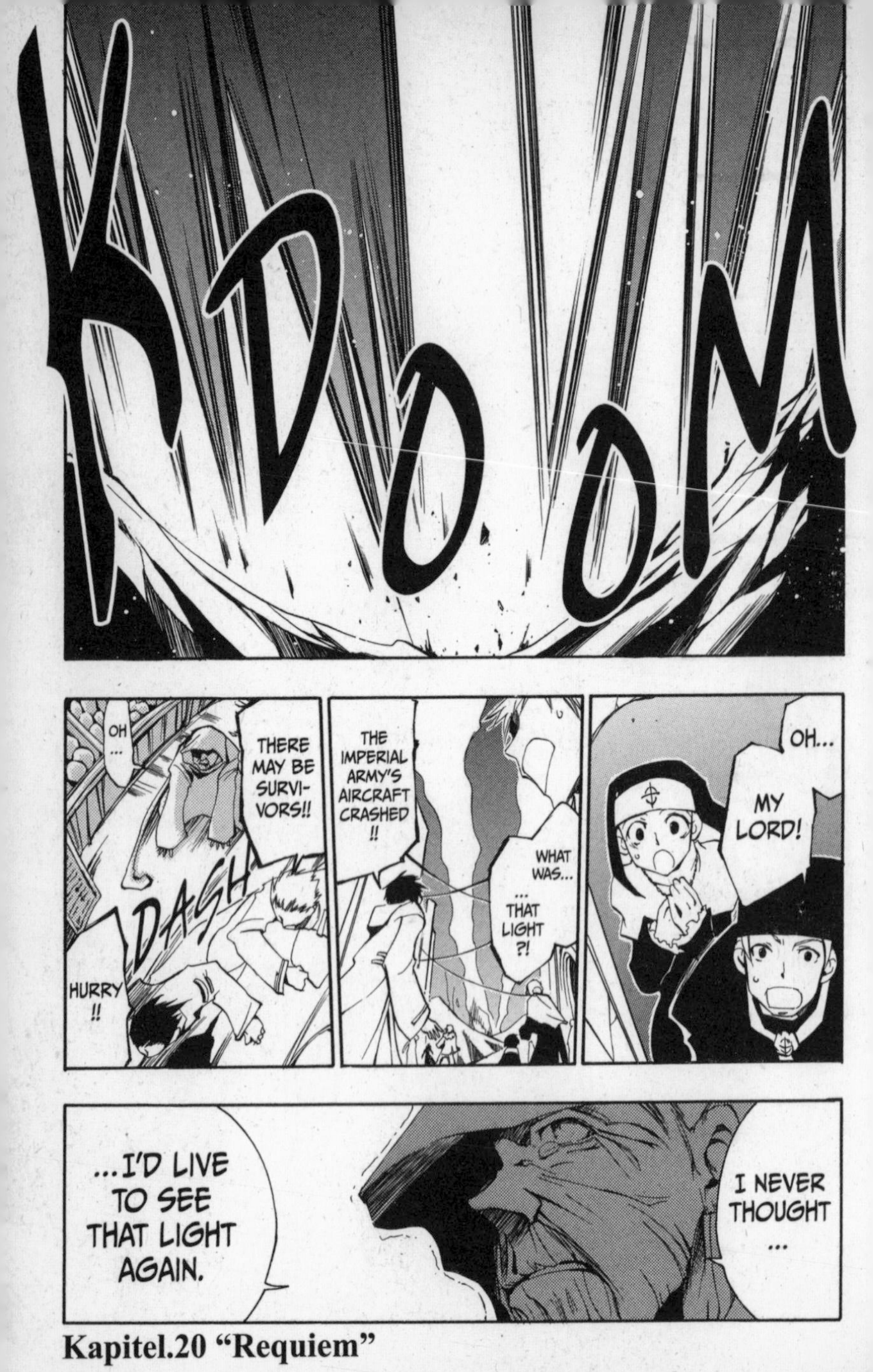
KDOOM
OH... MY LORD!
THE IMPERIAL ARMY'S AIRCRAFT CRASHED!!
WHAT WAS... ...THAT LIGHT?!
THERE MAY BE SURVIVORS!!
OH ...
DASH
HURRY!!
I NEVER THOUGHT ...
...I'D LIVE TO SEE THAT LIGHT AGAIN.

Kapitel.20 “Requiem”

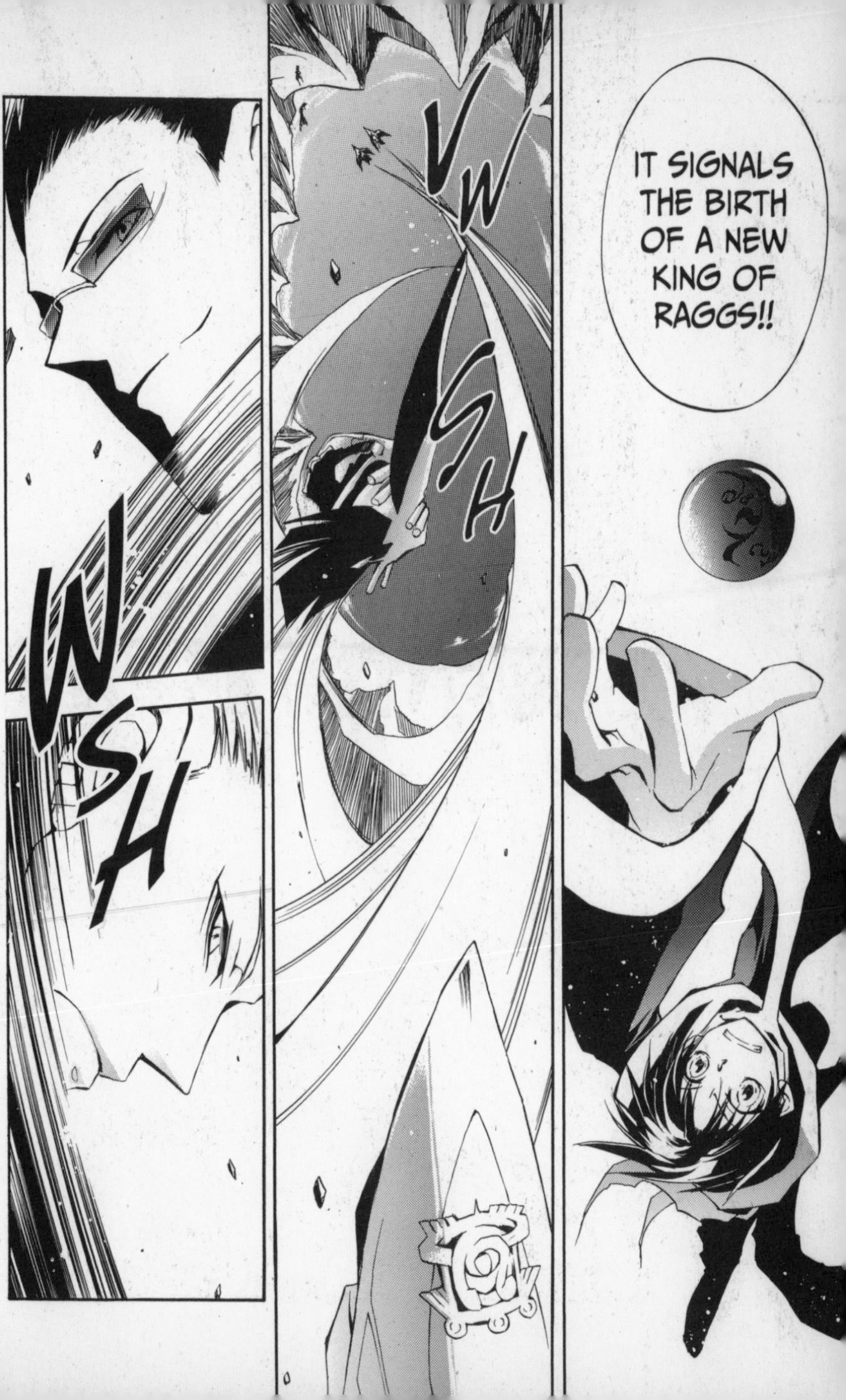
IT SIGNALS THE BIRTH OF A NEW KING OF RAGGS!!
VWSH
WSH

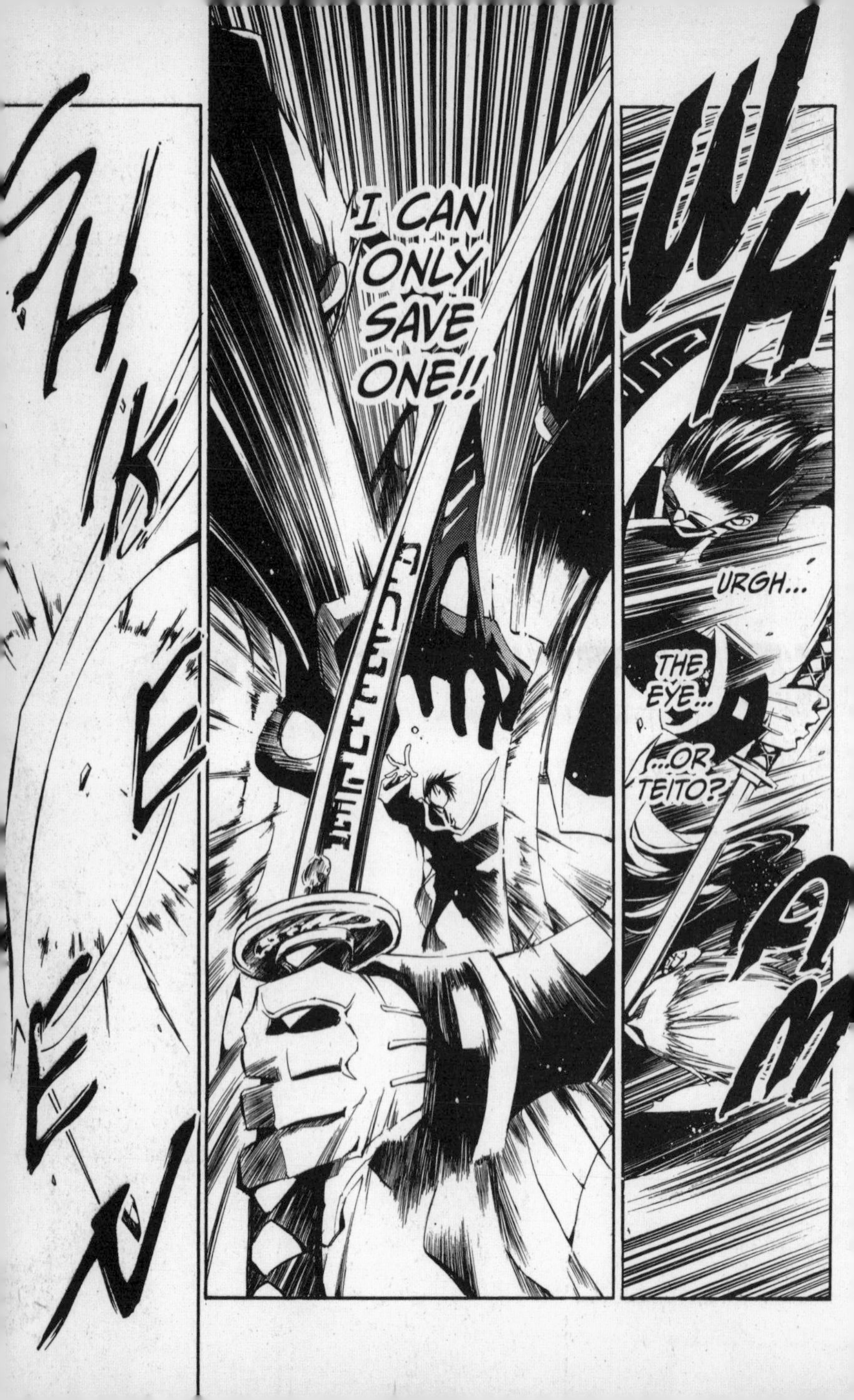
URGH...
THE EYE...
...OR TEITO?
I CAN ONLY SAVE ONE!!

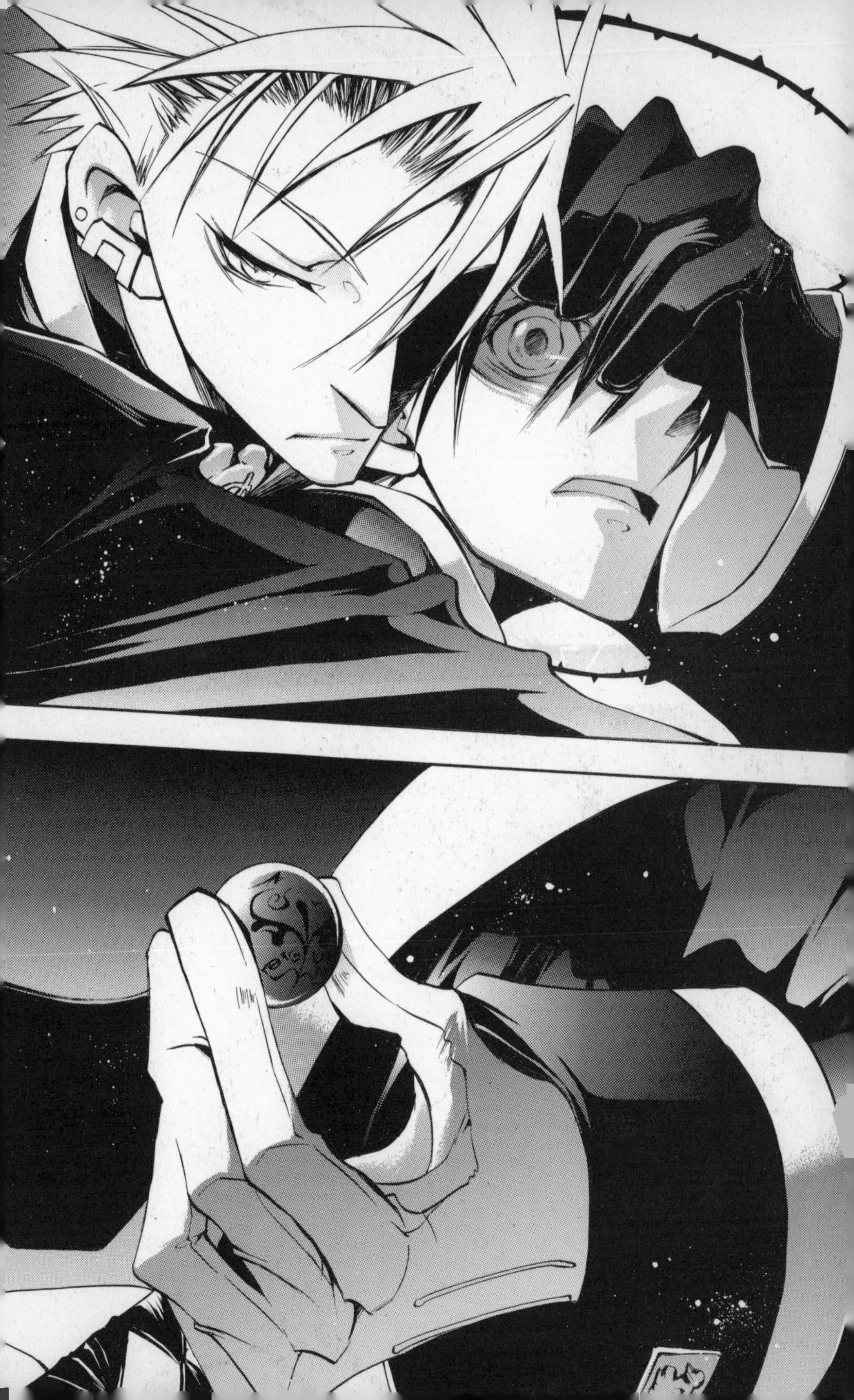

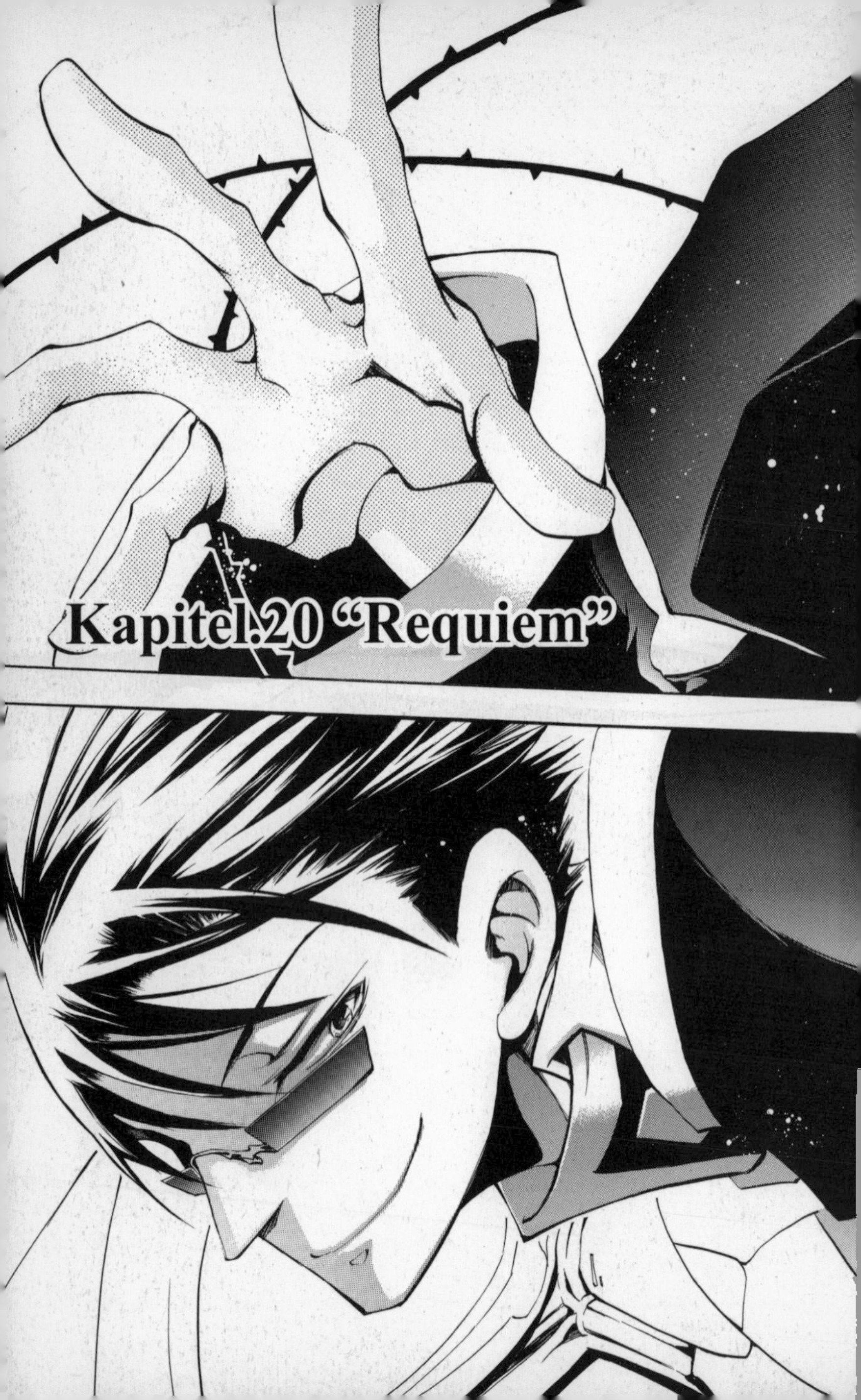
Kapitel.20 “Requiem”

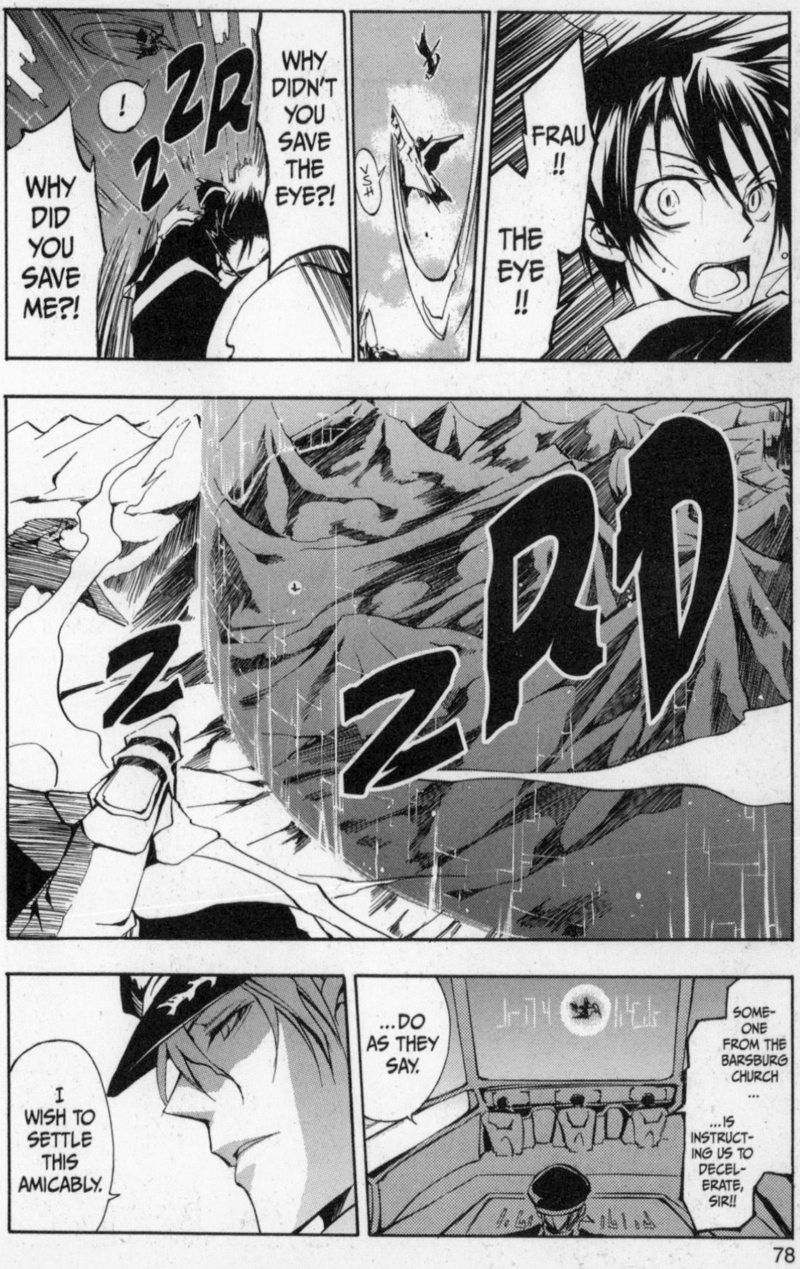
FRAU!!
THE EYE!!
WHY DIDN'T YOU SAVE THE EYE?!
!
ZZR
WHY DID YOU SAVE ME?!
ZZRD
SOME-ONE FROM THE BARSBURG CHURCH...
...IS INSTRUCT-ING US TO DECEL-ERATE, SIR!!
...DO AS THEY SAY.
I WISH TO SETTLE THIS AMICABLY.

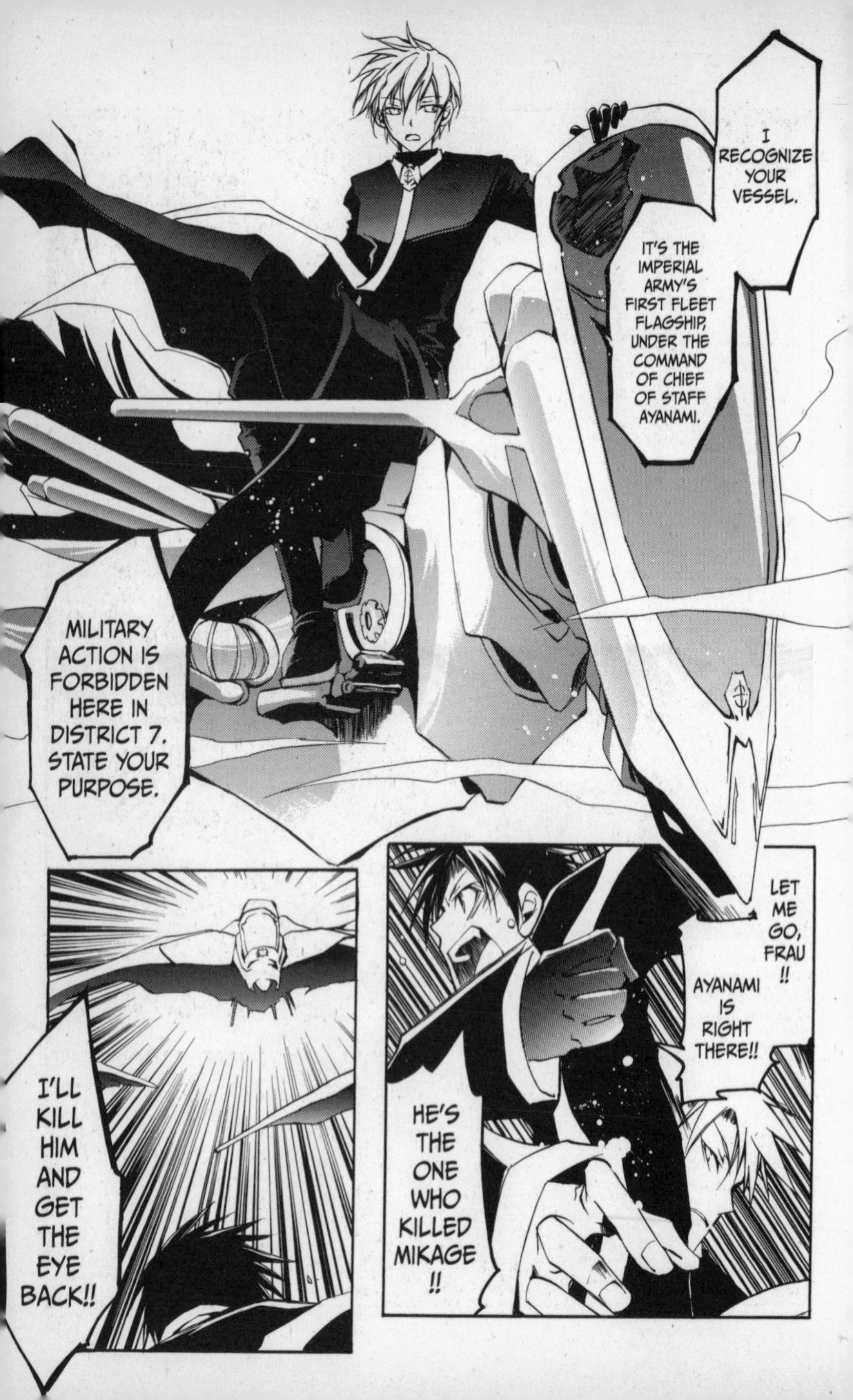
I RECOGNIZE YOUR VESSEL.
IT'S THE IMPERIAL ARMY'S FIRST FLEET FLAGSHIP, UNDER THE COMMAND OF CHIEF OF STAFF AYANAMI.
MILITARY ACTION IS FORBIDDEN HERE IN DISTRICT 7. STATE YOUR PURPOSE.
LET ME GO, FRAU!!
AYANAMI IS RIGHT THERE!!
HE'S THE ONE WHO KILLED MIKAGE!!
I'LL KILL HIM AND GET THE EYE BACK!!

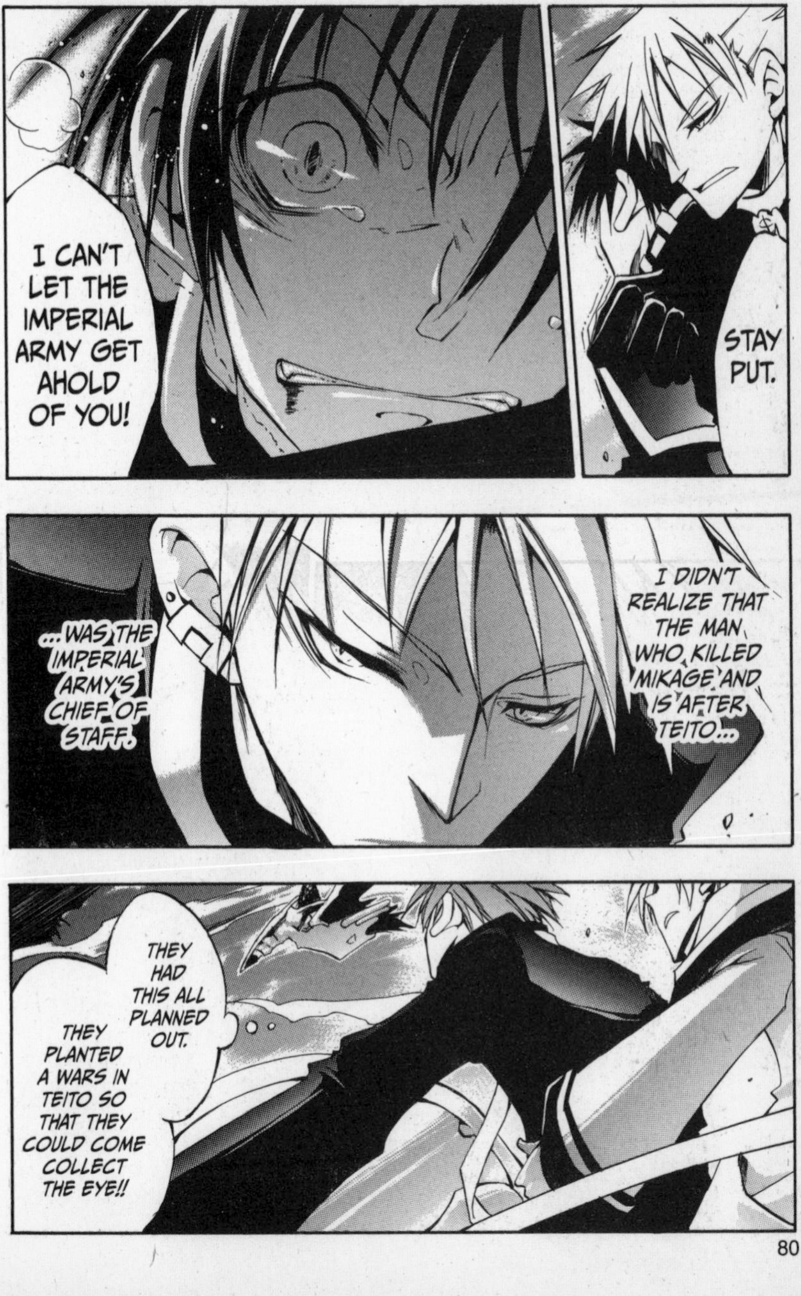
STAY PUT.
I CAN'T LET THE IMPERIAL ARMY GET AHOLD OF YOU!
I DIDN'T REALIZE THAT THE MAN WHO KILLED MIKAGE AND IS AFTER TEITO...
...WAS THE IMPERIAL ARMY'S CHIEF OF STAFF.
THEY HAD THIS ALL PLANNED OUT.
THEY PLANTED A WARS IN TEITO SO THAT THEY COULD COME COLLECT THE EYE!!

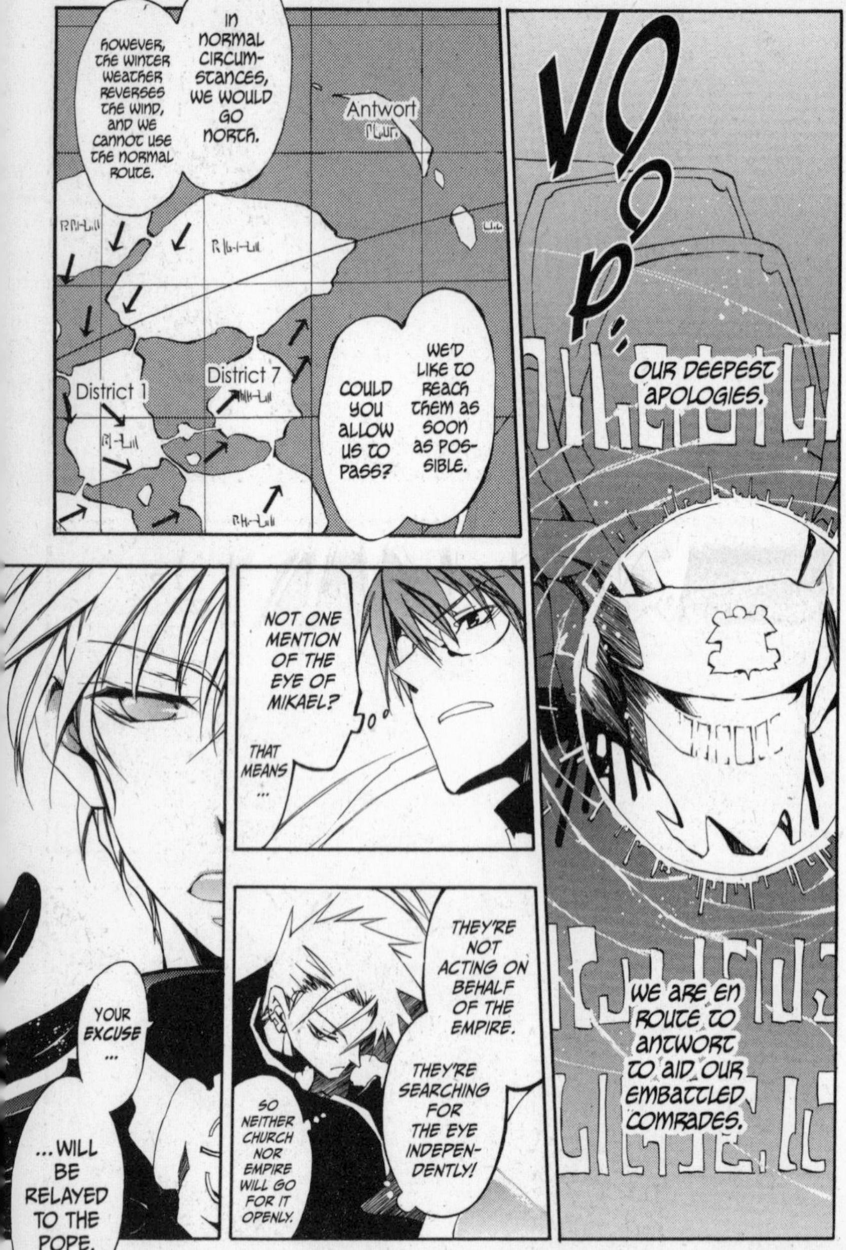
VOOP
OUR DEEPEST APOLOGIES.
WE ARE EN ROUTE TO ANTWORT TO AID OUR EMBATTLED COMRADES.
IN NORMAL CIRCUMSTANCES, WE WOULD GO NORTH.
HOWEVER, THE WINTER WEATHER REVERSES THE WIND, AND WE CANNOT USE THE NORMAL ROUTE.
Antwort
District 7
District 1
WE'D LIKE TO REACH THEM AS SOON AS POSSIBLE.
COULD YOU ALLOW US TO PASS?
NOT ONE MENTION OF THE EYE OF MIKAEL?
THAT MEANS ...
THEY'RE NOT ACTING ON BEHALF OF THE EMPIRE.
THEY'RE SEARCHING FOR THE EYE INDEPENDENTLY!
SO NEITHER CHURCH NOR EMPIRE WILL GO FOR IT OPENLY.
YOUR EXCUSE ...
...WILL BE RELAYED TO THE POPE.

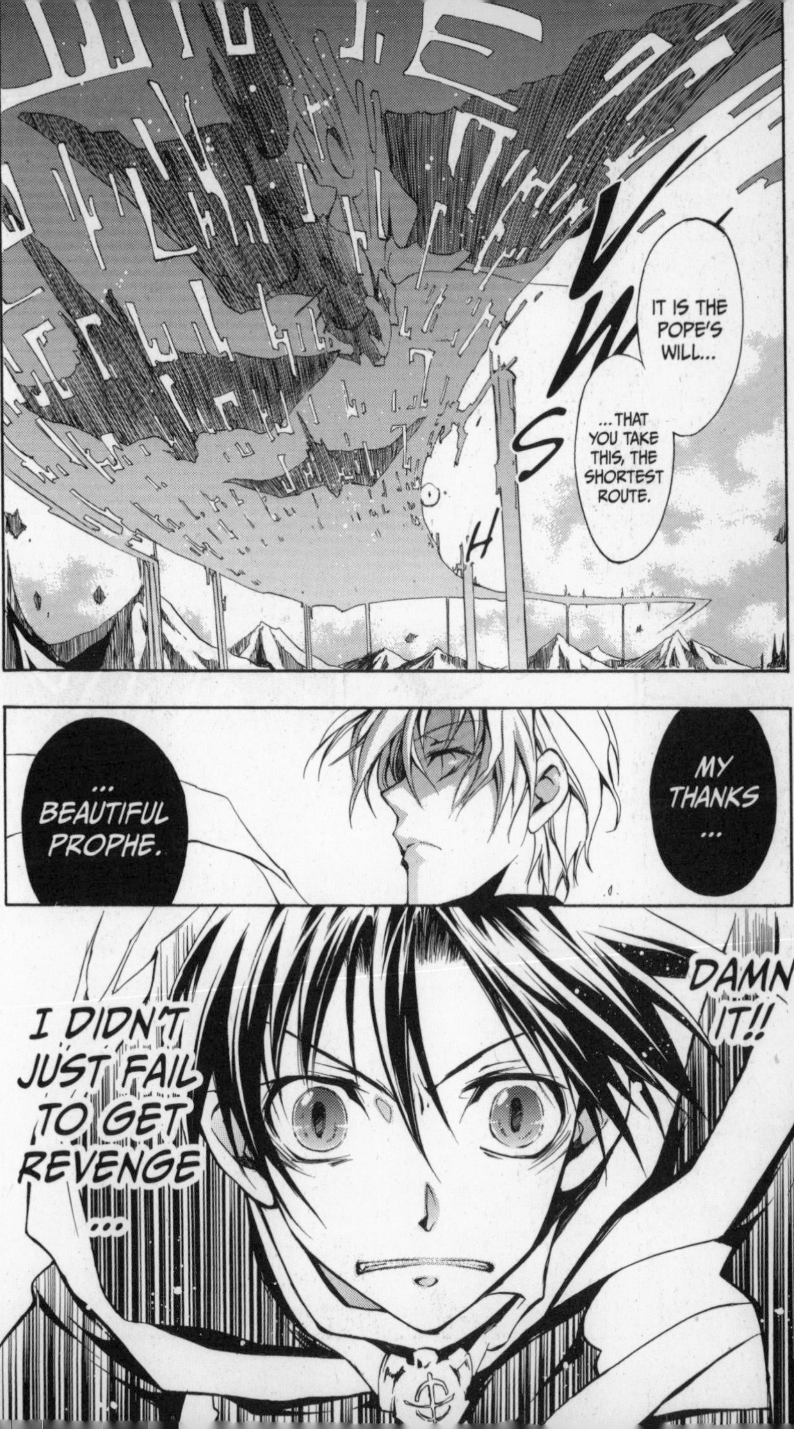

VWSH
IT IS THE POPE'S WILL...
...THAT YOU TAKE THIS, THE SHORTEST ROUTE.
MY THANKS...
...BEAUTIFUL PROPHE.
DAMN IT!!
I DIDN'T JUST FAIL TO GET REVENGE...

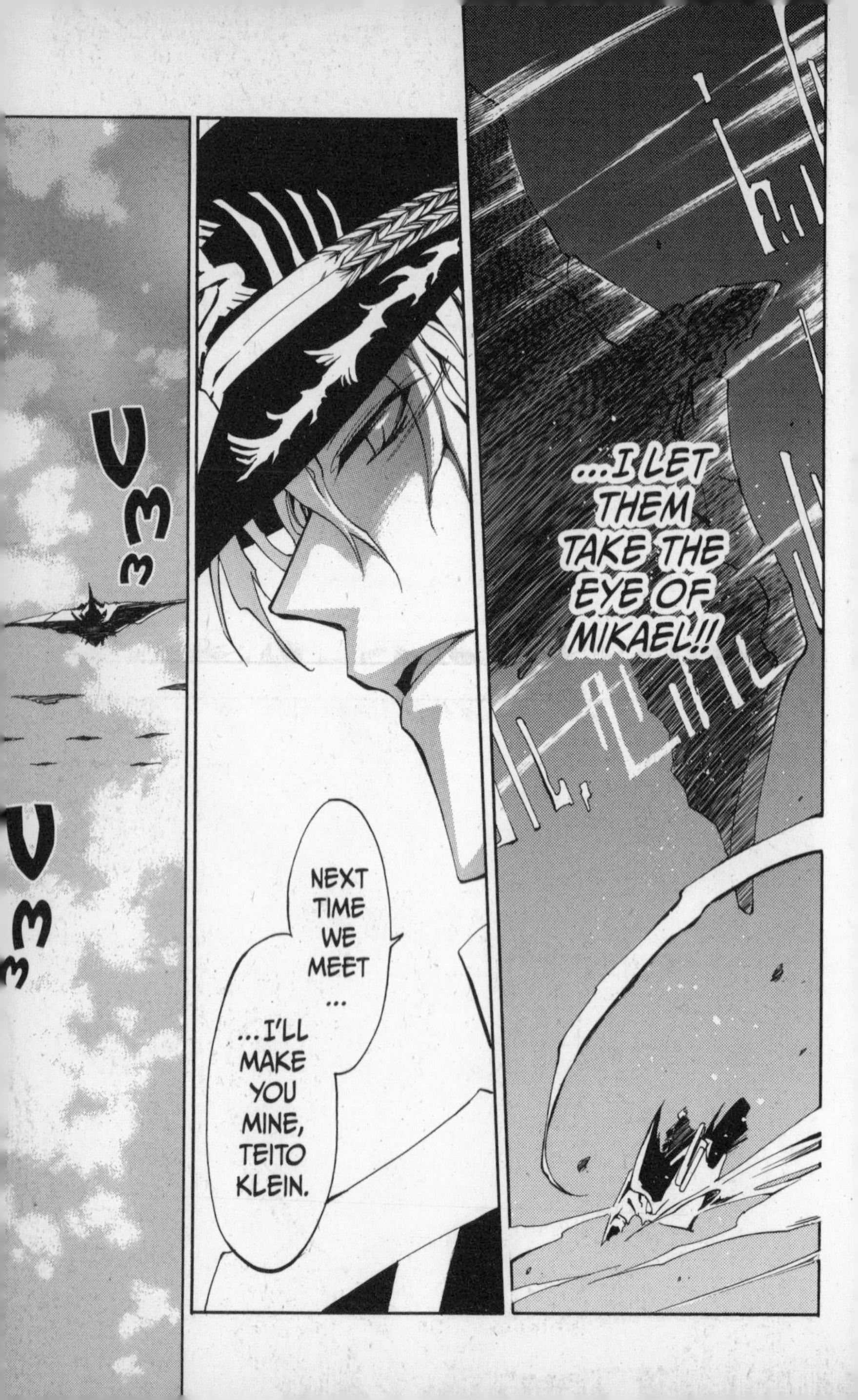
...I LET THEM TAKE THE EYE OF MIKAEL!!
NEXT TIME WE MEET... ...I'LL MAKE YOU MINE, TEITO KLEIN.

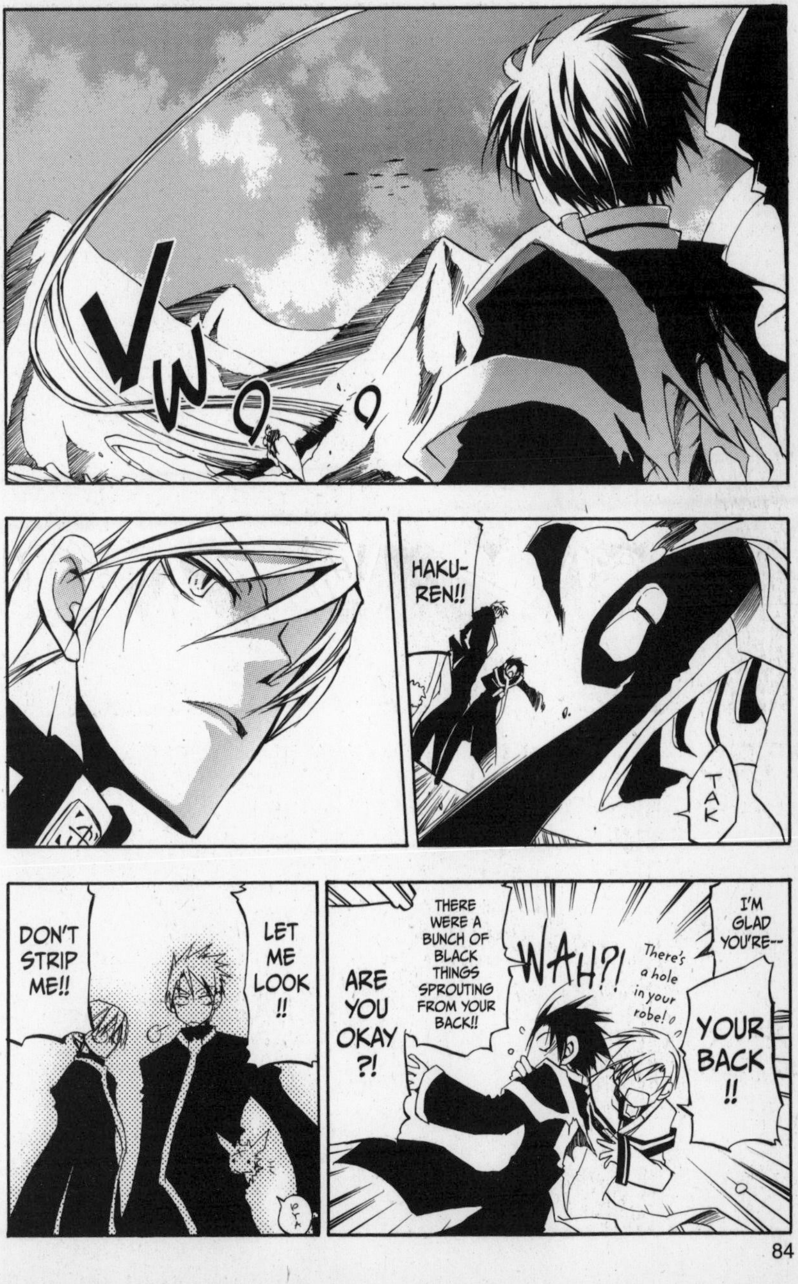

HAKU-REN!!
TAK
I'M GLAD YOU'RE--
YOUR BACK !!
There's a hole in your robe!
WAH?!
THERE WERE A BUNCH OF BLACK THINGS SPROUTING FROM YOUR BACK!!
ARE YOU OKAY ?!
LET ME LOOK !!
DON'T STRIP ME!!

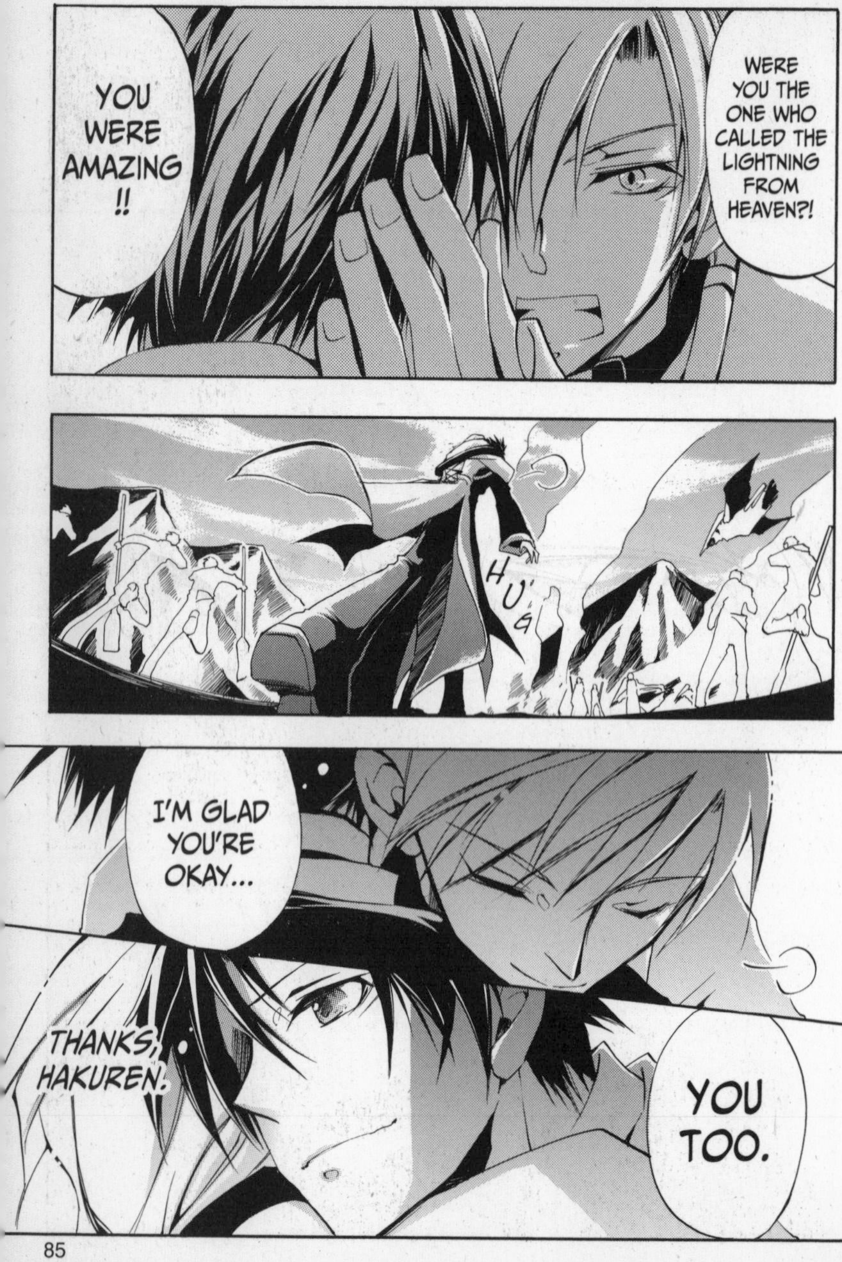
WERE YOU THE ONE WHO CALLED THE LIGHTNING FROM HEAVEN?!
YOU WERE AMAZING!!
HUG
I'M GLAD YOU'RE OKAY...
YOU TOO.
THANKS, HAKUREN.

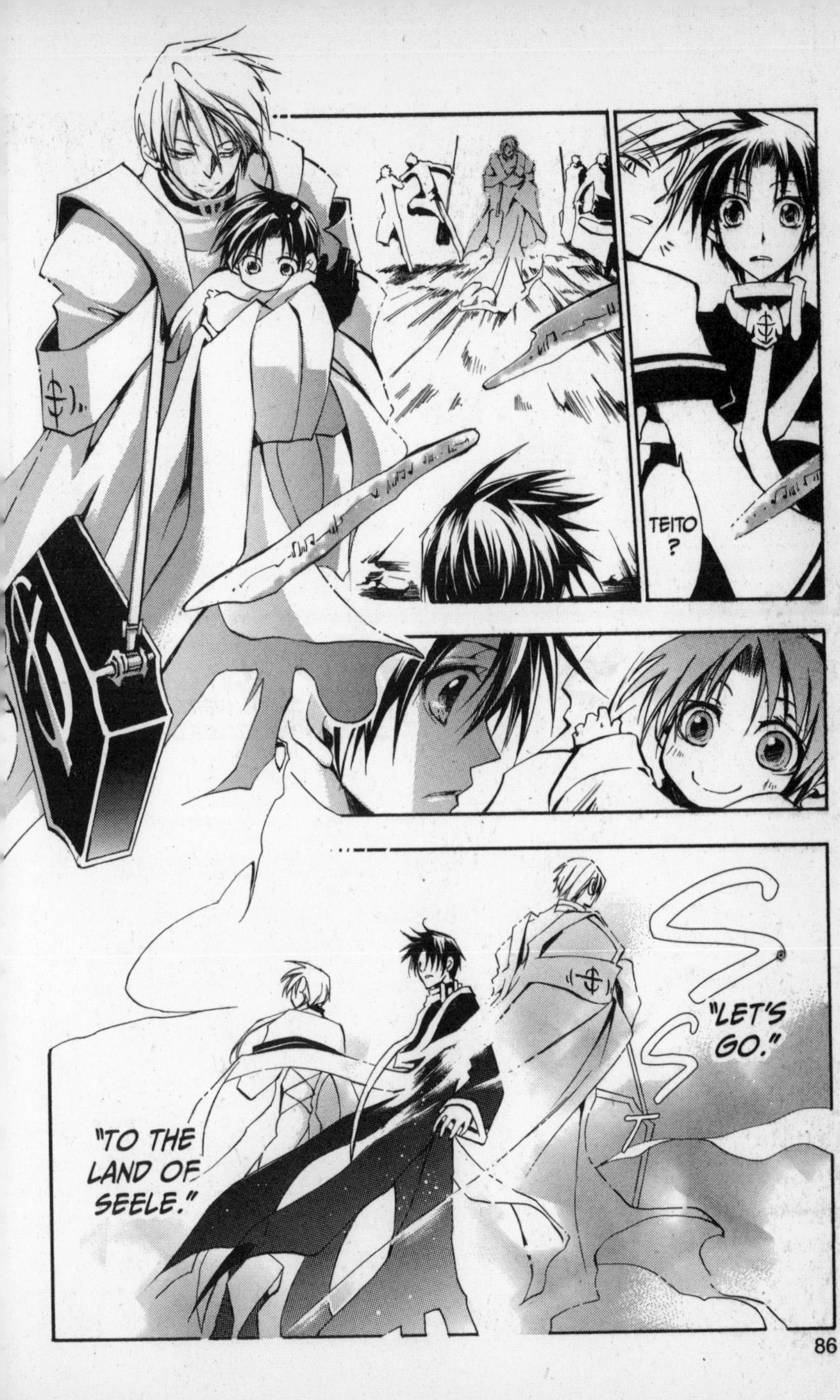
TEITO?
"LET'S GO."
"TO THE LAND OF SEELE."

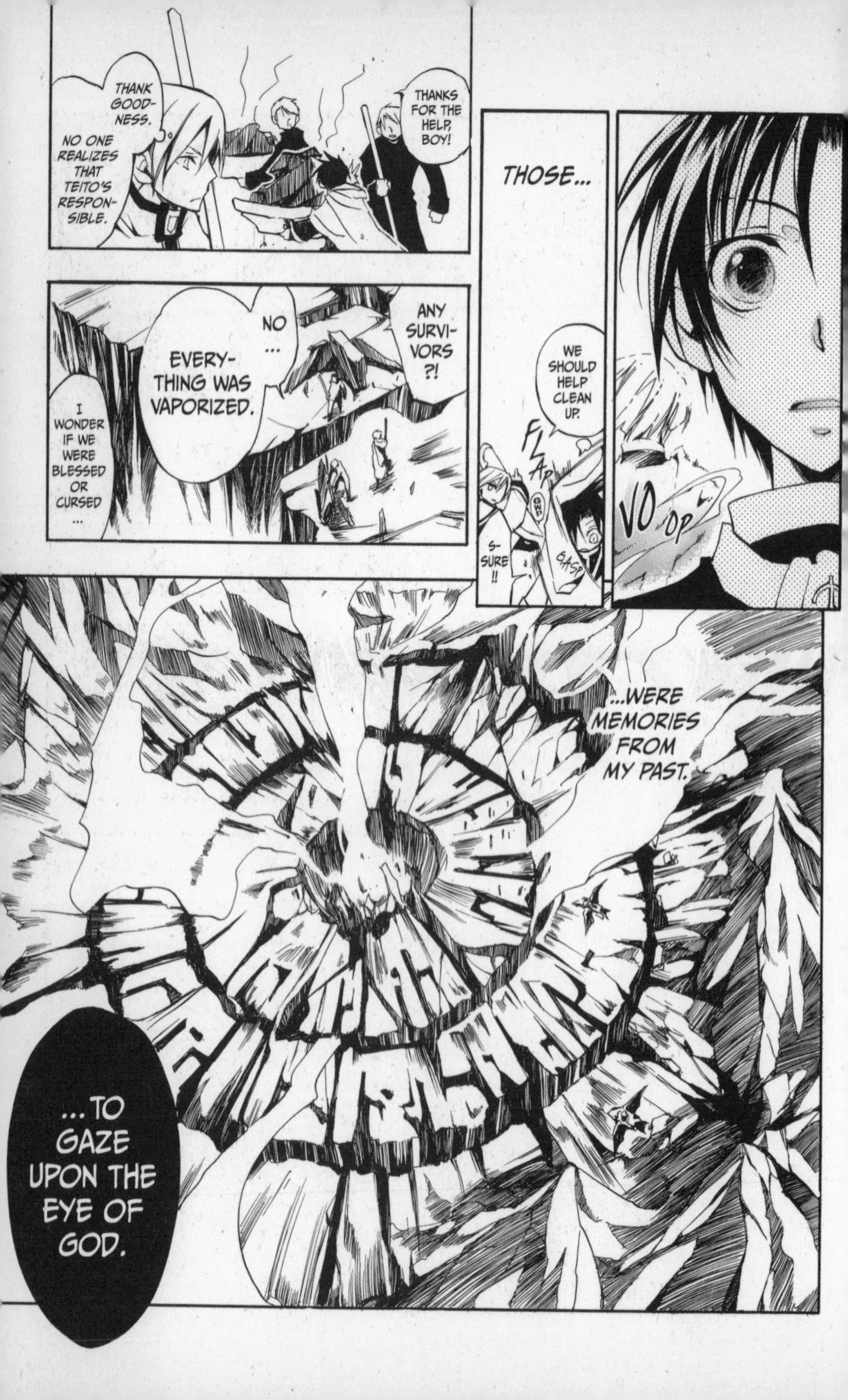
VOOP
THOSE...
WE SHOULD HELP CLEAN UP.
FLAP
GASP
S-SURE!!
THANKS FOR THE HELP, BOY!
THANK GOODNESS.
NO ONE REALIZES THAT TEITO'S RESPONSIBLE.
ANY SURVIVORS?!
NO...
EVERYTHING WAS VAPORIZED.
I WONDER IF WE WERE BLESSED OR CURSED...
...WERE MEMORIES FROM MY PAST.
...TO GAZE UPON THE EYE OF GOD.

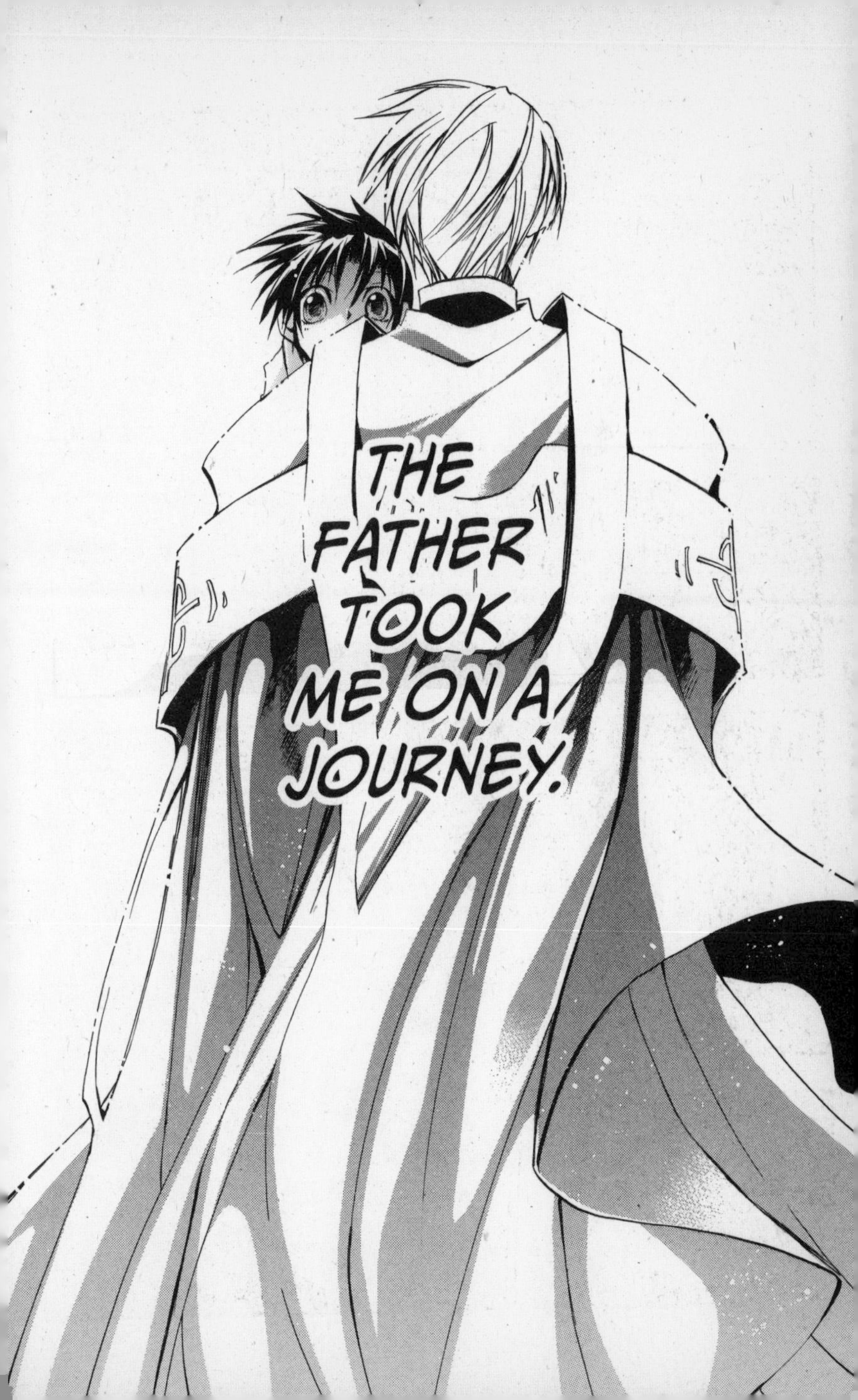
THE FATHER TOOK ME ON A JOURNEY.

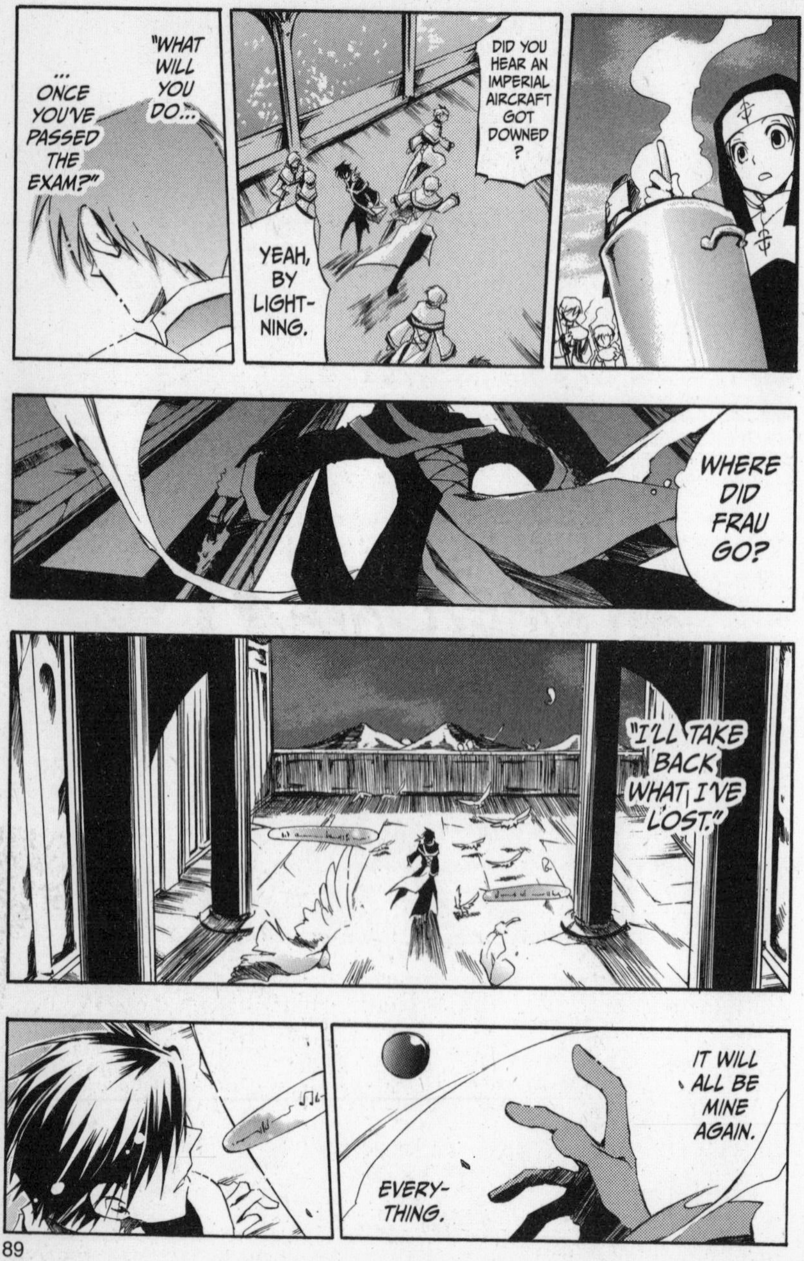
DID YOU HEAR AN IMPERIAL AIRCRAFT GOT DOWNED?
YEAH, BY LIGHTNING.
"WHAT WILL YOU DO...
... ONCE YOU'VE PASSED THE EXAM?"
WHERE DID FRAU GO?
"I'LL TAKE BACK WHAT I'VE LOST."
IT WILL ALL BE MINE AGAIN.
EVERYTHING.

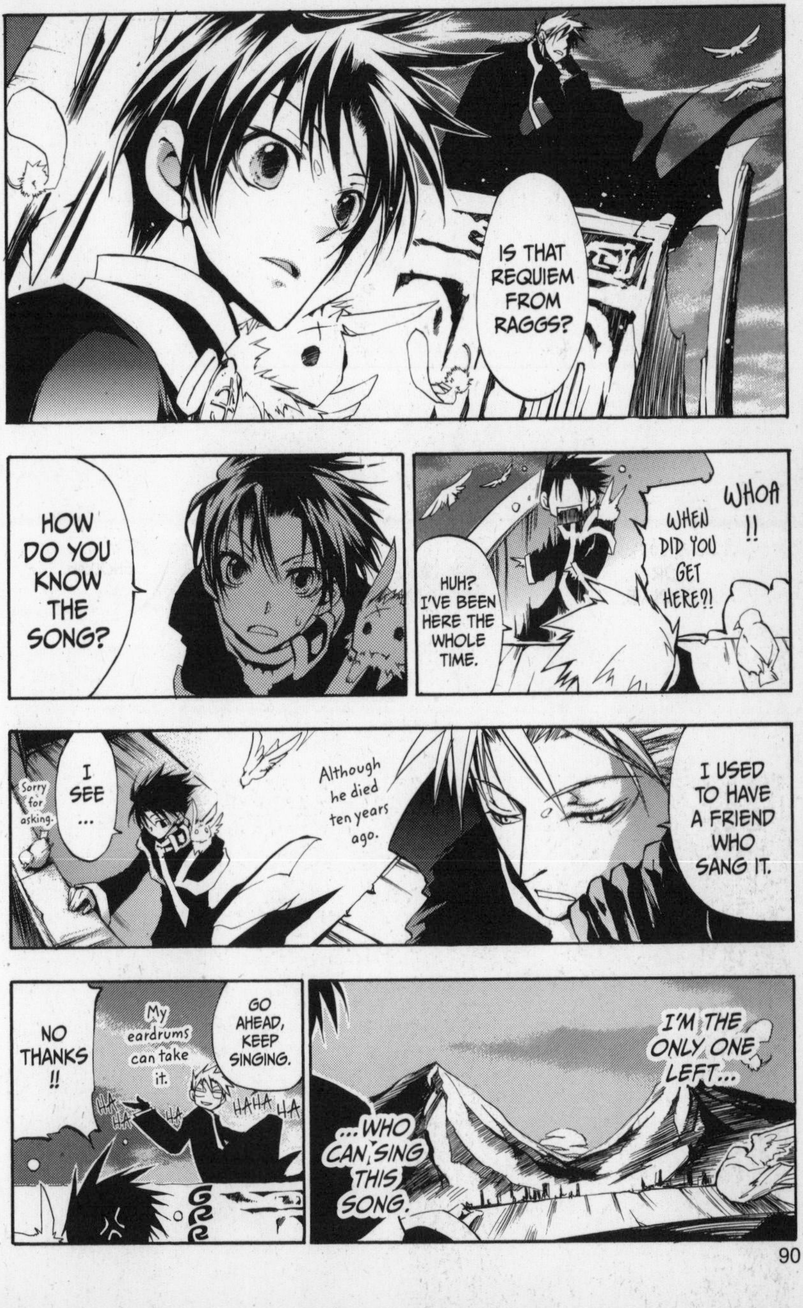
IS THAT REQUIEM FROM RAGGS?
WHOA !!
WHEN DID YOU GET HERE?!
HUH? I'VE BEEN HERE THE WHOLE TIME.
HOW DO YOU KNOW THE SONG?
I USED TO HAVE A FRIEND WHO SANG IT.
Although he died ten years ago.
I SEE ...
Sorry for asking.
I'M THE ONLY ONE LEFT...
...WHO CAN SING THIS SONG.
GO AHEAD, KEEP SINGING.
My eardrums can take it.
HAHA HA
HA HA
HA
NO THANKS !!
GRR

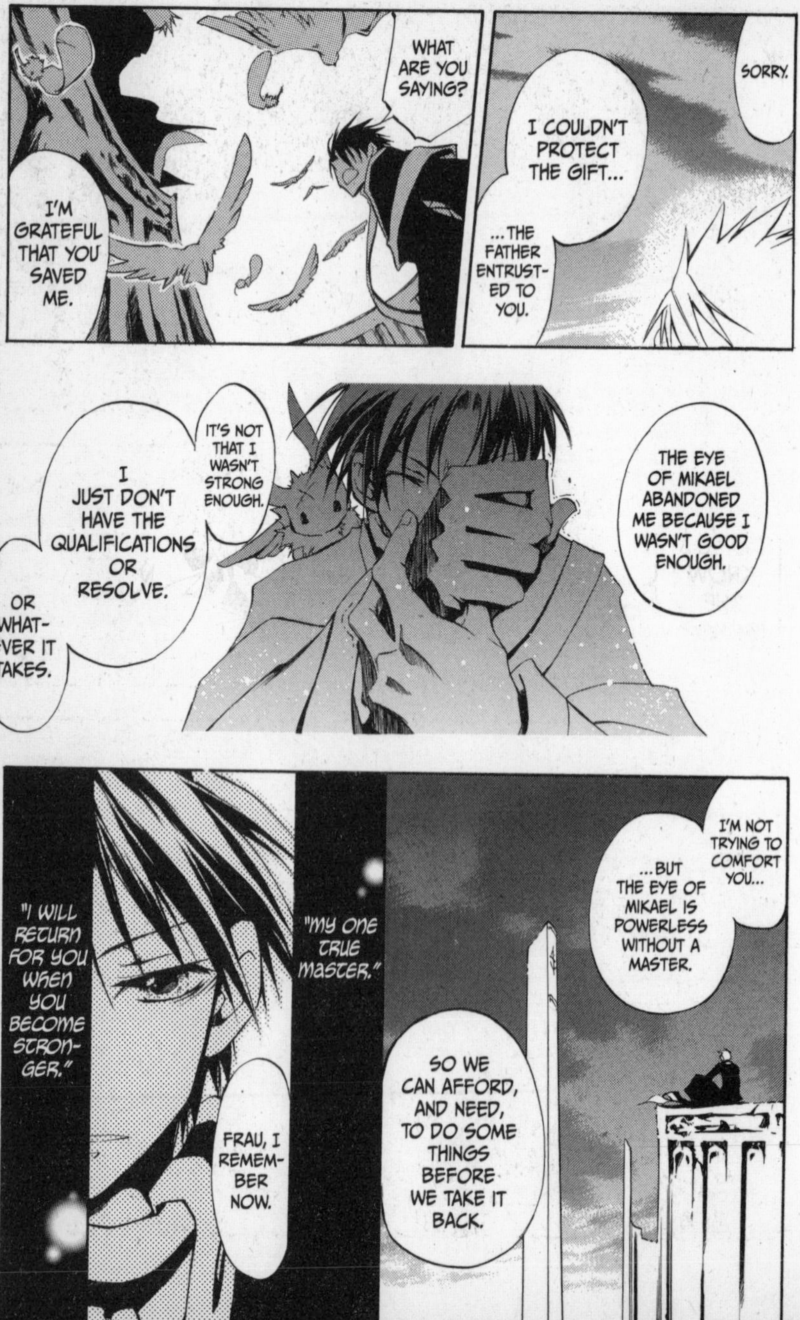
SORRY.
I COULDN'T PROTECT THE GIFT...
...THE FATHER ENTRUST-ED TO YOU.
WHAT ARE YOU SAYING?
I'M GRATEFUL THAT YOU SAVED ME.
THE EYE OF MIKAEL ABANDONED ME BECAUSE I WASN'T GOOD ENOUGH.
IT'S NOT THAT I WASN'T STRONG ENOUGH.
I JUST DON'T HAVE THE QUALIFICATIONS OR RESOLVE.
OR WHAT-EVER IT TAKES.
I'M NOT TRYING TO COMFORT YOU...
...BUT THE EYE OF MIKAEL IS POWERLESS WITHOUT A MASTER.
SO WE CAN AFFORD, AND NEED, TO DO SOME THINGS BEFORE WE TAKE IT BACK.
"MY ONE TRUE MASTER."
"I WILL RETURN FOR YOU WHEN YOU BECOME STRON-GER."
FRAU, I REMEM-BER NOW.

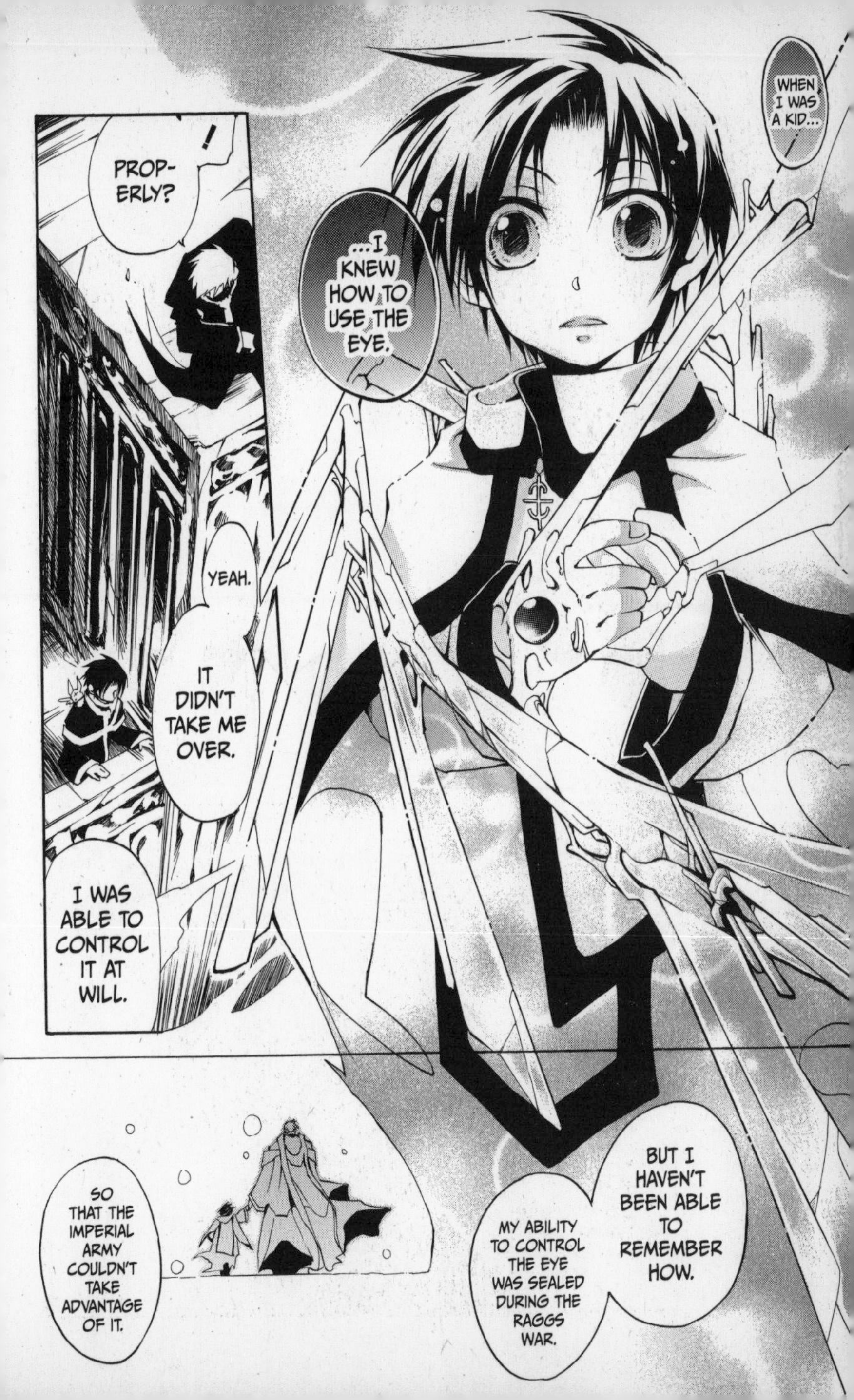
WHEN I WAS A KID...
...I KNEW HOW TO USE THE EYE.
!
PROPERLY?
YEAH.
IT DIDN'T TAKE ME OVER.
I WAS ABLE TO CONTROL IT AT WILL.
BUT I HAVEN'T BEEN ABLE TO REMEMBER HOW.
MY ABILITY TO CONTROL THE EYE WAS SEALED DURING THE RAGGS WAR.
SO THAT THE IMPERIAL ARMY COULDN'T TAKE ADVANTAGE OF IT.

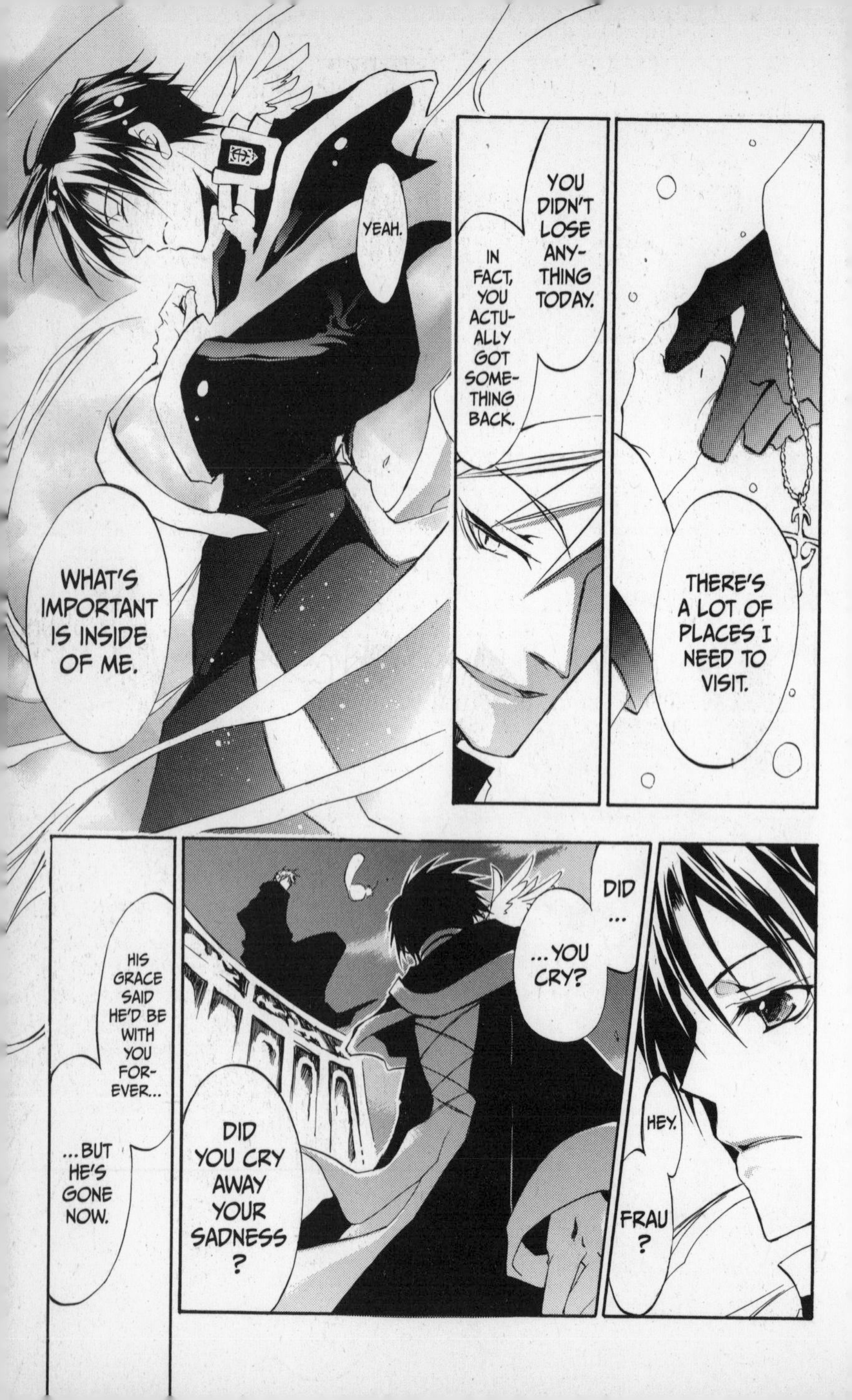
THERE'S A LOT OF PLACES I NEED TO VISIT.
YOU DIDN'T LOSE ANYTHING TODAY.
IN FACT, YOU ACTUALLY GOT SOMETHING BACK.
YEAH.
WHAT'S IMPORTANT IS INSIDE OF ME.
HEY.
FRAU?
DID...
...YOU CRY?
DID YOU CRY AWAY YOUR SADNESS?
HIS GRACE SAID HE'D BE WITH YOU FOREVER...
...BUT HE'S GONE NOW.

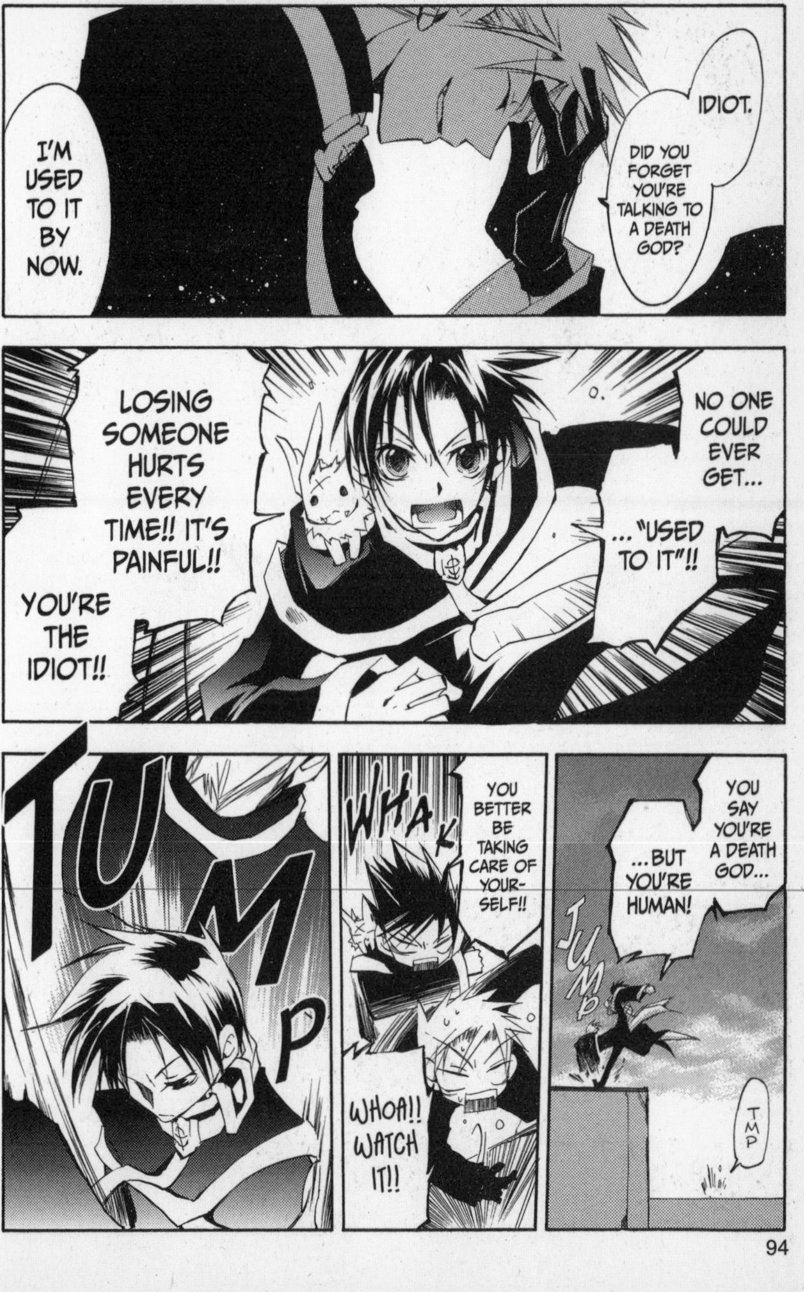

IDIOT.
DID YOU FORGET YOU'RE TALKING TO A DEATH GOD?
I'M USED TO IT BY NOW.
NO ONE COULD EVER GET...
..."USED TO IT"!!
LOSING SOMEONE HURTS EVERY TIME!! IT'S PAINFUL!!
YOU'RE THE IDIOT!!
YOU SAY YOU'RE A DEATH GOD...
...BUT YOU'RE HUMAN!
JUMP
TMP
WHAK
YOU BETTER BE TAKING CARE OF YOUR-SELF!!
WHOA!! WATCH IT!!
TUMP

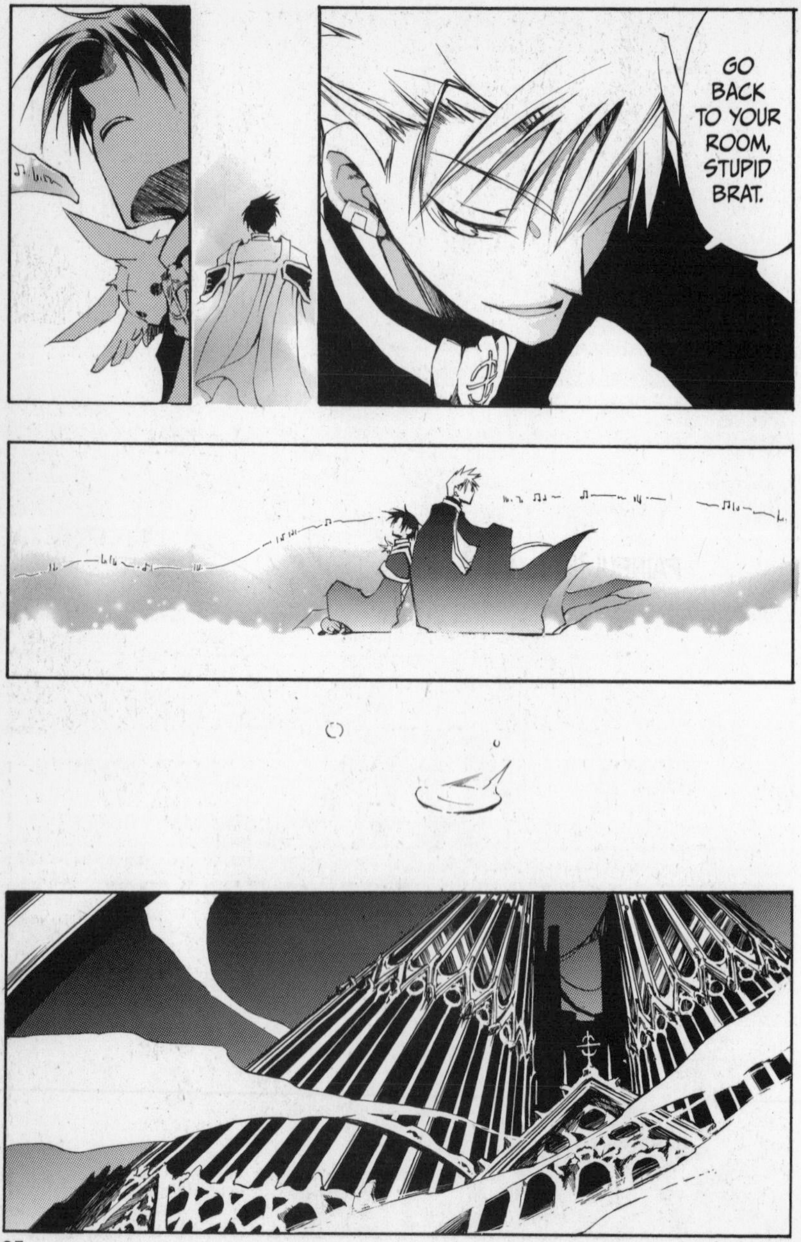
GO BACK TO YOUR ROOM, STUPID BRAT.

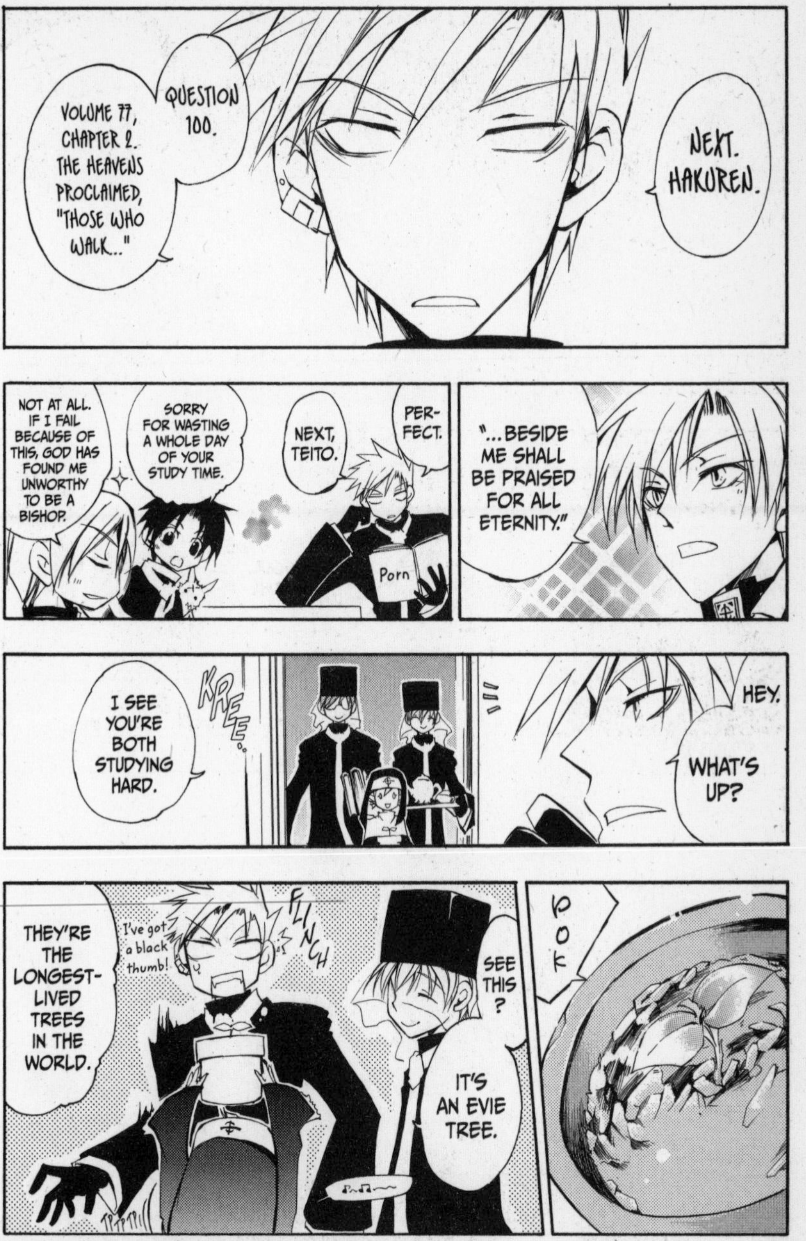
NEXT. HAKUREN.
QUESTION 100.
VOLUME 77, CHAPTER 2. THE HEAVENS PROCLAIMED, "THOSE WHO WALK..."
"...BESIDE ME SHALL BE PRAISED FOR ALL ETERNITY."
PER-FECT.
NEXT, TEITO.
Porn
SORRY FOR WASTING A WHOLE DAY OF YOUR STUDY TIME.
NOT AT ALL. IF I FAIL BECAUSE OF THIS, GOD HAS FOUND ME UNWORTHY TO BE A BISHOP.
HEY.
WHAT'S UP?
KREE
I SEE YOU'RE BOTH STUDYING HARD.
POK
SEE THIS?
IT'S AN EVIE TREE.
FLINCH
I've got a black thumb!
THEY'RE THE LONGEST-LIVED TREES IN THE WORLD.

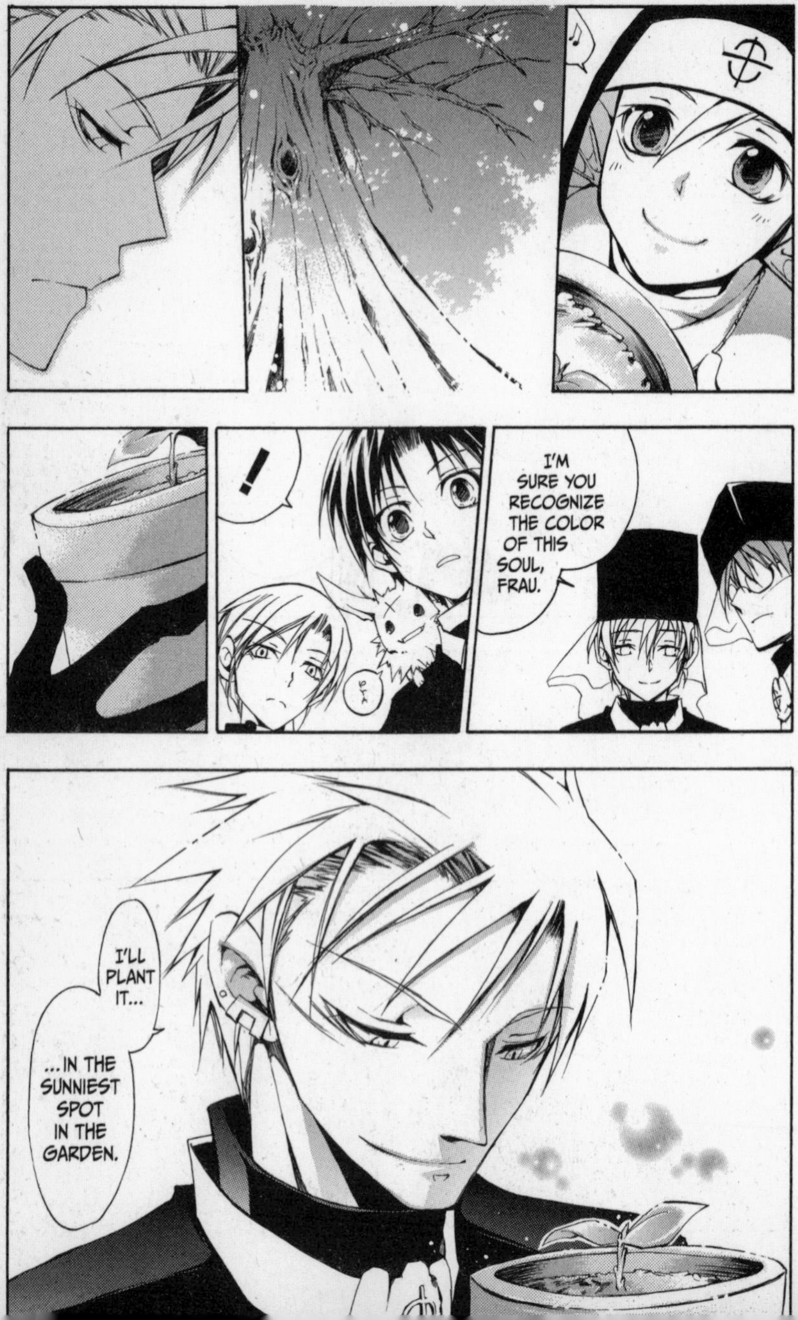
I'M SURE YOU RECOGNIZE THE COLOR OF THIS SOUL, FRAU.
!
I'LL PLANT IT...
...IN THE SUNNIEST SPOT IN THE GARDEN.

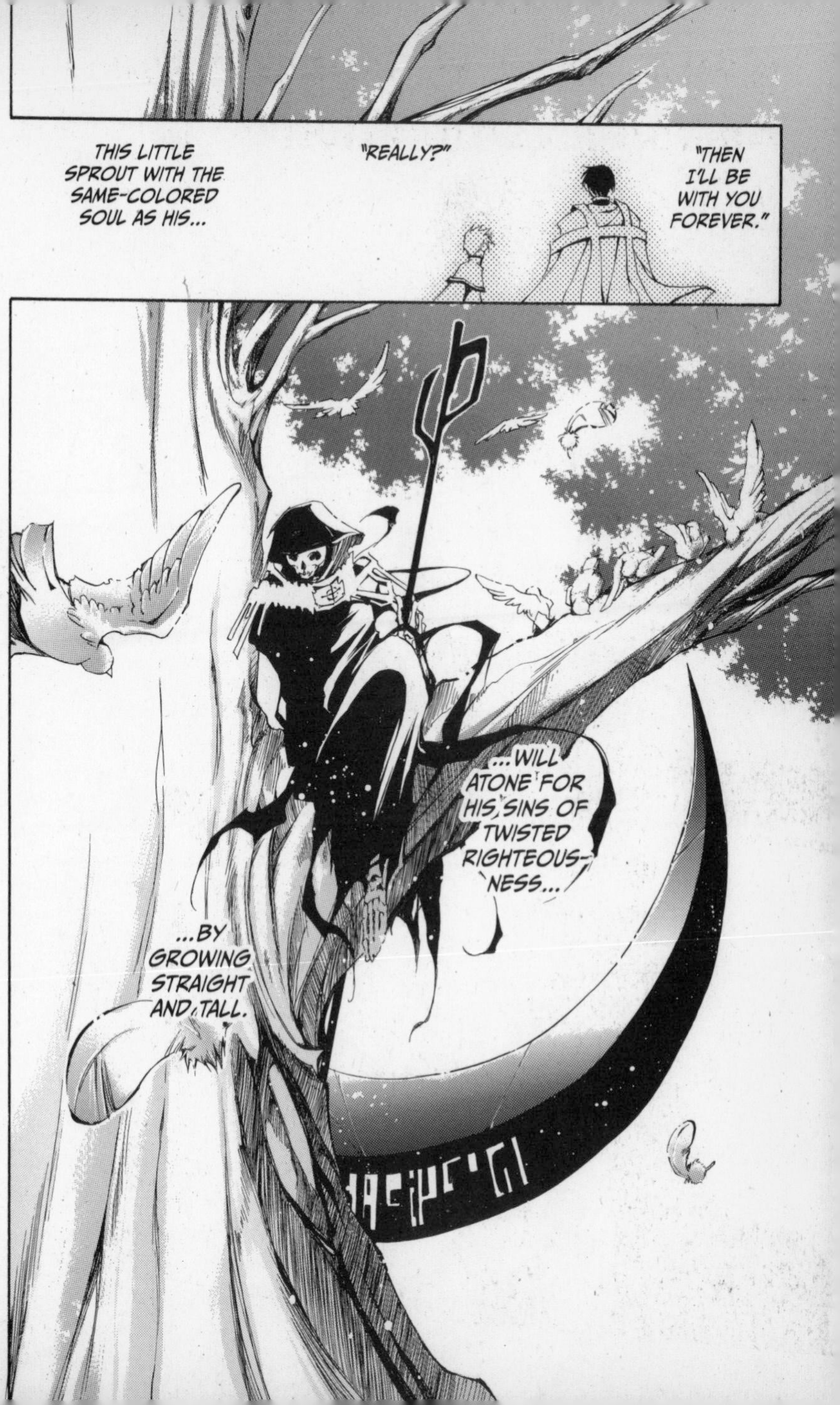
"THEN I'LL BE WITH YOU FOREVER."
"REALLY?"
THIS LITTLE SPROUT WITH THE SAME-COLORED SOUL AS HIS...
...WILL ATONE FOR HIS SINS OF TWISTED RIGHTEOUS-NESS...
...BY GROWING STRAIGHT AND TALL.

Kapitel.21 “Morning of the Bishop Examination”

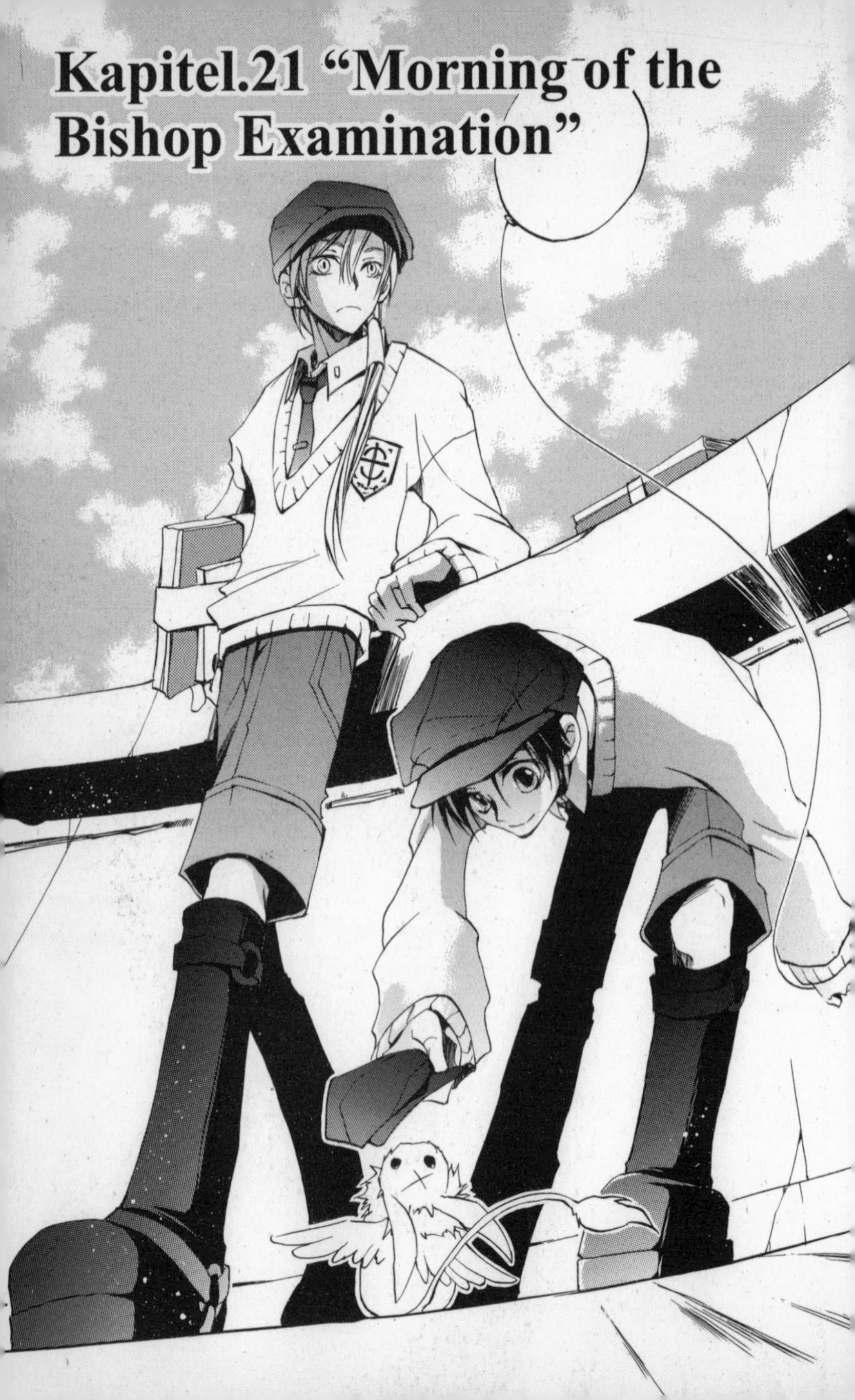

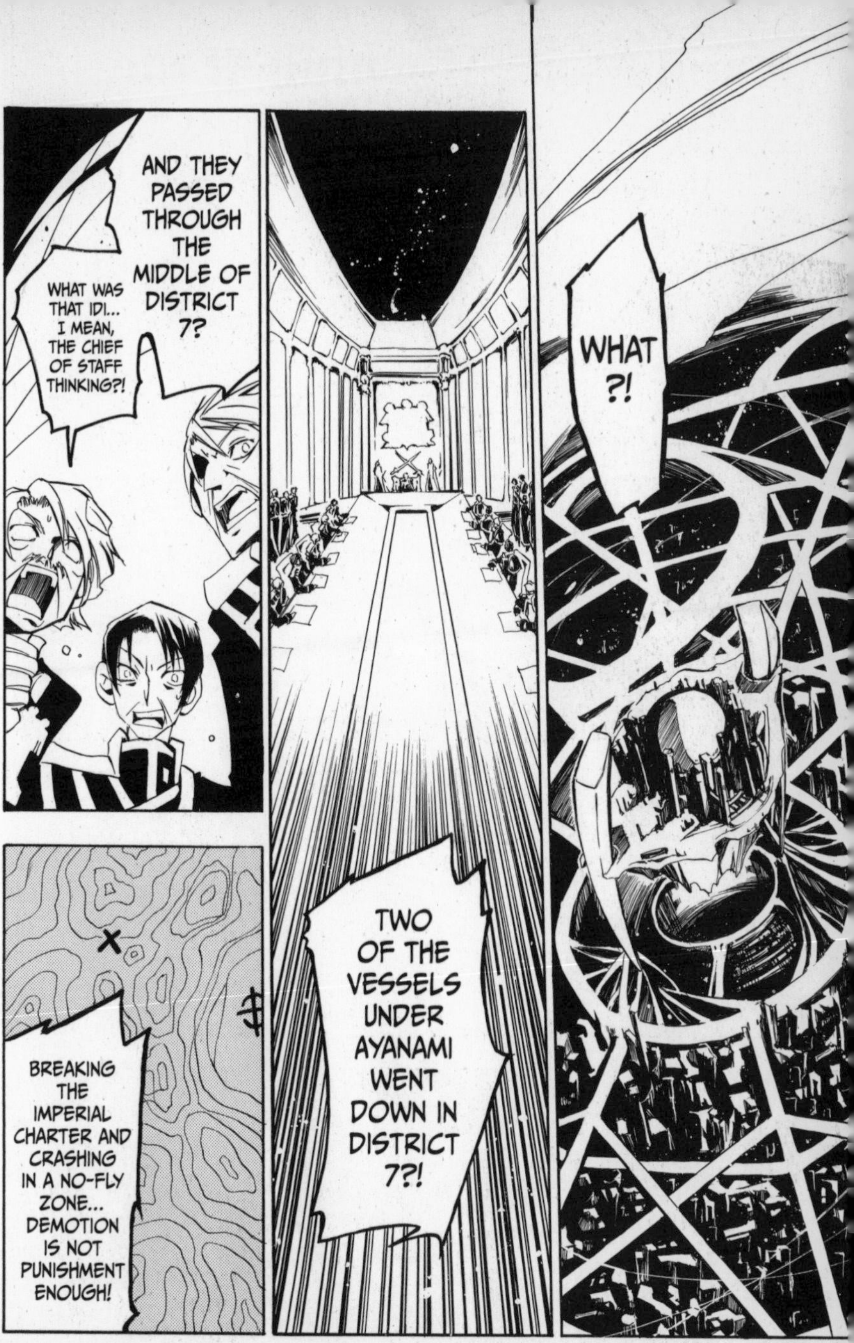
WHAT?!
TWO OF THE VESSELS UNDER AYANAMI WENT DOWN IN DISTRICT 7?!
AND THEY PASSED THROUGH THE MIDDLE OF DISTRICT 7?
WHAT WAS THAT IDI... I MEAN, THE CHIEF OF STAFF THINKING?!
BREAKING THE IMPERIAL CHARTER AND CRASHING IN A NO-FLY ZONE... DEMOTION IS NOT PUNISHMENT ENOUGH!

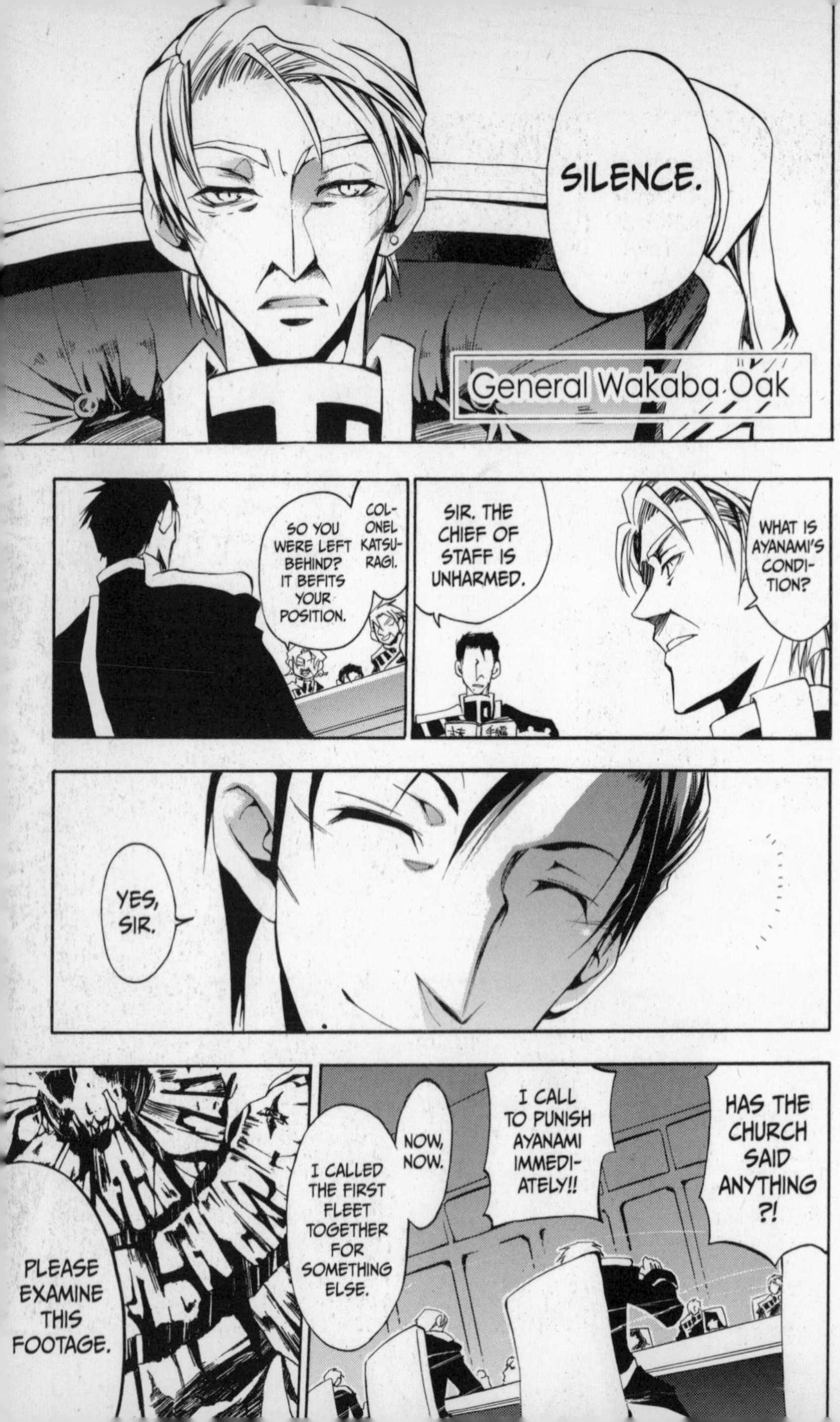
SILENCE.
General Wakaba Oak
WHAT IS AYANAMI'S CONDITION?
SIR. THE CHIEF OF STAFF IS UNHARMED.
COLONEL KATSURAGI.
SO YOU WERE LEFT BEHIND? IT BEFITS YOUR POSITION.
YES, SIR.
HAS THE CHURCH SAID ANYTHING?!
I CALL TO PUNISH AYANAMI IMMEDIATELY!!
NOW, NOW.
I CALLED THE FIRST FLEET TOGETHER FOR SOMETHING ELSE.
PLEASE EXAMINE THIS FOOTAGE.

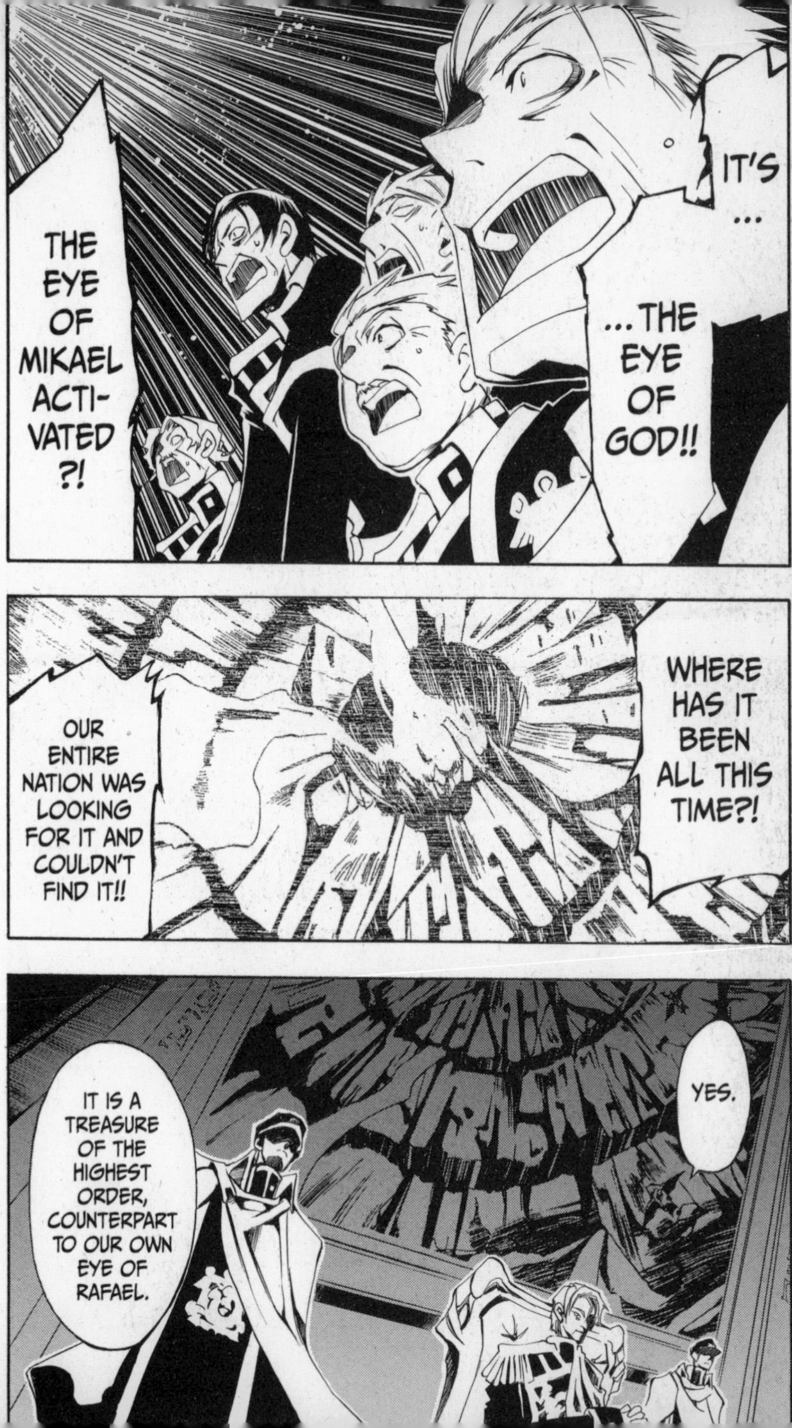
IT'S ...
...THE EYE OF GOD!!
THE EYE OF MIKAEL ACTIVATED?!
WHERE HAS IT BEEN ALL THIS TIME?!
OUR ENTIRE NATION WAS LOOKING FOR IT AND COULDN'T FIND IT!!
YES.
IT IS A TREASURE OF THE HIGHEST ORDER, COUNTERPART TO OUR OWN EYE OF RAFAEL.

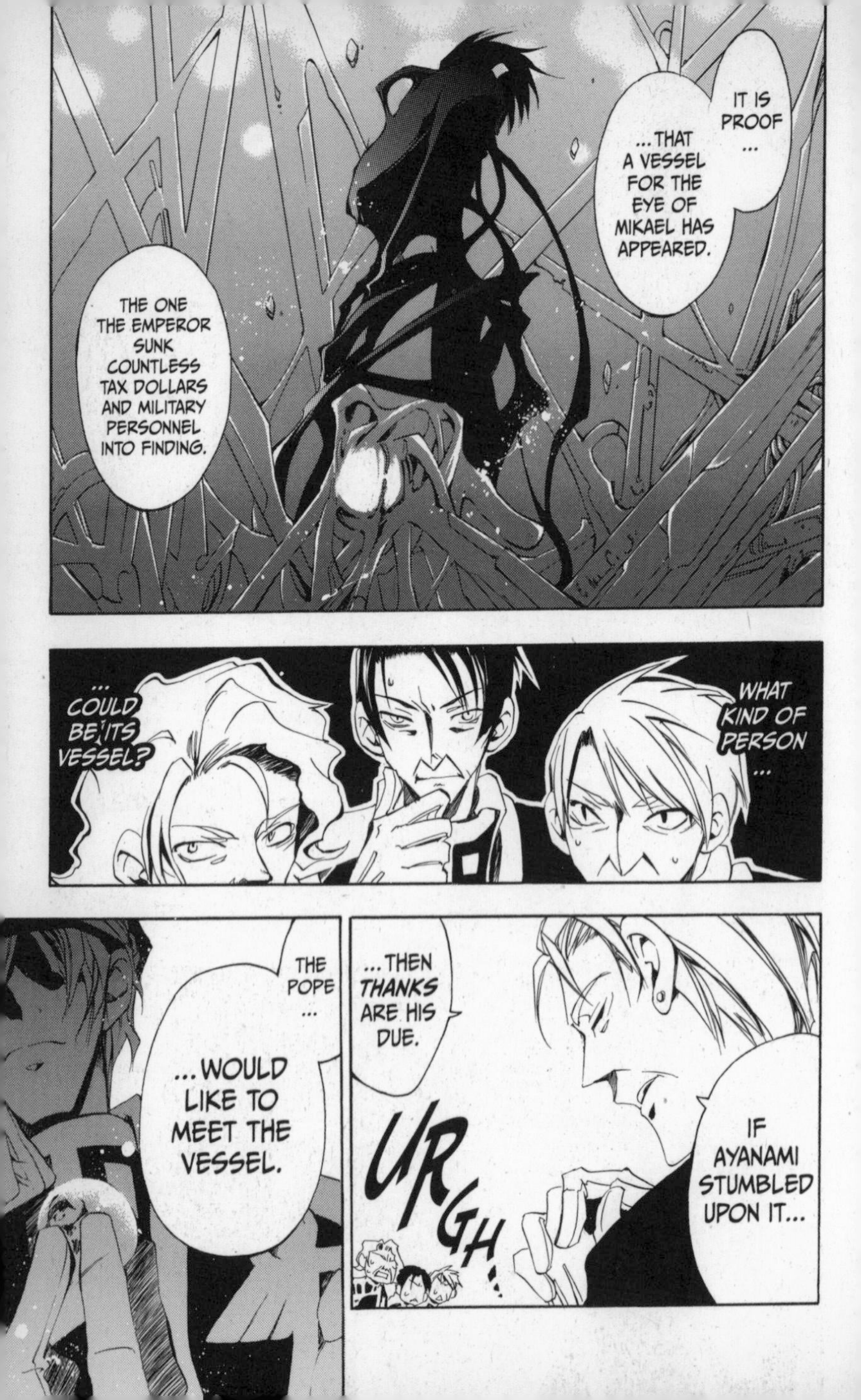
IT IS PROOF ...
...THAT A VESSEL FOR THE EYE OF MIKAEL HAS APPEARED.
THE ONE THE EMPEROR SUNK COUNTLESS TAX DOLLARS AND MILITARY PERSONNEL INTO FINDING.
WHAT KIND OF PERSON ...
... COULD BE ITS VESSEL?
IF AYANAMI STUMBLED UPON IT...
...THEN THANKS ARE HIS DUE.
URGH!!
THE POPE ...
...WOULD LIKE TO MEET THE VESSEL.

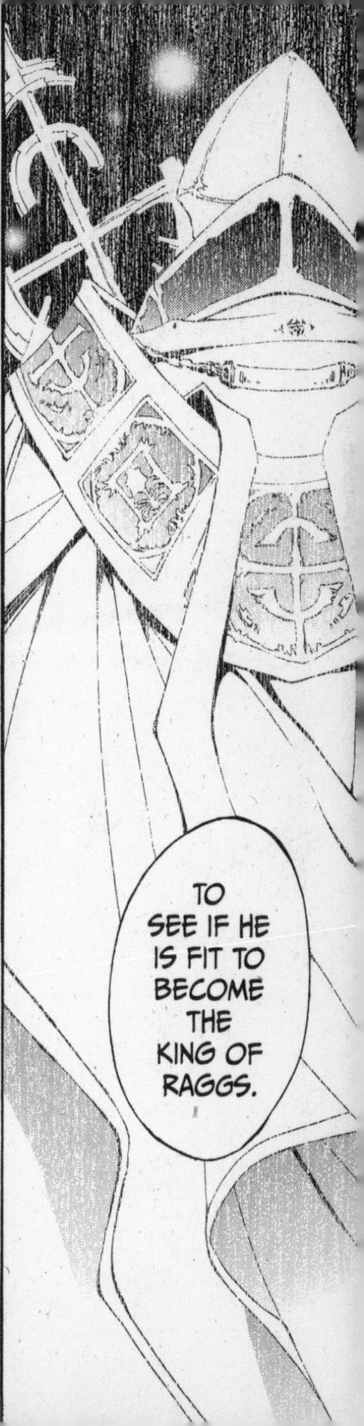
TO SEE IF HE IS FIT TO BECOME THE KING OF RAGGS.

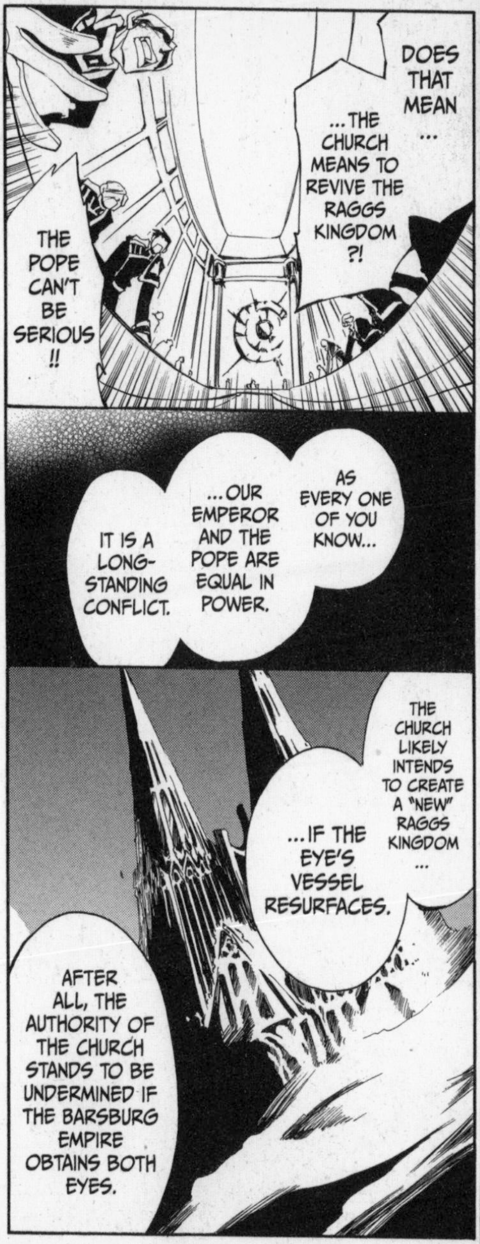
DOES THAT MEAN...
...THE CHURCH MEANS TO REVIVE THE RAGGS KINGDOM?!
THE POPE CAN'T BE SERIOUS!!
AS EVERY ONE OF YOU KNOW...
...OUR EMPEROR AND THE POPE ARE EQUAL IN POWER.
IT IS A LONG-STANDING CONFLICT.
THE CHURCH LIKELY INTENDS TO CREATE A "NEW" RAGGS KINGDOM...
...IF THE EYE'S VESSEL RESURFACES.
AFTER ALL, THE AUTHORITY OF THE CHURCH STANDS TO BE UNDERMINED IF THE BARSBURG EMPIRE OBTAINS BOTH EYES.

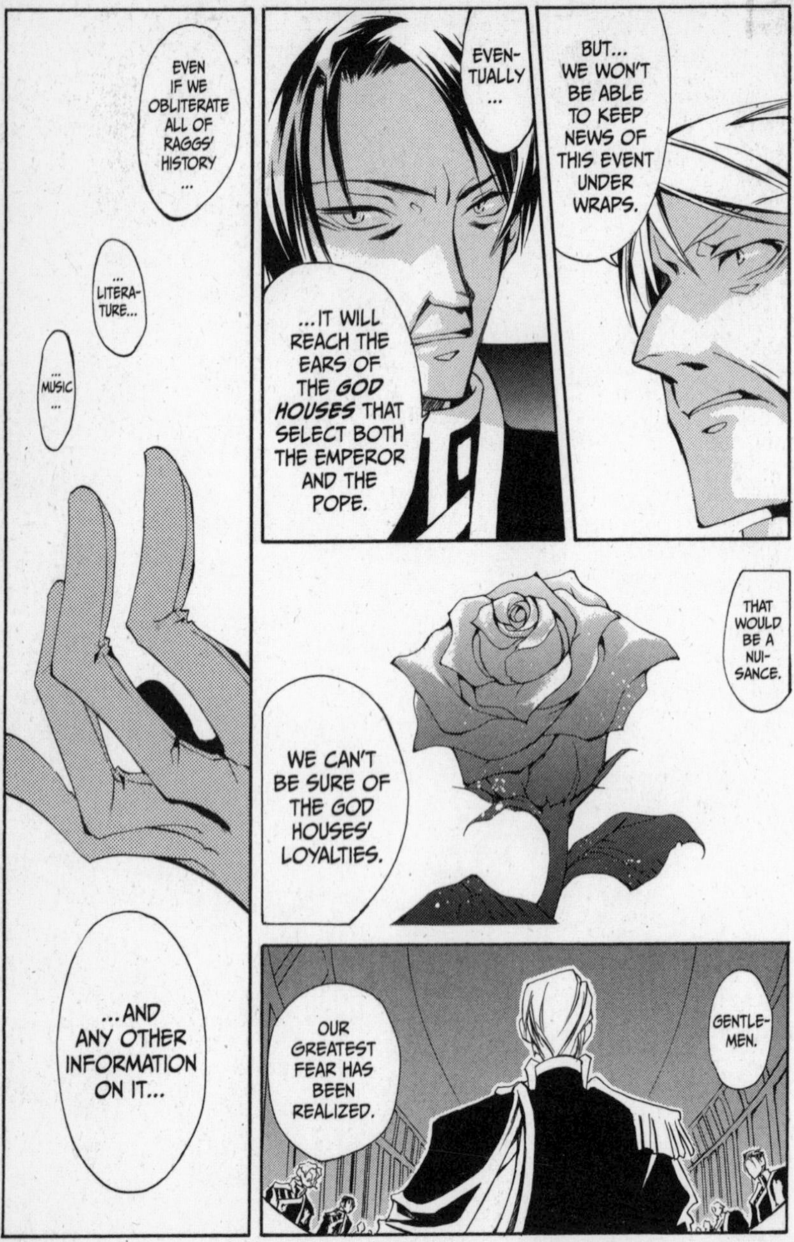
BUT... WE WON'T BE ABLE TO KEEP NEWS OF THIS EVENT UNDER WRAPS.
EVEN-TUALLY ...
...IT WILL REACH THE EARS OF THE *GOD HOUSES* THAT SELECT BOTH THE EMPEROR AND THE POPE.
THAT WOULD BE A NUI-SANCE.
WE CAN'T BE SURE OF THE GOD HOUSES' LOYALTIES.
GENTLE-MEN.
OUR GREATEST FEAR HAS BEEN REALIZED.
EVEN IF WE OBLITERATE ALL OF RAGGS' HISTORY ...
... LITERA-TURE...
... MUSIC ...
...AND ANY OTHER INFORMATION ON IT...

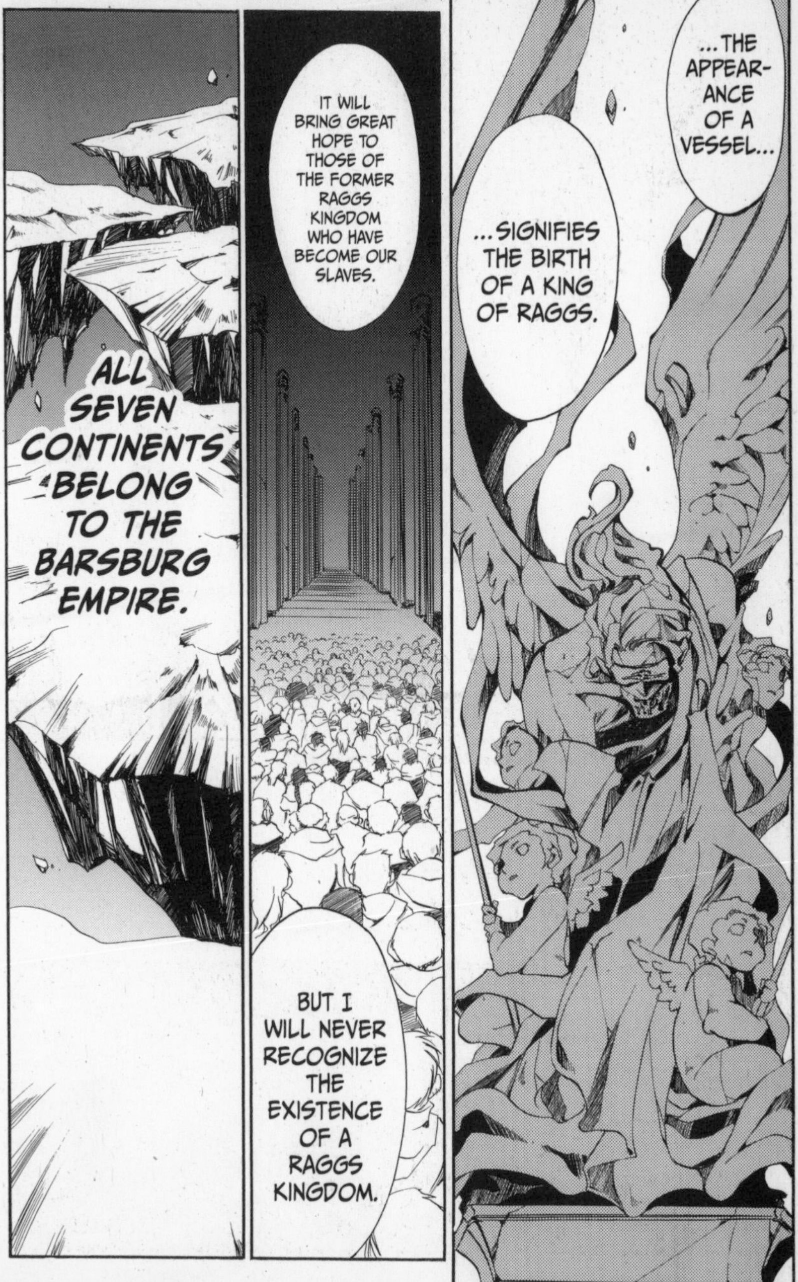
...THE APPEARANCE OF A VESSEL...
...SIGNIFIES THE BIRTH OF A KING OF RAGGS.
IT WILL BRING GREAT HOPE TO THOSE OF THE FORMER RAGGS KINGDOM WHO HAVE BECOME OUR SLAVES.
BUT I WILL NEVER RECOGNIZE THE EXISTENCE OF A RAGGS KINGDOM.
ALL SEVEN CONTINENTS BELONG TO THE BARSBURG EMPIRE.

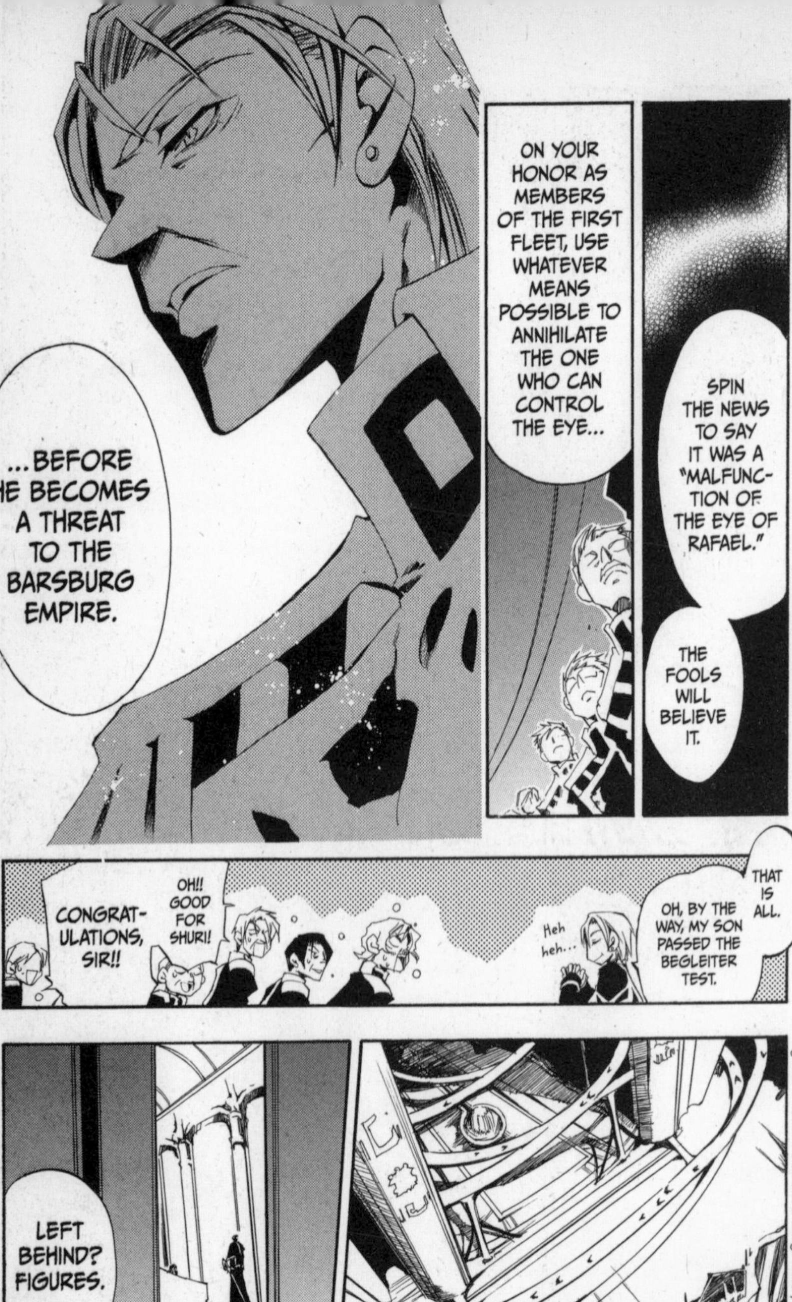
SPIN THE NEWS TO SAY IT WAS A "MALFUNCTION OF THE EYE OF RAFAEL."
THE FOOLS WILL BELIEVE IT.
ON YOUR HONOR AS MEMBERS OF THE FIRST FLEET, USE WHATEVER MEANS POSSIBLE TO ANNIHILATE THE ONE WHO CAN CONTROL THE EYE...
...BEFORE HE BECOMES A THREAT TO THE BARSBURG EMPIRE.
THAT IS ALL.
OH, BY THE WAY, MY SON PASSED THE BEGLEITER TEST.
Heh heh...
OH!! GOOD FOR SHURI!
CONGRATULATIONS, SIR!!
LEFT BEHIND? FIGURES.

Begleiter = Assistant to an officer of high military rank

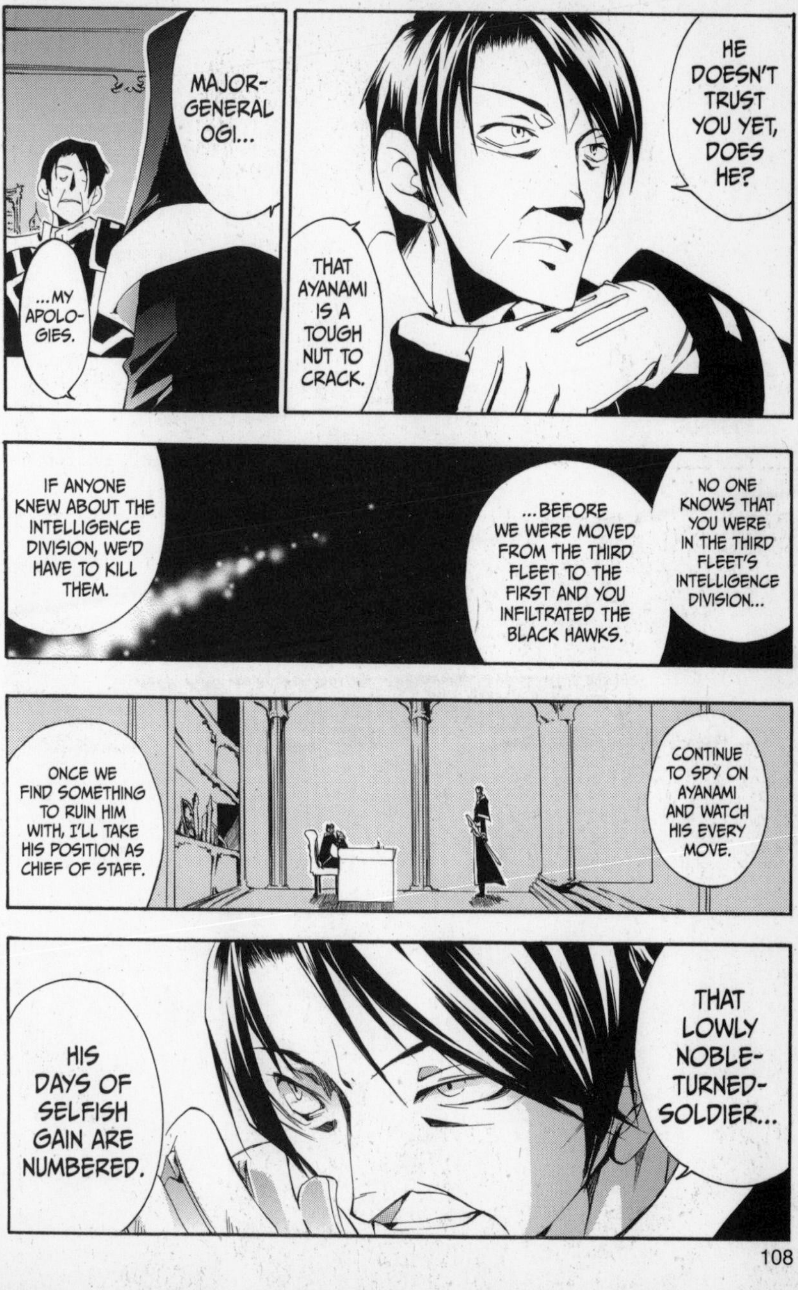
HE DOESN'T TRUST YOU YET, DOES HE?
THAT AYANAMI IS A TOUGH NUT TO CRACK.
MAJOR-GENERAL OGI...
...MY APOLOGIES.
NO ONE KNOWS THAT YOU WERE IN THE THIRD FLEET'S INTELLIGENCE DIVISION...
...BEFORE WE WERE MOVED FROM THE THIRD FLEET TO THE FIRST AND YOU INFILTRATED THE BLACK HAWKS.
IF ANYONE KNEW ABOUT THE INTELLIGENCE DIVISION, WE'D HAVE TO KILL THEM.
CONTINUE TO SPY ON AYANAMI AND WATCH HIS EVERY MOVE.
ONCE WE FIND SOMETHING TO RUIN HIM WITH, I'LL TAKE HIS POSITION AS CHIEF OF STAFF.
THAT LOWLY NOBLE-TURNED-SOLDIER...
HIS DAYS OF SELFISH GAIN ARE NUMBERED.

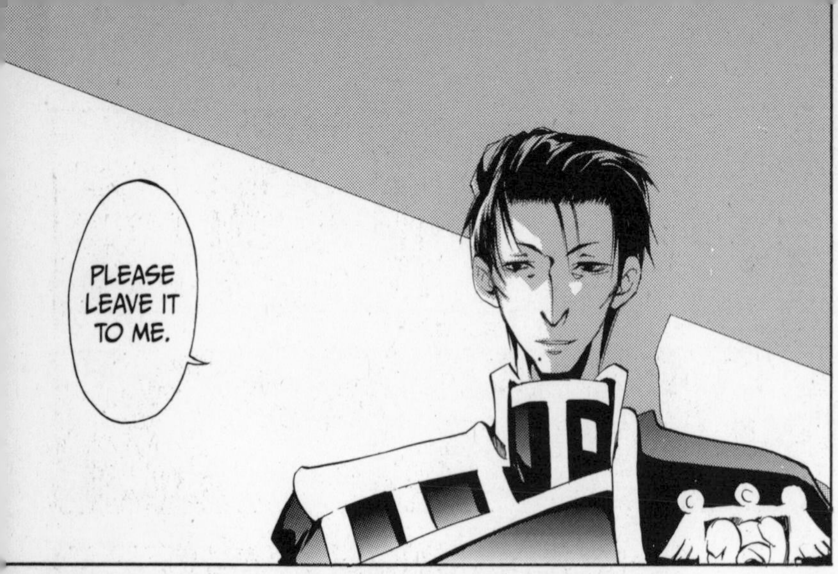
PLEASE LEAVE IT TO ME.

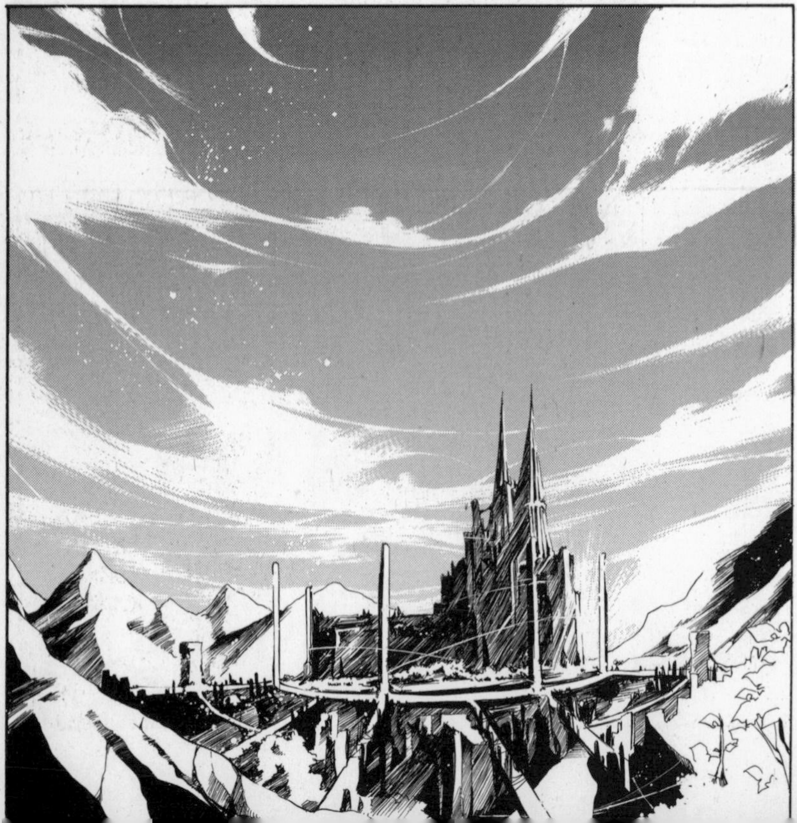

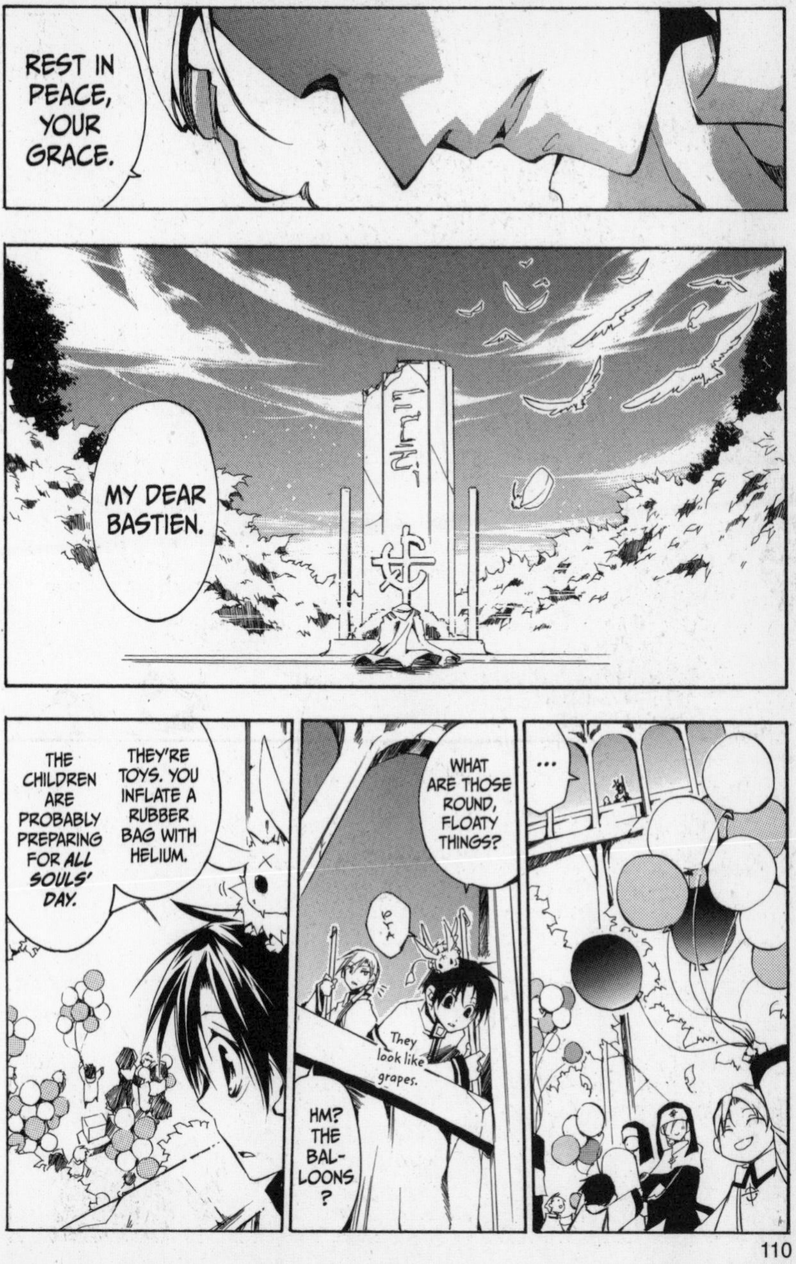
REST IN PEACE, YOUR GRACE.
MY DEAR BASTIEN.
...
WHAT ARE THOSE ROUND, FLOATY THINGS?
They look like grapes.
HM? THE BAL-LOONS?
THEY'RE TOYS. YOU INFLATE A RUBBER BAG WITH HELIUM.
THE CHILDREN ARE PROBABLY PREPARING FOR *ALL SOULS' DAY.*

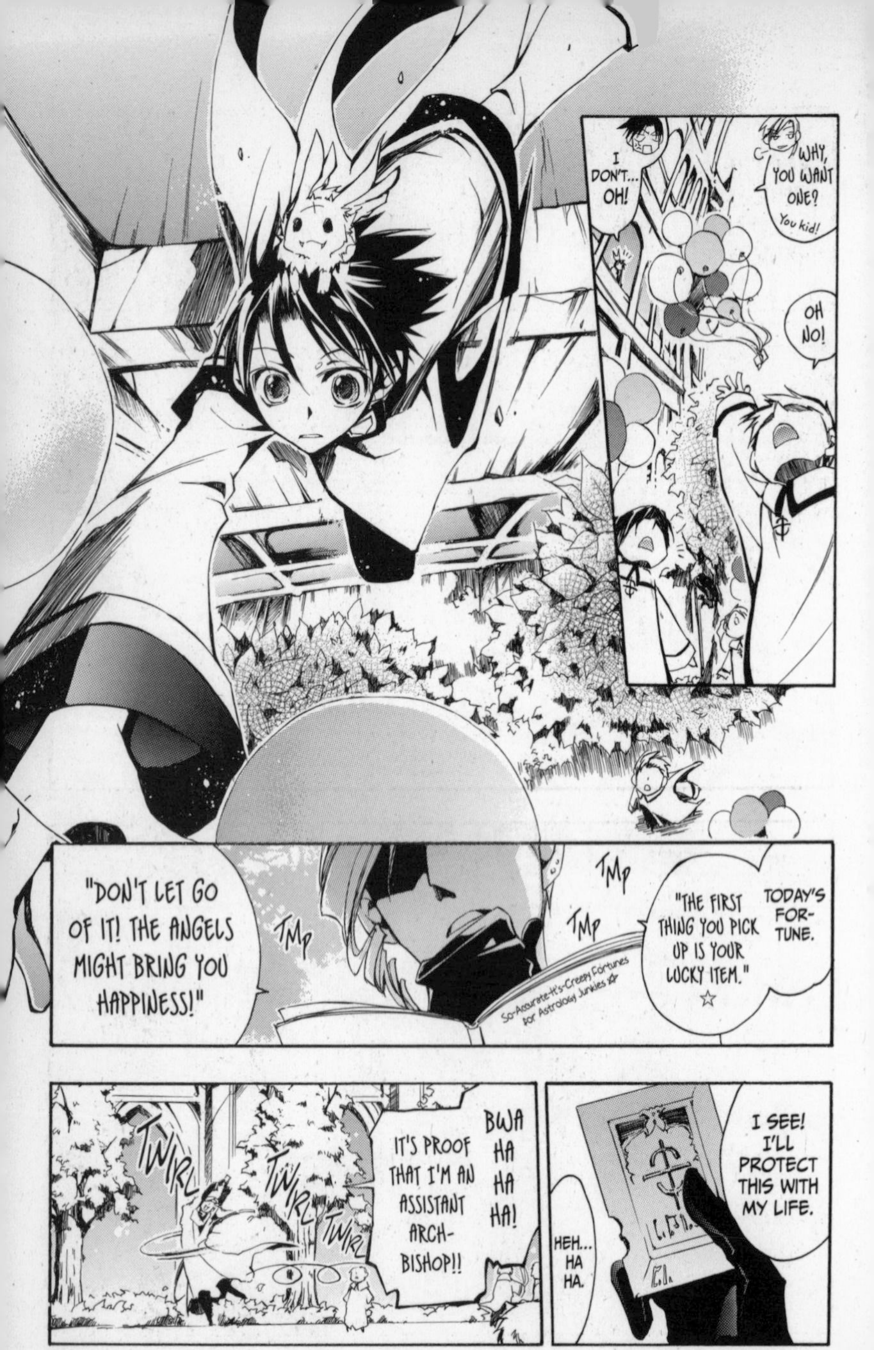
WHY, YOU WANT ONE? You kid!
I DON'T... OH!
OH NO!
TODAY'S FORTUNE.
"THE FIRST THING YOU PICK UP IS YOUR LUCKY ITEM." ☆
TMP
TMP
TMP
So-Accurate-It's-Creepy Fortunes for Astrology Junkies ☆
"DON'T LET GO OF IT! THE ANGELS MIGHT BRING YOU HAPPINESS!"
I SEE! I'LL PROTECT THIS WITH MY LIFE.
HEH... HA HA.
BWA HA HA HA!
IT'S PROOF THAT I'M AN ASSISTANT ARCH-BISHOP!!
TWIRL
TWIRL
TWIRL

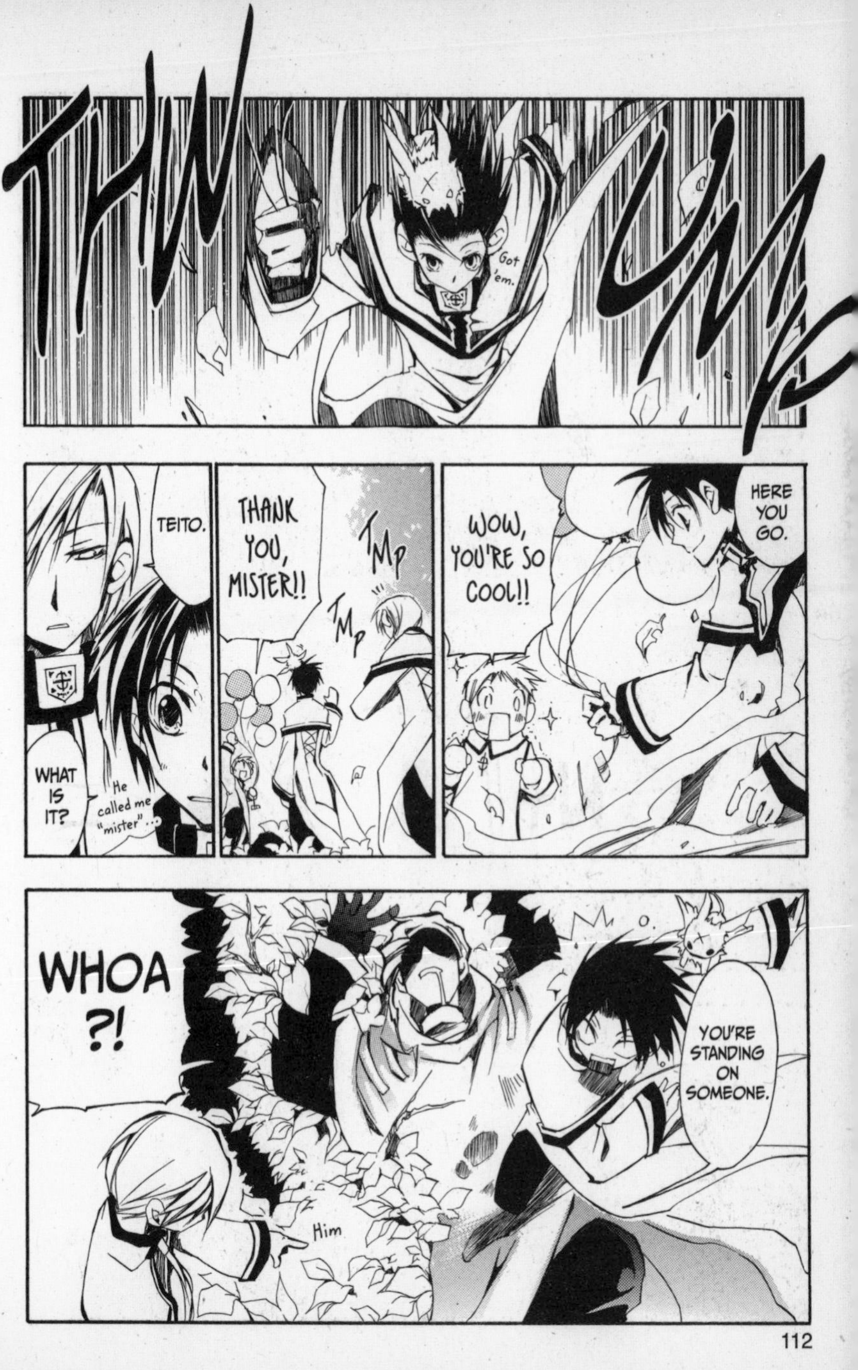

Got 'em.
HERE YOU GO.
WOW, YOU'RE SO COOL!!
THANK YOU, MISTER!!
TMP
TMP
TEITO.
WHAT IS IT?
He called me "mister"...
YOU'RE STANDING ON SOMEONE.
WHOA?!
Him

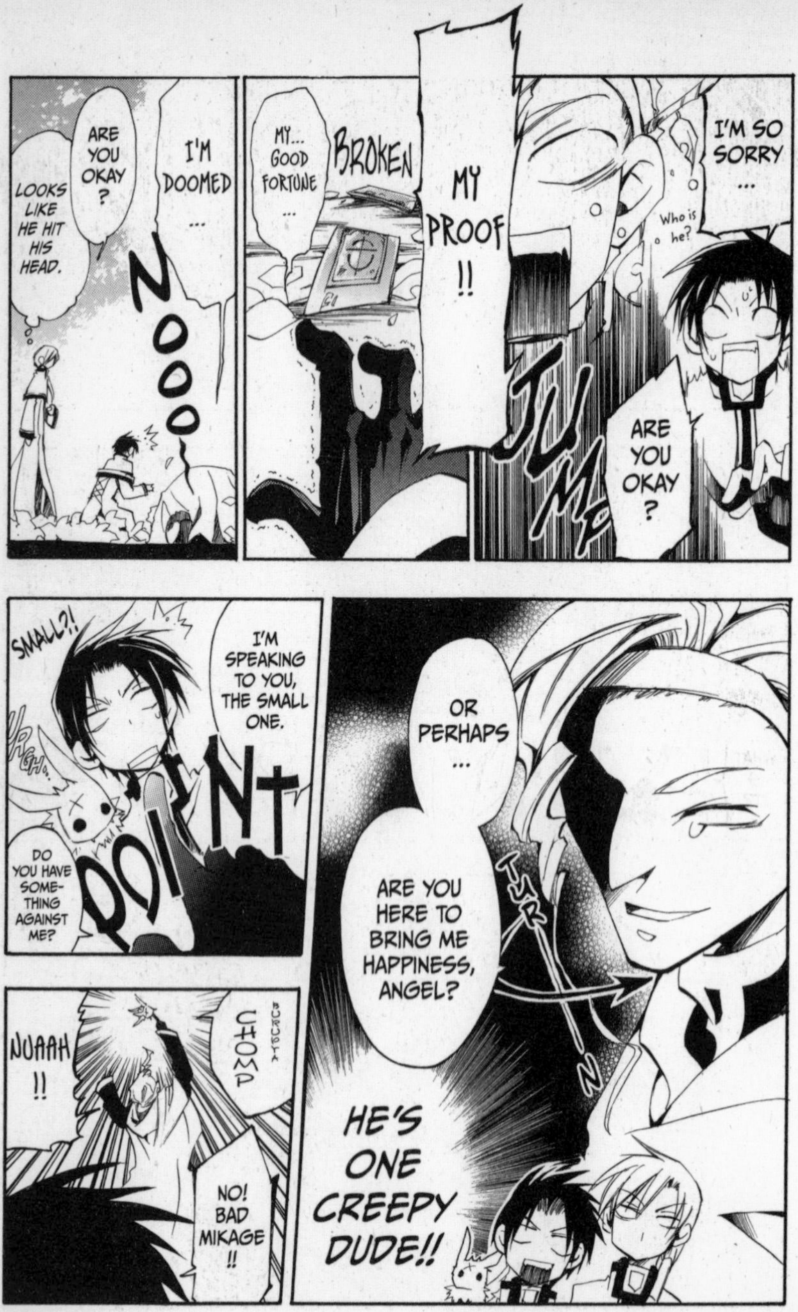
I'M SO SORRY ...
Who is he?
ARE YOU OKAY ?
JUMP
MY PROOF !!
BROKEN
MY... GOOD FORTUNE ...
I'M DOOMED ...
ARE YOU OKAY ?
LOOKS LIKE HE HIT HIS HEAD.
NOOOO
OR PERHAPS ...
ARE YOU HERE TO BRING ME HAPPINESS, ANGEL?
TURN
HE'S ONE CREEPY DUDE!!
I'M SPEAKING TO YOU, THE SMALL ONE.
SMALL?!
POINT
URGH..
DO YOU HAVE SOME-THING AGAINST ME?
CHOMP
NUAAH !!
NO! BAD MIKAGE !!

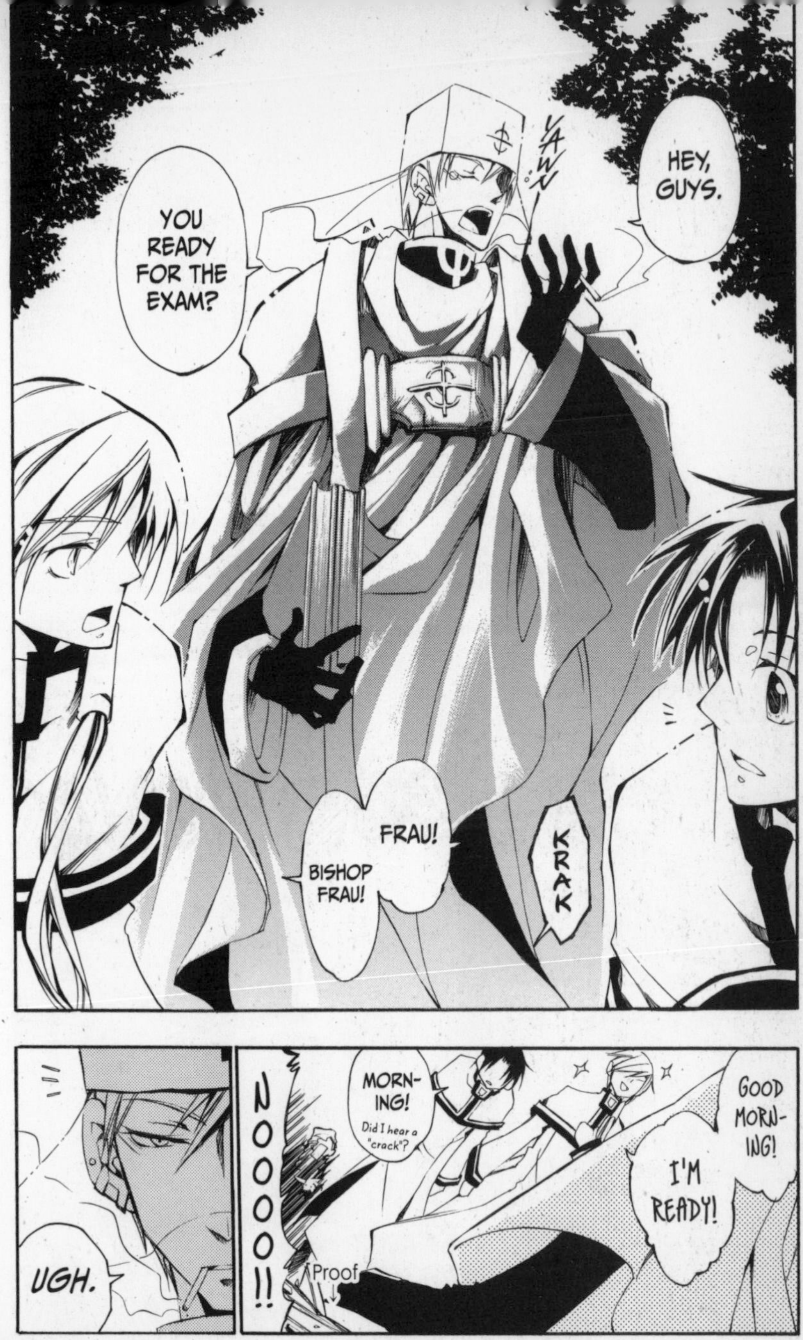
HEY, GUYS.
YAWN
YOU READY FOR THE EXAM?
KRAK
FRAU!
BISHOP FRAU!
GOOD MORNING!
I'M READY!
MORNING!
Did I hear a "crack"?
NOOOOO!!
Proof
UGH.

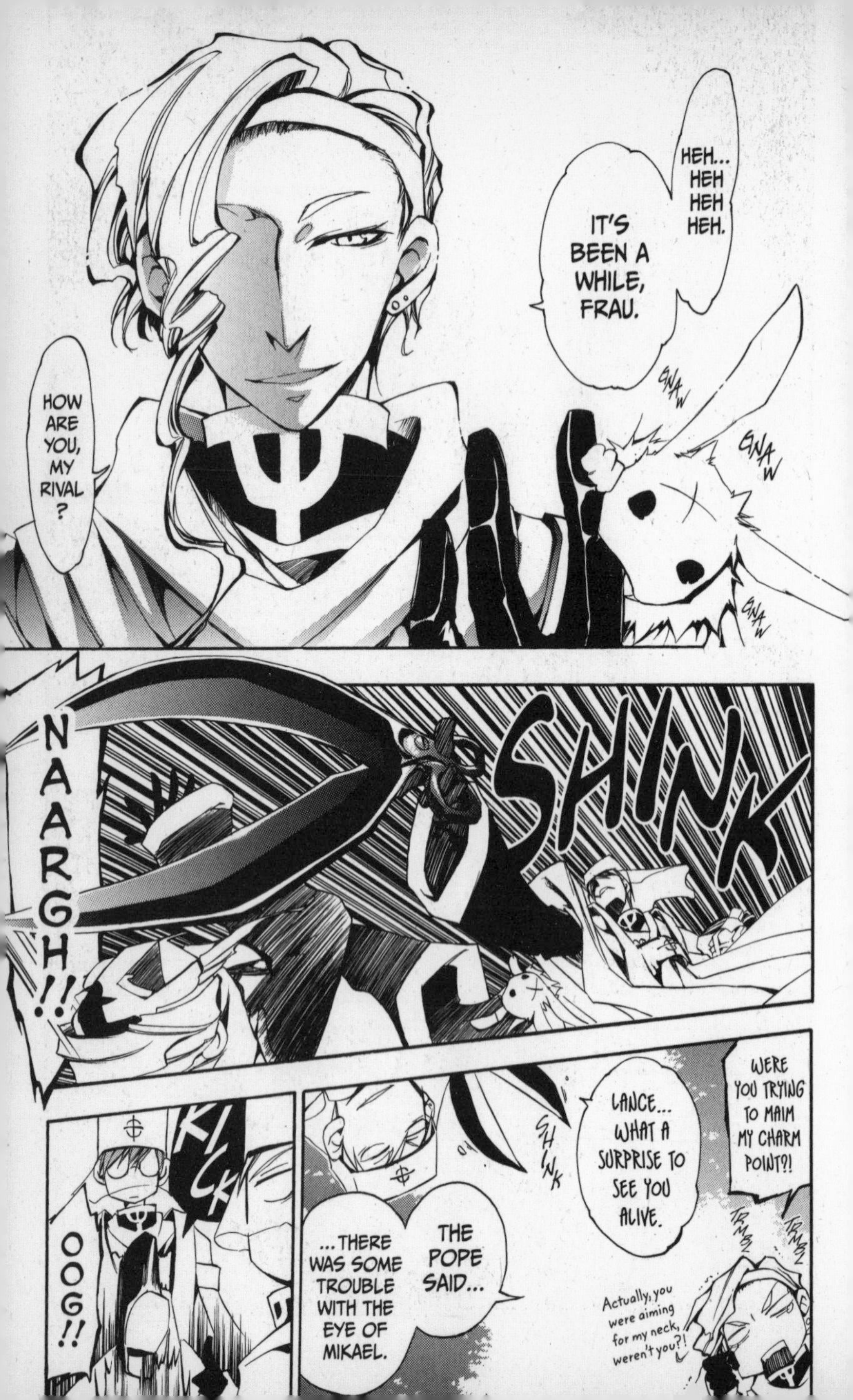
HEH... HEH HEH HEH.
IT'S BEEN A WHILE, FRAU.
GNAW
GNAW
GNAW
HOW ARE YOU, MY RIVAL?
SHINK
NAARGH!!
WERE YOU TRYING TO MAIM MY CHARM POINT?!
LANCE... WHAT A SURPRISE TO SEE YOU ALIVE.
SHINK
TRMBL
TRMBL
Actually, you were aiming for my neck, weren't you?!
THE POPE SAID...
...THERE WAS SOME TROUBLE WITH THE EYE OF MIKAEL.
KICK
OOG!!

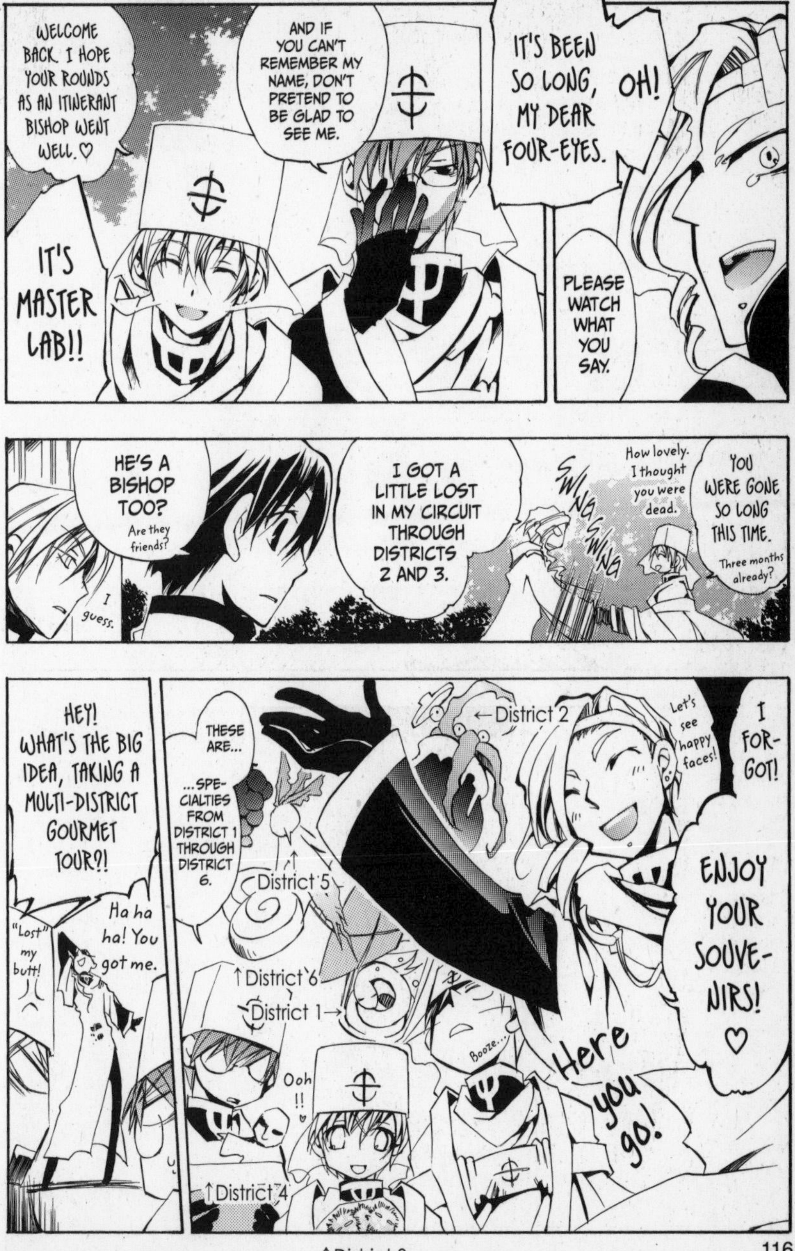
OH!
IT'S BEEN SO LONG, MY DEAR FOUR-EYES.
PLEASE WATCH WHAT YOU SAY.
AND IF YOU CAN'T REMEMBER MY NAME, DON'T PRETEND TO BE GLAD TO SEE ME.
WELCOME BACK. I HOPE YOUR ROUNDS AS AN ITINERANT BISHOP WENT WELL. ♡
IT'S MASTER LAB!!
YOU WERE GONE SO LONG THIS TIME.
Three months already?
How lovely. I thought you were dead.
SWING SWING
I GOT A LITTLE LOST IN MY CIRCUIT THROUGH DISTRICTS 2 AND 3.
HE'S A BISHOP TOO?
Are they friends?
I guess.
I FORGOT!
Let's see happy faces!
ENJOY YOUR SOUVENIRS! ♡
←District 2
THESE ARE...
...SPECIALTIES FROM DISTRICT 1 THROUGH DISTRICT 6.
↑District 5
↑District 6
District 1→
Booze...
Here you go!
Ooh!!
↑District 4
↑District 3
HEY! WHAT'S THE BIG IDEA, TAKING A MULTI-DISTRICT GOURMET TOUR?!
Ha ha ha! You got me.
"Lost" my butt!

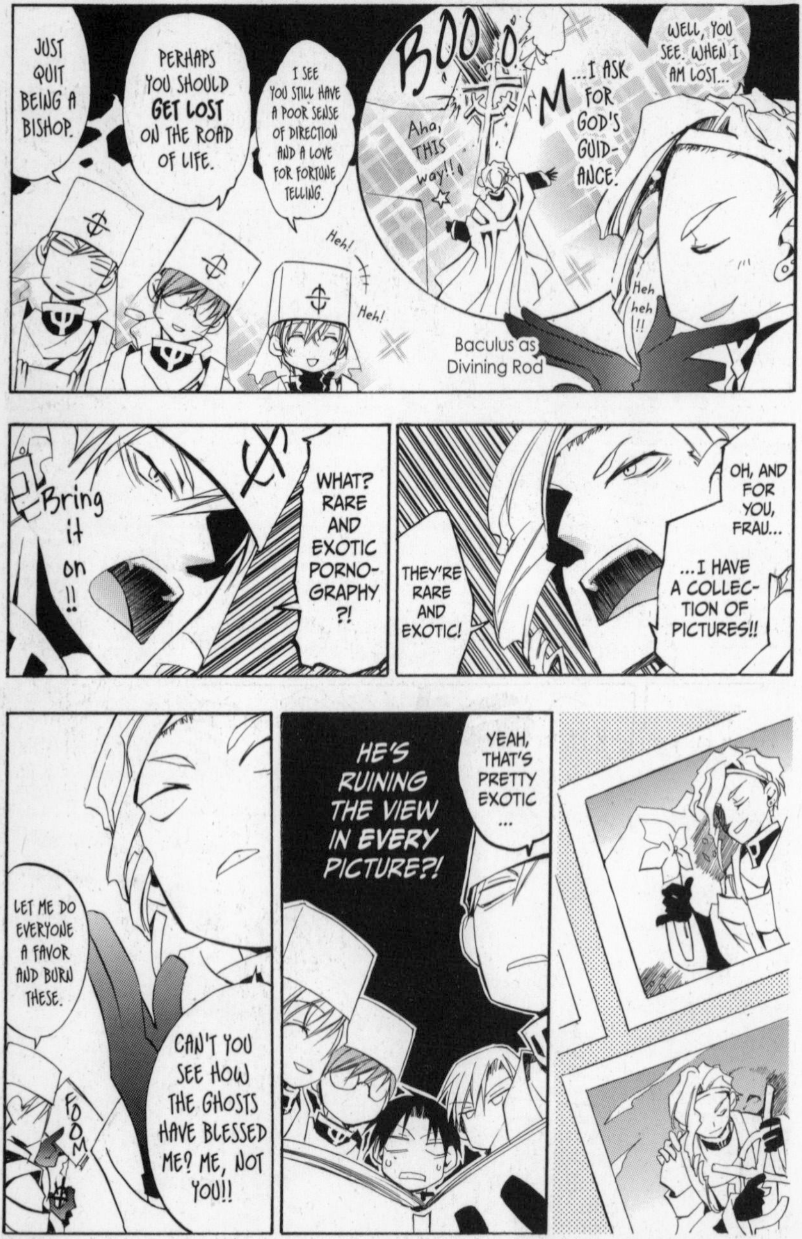
WELL, YOU SEE. WHEN I AM LOST...
...I ASK FOR GOD'S GUID-ANCE.
BOOOM
Aha, THIS way!!
Heh heh!!
Baculus as Divining Rod
I SEE YOU STILL HAVE A POOR SENSE OF DIRECTION AND A LOVE FOR FORTUNE TELLING.
Heh! Heh!
PERHAPS YOU SHOULD **GET LOST** ON THE ROAD OF LIFE.
JUST QUIT BEING A BISHOP.
OH, AND FOR YOU, FRAU...
...I HAVE A COLLEC-TION OF PICTURES!!
THEY'RE RARE AND EXOTIC!
WHAT? RARE AND EXOTIC PORNO-GRAPHY?!
Bring it on!!
YEAH, THAT'S PRETTY EXOTIC...
HE'S RUINING THE VIEW IN EVERY PICTURE?!
LET ME DO EVERYONE A FAVOR AND BURN THESE.
CAN'T YOU SEE HOW THE GHOSTS HAVE BLESSED ME? ME, NOT YOU!!
FOOOM

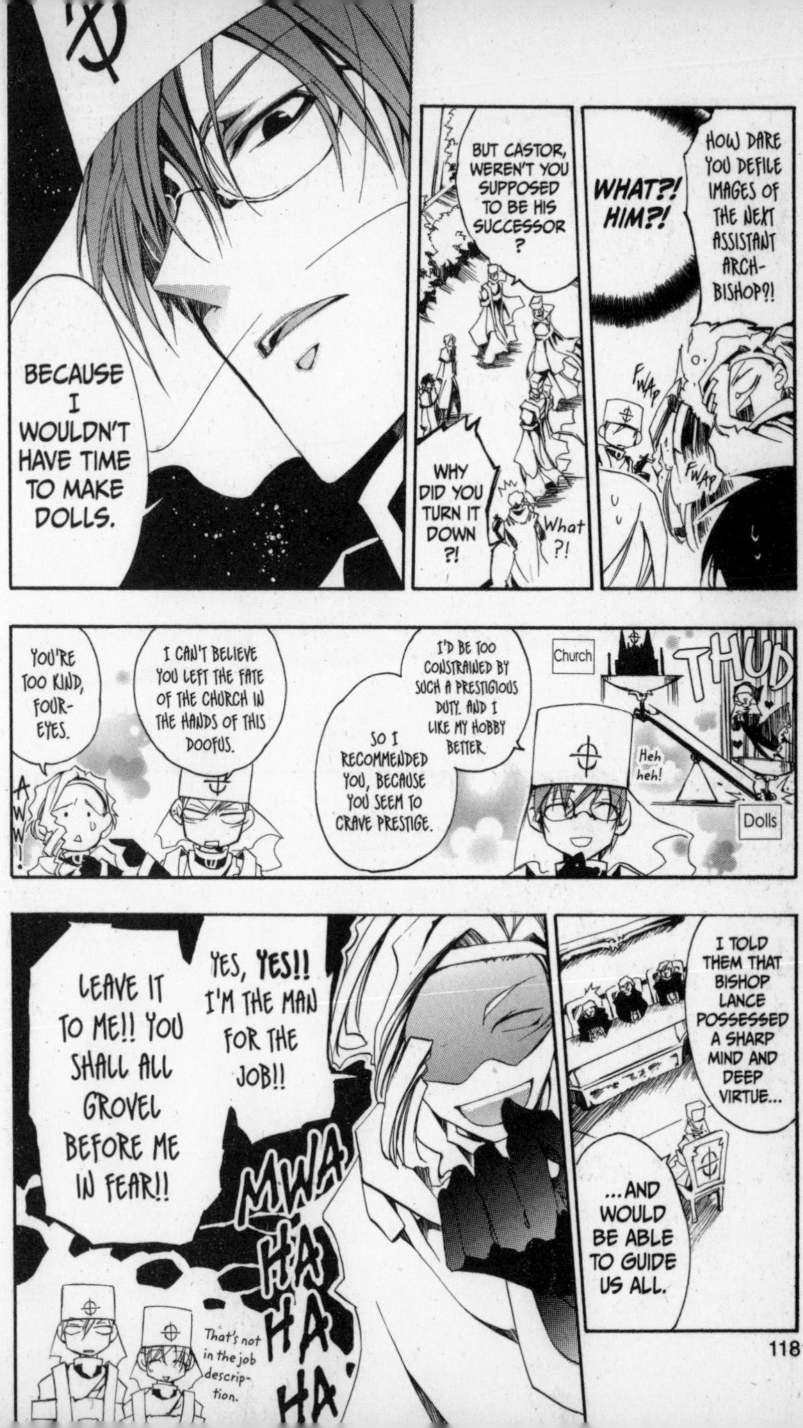
HOW DARE YOU DEFILE IMAGES OF THE NEXT ASSISTANT ARCH-BISHOP?!
WHAT?! HIM?!
FWAP
FWAP
BUT CASTOR, WEREN'T YOU SUPPOSED TO BE HIS SUCCESSOR?
WHY DID YOU TURN IT DOWN?!
What?!
BECAUSE I WOULDN'T HAVE TIME TO MAKE DOLLS.
THUD
Church
Dolls
Heh heh!
I'D BE TOO CONSTRAINED BY SUCH A PRESTIGIOUS DUTY. AND I LIKE MY HOBBY BETTER.
SO I RECOMMENDED YOU, BECAUSE YOU SEEM TO CRAVE PRESTIGE.
I CAN'T BELIEVE YOU LEFT THE FATE OF THE CHURCH IN THE HANDS OF THIS DOOFUS.
YOU'RE TOO KIND, FOUR-EYES.
AWWW!
I TOLD THEM THAT BISHOP LANCE POSSESSED A SHARP MIND AND DEEP VIRTUE...
...AND WOULD BE ABLE TO GUIDE US ALL.
YES, YES!! I'M THE MAN FOR THE JOB!!
LEAVE IT TO ME!! YOU SHALL ALL GROVEL BEFORE ME IN FEAR!!
MWA HA HA HA
That's not in the job description.

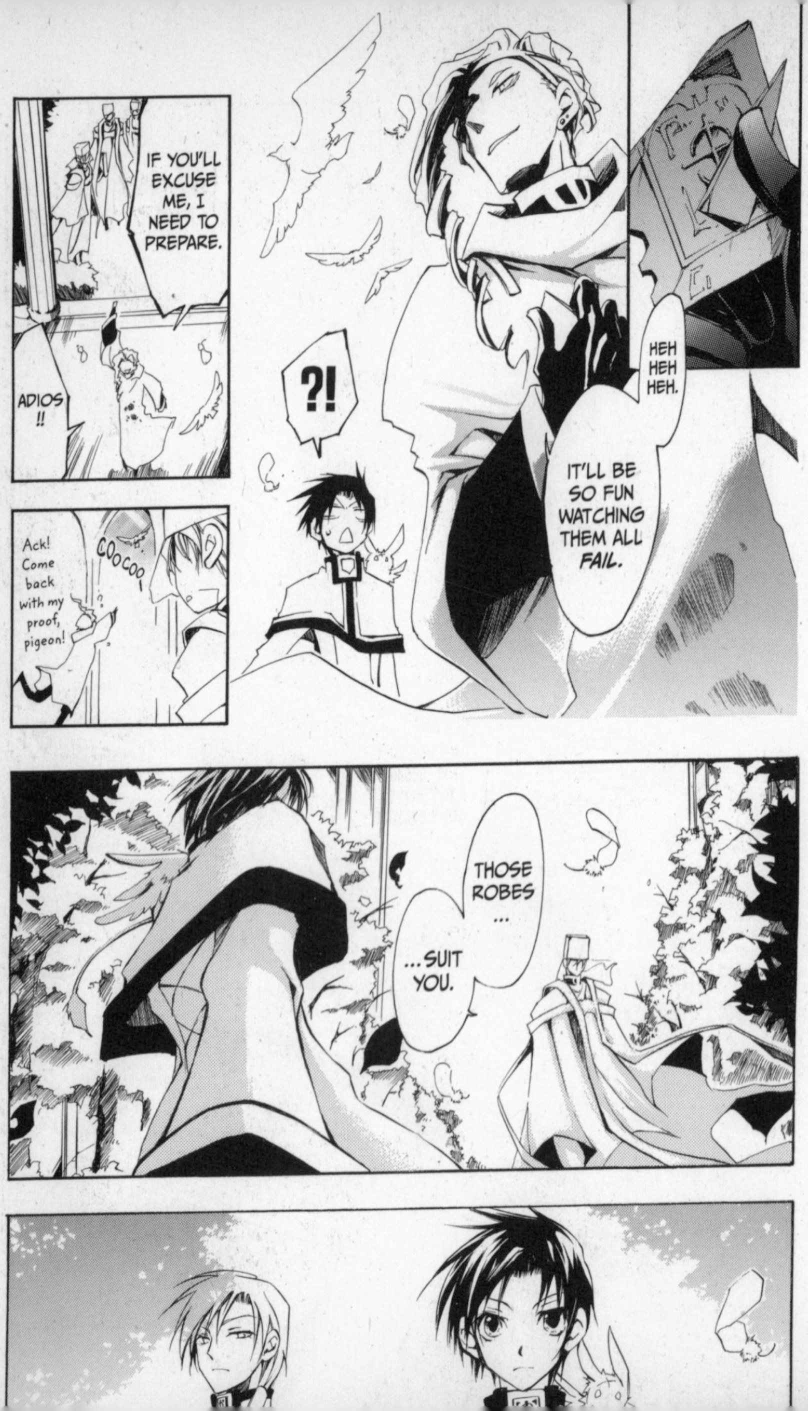
HEH HEH HEH.
IT'LL BE SO FUN WATCHING THEM ALL FAIL.
?!
IF YOU'LL EXCUSE ME, I NEED TO PREPARE.
ADIOS !!
COOCOO
Ack! Come back with my proof, pigeon!
THOSE ROBES ...
...SUIT YOU.

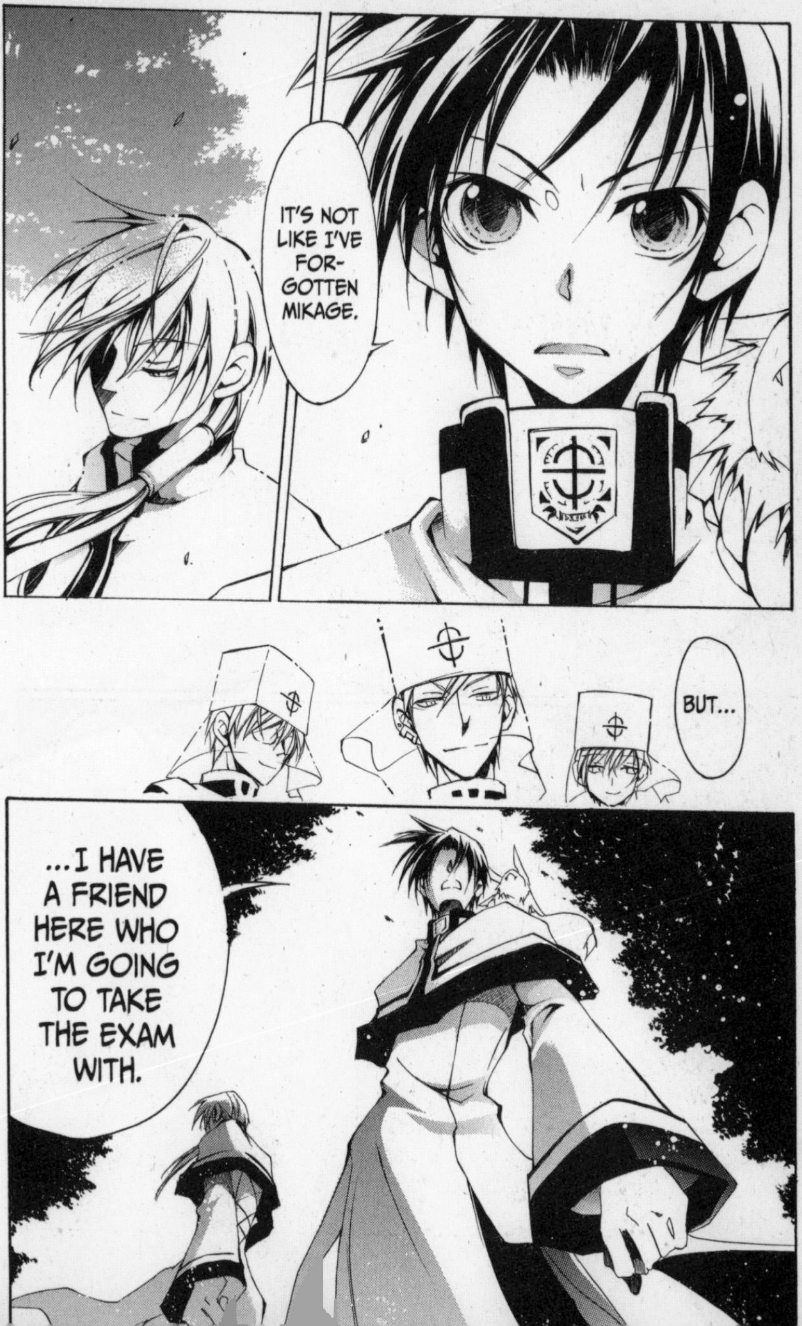
IT'S NOT LIKE I'VE FOR-GOTTEN MIKAGE.
BUT...
...I HAVE A FRIEND HERE WHO I'M GOING TO TAKE THE EXAM WITH.

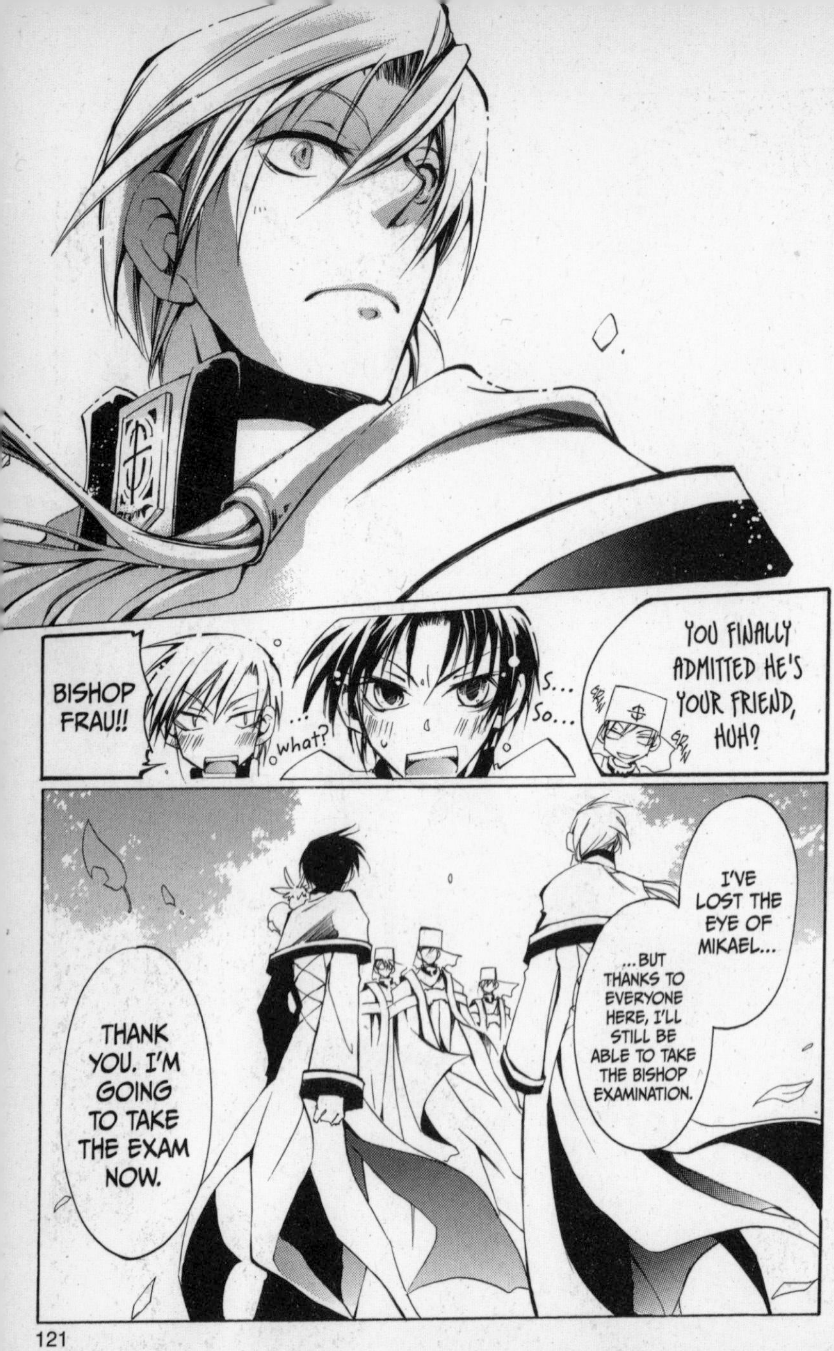
YOU FINALLY ADMITTED HE'S YOUR FRIEND, HUH?
GRIN GRIN
S... So...
...what?
BISHOP FRAU!!
I'VE LOST THE EYE OF MIKAEL...
...BUT THANKS TO EVERYONE HERE, I'LL STILL BE ABLE TO TAKE THE BISHOP EXAMINATION.
THANK YOU. I'M GOING TO TAKE THE EXAM NOW.

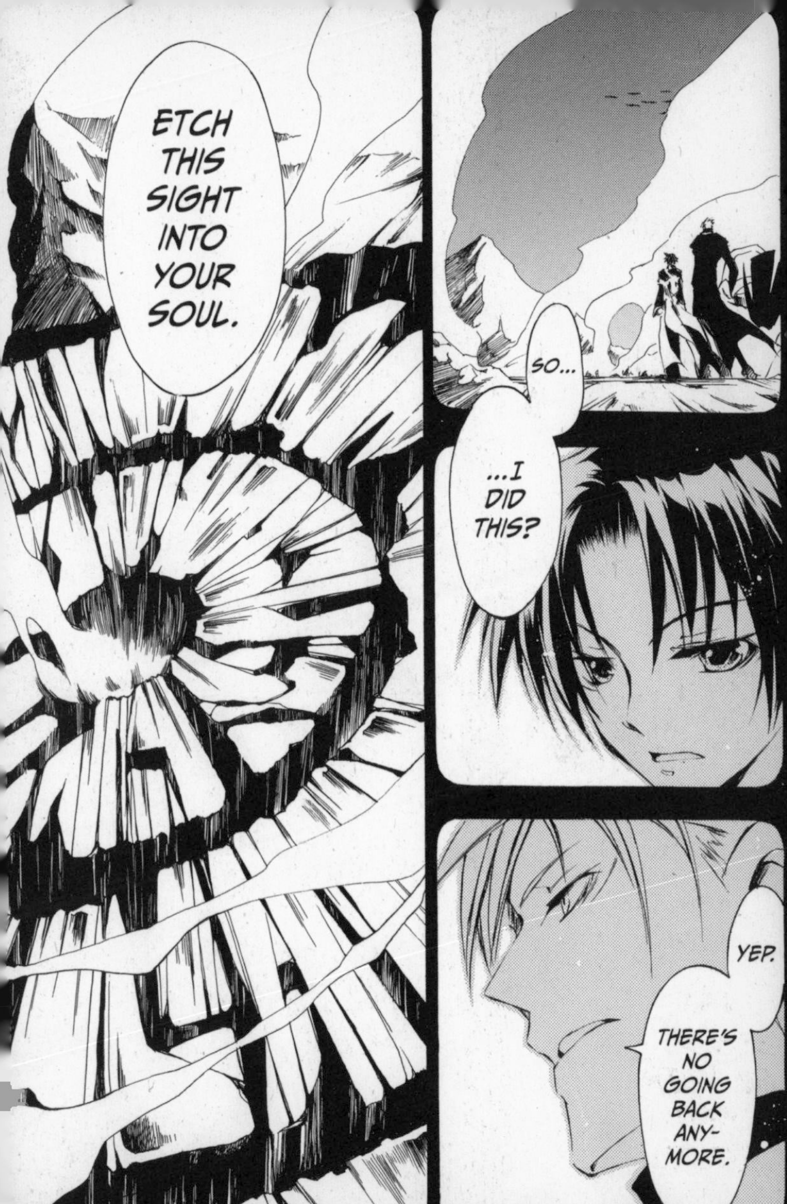
SO...
...I DID THIS?
YEP.
THERE'S NO GOING BACK ANY-MORE.
ETCH THIS SIGHT INTO YOUR SOUL.

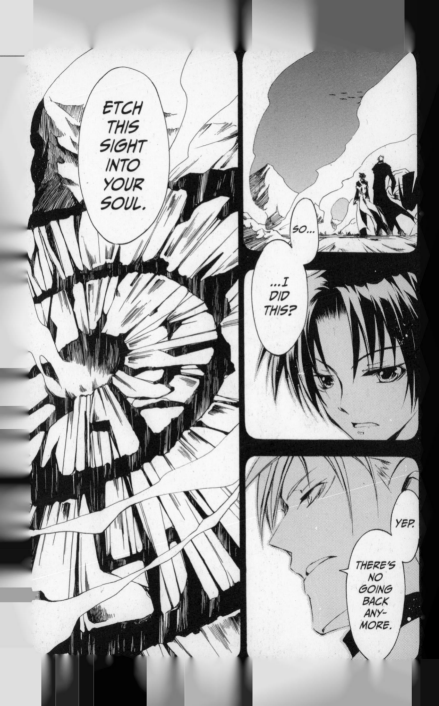

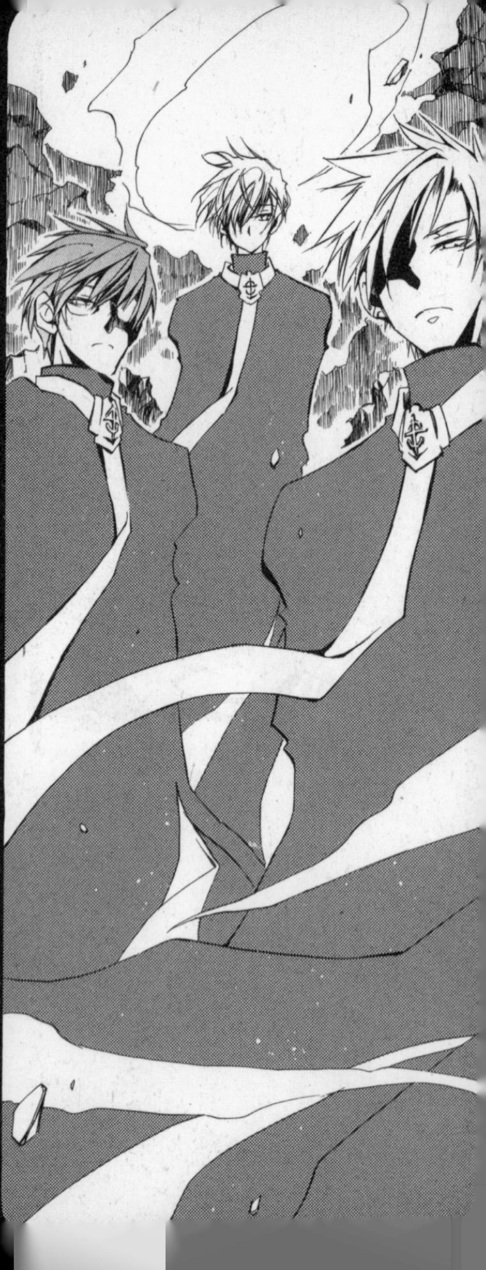

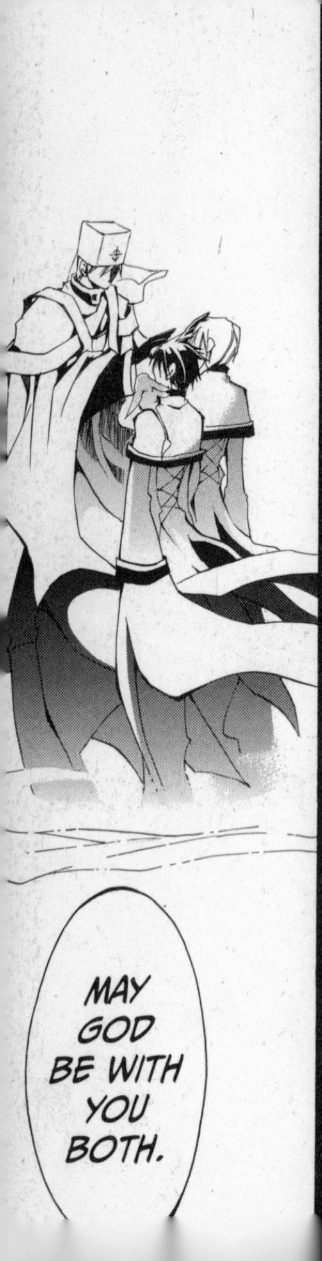
MAY GOD BE WITH YOU BOTH.

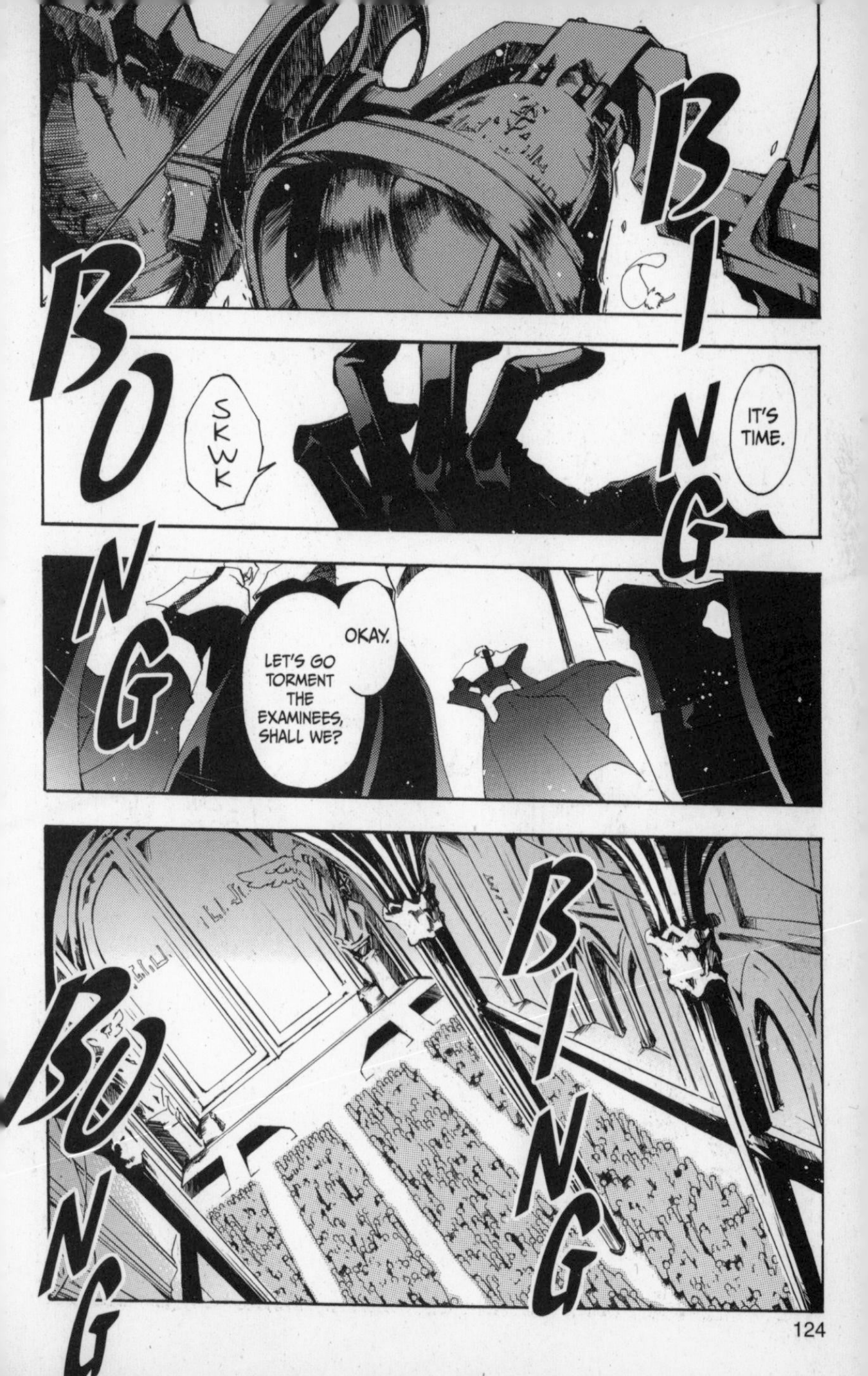
BING
BONG
IT'S TIME.
SKWK
OKAY.
LET'S GO TORMENT THE EXAMINEES, SHALL WE?
BING
BONG
BING
BONG

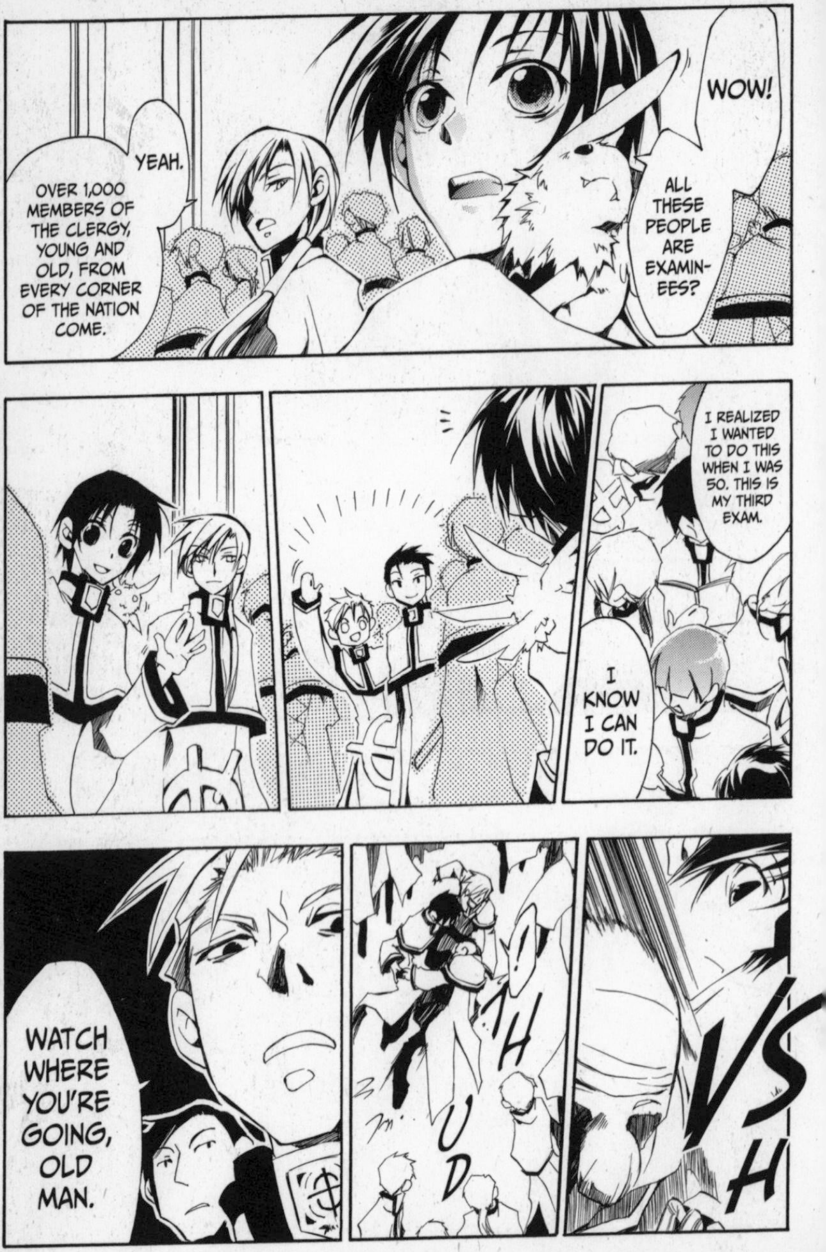
WOW!
ALL THESE PEOPLE ARE EXAMINEES?
YEAH.
OVER 1,000 MEMBERS OF THE CLERGY, YOUNG AND OLD, FROM EVERY CORNER OF THE NATION COME.
I REALIZED I WANTED TO DO THIS WHEN I WAS 50. THIS IS MY THIRD EXAM.
I KNOW I CAN DO IT.
!
WATCH WHERE YOU'RE GOING, OLD MAN.

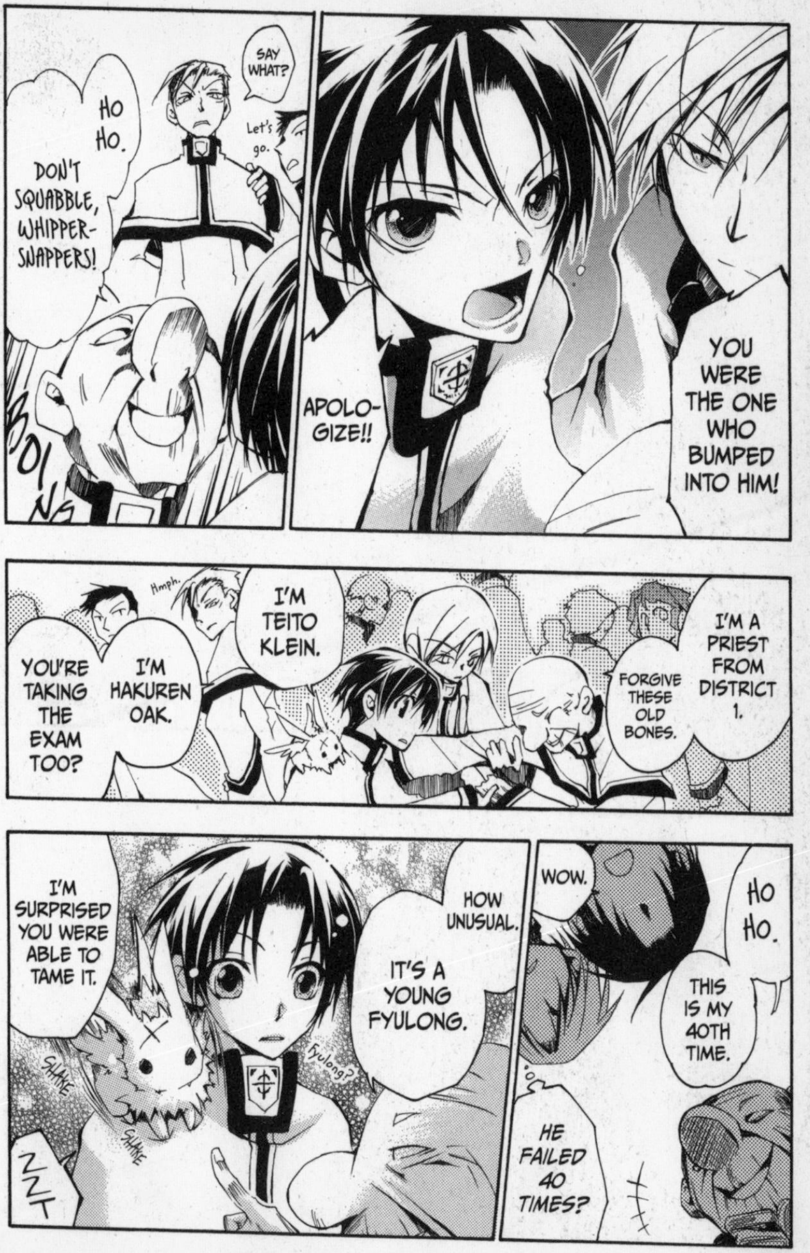
YOU WERE THE ONE WHO BUMPED INTO HIM!
APOLO-GIZE!!
SAY WHAT?
Let's go.
HO HO.
DON'T SQUABBLE, WHIPPER-SNAPPERS!
BOING
I'M A PRIEST FROM DISTRICT 1.
FORGIVE THESE OLD BONES.
I'M TEITO KLEIN.
Hmph.
I'M HAKUREN OAK.
YOU'RE TAKING THE EXAM TOO?
HO HO.
THIS IS MY 40TH TIME.
WOW.
HE FAILED 40 TIMES?
HOW UNUSUAL.
IT'S A YOUNG FYULONG.
Fyulong?
I'M SURPRISED YOU WERE ABLE TO TAME IT.
SHAKE
SHAKE
ZZT

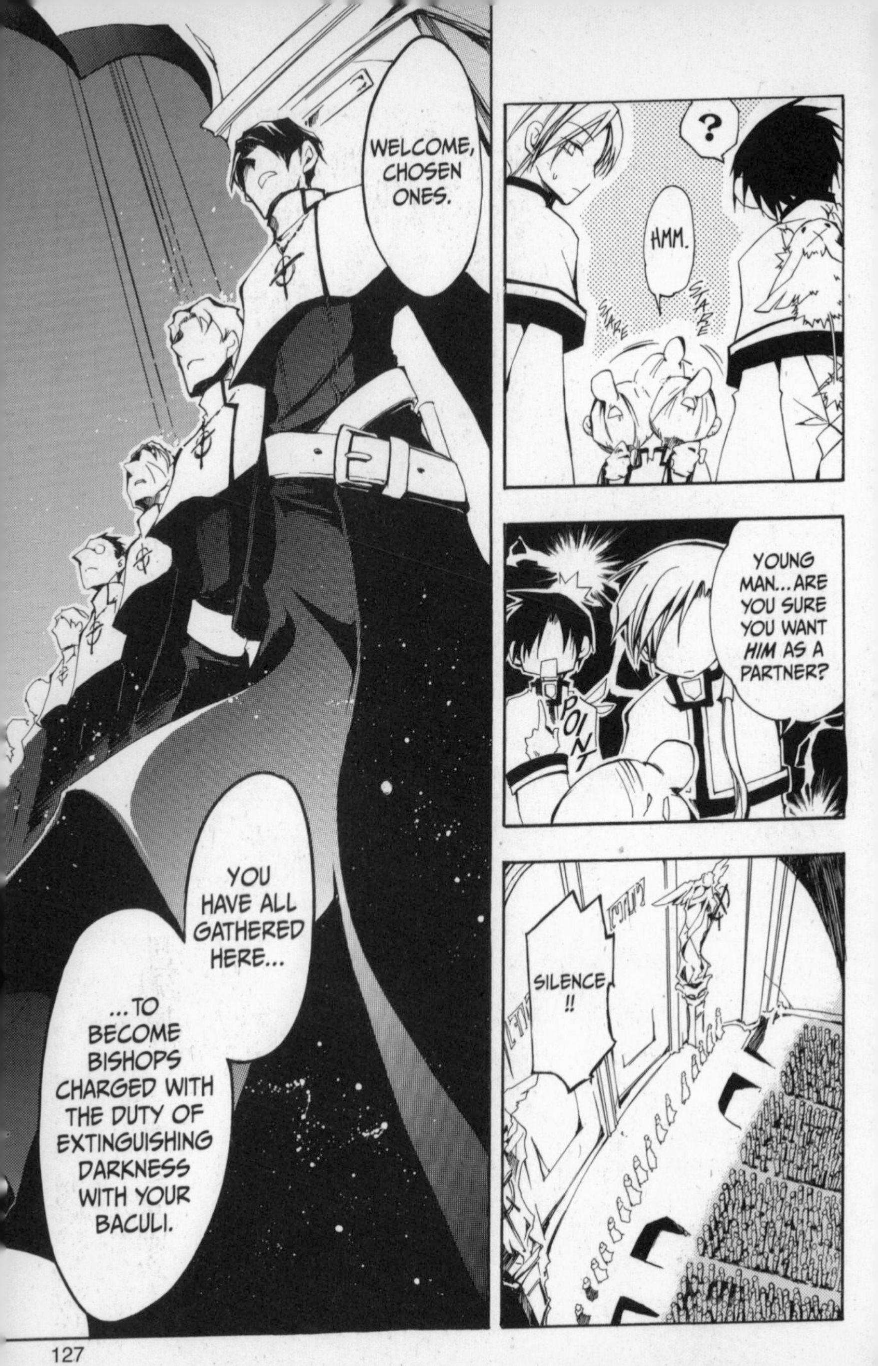
?
HMM.
STARE
STARE
YOUNG MAN... ARE YOU SURE YOU WANT *HIM* AS A PARTNER?
POINT
SILENCE !!
WELCOME, CHOSEN ONES.
YOU HAVE ALL GATHERED HERE...
...TO BECOME BISHOPS CHARGED WITH THE DUTY OF EXTINGUISHING DARKNESS WITH YOUR BACULI.

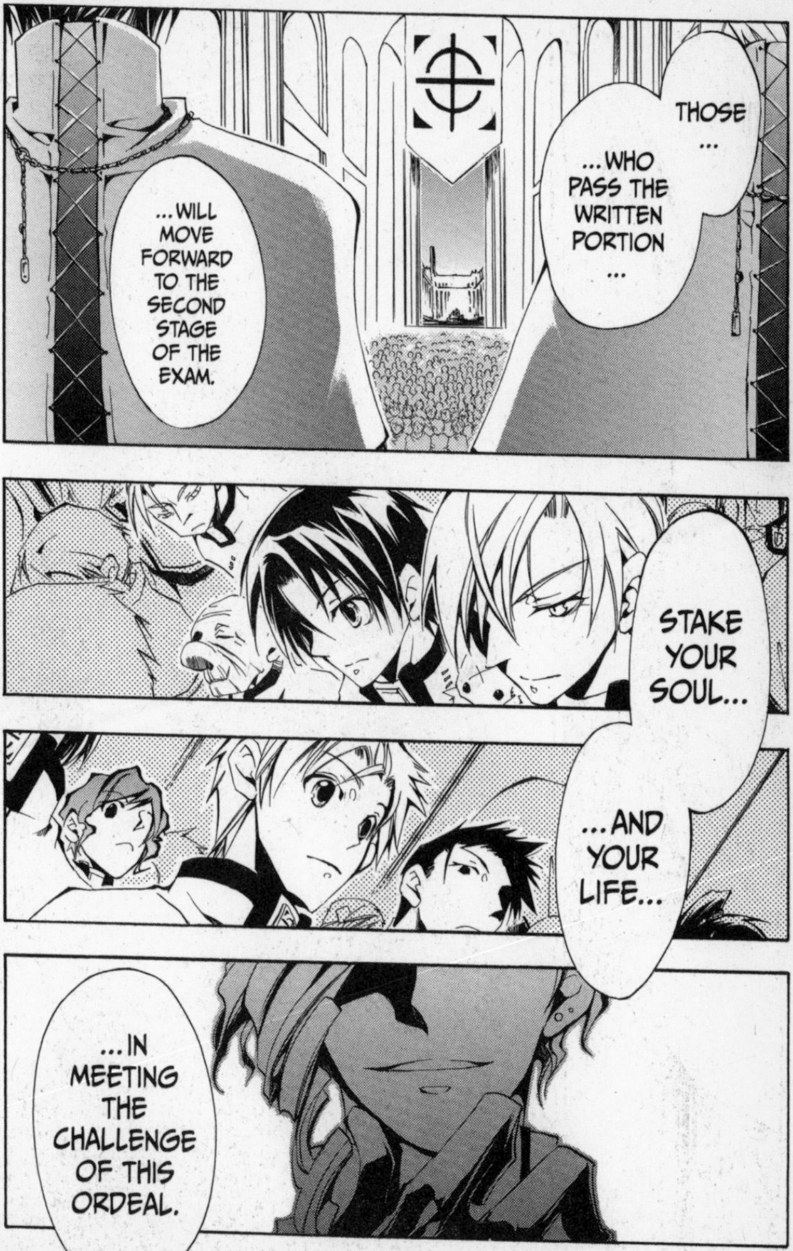
THOSE ...
...WHO PASS THE WRITTEN PORTION ...
...WILL MOVE FORWARD TO THE SECOND STAGE OF THE EXAM.
STAKE YOUR SOUL...
...AND YOUR LIFE...
...IN MEETING THE CHALLENGE OF THIS ORDEAL.

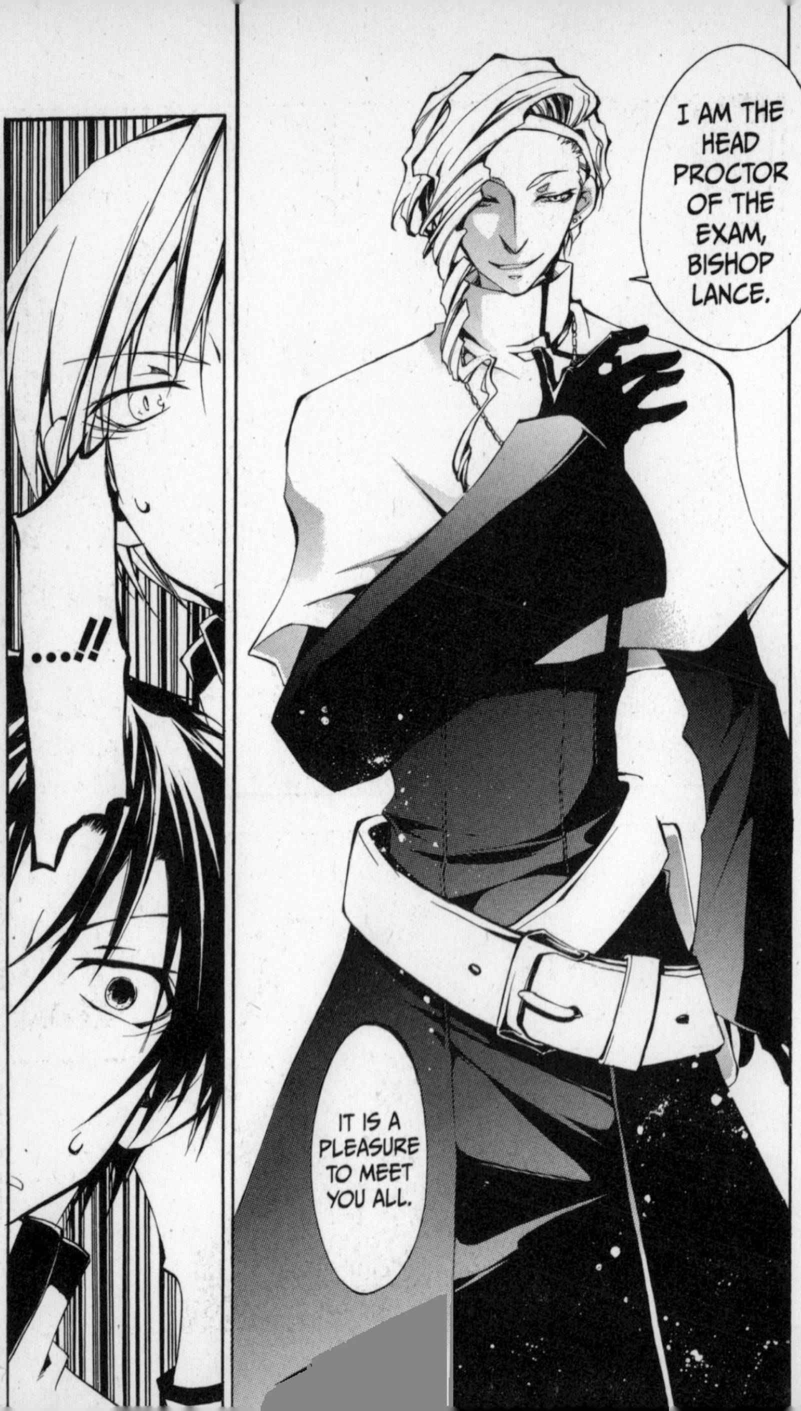
I AM THE HEAD PROCTOR OF THE EXAM, BISHOP LANCE.
IT IS A PLEASURE TO MEET YOU ALL.
...!!

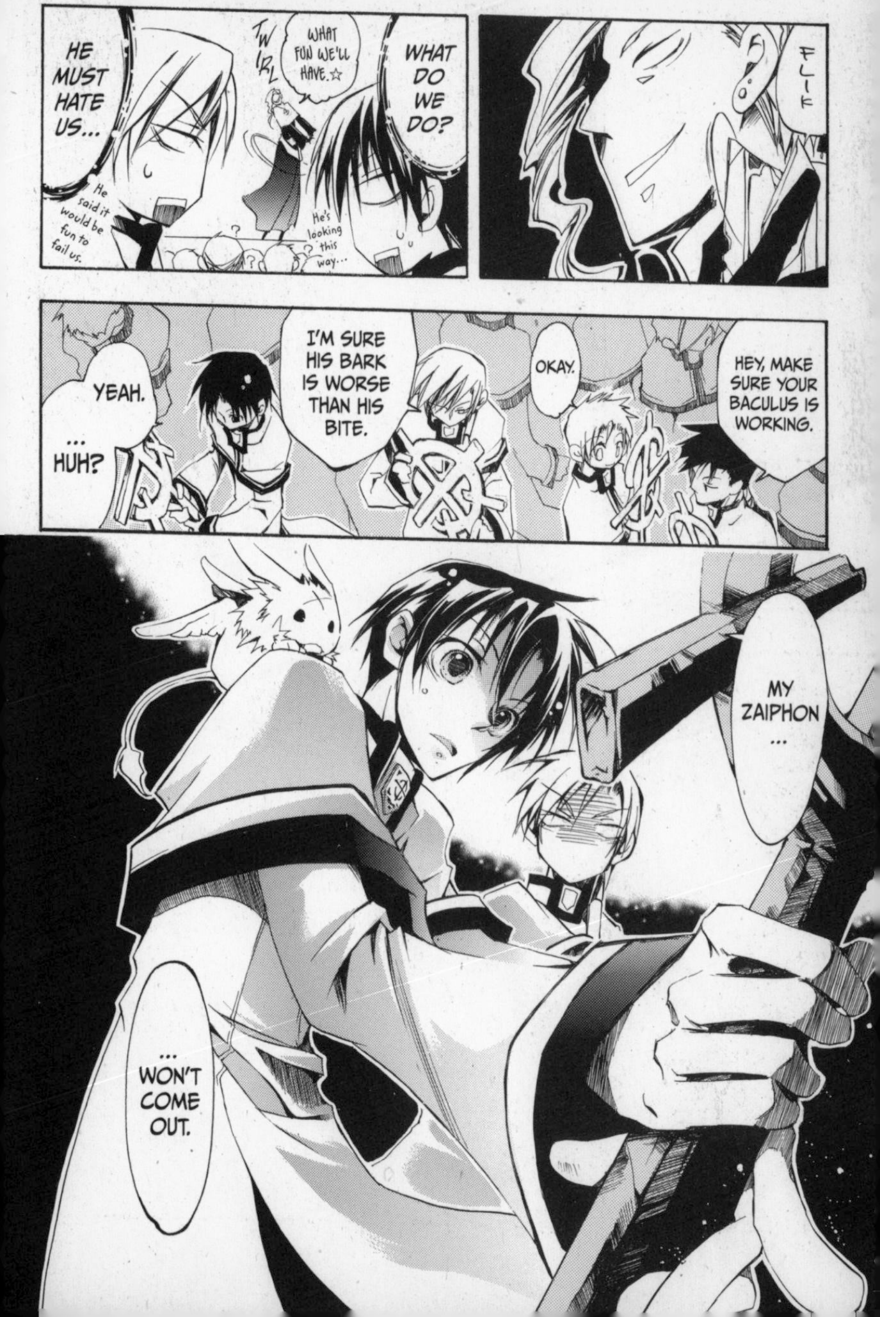
FLIK
WHAT DO WE DO?
WHAT FUN WE'LL HAVE.☆
TWIRL
He's looking this way...
HE MUST HATE US...
He said it would be fun to fail us.
HEY, MAKE SURE YOUR BACULUS IS WORKING.
OKAY.
I'M SURE HIS BARK IS WORSE THAN HIS BITE.
YEAH.
... HUH?
MY ZAIPHON ...
... WON'T COME OUT.

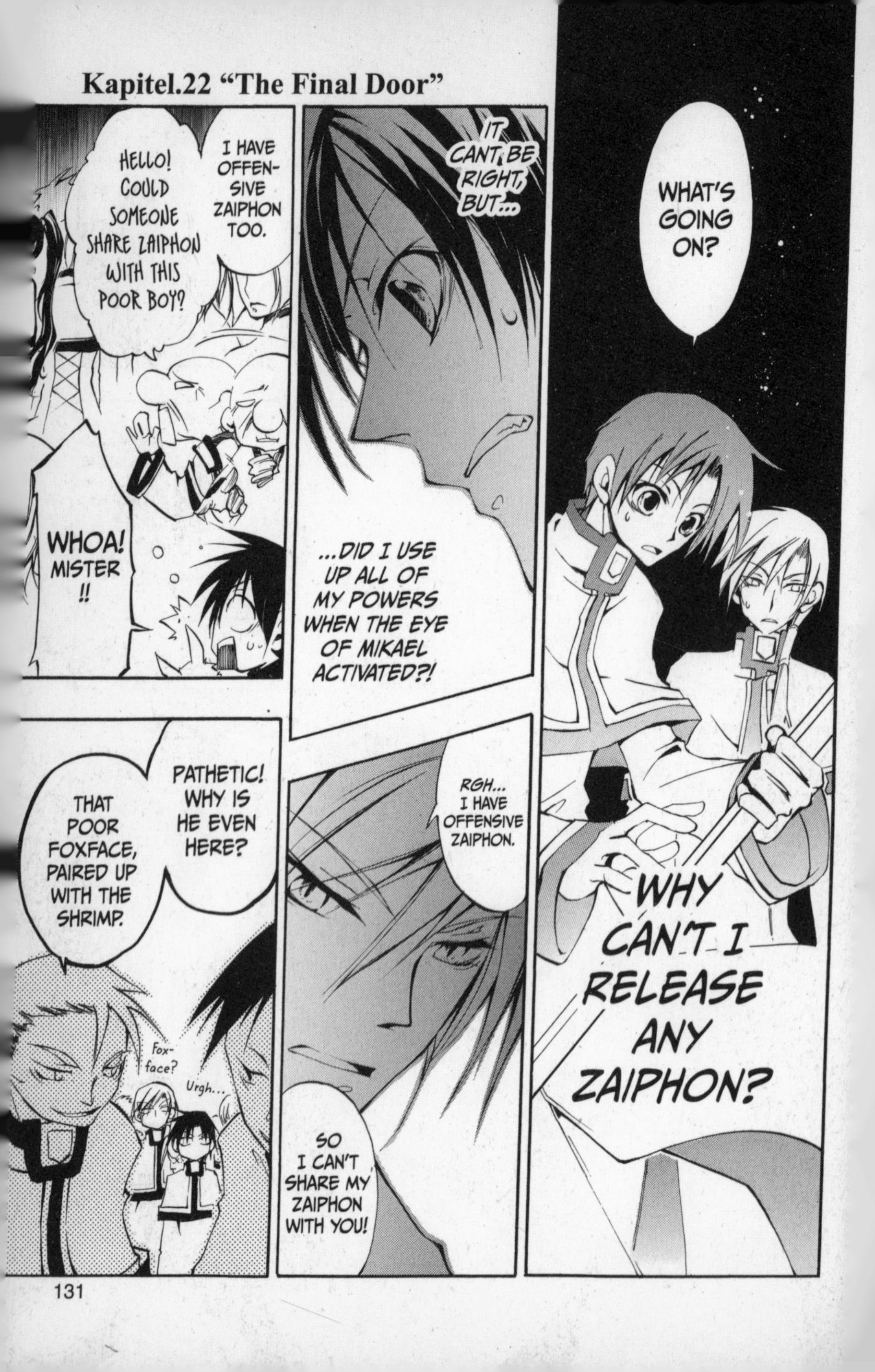
WHAT'S GOING ON?
WHY CAN'T I RELEASE ANY ZAIPHON?
IT CANT BE RIGHT, BUT...
...DID I USE UP ALL OF MY POWERS WHEN THE EYE OF MIKAEL ACTIVATED?!
I HAVE OFFEN-SIVE ZAIPHON TOO.
HELLO! COULD SOMEONE SHARE ZAIPHON WITH THIS POOR BOY?
WHOA! MISTER !!
RGH... I HAVE OFFENSIVE ZAIPHON.
SO I CAN'T SHARE MY ZAIPHON WITH YOU!
PATHETIC! WHY IS HE EVEN HERE?
THAT POOR FOXFACE, PAIRED UP WITH THE SHRIMP.
Fox-face?
Urgh...

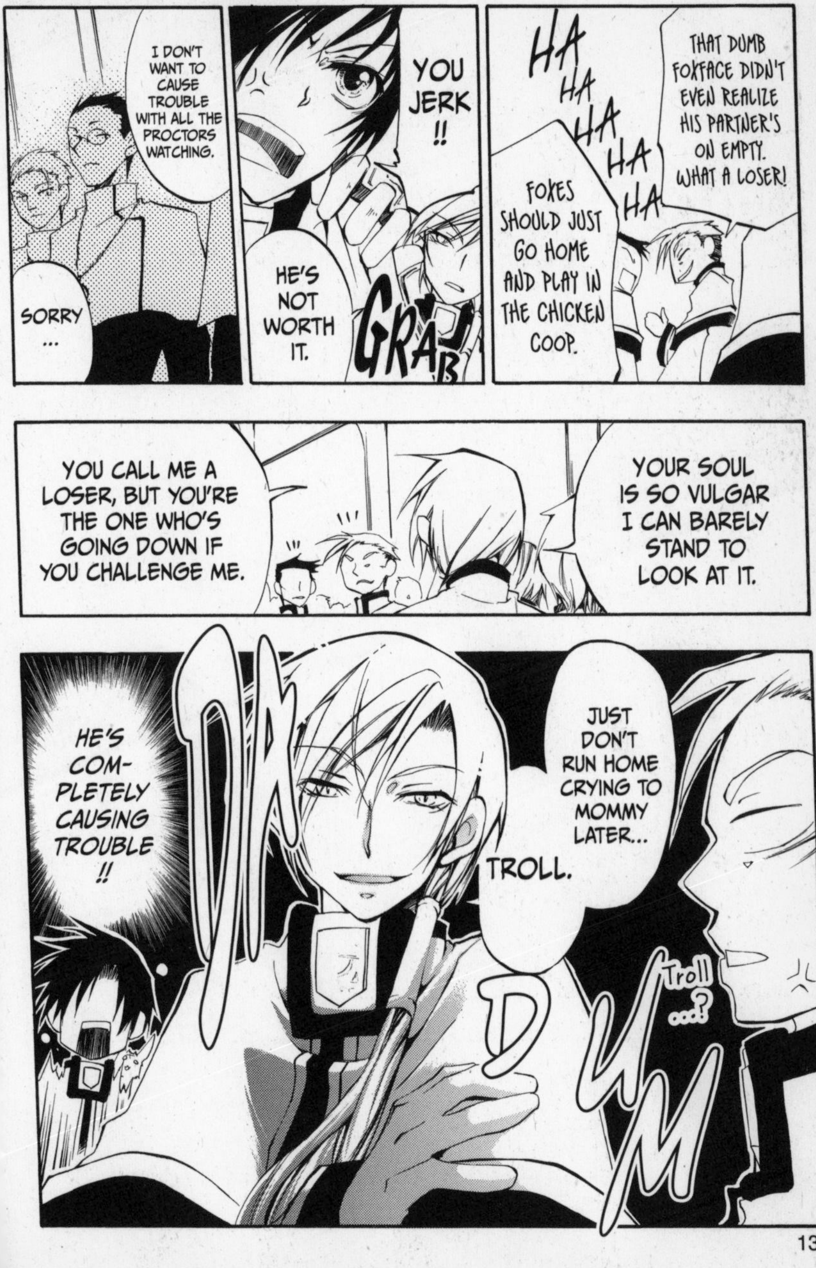
HA HA HA HA HA
THAT DUMB FOXFACE DIDN'T EVEN REALIZE HIS PARTNER'S ON EMPTY. WHAT A LOSER!
FOXES SHOULD JUST GO HOME AND PLAY IN THE CHICKEN COOP.
YOU JERK !!
HE'S NOT WORTH IT.
GRAB
I DON'T WANT TO CAUSE TROUBLE WITH ALL THE PROCTORS WATCHING.
SORRY ...
YOUR SOUL IS SO VULGAR I CAN BARELY STAND TO LOOK AT IT.
YOU CALL ME A LOSER, BUT YOU'RE THE ONE WHO'S GOING DOWN IF YOU CHALLENGE ME.
JUST DON'T RUN HOME CRYING TO MOMMY LATER...
TROLL.
DUM
Troll ...?
HE'S COM-PLETELY CAUSING TROUBLE !!

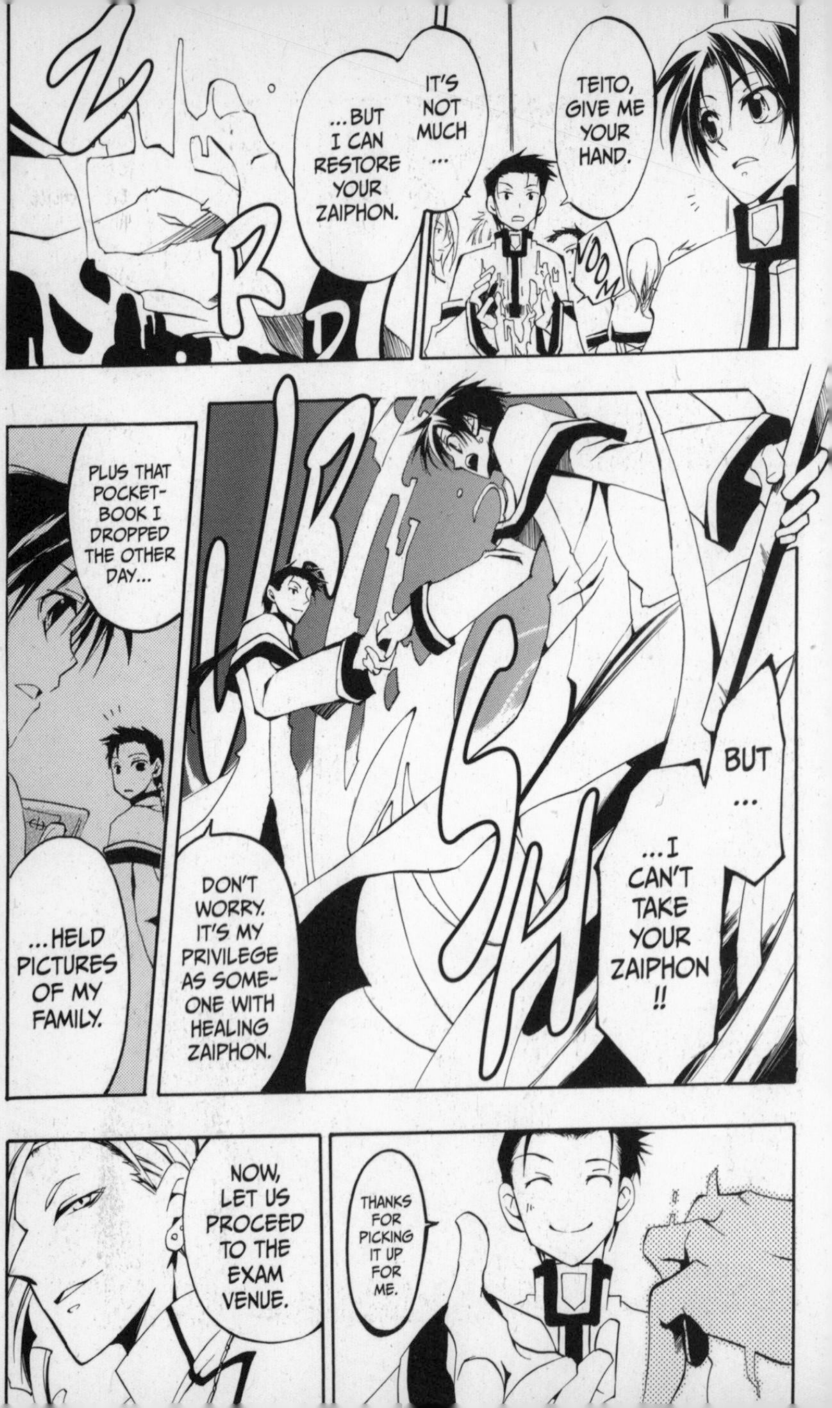
TEITO, GIVE ME YOUR HAND.
IT'S NOT MUCH...
...BUT I CAN RESTORE YOUR ZAIPHON.
BUT...
...I CAN'T TAKE YOUR ZAIPHON!!
DON'T WORRY. IT'S MY PRIVILEGE AS SOME-ONE WITH HEALING ZAIPHON.
PLUS THAT POCKET-BOOK I DROPPED THE OTHER DAY...
...HELD PICTURES OF MY FAMILY.
THANKS FOR PICKING IT UP FOR ME.
NOW, LET US PROCEED TO THE EXAM VENUE.

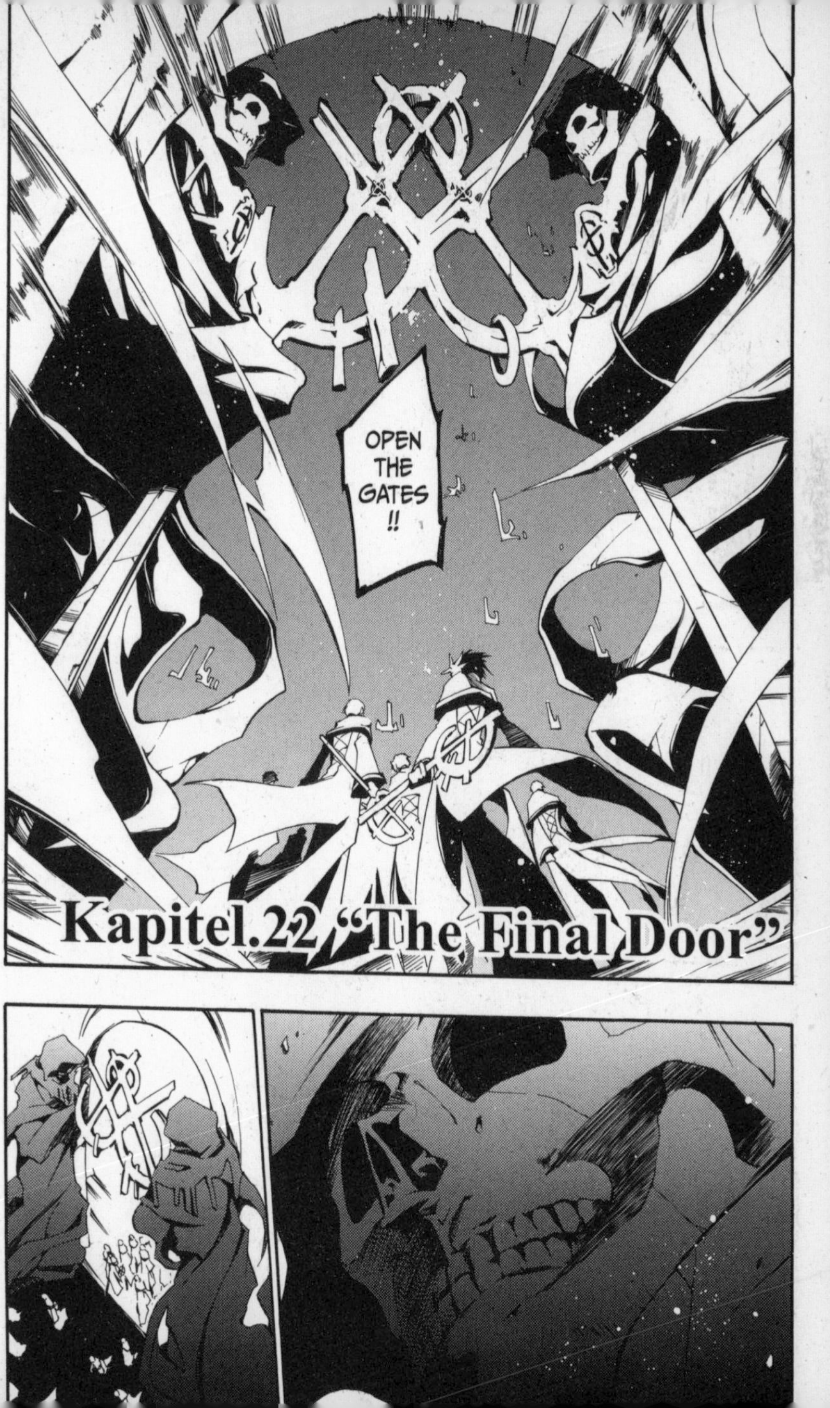
OPEN THE GATES !!
Kapitel.22 "The Final Door"

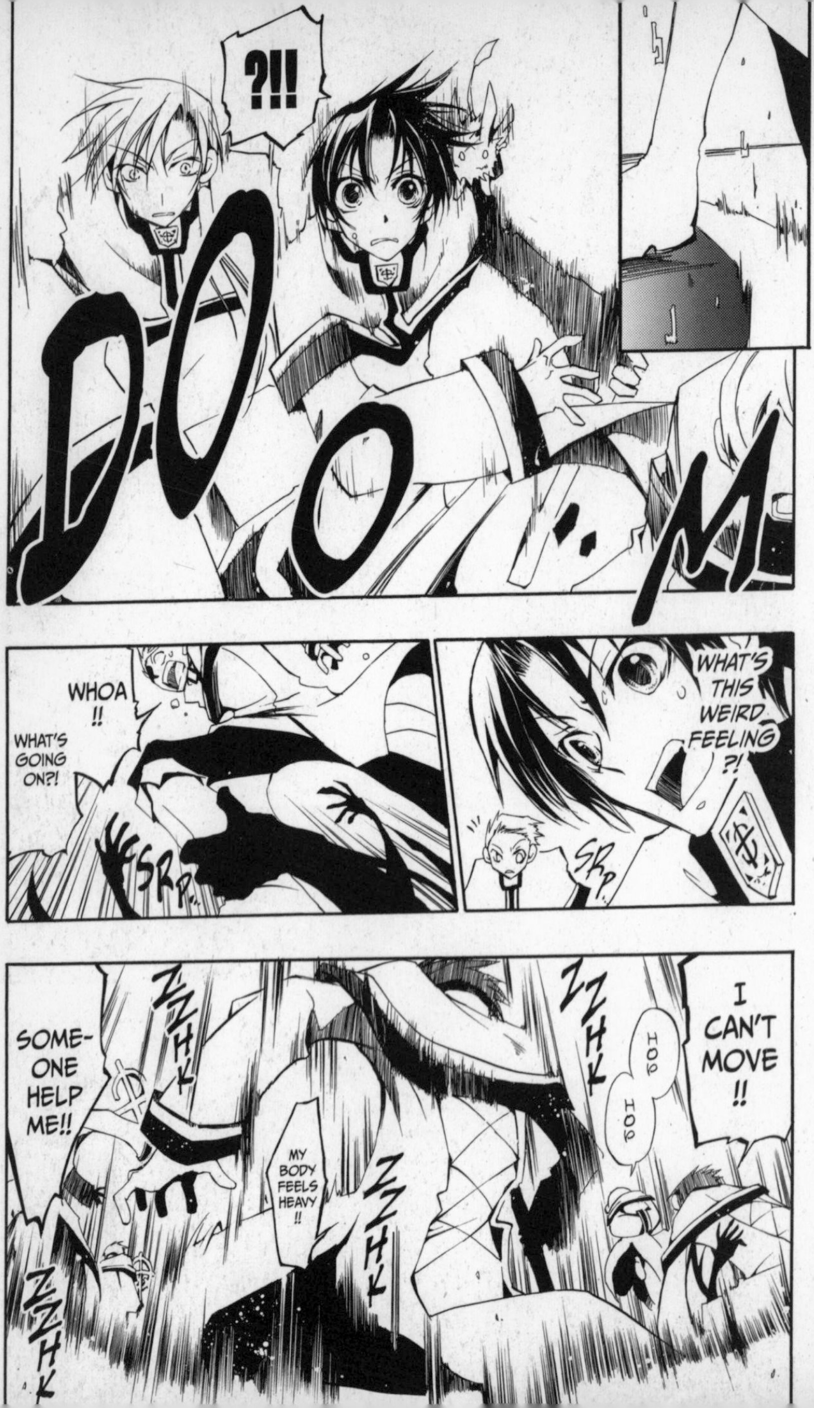
?!!
DOOOM
WHAT'S THIS WEIRD FEELING ?!
SRP
WHOA !!
WHAT'S GOING ON?!
SRP
I CAN'T MOVE !!
HOP
HOP
ZZHK
ZZHK
MY BODY FEELS HEAVY !!
SOME-ONE HELP ME!!
ZZHK
ZZHK

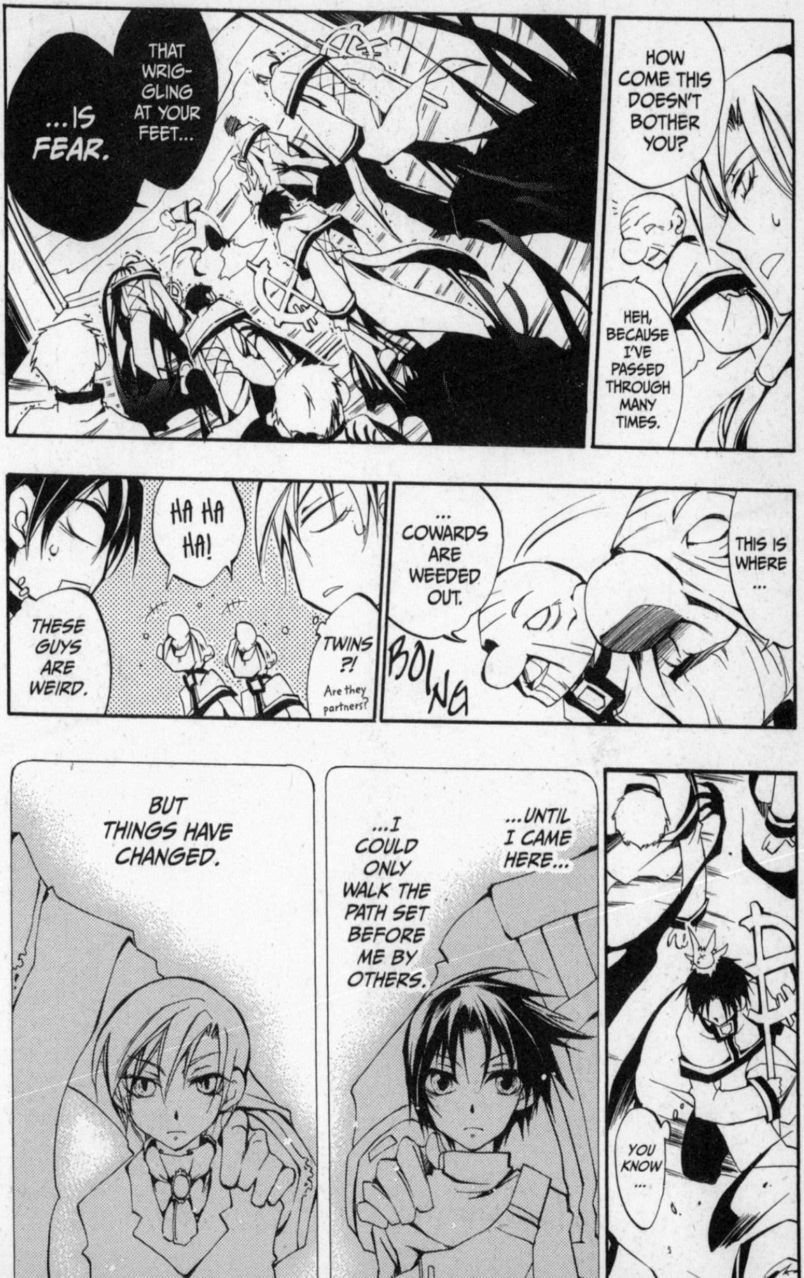
HOW COME THIS DOESN'T BOTHER YOU?
HEH, BECAUSE I'VE PASSED THROUGH MANY TIMES.
THAT WRIG-GLING AT YOUR FEET...
...IS FEAR.
THIS IS WHERE ...
... COWARDS ARE WEEDED OUT.
BOING
HA HA HA!
TWINS?!
Are they partners?
THESE GUYS ARE WEIRD.
YOU KNOW ...
...UNTIL I CAME HERE...
...I COULD ONLY WALK THE PATH SET BEFORE ME BY OTHERS.
BUT THINGS HAVE CHANGED.

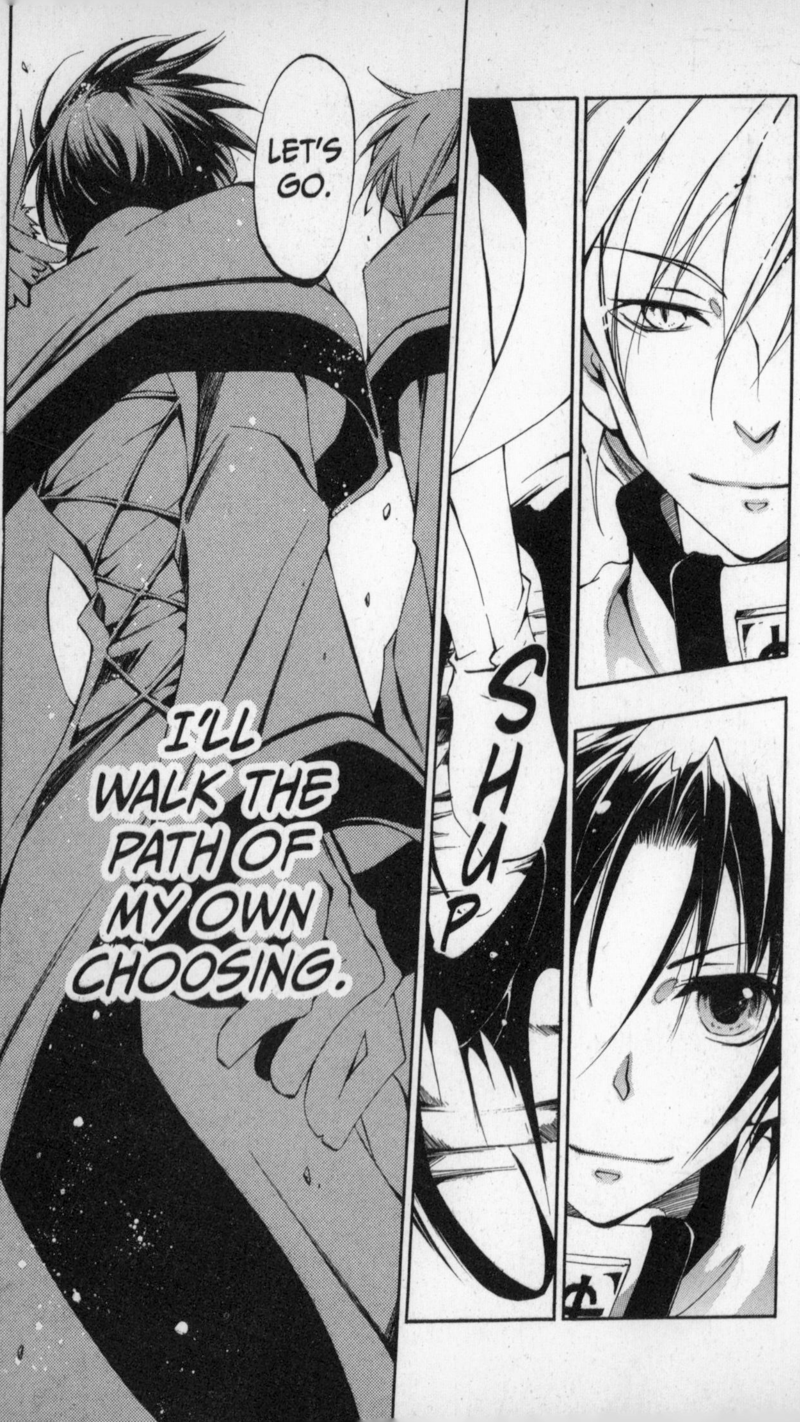
SHUP
LET'S GO.
I'LL WALK THE PATH OF MY OWN CHOOSING.

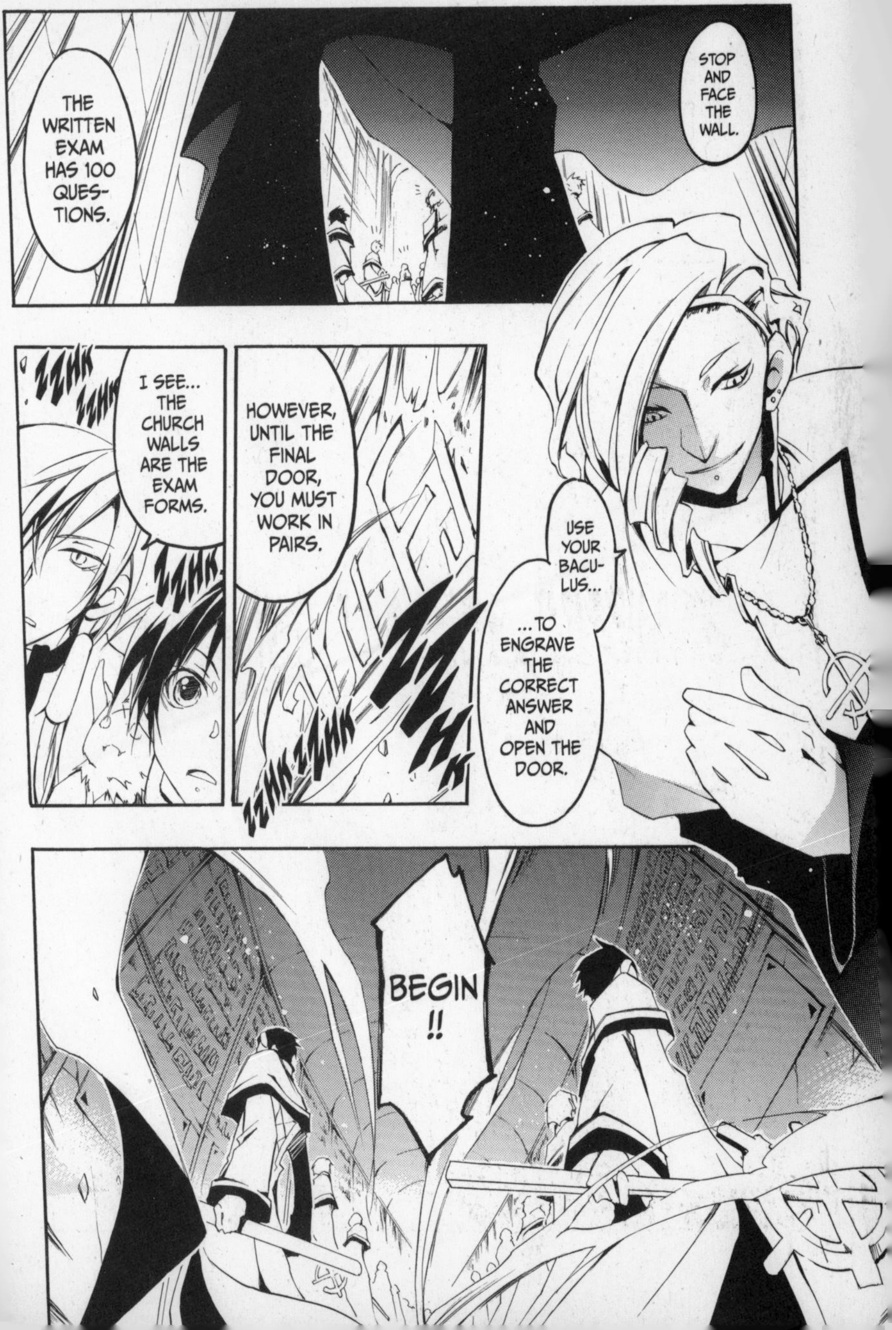
STOP AND FACE THE WALL.
THE WRITTEN EXAM HAS 100 QUES-TIONS.
USE YOUR BACU-LUS...
...TO ENGRAVE THE CORRECT ANSWER AND OPEN THE DOOR.
ZZHK ZZHK
HOWEVER, UNTIL THE FINAL DOOR, YOU MUST WORK IN PAIRS.
ZZHK
I SEE... THE CHURCH WALLS ARE THE EXAM FORMS.
ZZHK ZZHK
BEGIN!!

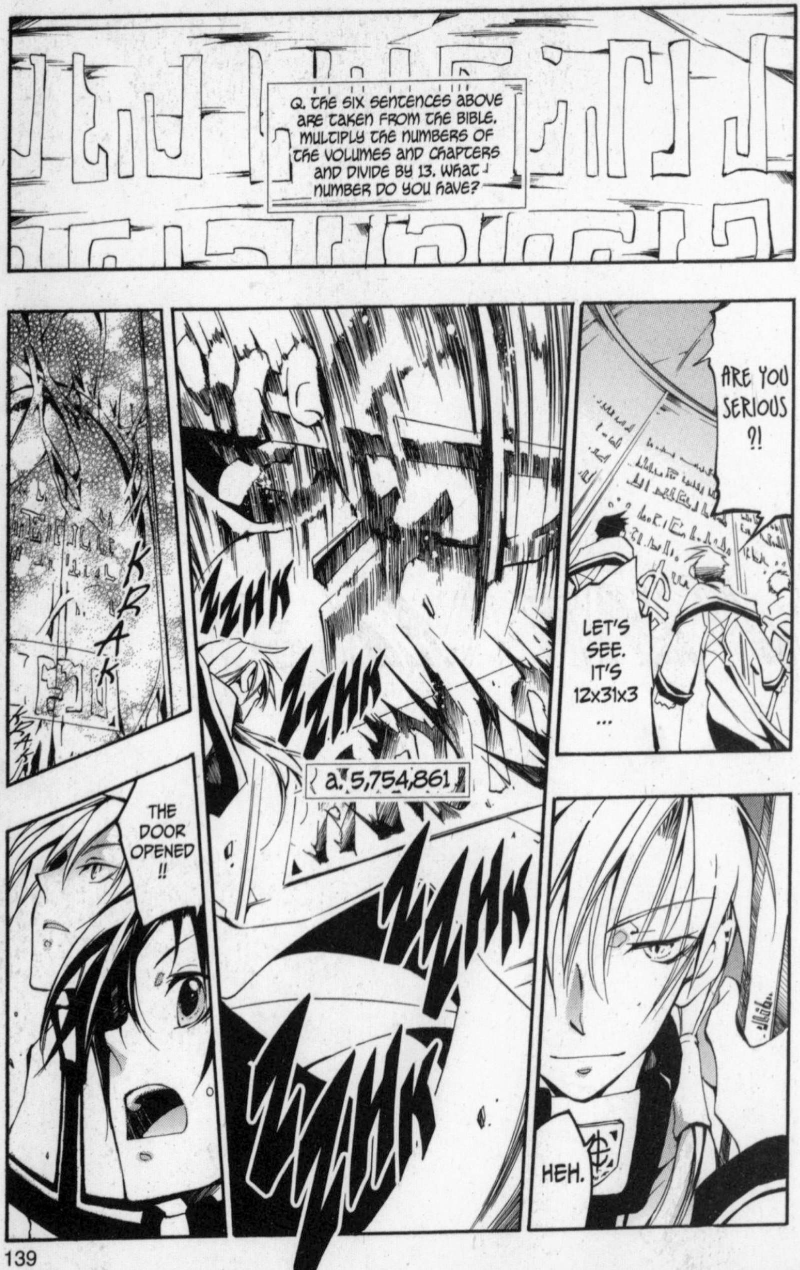

Q. THE SIX SENTENCES ABOVE ARE TAKEN FROM THE BIBLE. MULTIPLY THE NUMBERS OF THE VOLUMES AND CHAPTERS AND DIVIDE BY 13. WHAT NUMBER DO YOU HAVE?
ARE YOU SERIOUS ?!
LET'S SEE. IT'S 12x31x3 ...
ZZHK
ZZHK
a. 5,754,861
KRAK
HEH.
ZZHK
ZZHK
THE DOOR OPENED !!

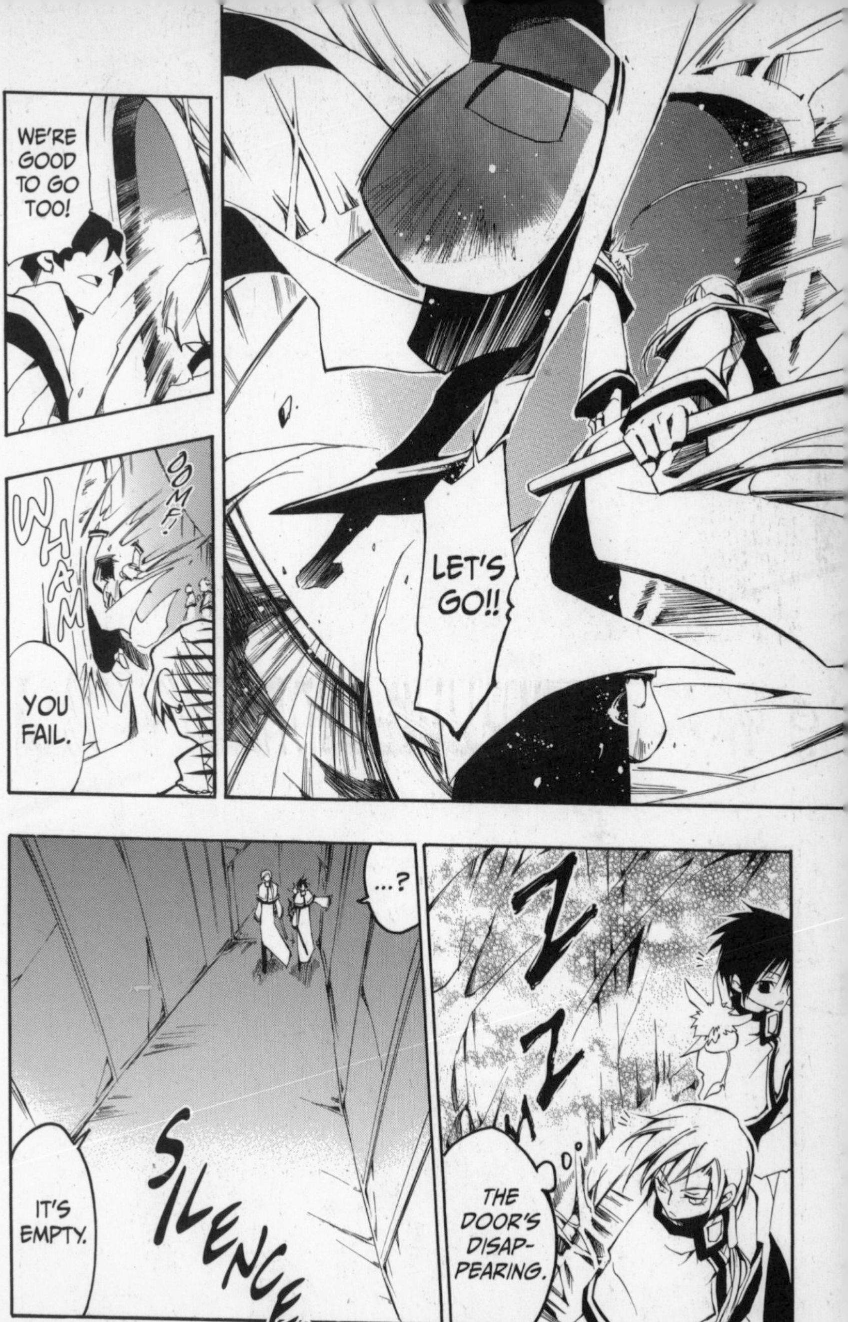
LET'S GO!!
WE'RE GOOD TO GO TOO!
OOMF!
WHAM
YOU FAIL.
ZZ
THE DOOR'S DISAP-PEARING.
...?
IT'S EMPTY.
SILENCE...

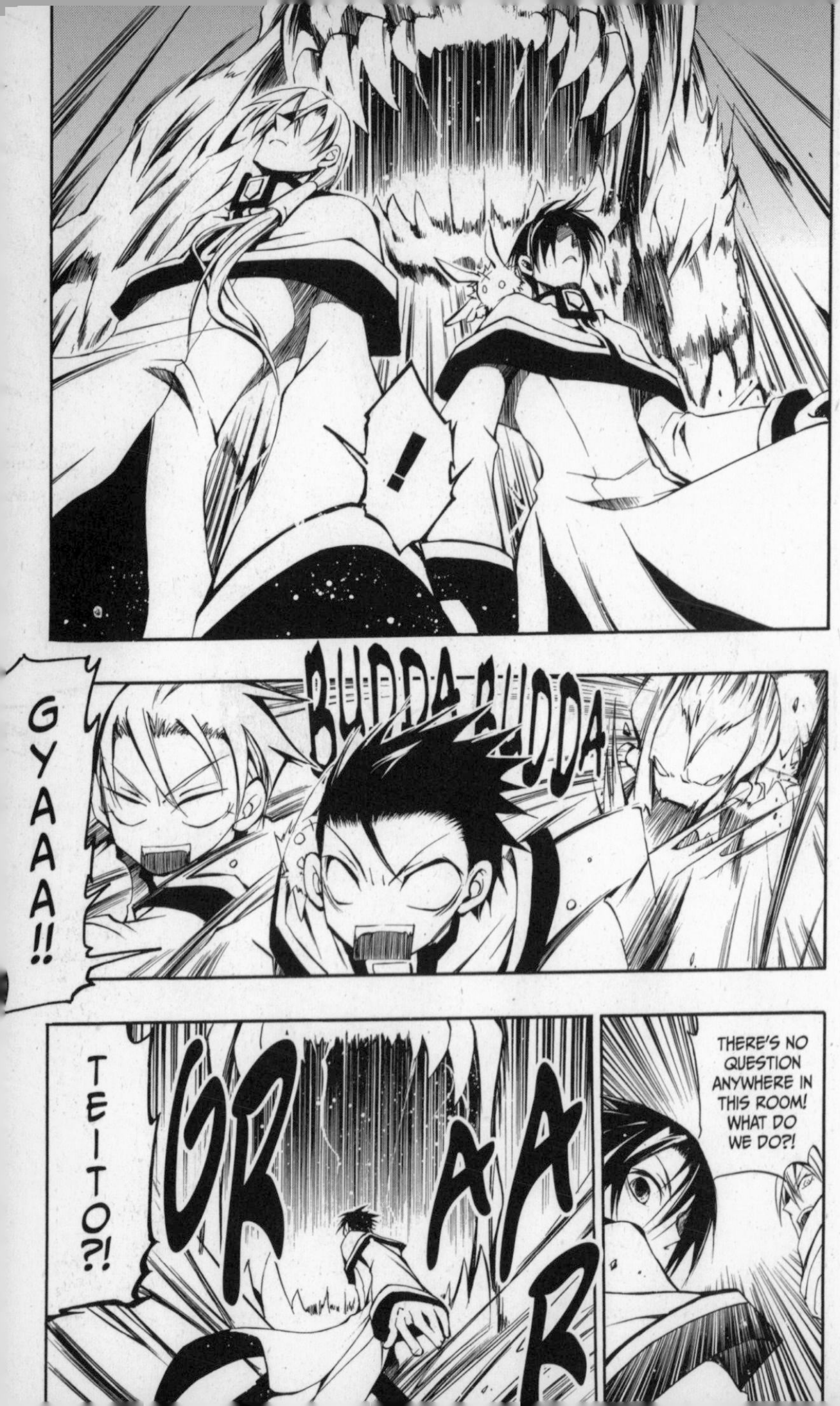
!
BUDDA BUDDA
GYAAAA!!
THERE'S NO QUESTION ANYWHERE IN THIS ROOM! WHAT DO WE DO?!
GRAAR
TEITO?!

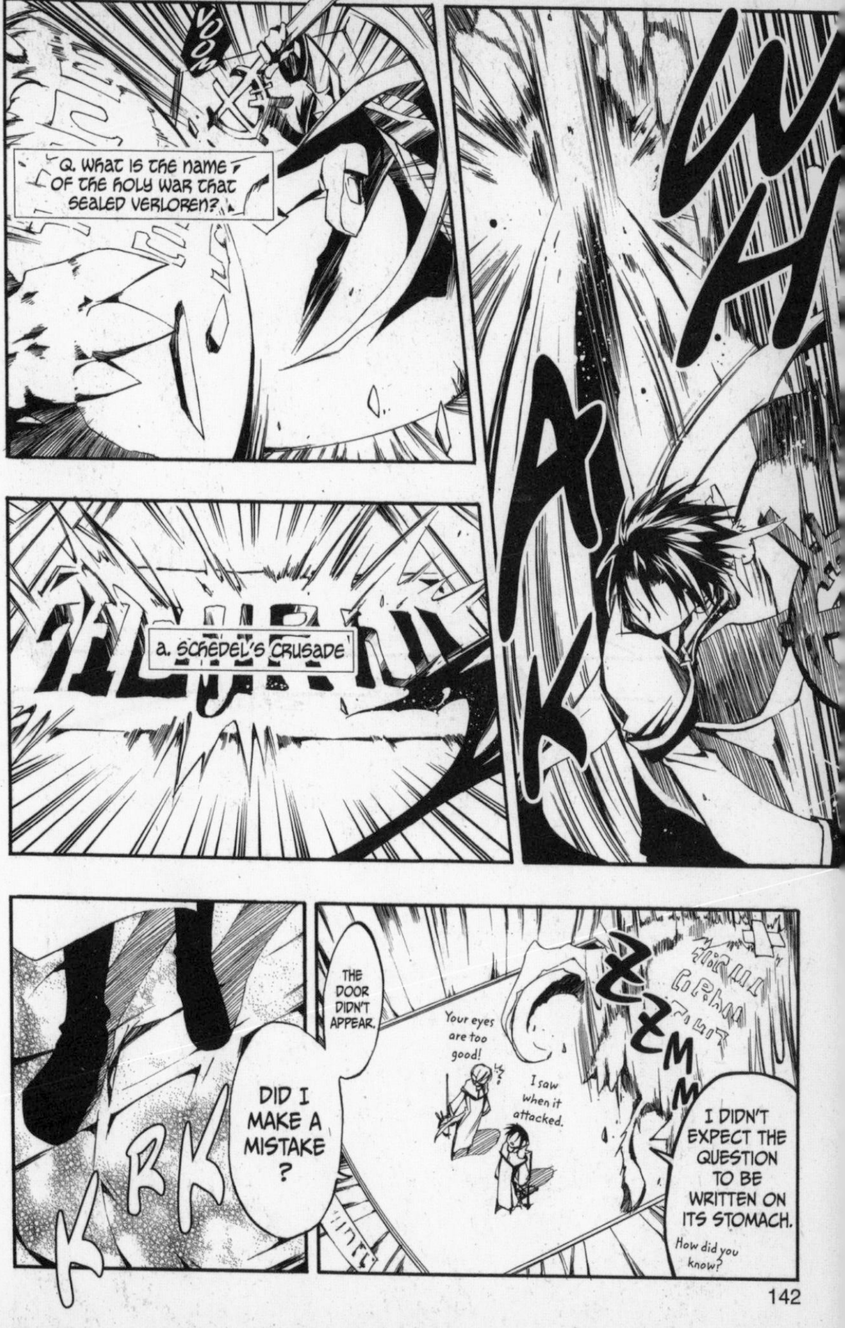
VOOM
Q. WHAT IS THE NAME OF THE HOLY WAR THAT SEALED VERLOREN?
a. SCHEDEL'S CRUSADE
I DIDN'T EXPECT THE QUESTION TO BE WRITTEN ON ITS STOMACH.
How did you know?
I saw when it attacked.
Your eyes are too good!
THE DOOR DIDN'T APPEAR.
DID I MAKE A MISTAKE?
KRK

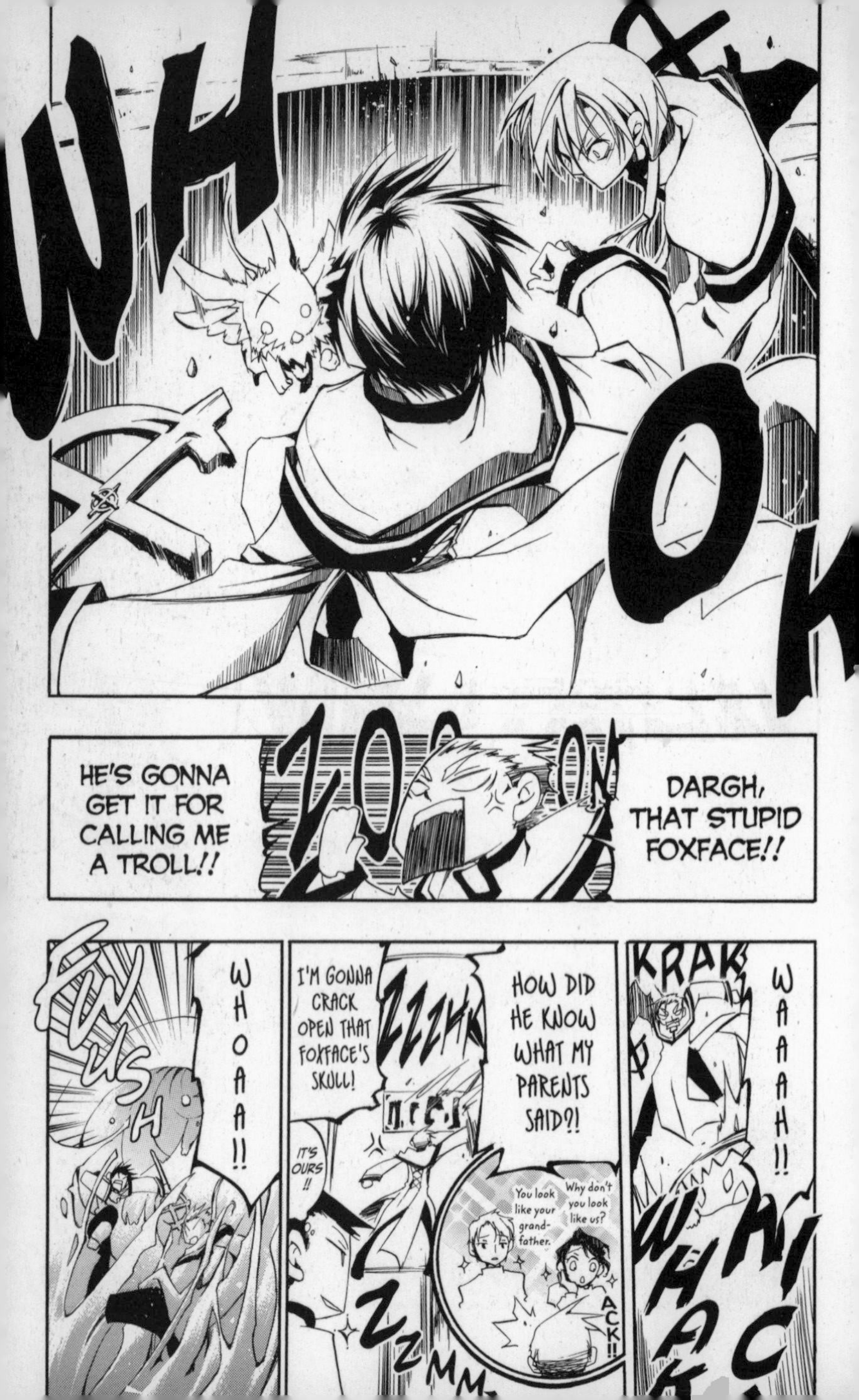
WH
OK
DARGH, THAT STUPID FOXFACE!!
HE'S GONNA GET IT FOR CALLING ME A TROLL!!
KRAK
WAAAAH!!
HOW DID HE KNOW WHAT MY PARENTS SAID?!
I'M GONNA CRACK OPEN THAT FOXFACE'S SKULL!
ZZZK
IT'S OURS!!
Why don't you look like us?
You look like your grand-father.
ACK!!
WHOAAA!!
FWUSH

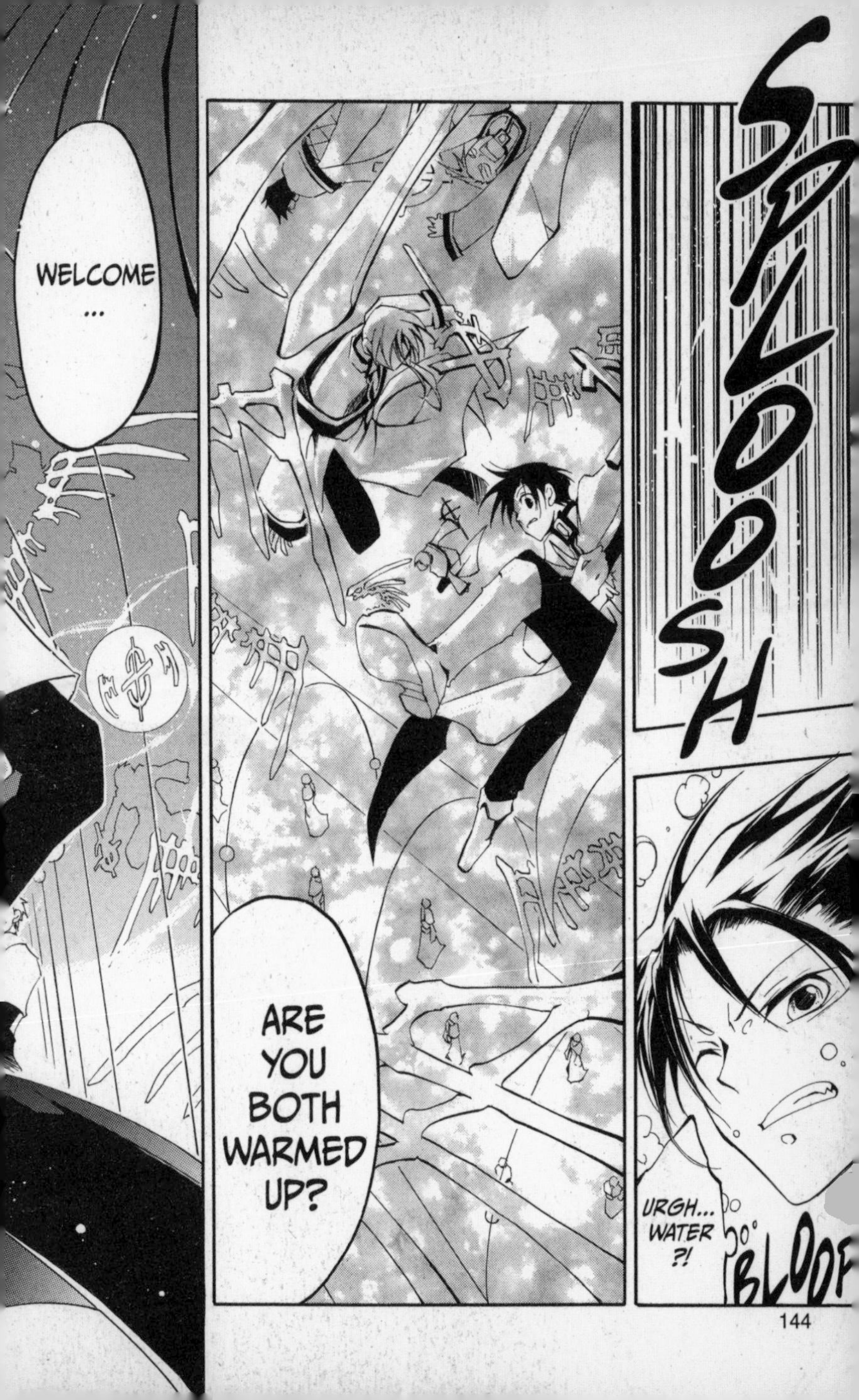
SWOOOSH
URGH... WATER?!
BLOOP
ARE YOU BOTH WARMED UP?
WELCOME...

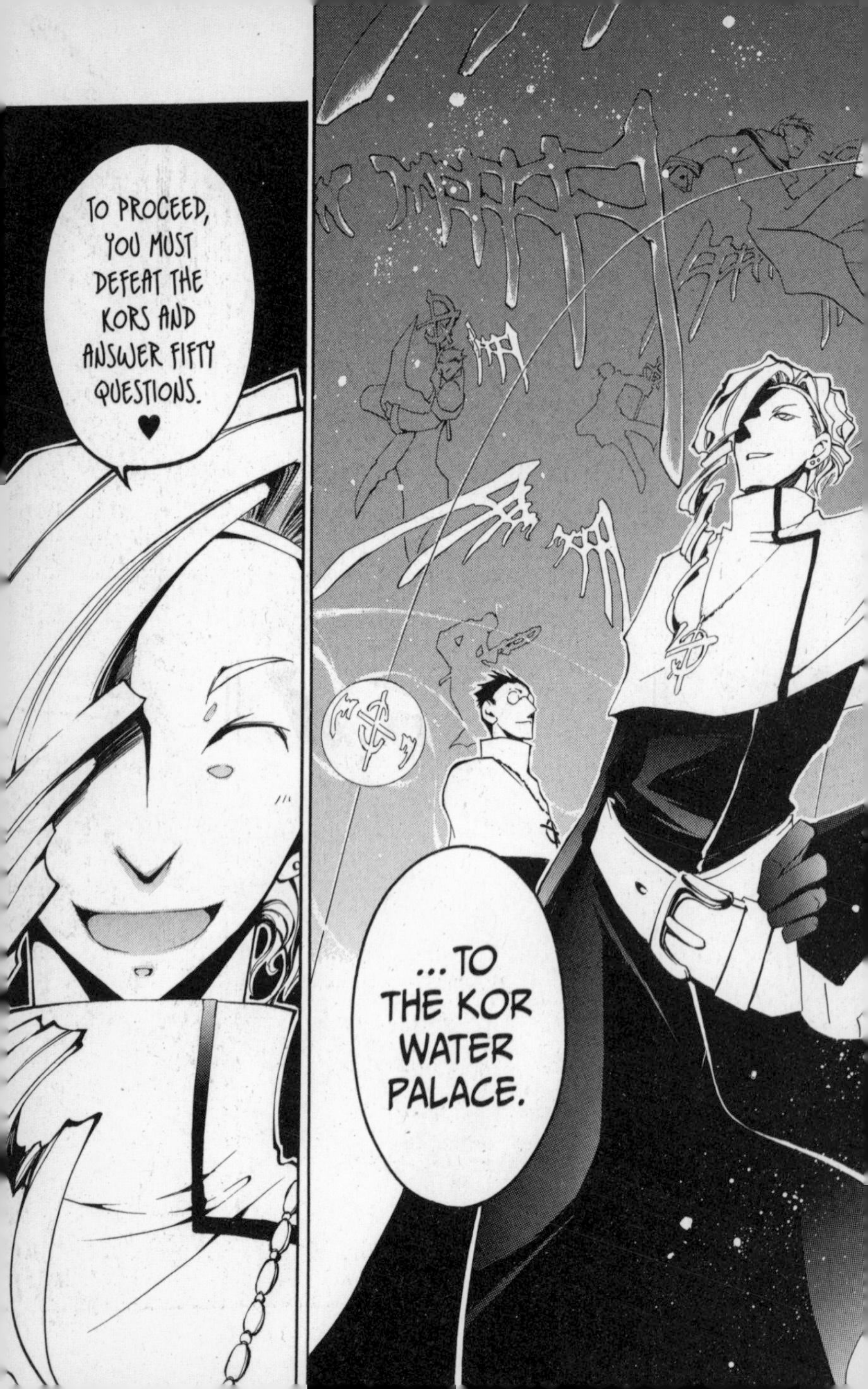
...TO THE KOR WATER PALACE.
TO PROCEED, YOU MUST DEFEAT THE KORS AND ANSWER FIFTY QUESTIONS. ♥

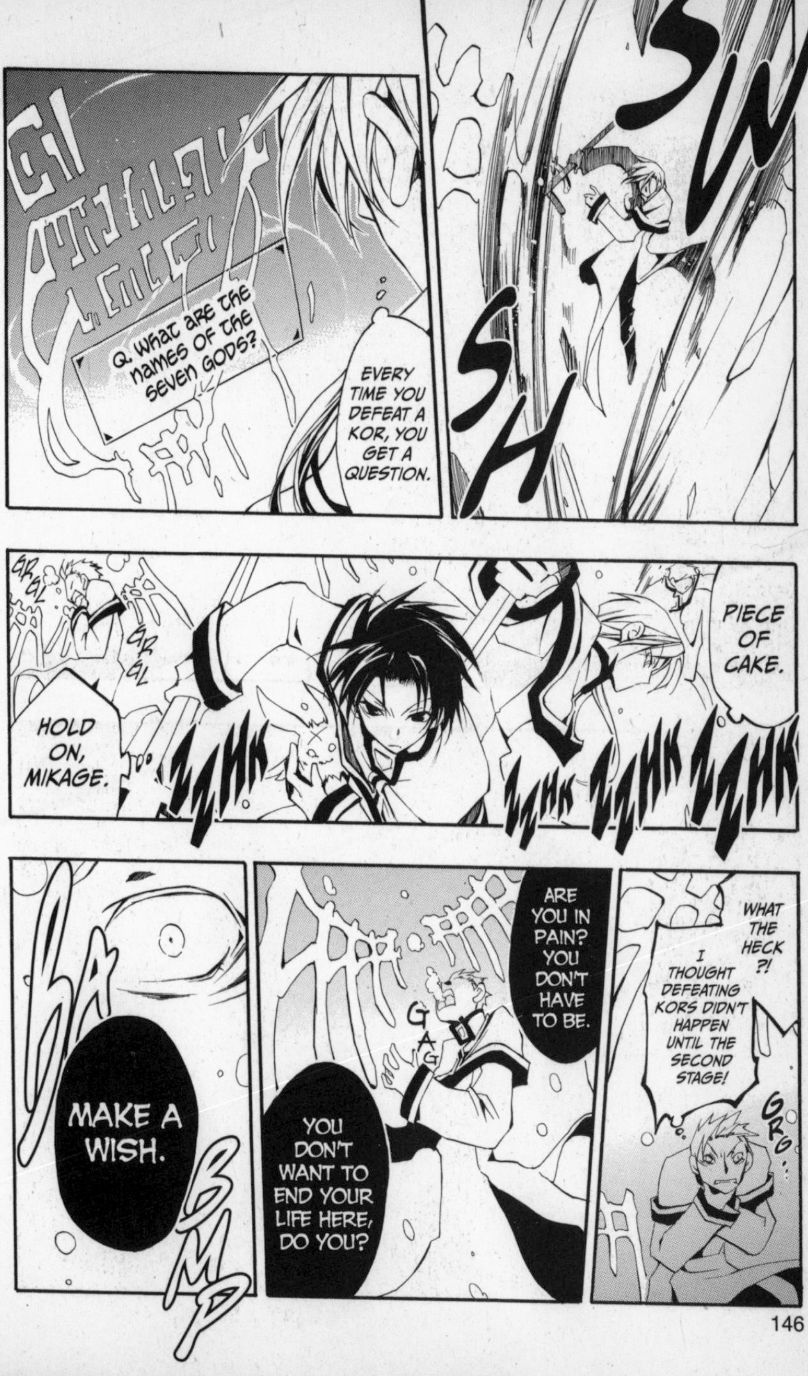
SW
SH
EVERY TIME YOU DEFEAT A KOR, YOU GET A QUESTION.
Q. What are the names of the seven gods?
PIECE OF CAKE.
ZZHK ZZHK ZZHK ZZHK
HOLD ON, MIKAGE.
GRGL
GRGL
WHAT THE HECK ?!
I THOUGHT DEFEATING KORS DIDN'T HAPPEN UNTIL THE SECOND STAGE!
GRG...
ARE YOU IN PAIN? YOU DON'T HAVE TO BE.
GAG
YOU DON'T WANT TO END YOUR LIFE HERE, DO YOU?
BA
MAKE A WISH.
BMP

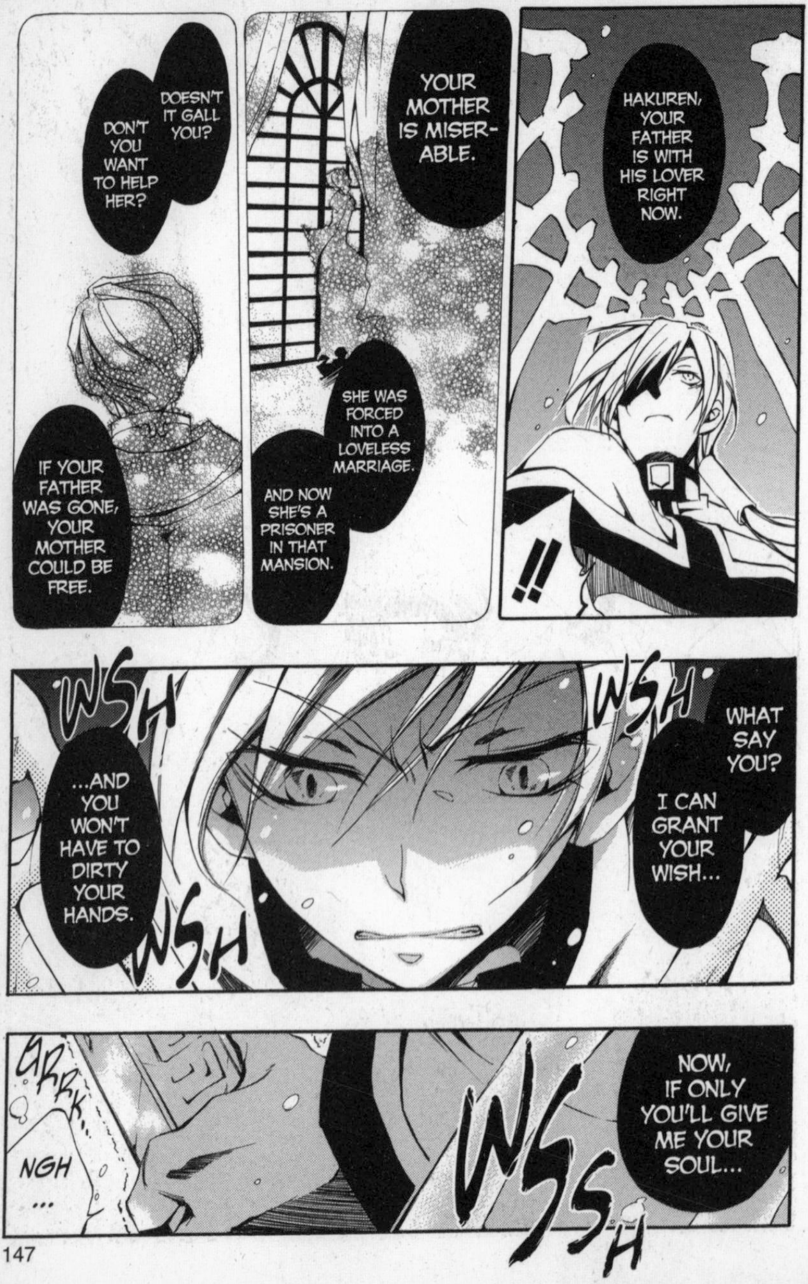
HAKUREN, YOUR FATHER IS WITH HIS LOVER RIGHT NOW.
!!
YOUR MOTHER IS MISER-ABLE.
SHE WAS FORCED INTO A LOVELESS MARRIAGE.
AND NOW SHE'S A PRISONER IN THAT MANSION.
DOESN'T IT GALL YOU?
DON'T YOU WANT TO HELP HER?
IF YOUR FATHER WAS GONE, YOUR MOTHER COULD BE FREE.
WSH
WHAT SAY YOU?
I CAN GRANT YOUR WISH...
WSH
...AND YOU WON'T HAVE TO DIRTY YOUR HANDS.
WSH
NOW, IF ONLY YOU'LL GIVE ME YOUR SOUL...
WSSH
GRRK...
NGH...

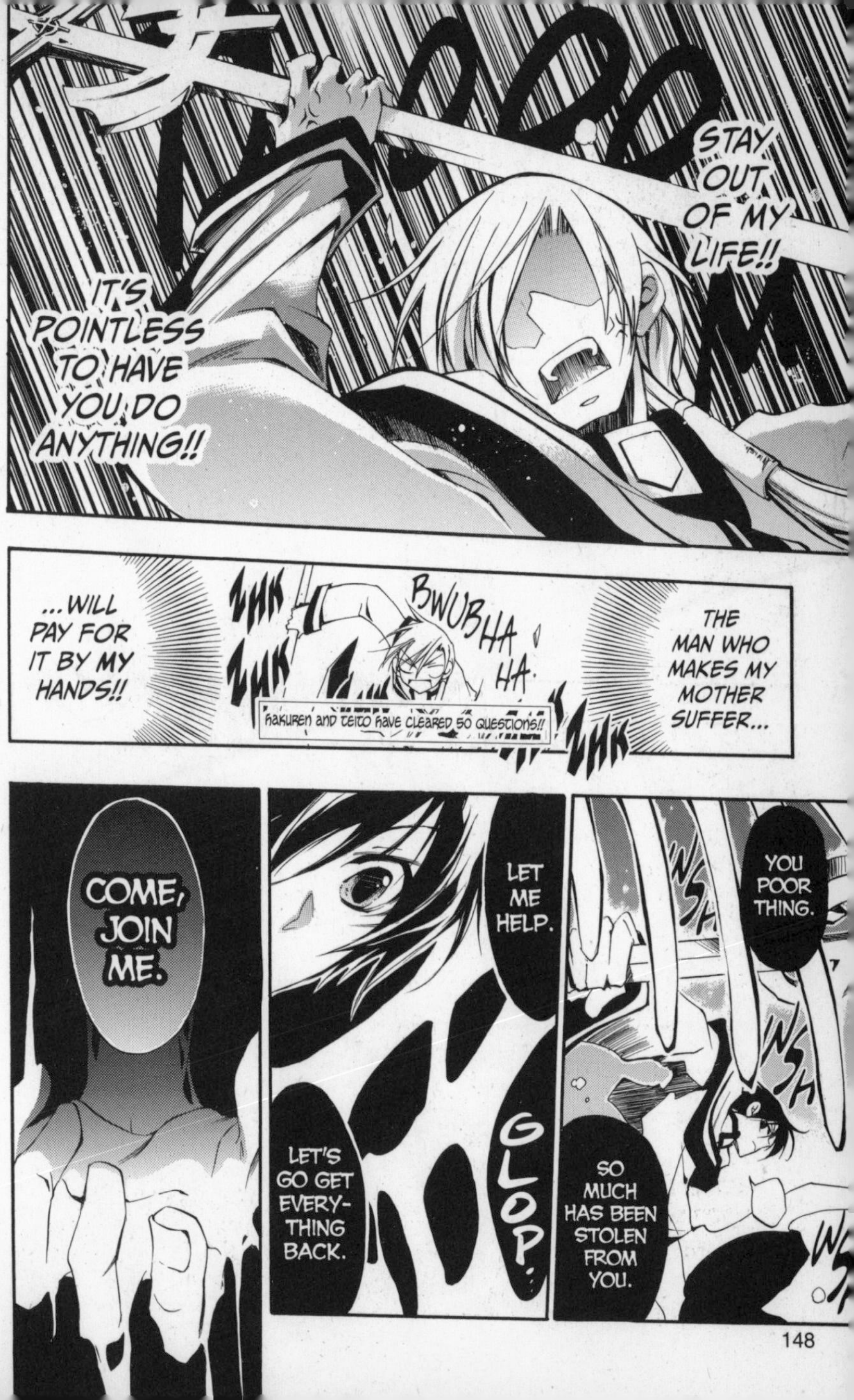
STAY OUT OF MY LIFE!!
IT'S POINTLESS TO HAVE YOU DO ANYTHING!!
THE MAN WHO MAKES MY MOTHER SUFFER...
ZHK
BWUBHA HA HA
ZHK
ZHK
...WILL PAY FOR IT BY MY HANDS!!
Hakuren and Teito have cleared 50 questions!!
YOU POOR THING.
SO MUCH HAS BEEN STOLEN FROM YOU.
LET ME HELP.
GLOP.
LET'S GO GET EVERY-THING BACK.
COME, JOIN ME.

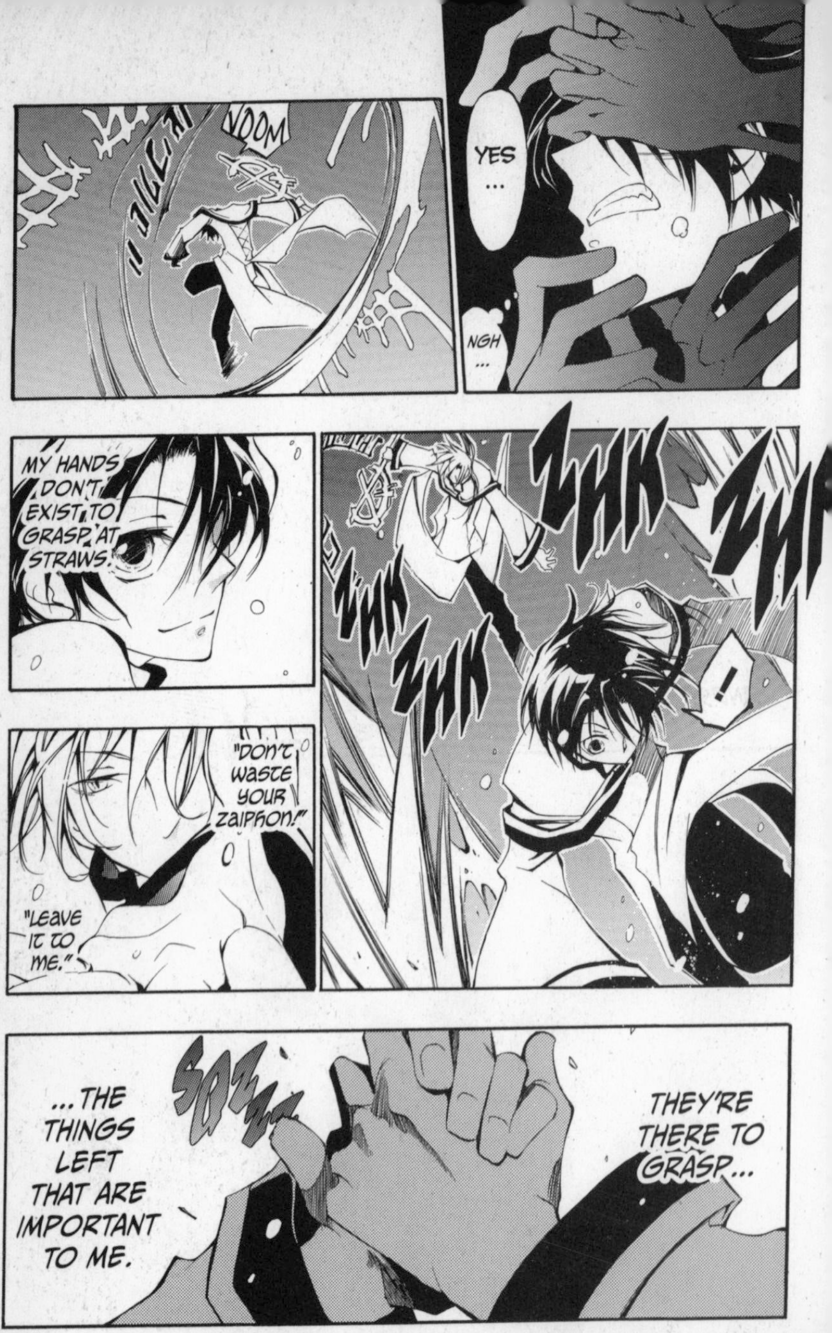
YES ...
NGH ...
VOOM
ZHK
ZHK
ZHK
ZHK
ZHK
!
MY HANDS DON'T EXIST TO GRASP AT STRAWS.
"DON'T WASTE YOUR ZAIPHON!"
"LEAVE IT TO ME."
THEY'RE THERE TO GRASP...
...THE THINGS LEFT THAT ARE IMPORTANT TO ME.

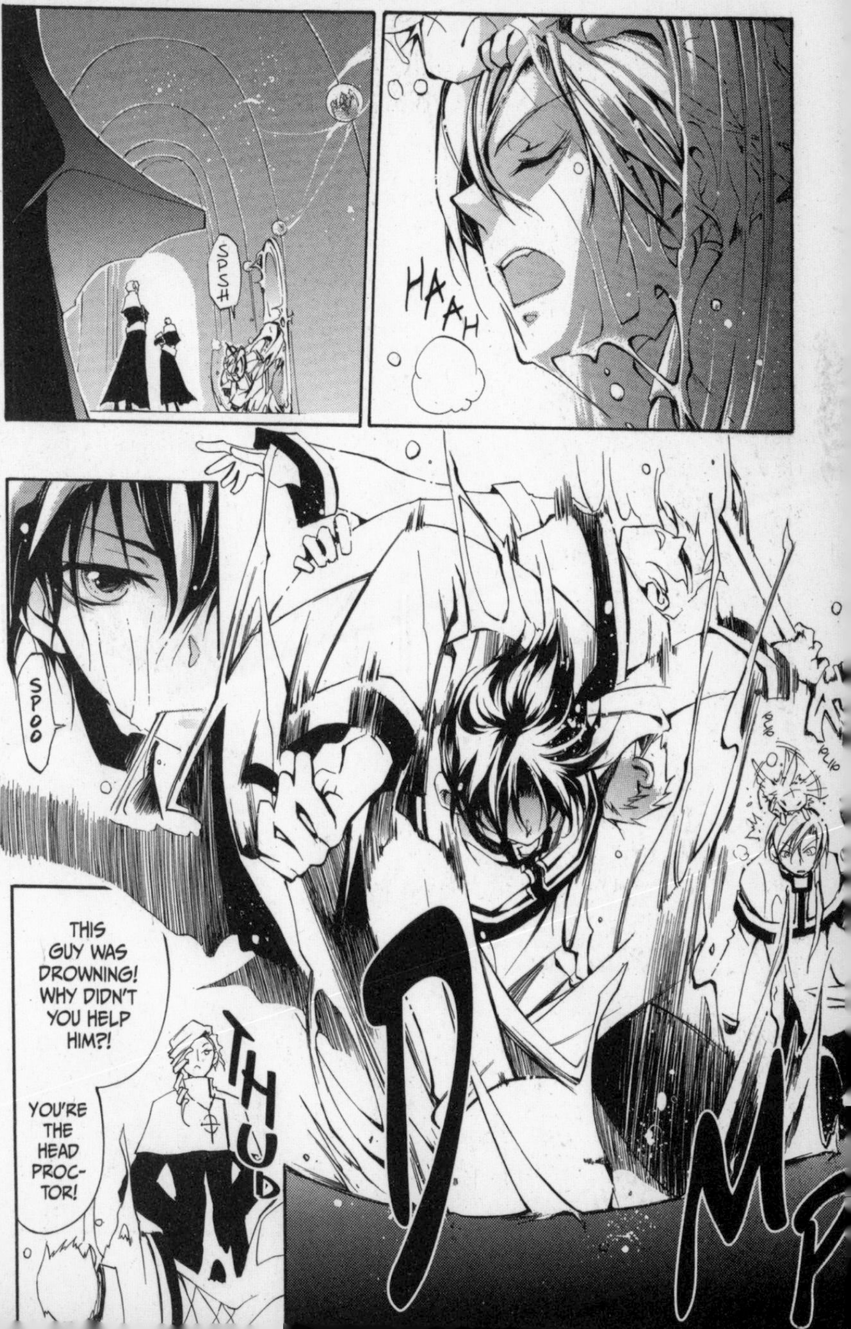
HAAH
SPSH
SPOO
THIS GUY WAS DROWNING! WHY DIDN'T YOU HELP HIM?!
YOU'RE THE HEAD PROCTOR!
THUD

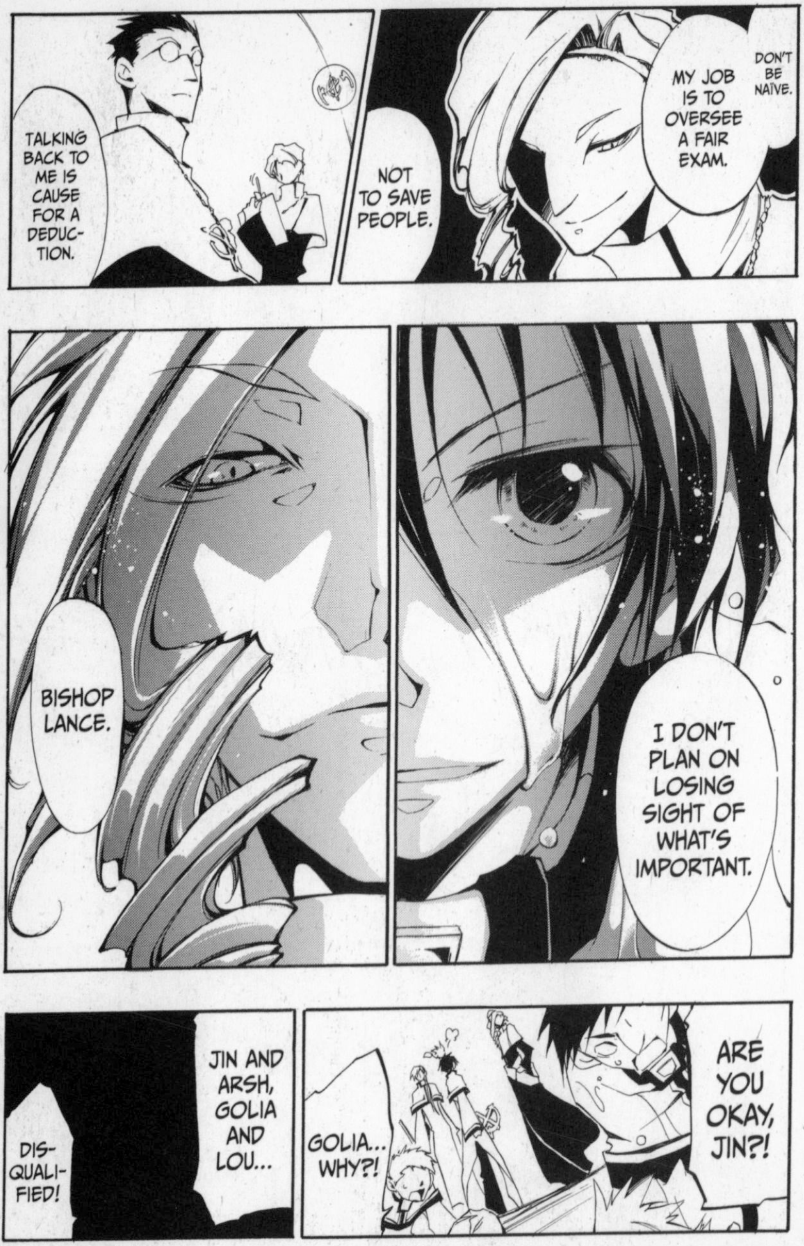
DON'T BE NAÏVE.
MY JOB IS TO OVERSEE A FAIR EXAM.
NOT TO SAVE PEOPLE.
TALKING BACK TO ME IS CAUSE FOR A DEDUC-TION.
I DON'T PLAN ON LOSING SIGHT OF WHAT'S IMPORTANT.
BISHOP LANCE.
ARE YOU OKAY, JIN?!
GOLIA... WHY?!
JIN AND ARSH, GOLIA AND LOU...
DIS-QUALI-FIED!

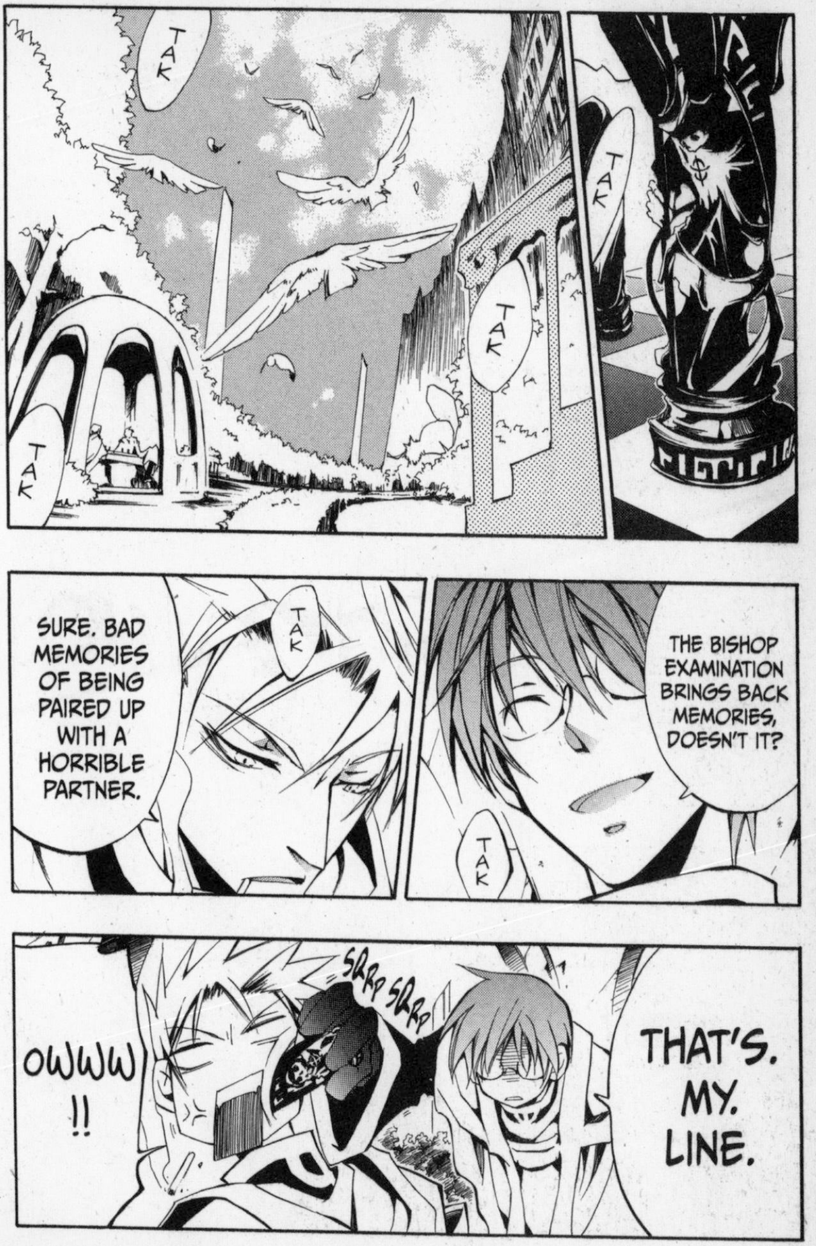
TAK
TAK
TAK
TAK
THE BISHOP EXAMINATION BRINGS BACK MEMORIES, DOESN'T IT?
TAK
TAK
SURE. BAD MEMORIES OF BEING PAIRED UP WITH A HORRIBLE PARTNER.
THAT'S. MY. LINE.
SRRP SRRP
OWWW !!

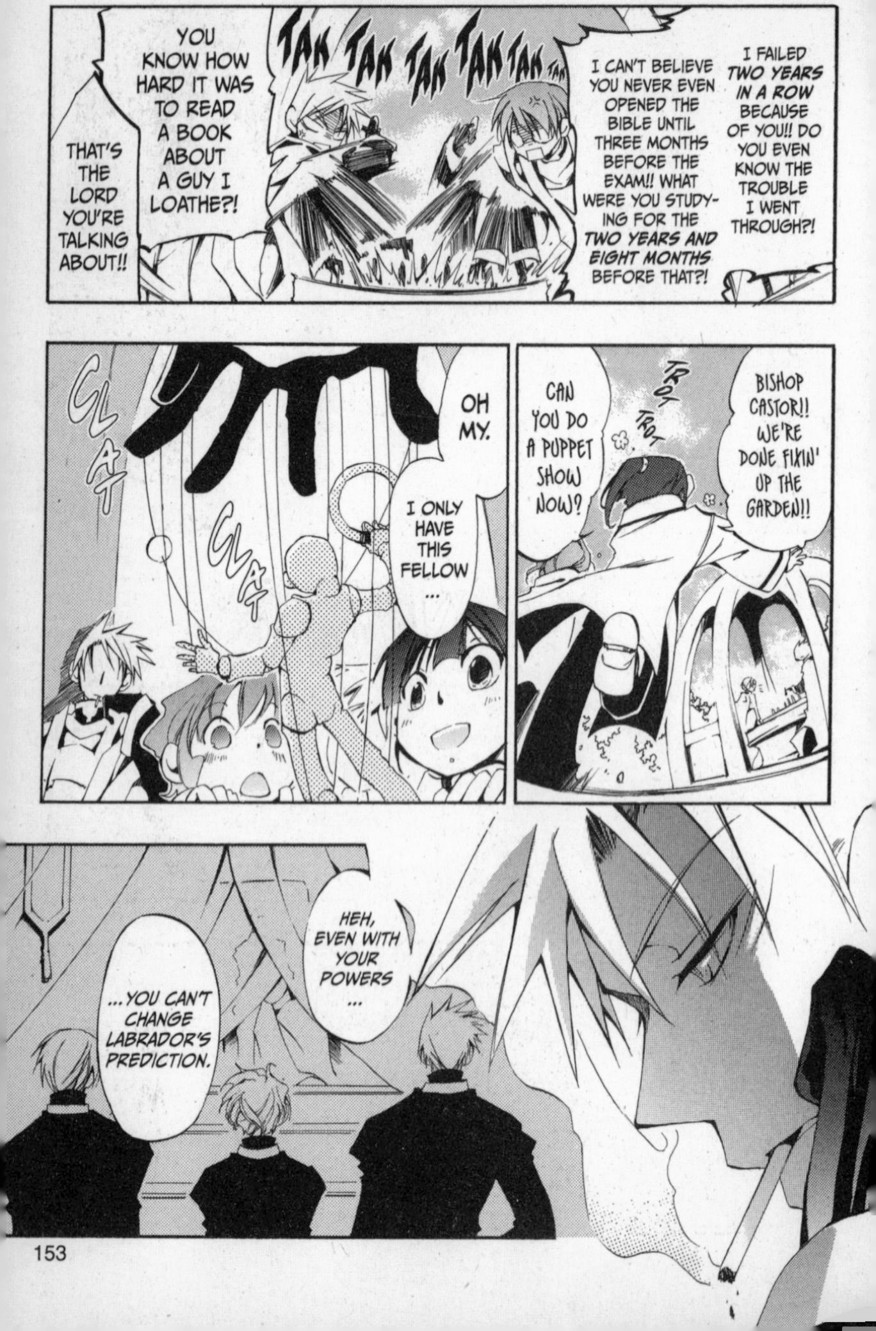
I FAILED TWO YEARS IN A ROW BECAUSE OF YOU!! DO YOU EVEN KNOW THE TROUBLE I WENT THROUGH?!
I CAN'T BELIEVE YOU NEVER EVEN OPENED THE BIBLE UNTIL THREE MONTHS BEFORE THE EXAM!! WHAT WERE YOU STUDYING FOR THE TWO YEARS AND EIGHT MONTHS BEFORE THAT?!
TAK TAK TAK TAK TAK TAK
YOU KNOW HOW HARD IT WAS TO READ A BOOK ABOUT A GUY I LOATHE?!
THAT'S THE LORD YOU'RE TALKING ABOUT!!
BISHOP CASTOR!! WE'RE DONE FIXIN' UP THE GARDEN!!
TROT TROT
CAN YOU DO A PUPPET SHOW NOW?
OH MY.
I ONLY HAVE THIS FELLOW ...
CLAT
CLAT
HEH, EVEN WITH YOUR POWERS ...
...YOU CAN'T CHANGE LABRADOR'S PREDICTION.

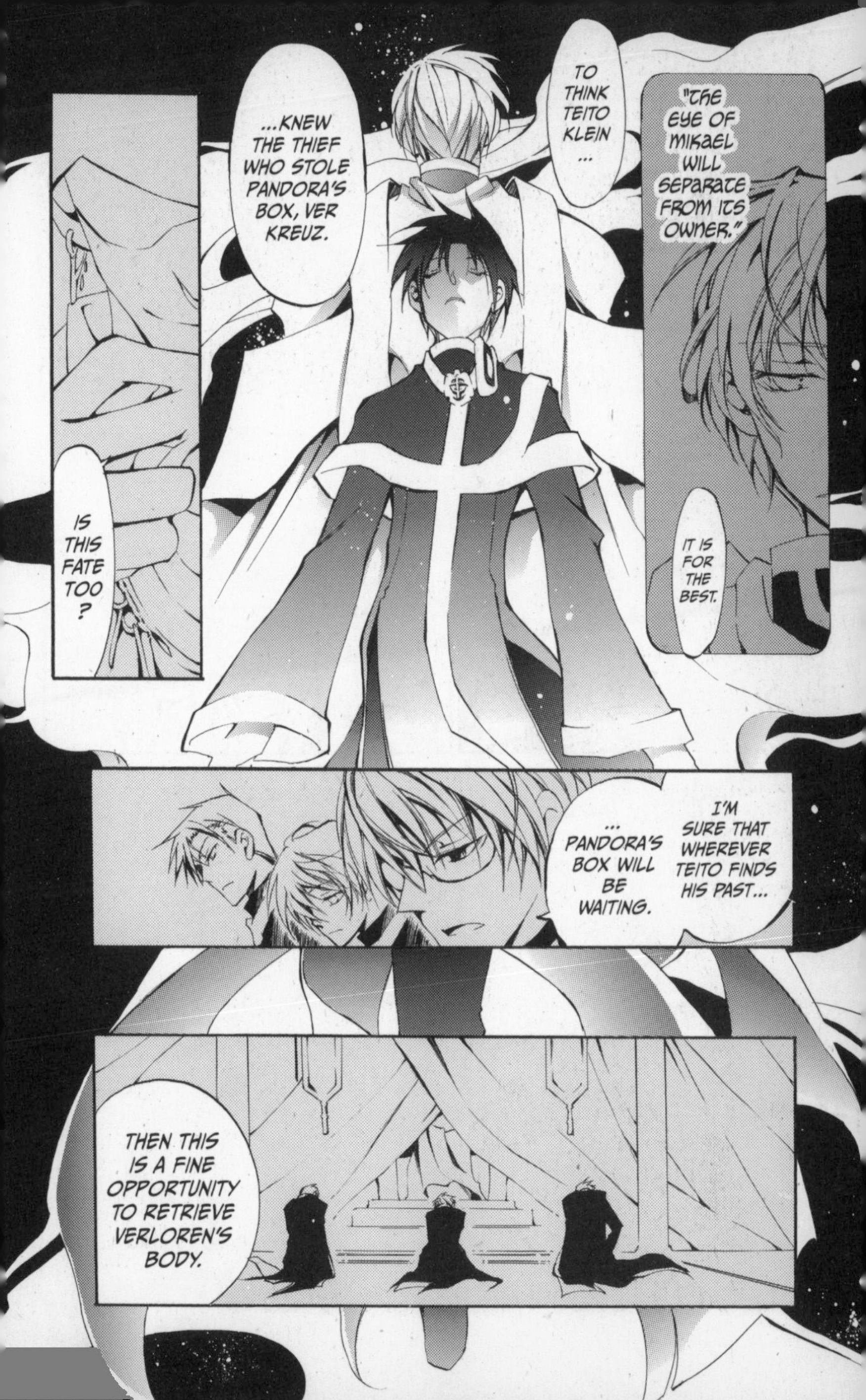
"THE EYE OF MIKAEL WILL SEPARATE FROM ITS OWNER."
IT IS FOR THE BEST.
TO THINK TEITO KLEIN ...
...KNEW THE THIEF WHO STOLE PANDORA'S BOX, VER KREUZ.
IS THIS FATE TOO?
I'M SURE THAT WHEREVER TEITO FINDS HIS PAST...
...PANDORA'S BOX WILL BE WAITING.
THEN THIS IS A FINE OPPORTUNITY TO RETRIEVE VERLOREN'S BODY.

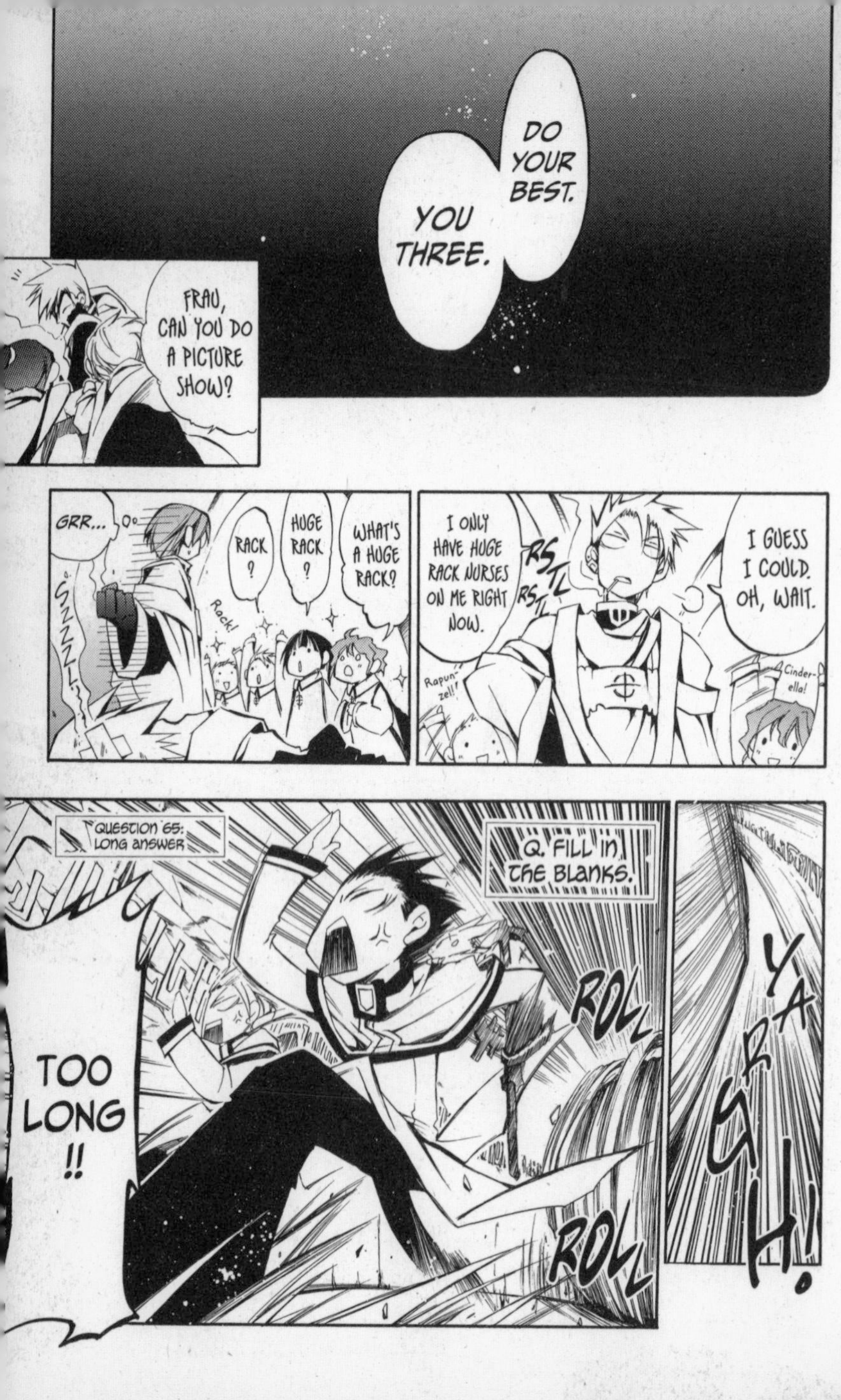

DO YOUR BEST.
YOU THREE.
FRAU, CAN YOU DO A PICTURE SHOW?
I GUESS I COULD. OH, WAIT.
Cinderella!
RSTL RSTL
I ONLY HAVE HUGE RACK NURSES ON ME RIGHT NOW.
Rapunzell!
WHAT'S A HUGE RACK?
HUGE RACK?
RACK?
Rack!
GRR...
SZZZL
YAGRRGH!
Q. FILL IN THE BLANKS.
QUESTION 65: LONG ANSWER
ROLL
ROLL
TOO LONG!!

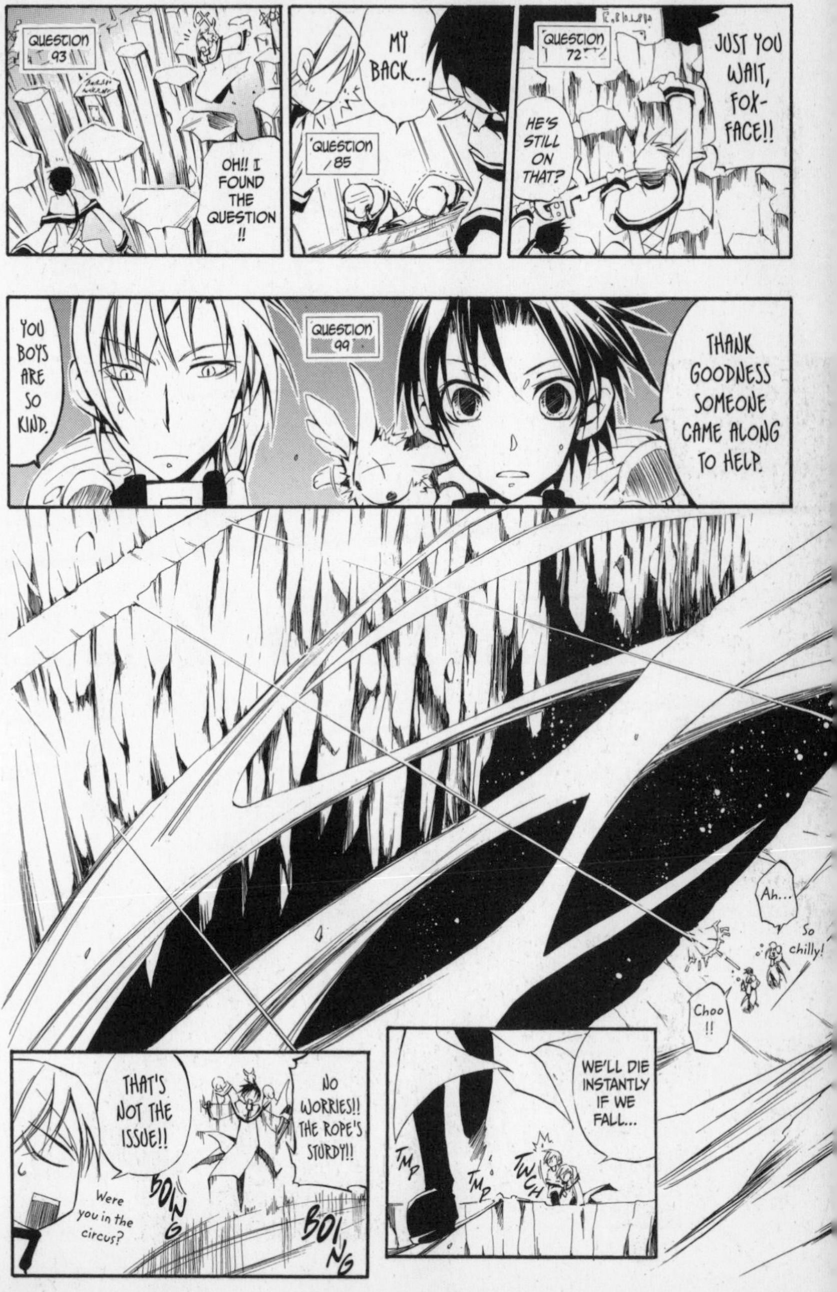
QUESTION 72
JUST YOU WAIT, FOX-FACE!!
HE'S STILL ON THAT?
MY BACK...
QUESTION 85
QUESTION 93
OH!! I FOUND THE QUESTION !!
THANK GOODNESS SOMEONE CAME ALONG TO HELP.
QUESTION 99
YOU BOYS ARE SO KIND.
Ah...
So chilly!
Choo !!
WE'LL DIE INSTANTLY IF WE FALL...
TWCH
TMP
TMP
NO WORRIES!! THE ROPE'S STURDY!!
THAT'S NOT THE ISSUE!!
BOING
BOING
Were you in the circus?

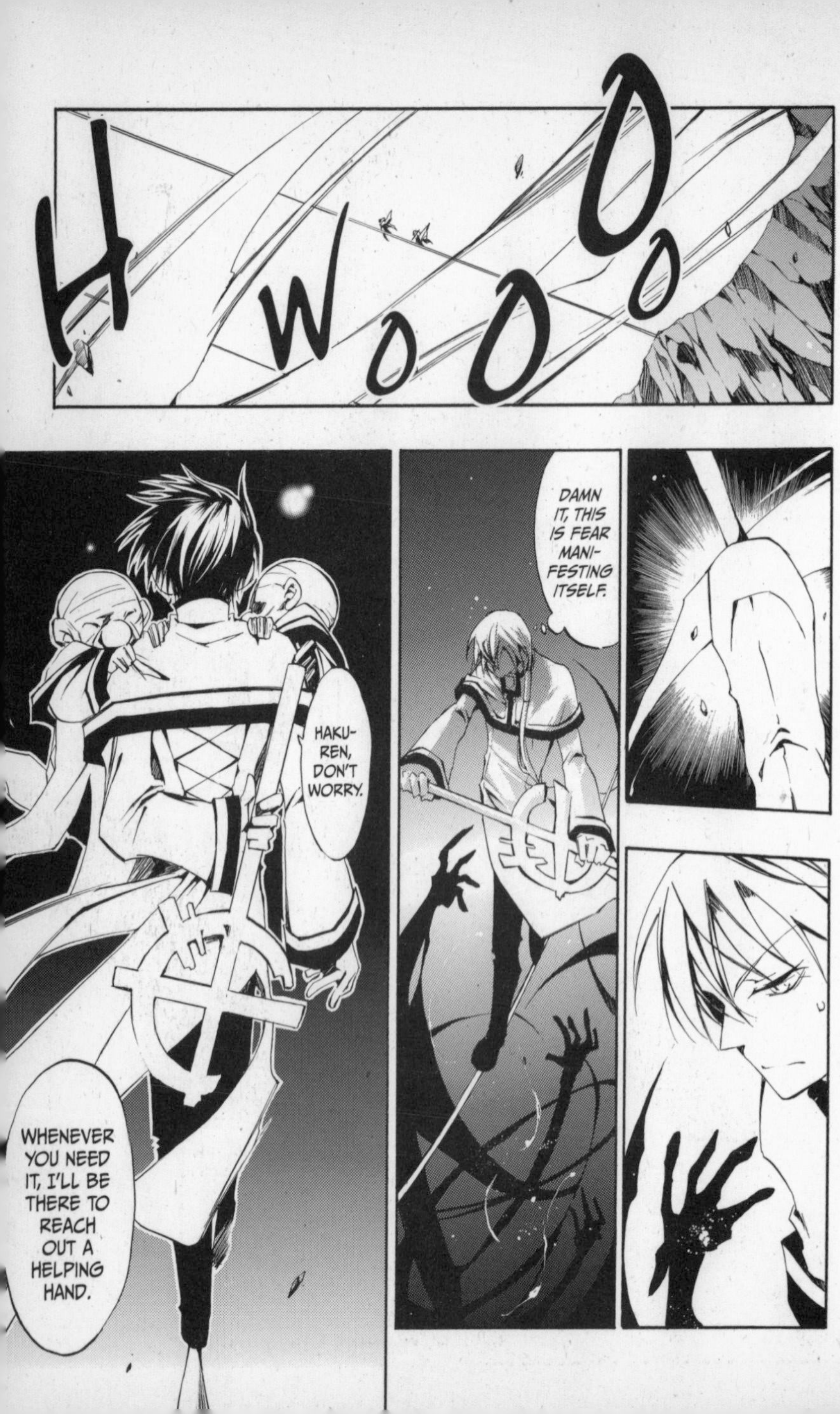
HWOOOOO
DAMN IT, THIS IS FEAR MANI-FESTING ITSELF.
HAKU-REN, DON'T WORRY.
WHENEVER YOU NEED IT, I'LL BE THERE TO REACH OUT A HELPING HAND.

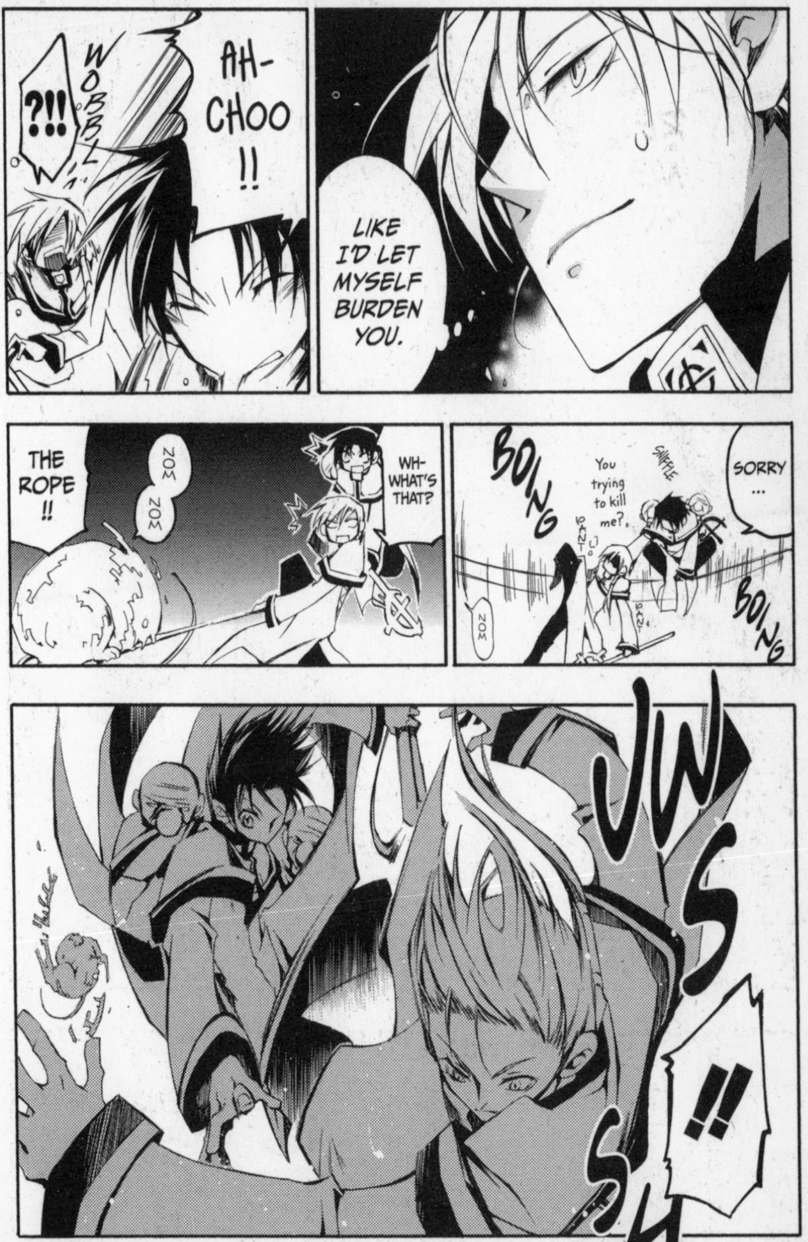
LIKE I'D LET MYSELF BURDEN YOU.
AH-CHOO!!
WOBBL
?!!
SORRY...
SNIFFLE
You trying to kill me?
BOING
BOING
NOM
WH-WHAT'S THAT?
NOM NOM
THE ROPE!!
SWISH
!!

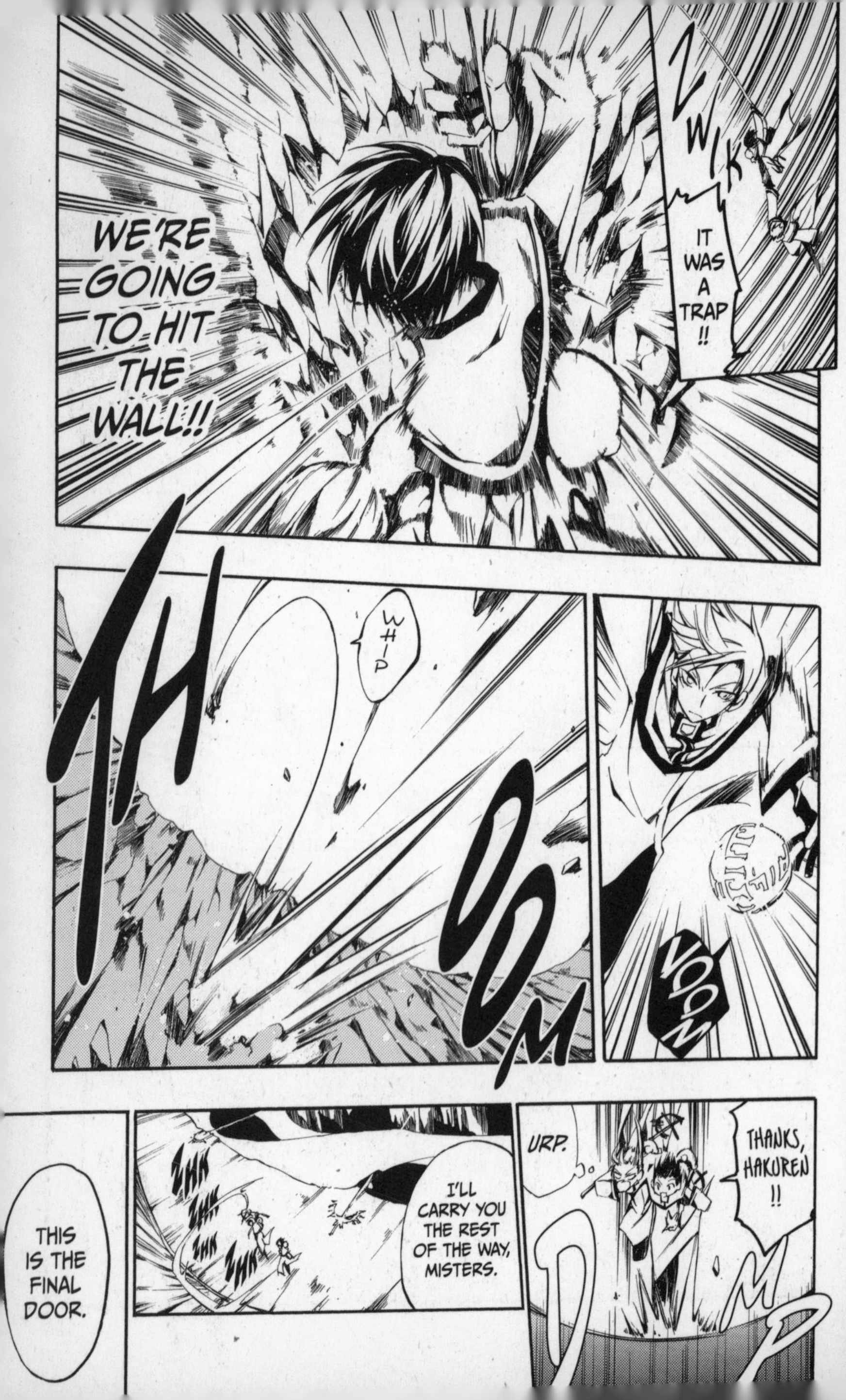
ZWIK
IT WAS A TRAP!!
WE'RE GOING TO HIT THE WALL!!
VOOM
WHIP
THOOM
THANKS, HAKUREN!!
URP.
I'LL CARRY YOU THE REST OF THE WAY, MISTERS.
ZHK ZHK ZHK ZHK
THIS IS THE FINAL DOOR.

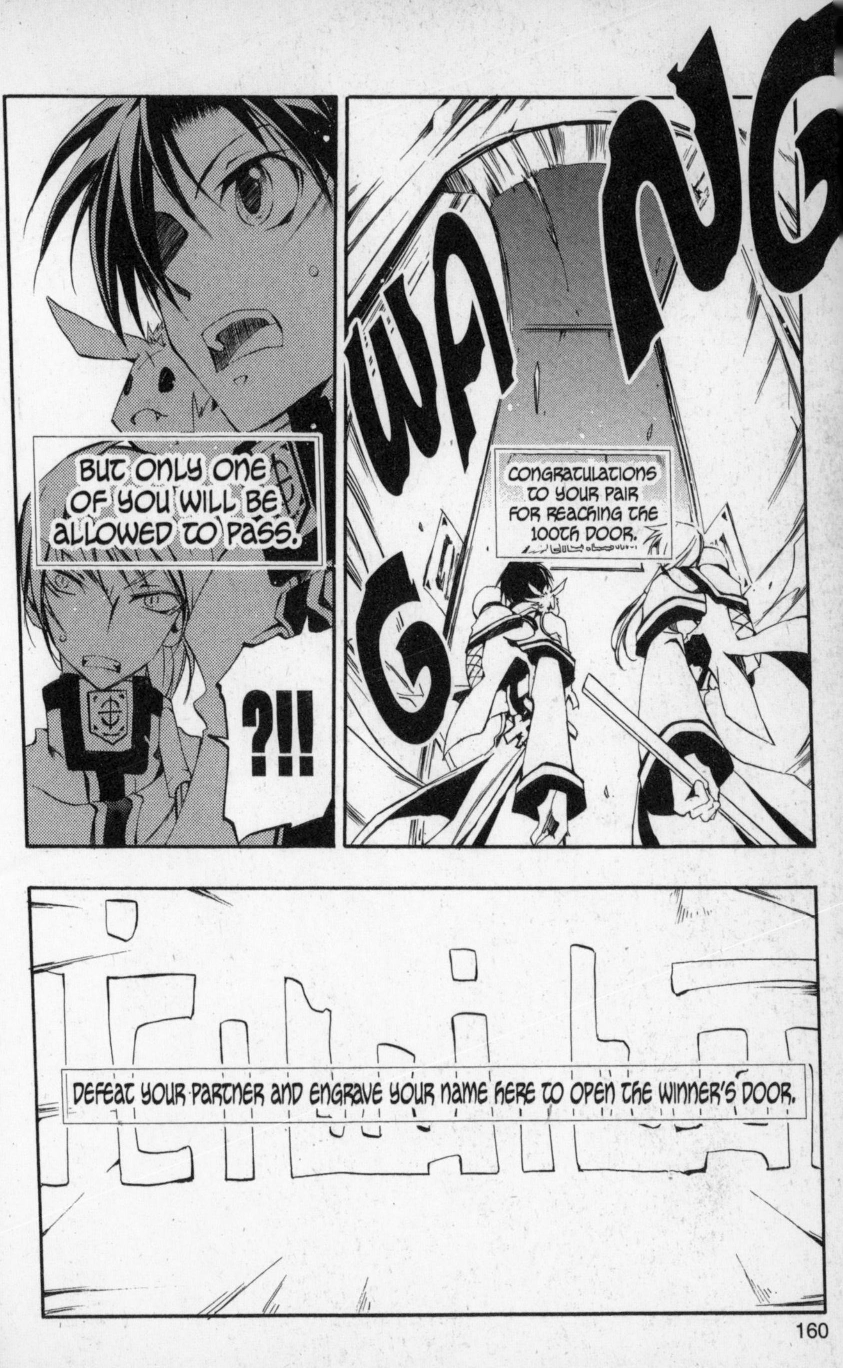
GWANG
CONGRATULATIONS TO YOUR PAIR FOR REACHING THE 100TH DOOR.
BUT ONLY ONE OF YOU WILL BE ALLOWED TO PASS.
?!!
DEFEAT YOUR PARTNER AND ENGRAVE YOUR NAME HERE TO OPEN THE WINNER'S DOOR.

Kapitel.23 "The Bridge of Trials"

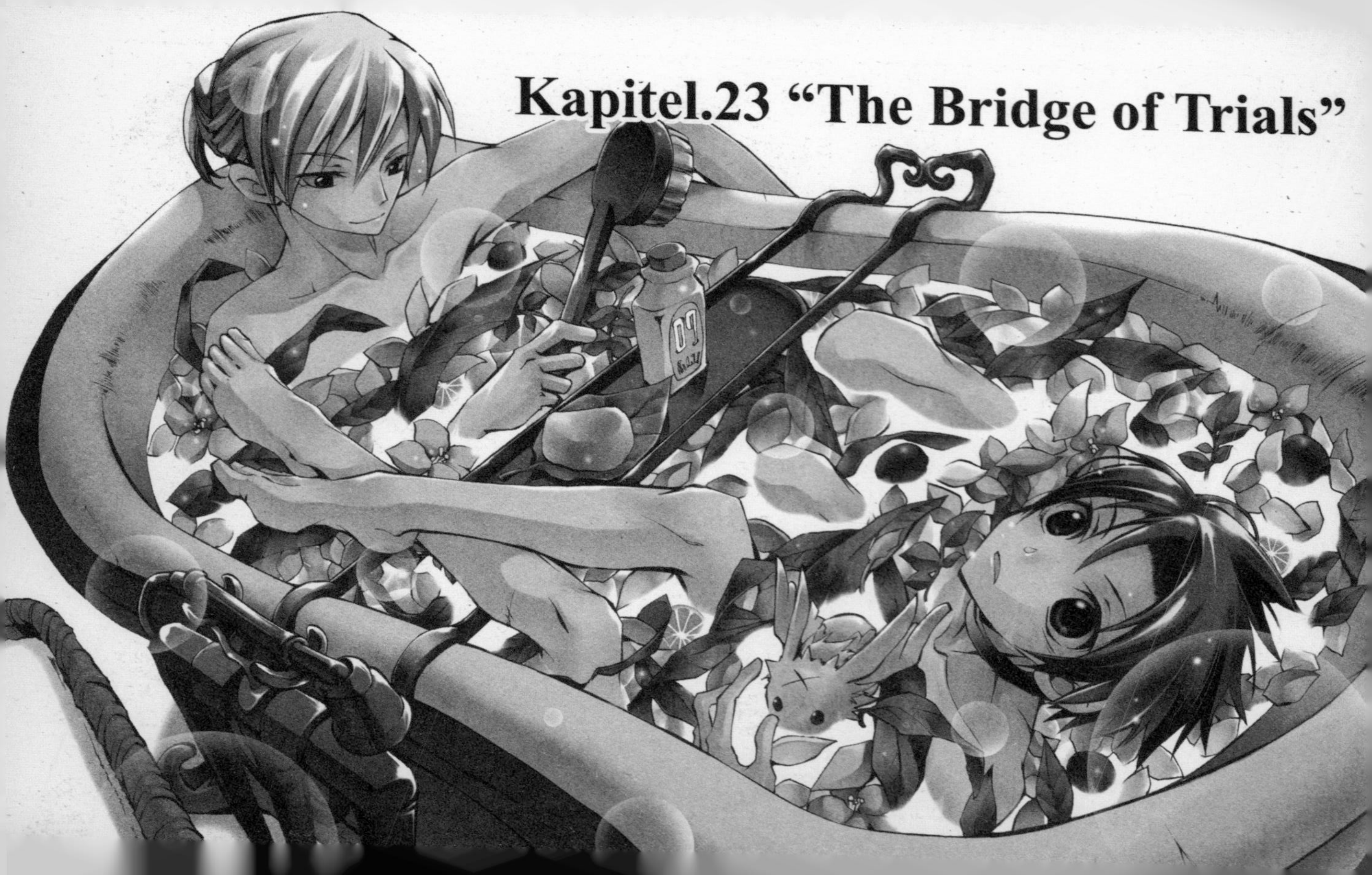

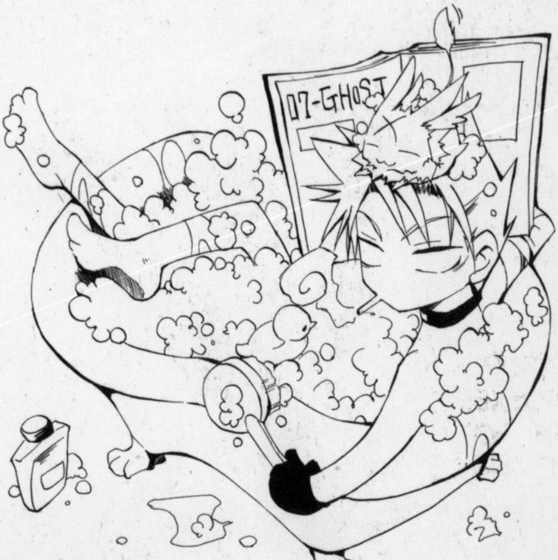
07-GHOST

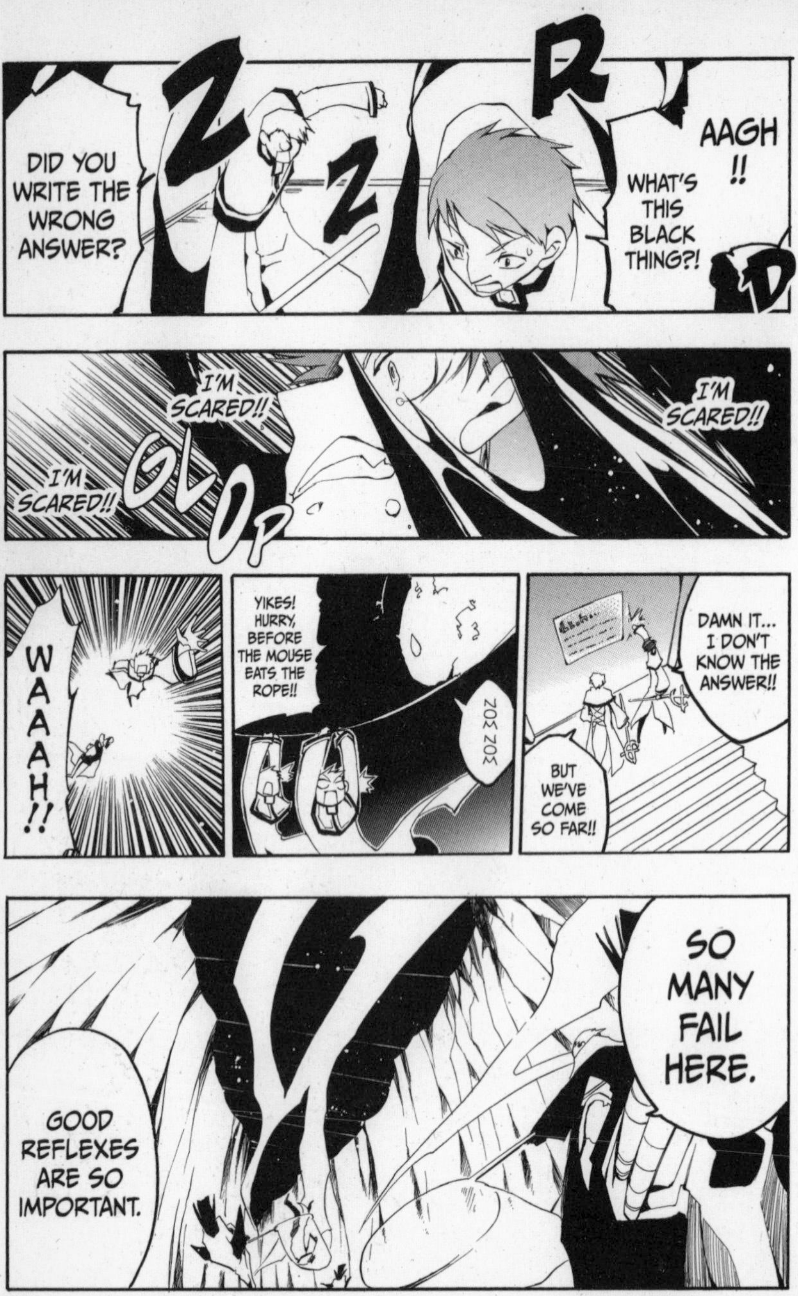
R
AAGH!!
WHAT'S THIS BLACK THING?!
Z
Z
D
DID YOU WRITE THE WRONG ANSWER?
I'M SCARED!!
I'M SCARED!!
GLOP
I'M SCARED!!
DAMN IT... I DON'T KNOW THE ANSWER!!
BUT WE'VE COME SO FAR!!
YIKES! HURRY, BEFORE THE MOUSE EATS THE ROPE!!
NOM NOM
WAAAAH!!
SO MANY FAIL HERE.
GOOD REFLEXES ARE SO IMPORTANT.

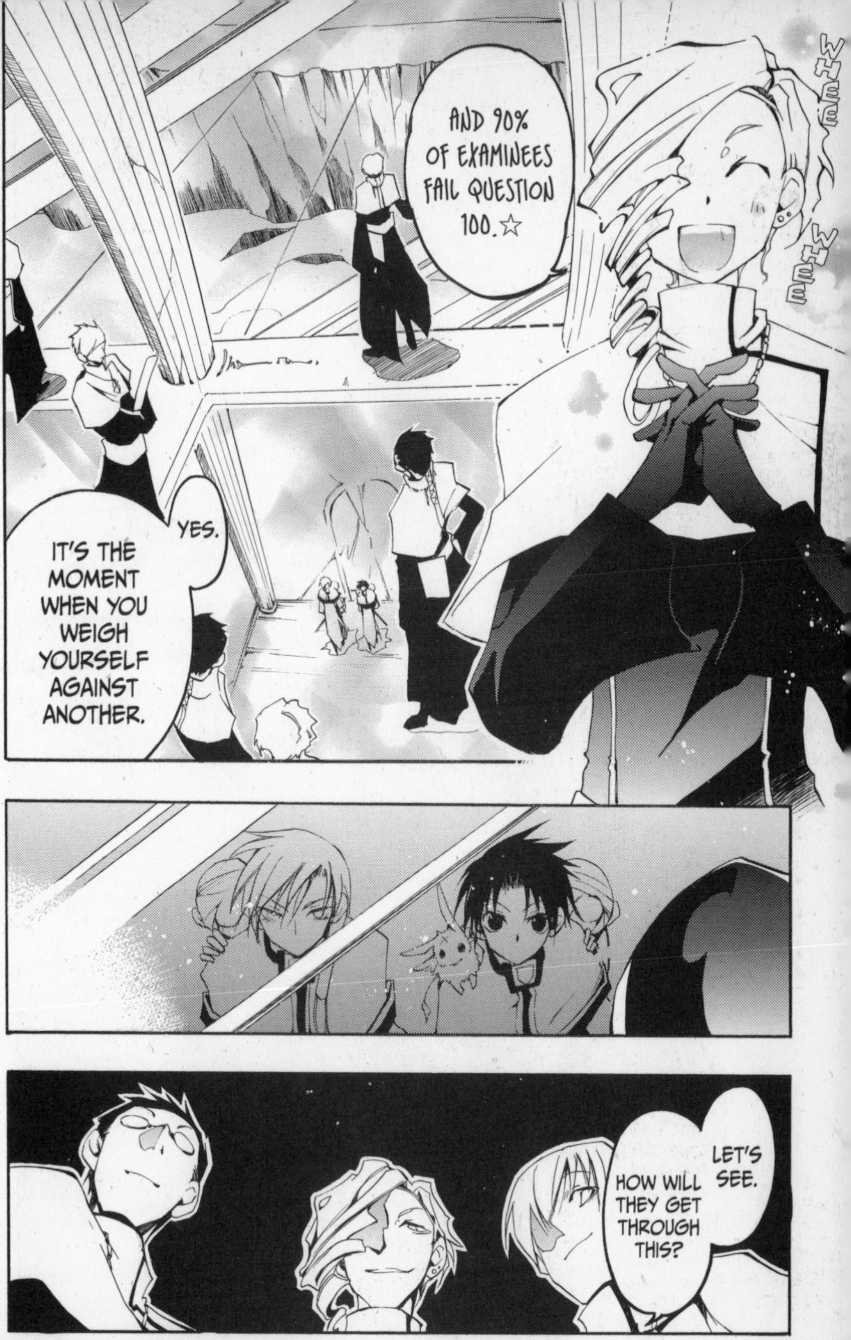
WHEE WHEE
AND 90% OF EXAMINEES FAIL QUESTION 100.☆
YES.
IT'S THE MOMENT WHEN YOU WEIGH YOURSELF AGAINST ANOTHER.
LET'S SEE.
HOW WILL THEY GET THROUGH THIS?

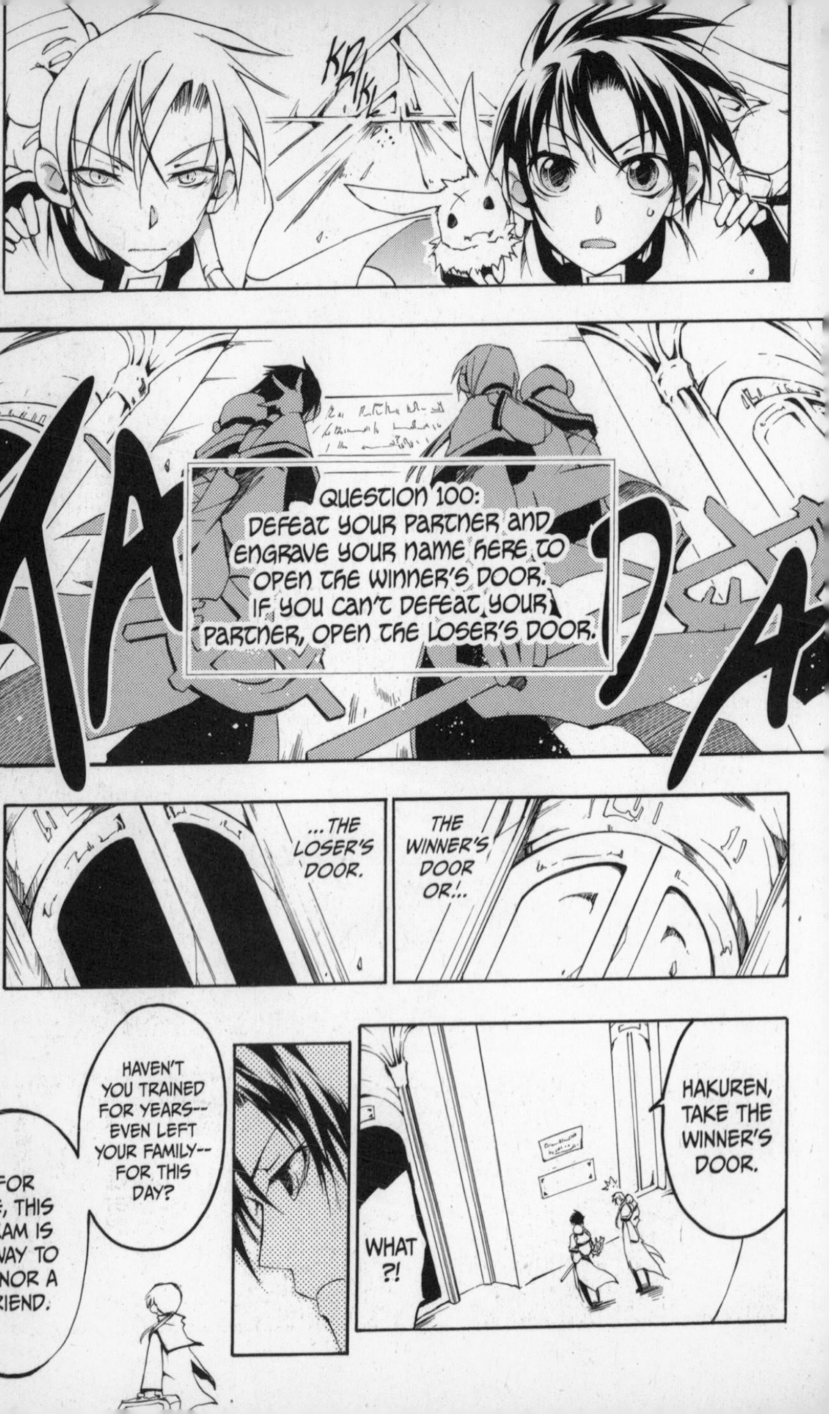
QUESTION 100:
DEFEAT YOUR PARTNER AND ENGRAVE YOUR NAME HERE TO OPEN THE WINNER'S DOOR. IF YOU CAN'T DEFEAT YOUR PARTNER, OPEN THE LOSER'S DOOR.
THE WINNER'S DOOR OR!..
...THE LOSER'S DOOR.
HAKUREN, TAKE THE WINNER'S DOOR.
WHAT ?!
HAVEN'T YOU TRAINED FOR YEARS-- EVEN LEFT YOUR FAMILY-- FOR THIS DAY?
FOR ME, THIS EXAM IS A WAY TO HONOR A FRIEND.

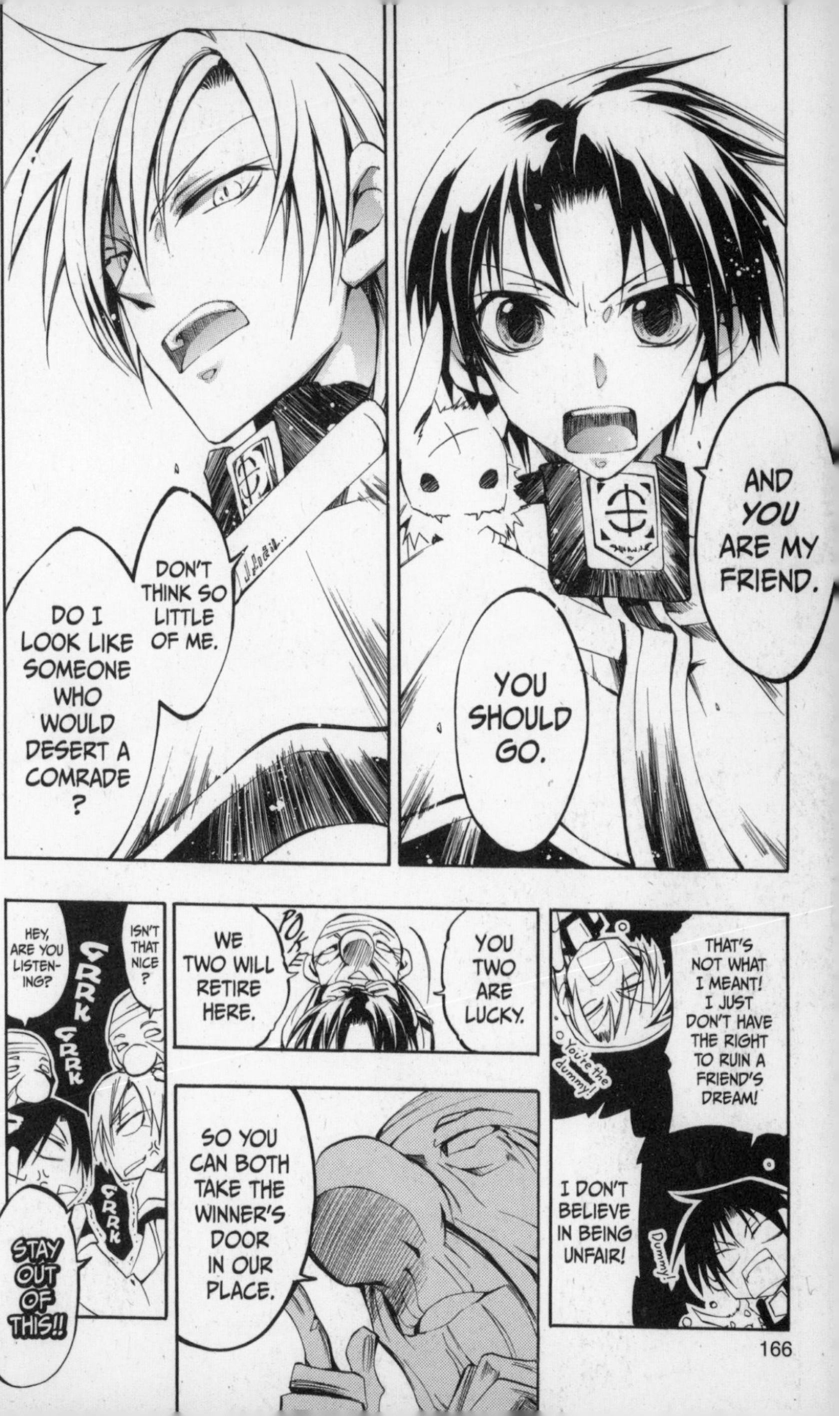
AND YOU ARE MY FRIEND.
YOU SHOULD GO.
DON'T THINK SO LITTLE OF ME.
DO I LOOK LIKE SOMEONE WHO WOULD DESERT A COMRADE?
THAT'S NOT WHAT I MEANT! I JUST DON'T HAVE THE RIGHT TO RUIN A FRIEND'S DREAM!
You're the dummy!
I DON'T BELIEVE IN BEING UNFAIR!
Dummy!
YOU TWO ARE LUCKY.
POKE
WE TWO WILL RETIRE HERE.
SO YOU CAN BOTH TAKE THE WINNER'S DOOR IN OUR PLACE.
ISN'T THAT NICE?
HEY, ARE YOU LISTENING?
GRRK
GRRK
GRRK
STAY OUT OF THIS!!

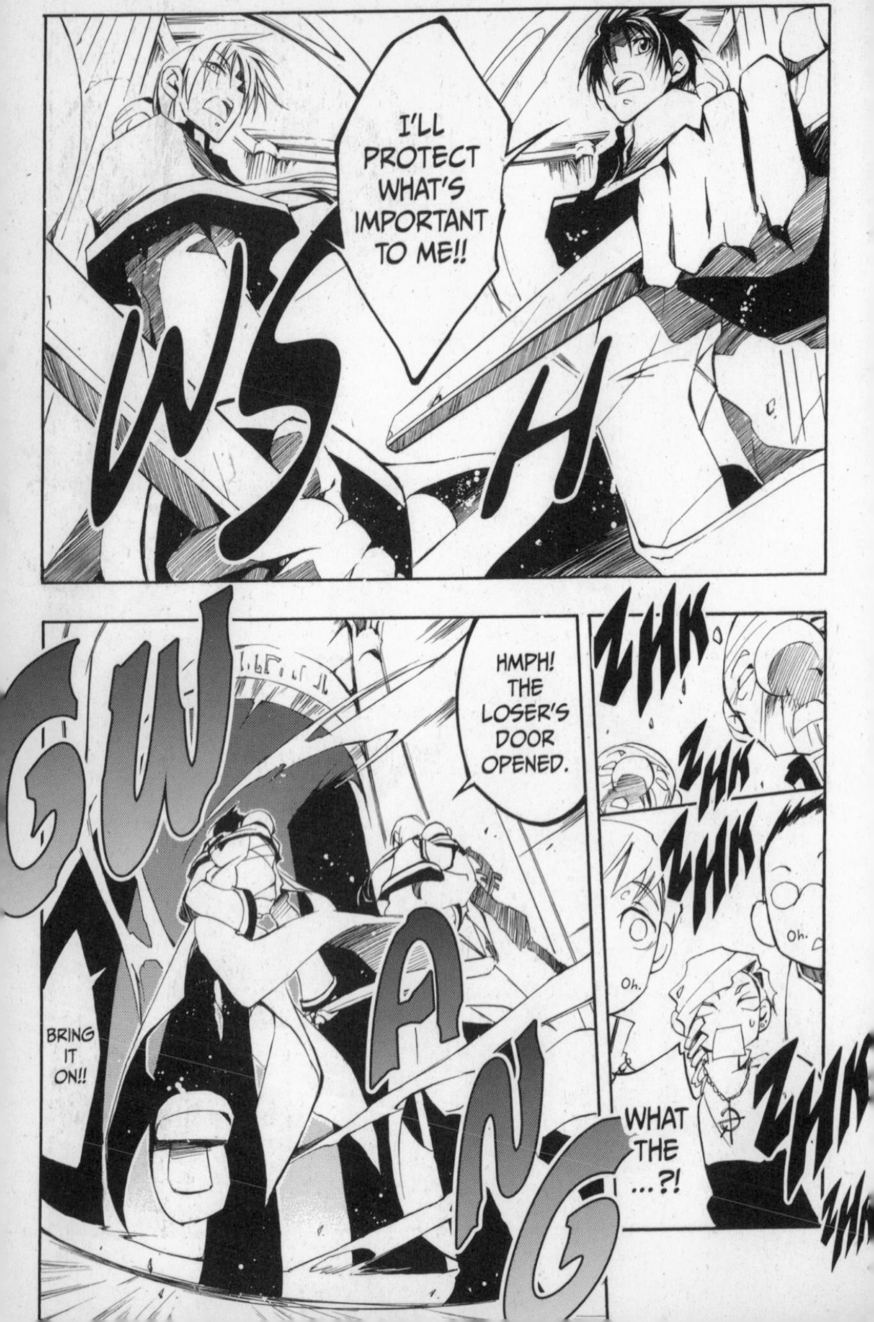
I'LL PROTECT WHAT'S IMPORTANT TO ME!!
WSH
ZHK
ZHK
ZHK
Oh.
Oh.
WHAT THE ...?!
ZHK
HMPH! THE LOSER'S DOOR OPENED.
GWANG
BRING IT ON!!

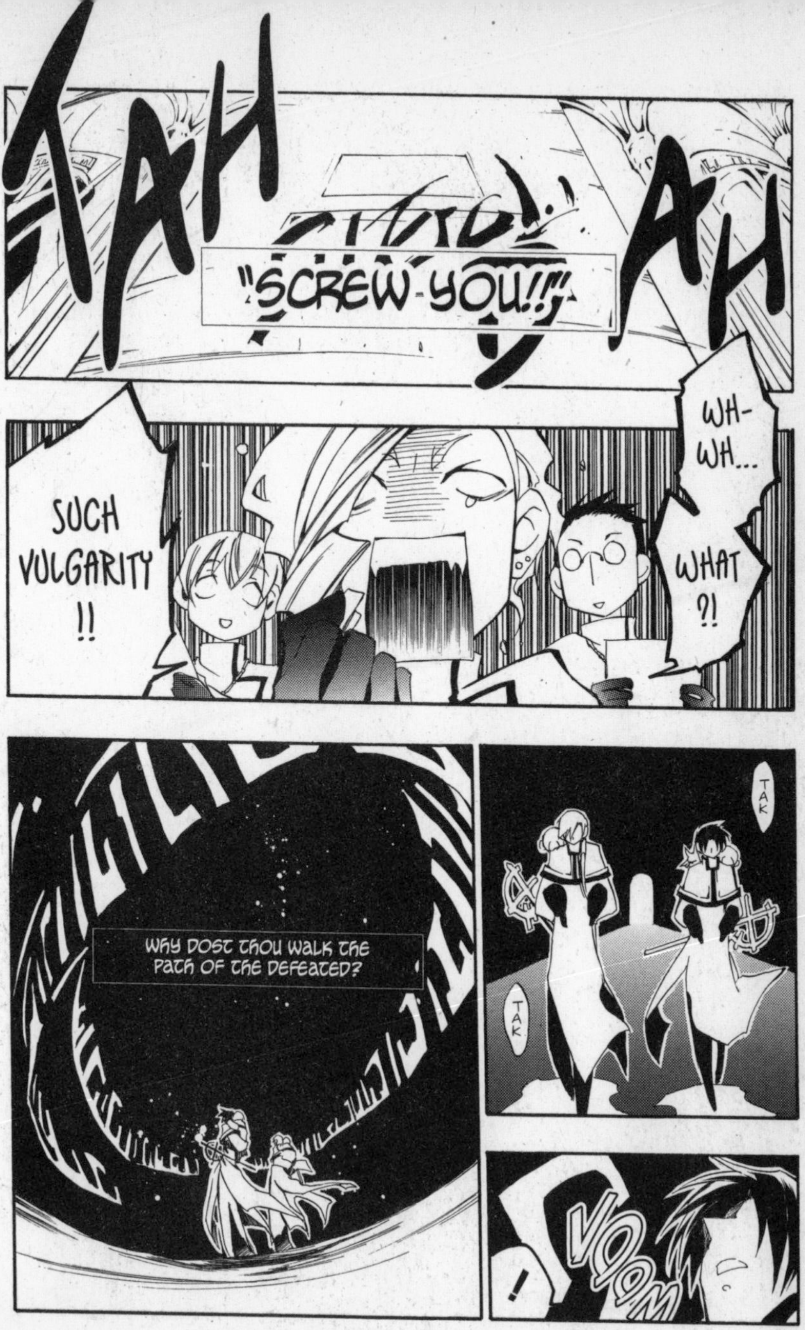
AAH
"SCREW YOU!!"
AH
WH- WH... WHAT?!
SUCH VULGARITY!!
TAK
TAK
VOOM
!
WHY DOST THOU WALK THE PATH OF THE DEFEATED?

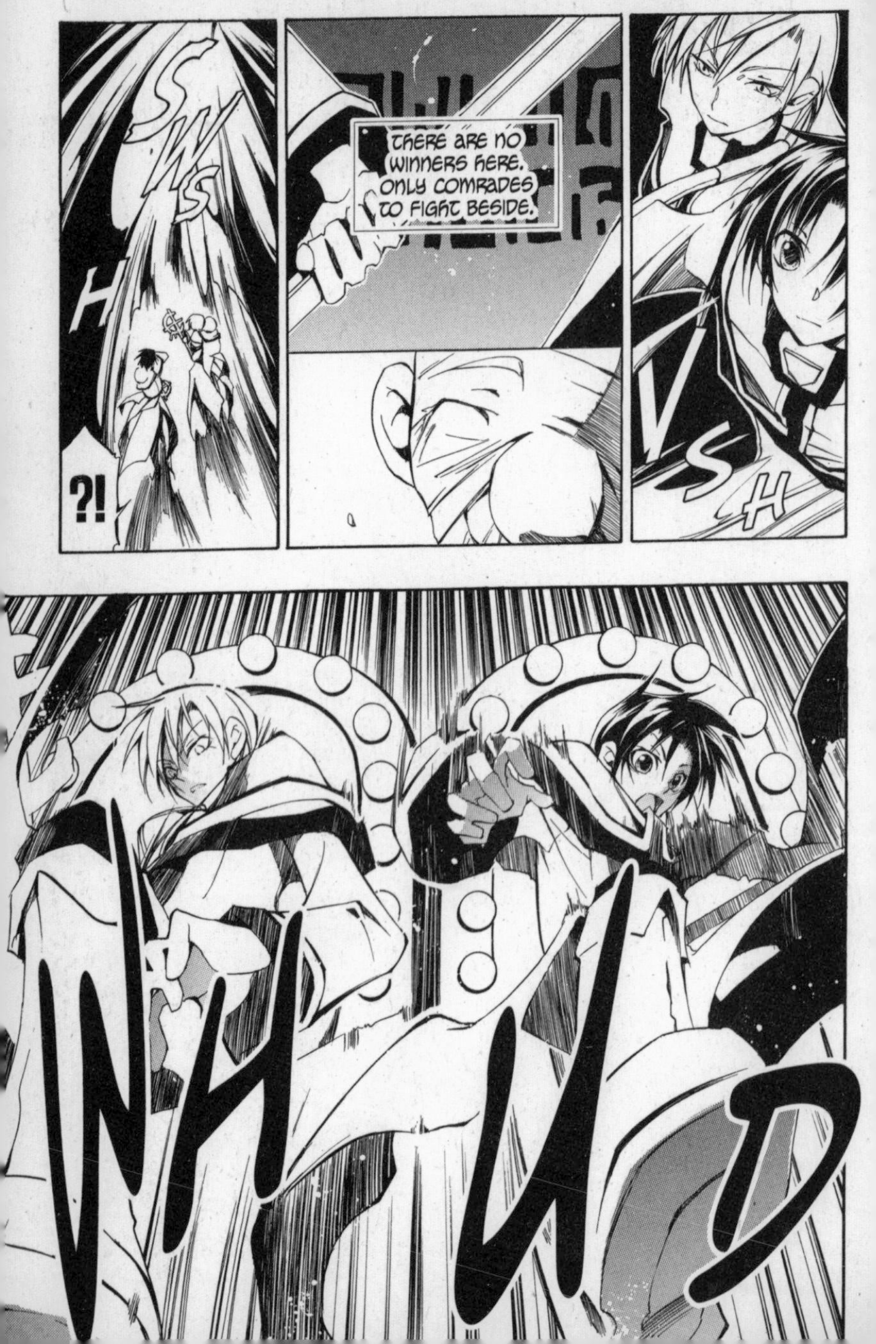
VSH
THERE ARE NO WINNERS HERE. ONLY COMRADES TO FIGHT BESIDE.
SWSH
?!
THUD

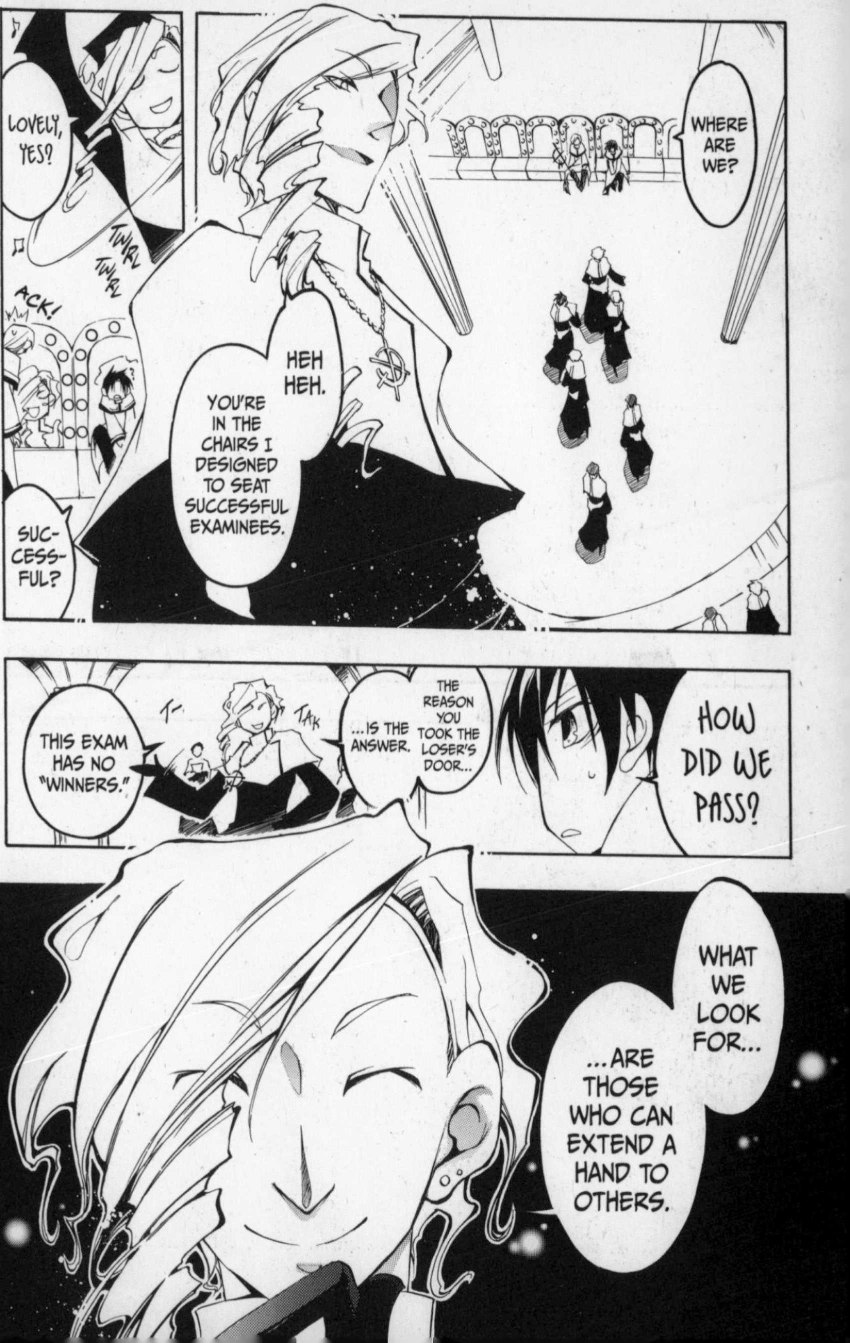
WHERE ARE WE?
HEH HEH.
YOU'RE IN THE CHAIRS I DESIGNED TO SEAT SUCCESSFUL EXAMINEES.
LOVELY, YES?
TWIRL TWIRL
ACK!
SUC-CESS-FUL?
HOW DID WE PASS?
THE REASON YOU TOOK THE LOSER'S DOOR...
...IS THE ANSWER.
TAK
THIS EXAM HAS NO "WINNERS."
WHAT WE LOOK FOR...
...ARE THOSE WHO CAN EXTEND A HAND TO OTHERS.

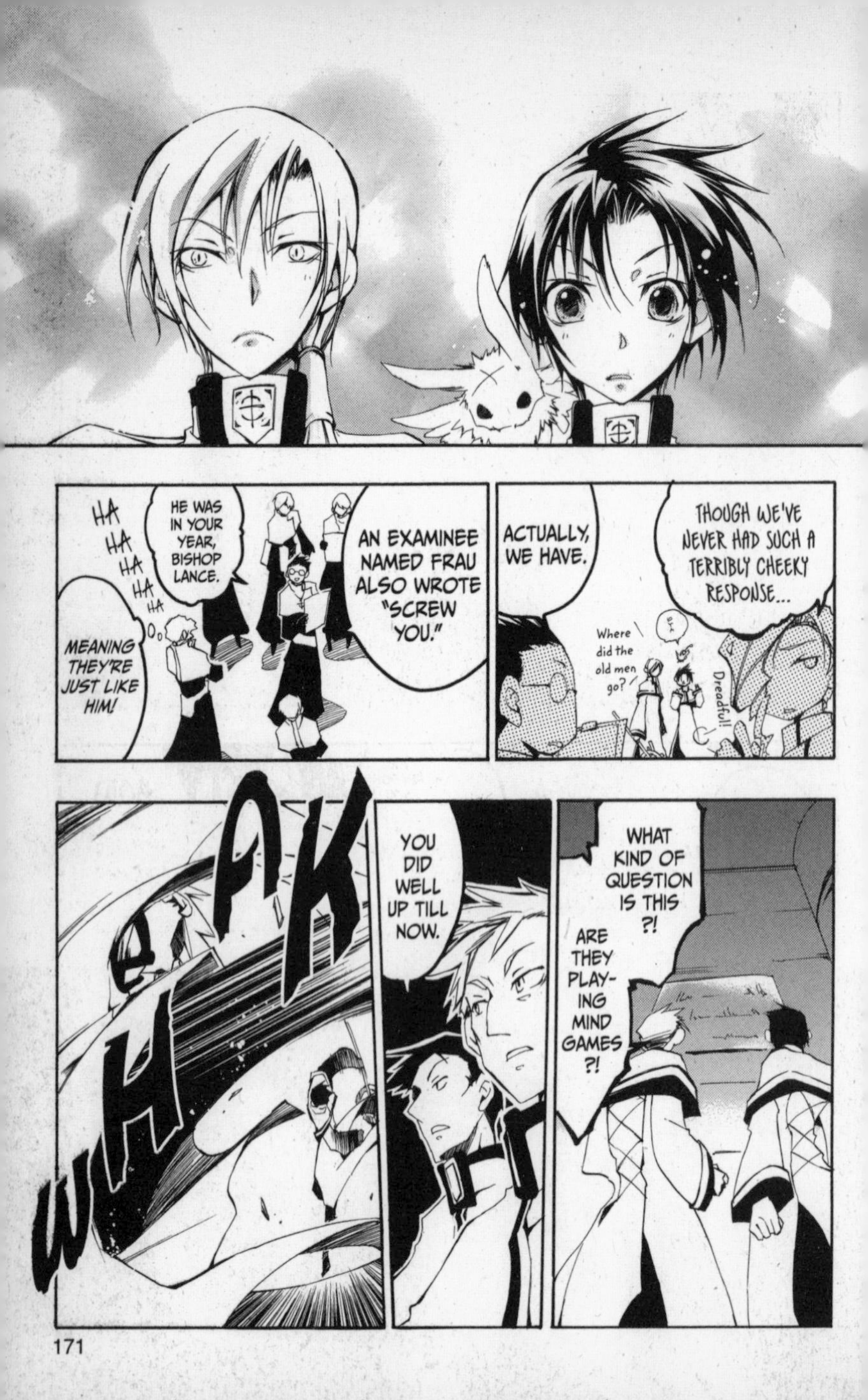
THOUGH WE'VE NEVER HAD SUCH A TERRIBLY CHEEKY RESPONSE...
Dreadful!
ACTUALLY, WE HAVE.
Where did the old men go?
AN EXAMINEE NAMED FRAU ALSO WROTE "SCREW YOU."
HE WAS IN YOUR YEAR, BISHOP LANCE.
HA HA HA HA HA
MEANING THEY'RE JUST LIKE HIM!
WHAT KIND OF QUESTION IS THIS?!
ARE THEY PLAYING MIND GAMES?!
YOU DID WELL UP TILL NOW.
WHAPK

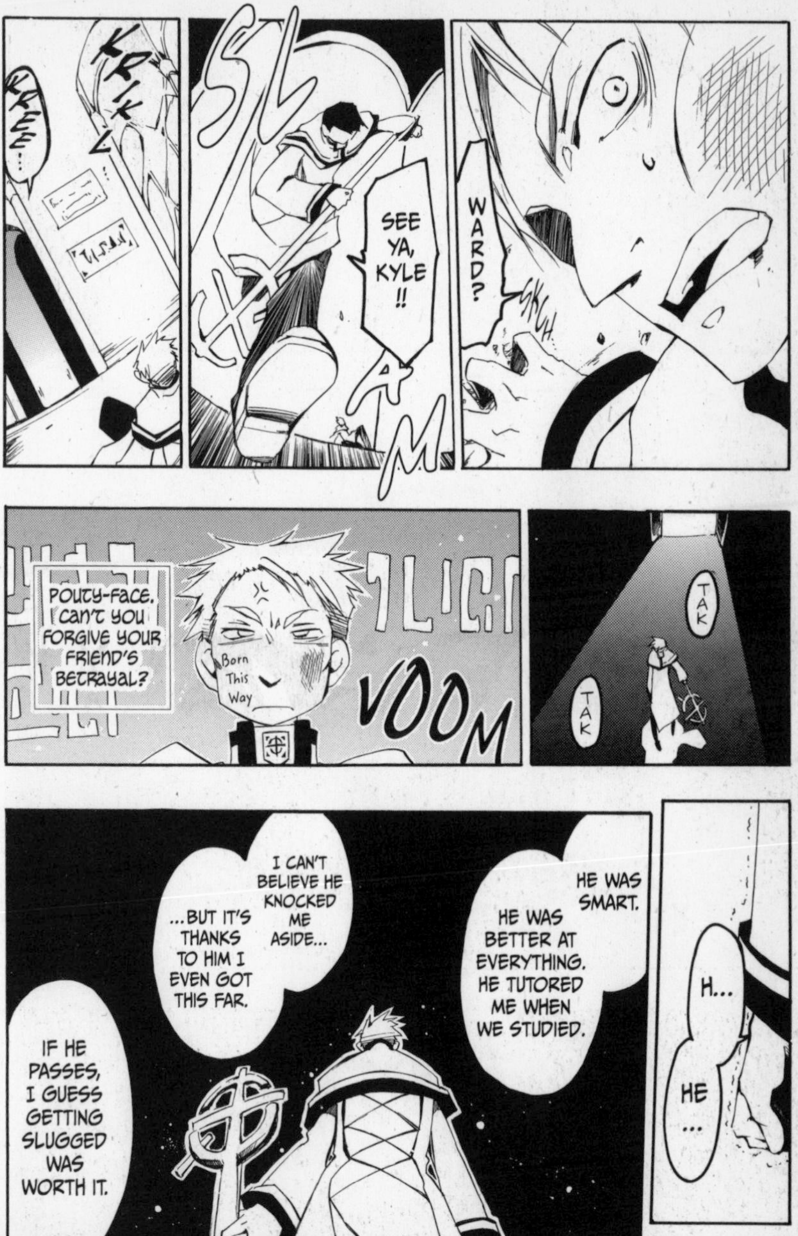

WARD?
SLAM
SEE YA, KYLE !!
KRRK
KREEE...
TAK
TAK
POUTY-FACE. CAN'T YOU FORGIVE YOUR FRIEND'S BETRAYAL?
Born This Way
VOOM
H...
HE ...
HE WAS SMART.
HE WAS BETTER AT EVERYTHING. HE TUTORED ME WHEN WE STUDIED.
I CAN'T BELIEVE HE KNOCKED ME ASIDE...
...BUT IT'S THANKS TO HIM I EVEN GOT THIS FAR.
IF HE PASSES, I GUESS GETTING SLUGGED WAS WORTH IT.

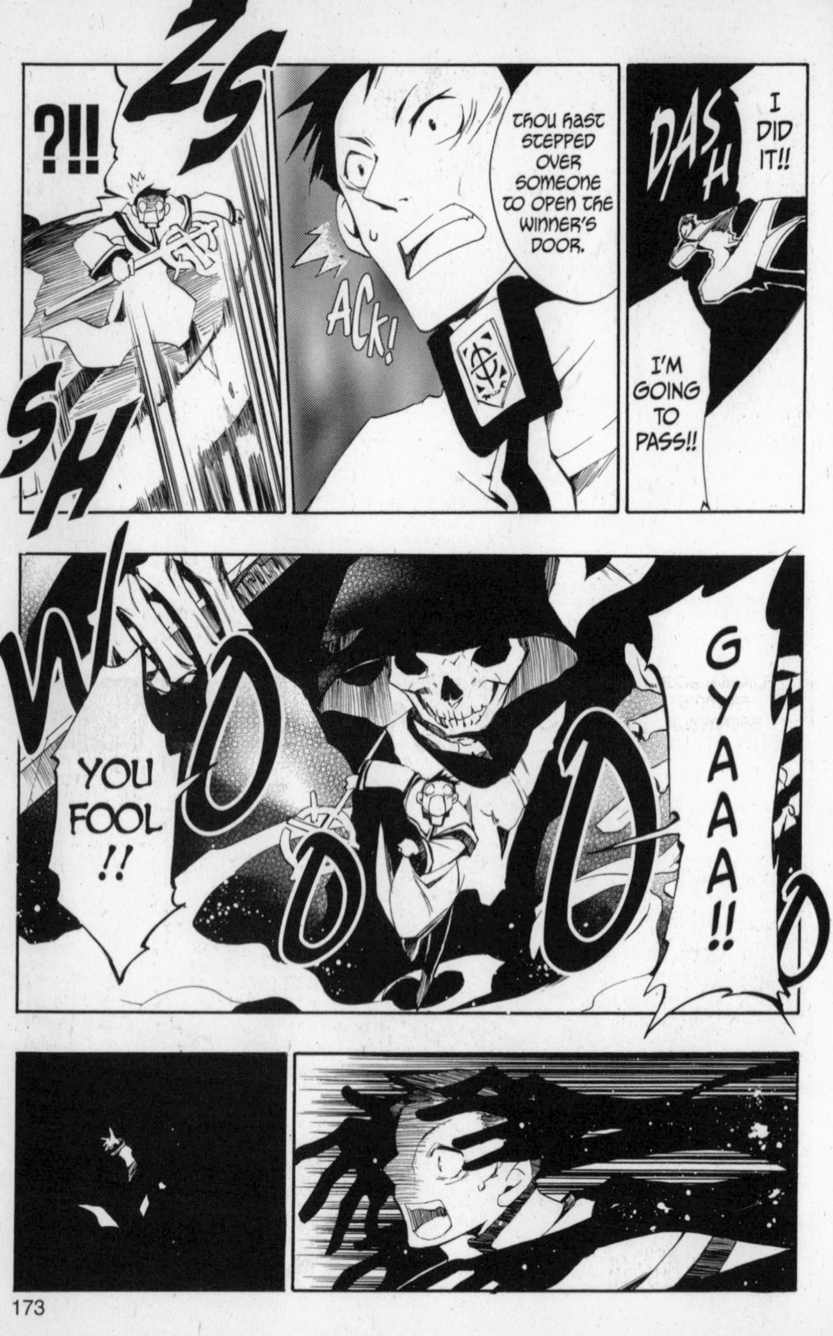
DASH
I DID IT!!
I'M GOING TO PASS!!
THOU HAST STEPPED OVER SOMEONE TO OPEN THE WINNER'S DOOR.
ACK!
ZS
?!!
SH
GYAAA!!
YOU FOOL!!

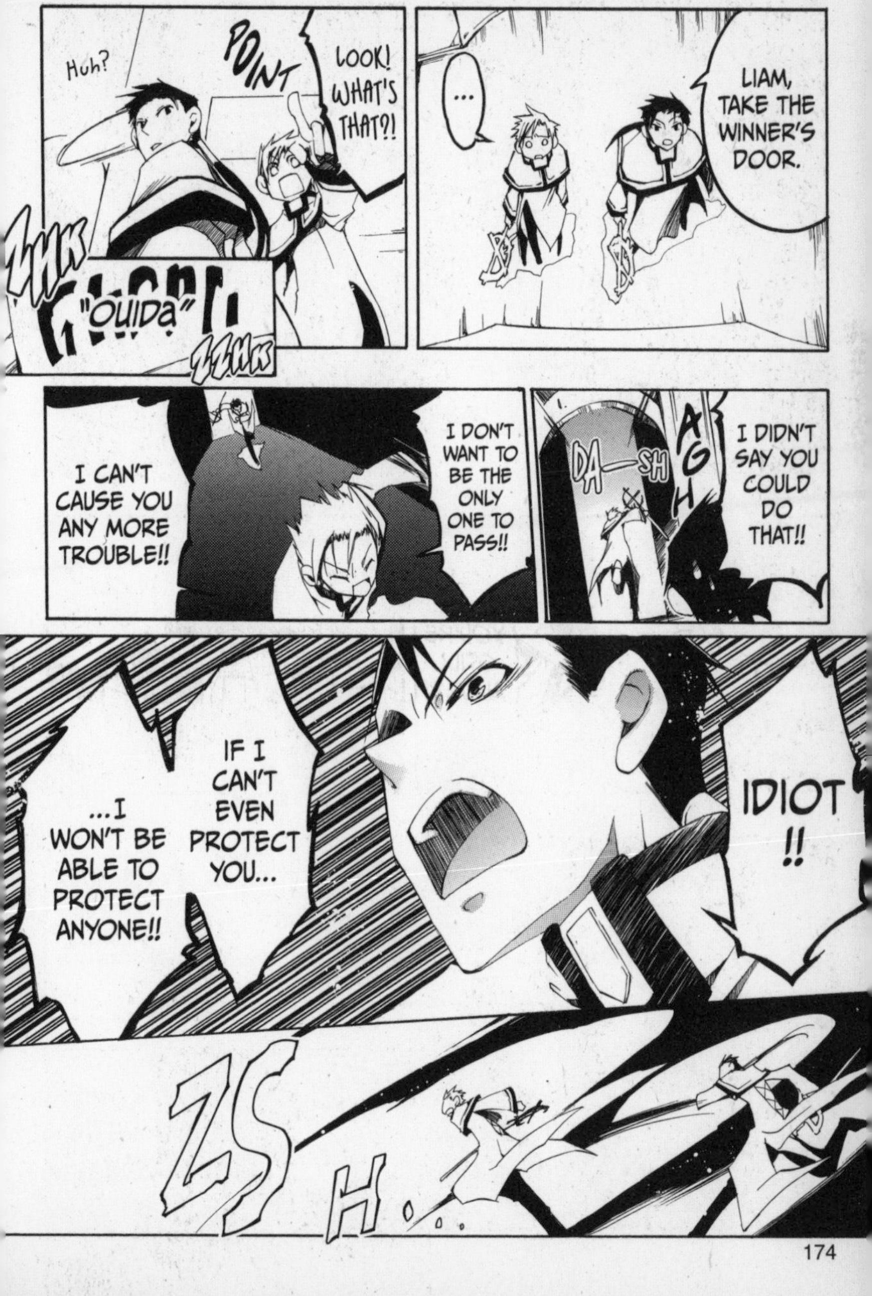
LIAM, TAKE THE WINNER'S DOOR.
...
LOOK! WHAT'S THAT?!
POINT
Huh?
ZHHS
"OUIDA"
ZZHHS
I DIDN'T SAY YOU COULD DO THAT!!
AGH
DA-SH
I DON'T WANT TO BE THE ONLY ONE TO PASS!!
I CAN'T CAUSE YOU ANY MORE TROUBLE!!
IDIOT!!
IF I CAN'T EVEN PROTECT YOU...
...I WON'T BE ABLE TO PROTECT ANYONE!!
ZSH...

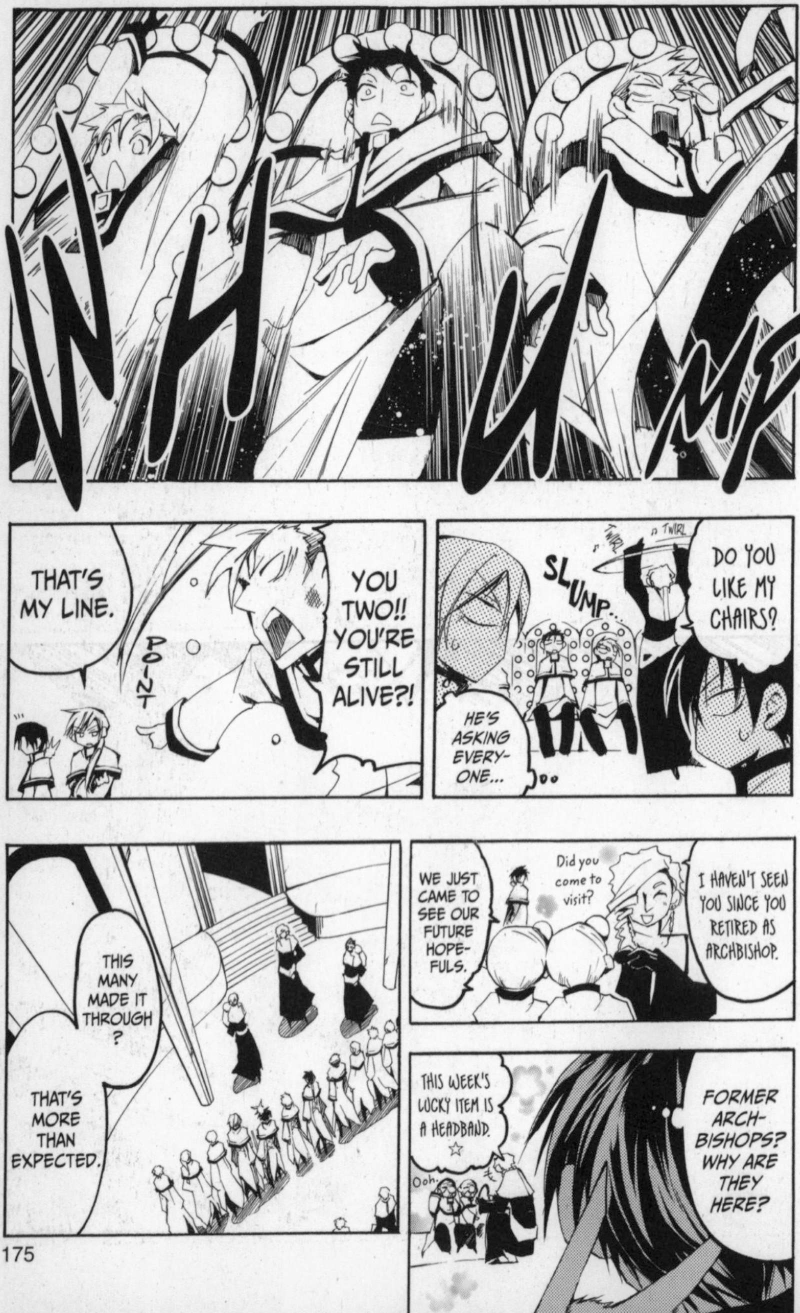
WHUMP
TWIRL
TWIRL
DO YOU LIKE MY CHAIRS?
SLUMP...
HE'S ASKING EVERY-ONE...
YOU TWO!! YOU'RE STILL ALIVE?!
POINT
THAT'S MY LINE.
I HAVEN'T SEEN YOU SINCE YOU RETIRED AS ARCHBISHOP.
Did you come to visit?
WE JUST CAME TO SEE OUR FUTURE HOPE-FULS.
FORMER ARCH-BISHOPS? WHY ARE THEY HERE?
THIS WEEK'S LUCKY ITEM IS A HEADBAND. ☆
Ooh.
THIS MANY MADE IT THROUGH?
THAT'S MORE THAN EXPECTED.

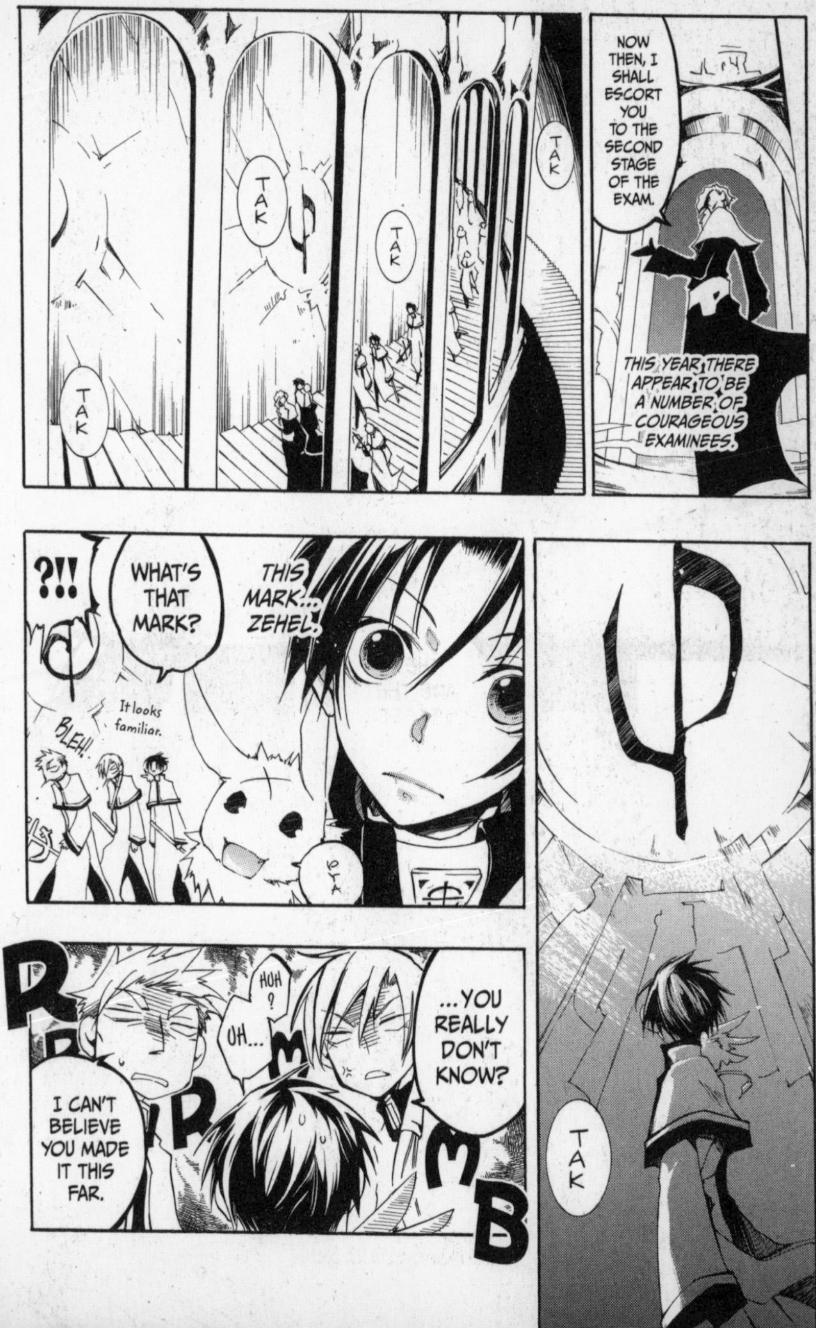
NOW THEN, I SHALL ESCORT YOU TO THE SECOND STAGE OF THE EXAM.
THIS YEAR THERE APPEAR TO BE A NUMBER OF COURAGEOUS EXAMINEES.
TAK
TAK
TAK
TAK
TAK
THIS MARK... ZEHEL.
WHAT'S THAT MARK?
?!!
It looks familiar.
BLEH!
...YOU REALLY DON'T KNOW?
HUH?
OH...
I CAN'T BELIEVE YOU MADE IT THIS FAR.

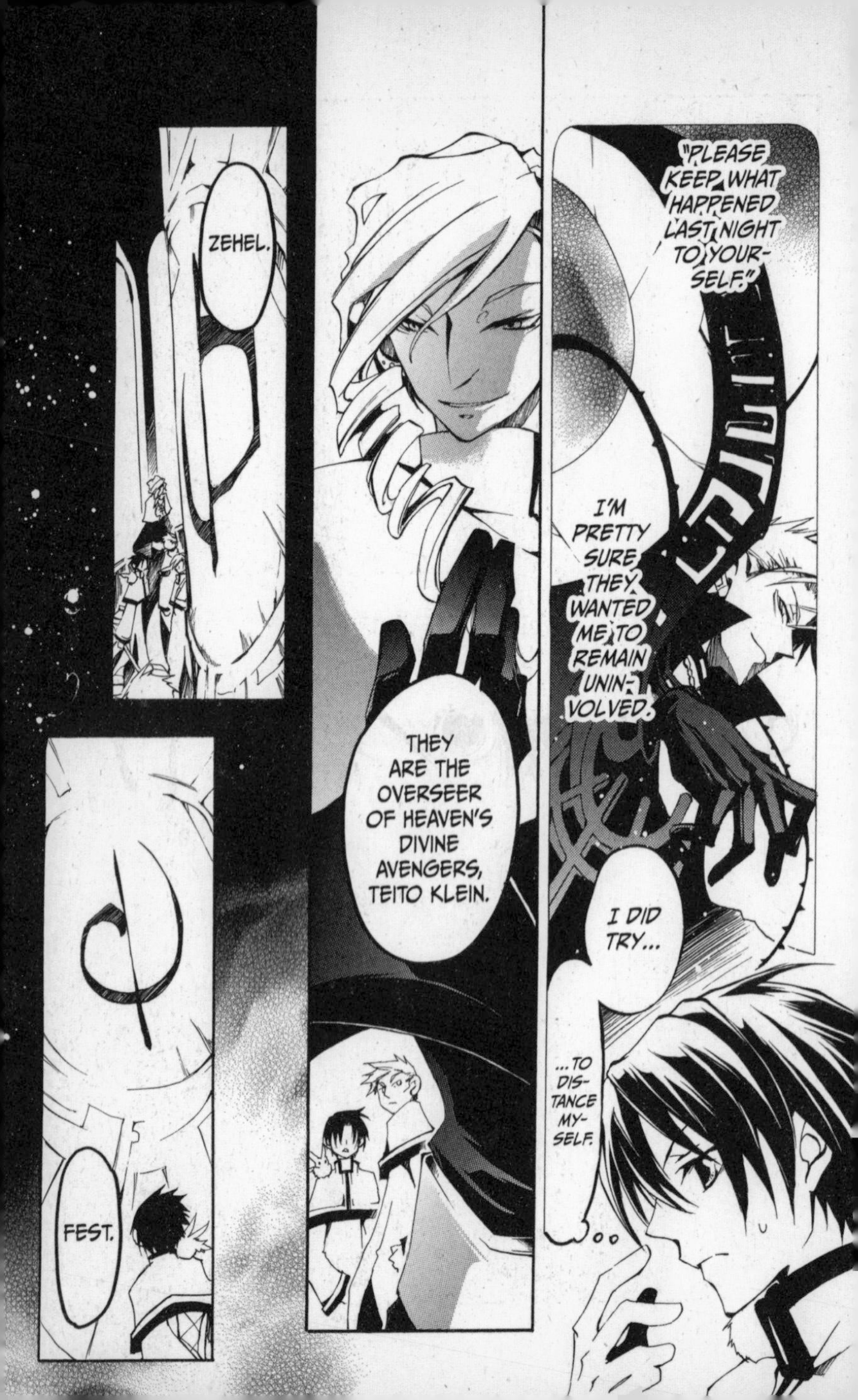
"PLEASE KEEP WHAT HAPPENED LAST NIGHT TO YOURSELF."
I'M PRETTY SURE THEY WANTED ME TO REMAIN UNINVOLVED.
I DID TRY...
...TO DISTANCE MYSELF.
THEY ARE THE OVERSEER OF HEAVEN'S DIVINE AVENGERS, TEITO KLEIN.
ZEHEL.
FEST.

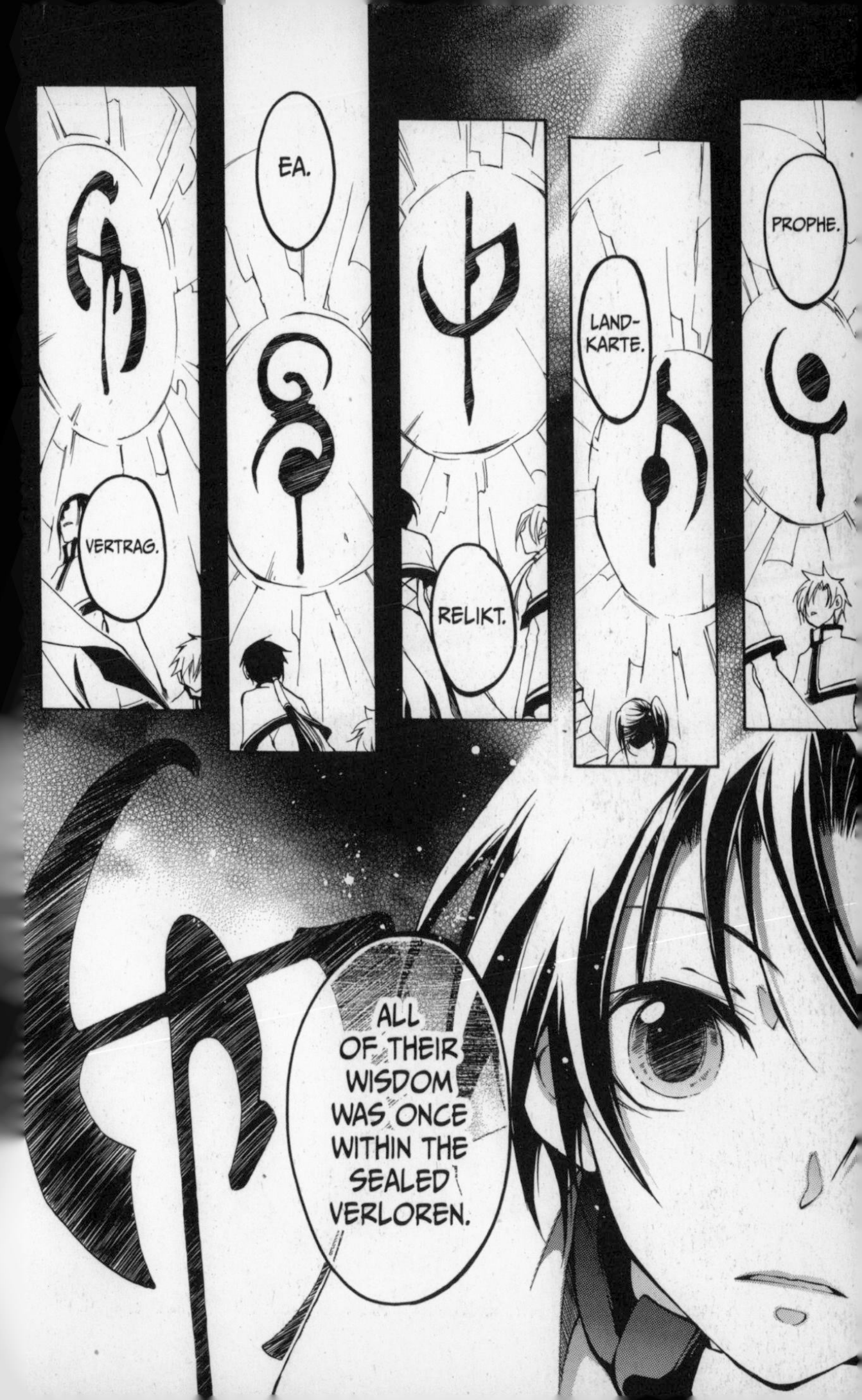
PROPHE.
LAND-KARTE.
RELIKT.
EA.
VERTRAG.
ALL OF THEIR WISDOM WAS ONCE WITHIN THE SEALED VERLOREN.

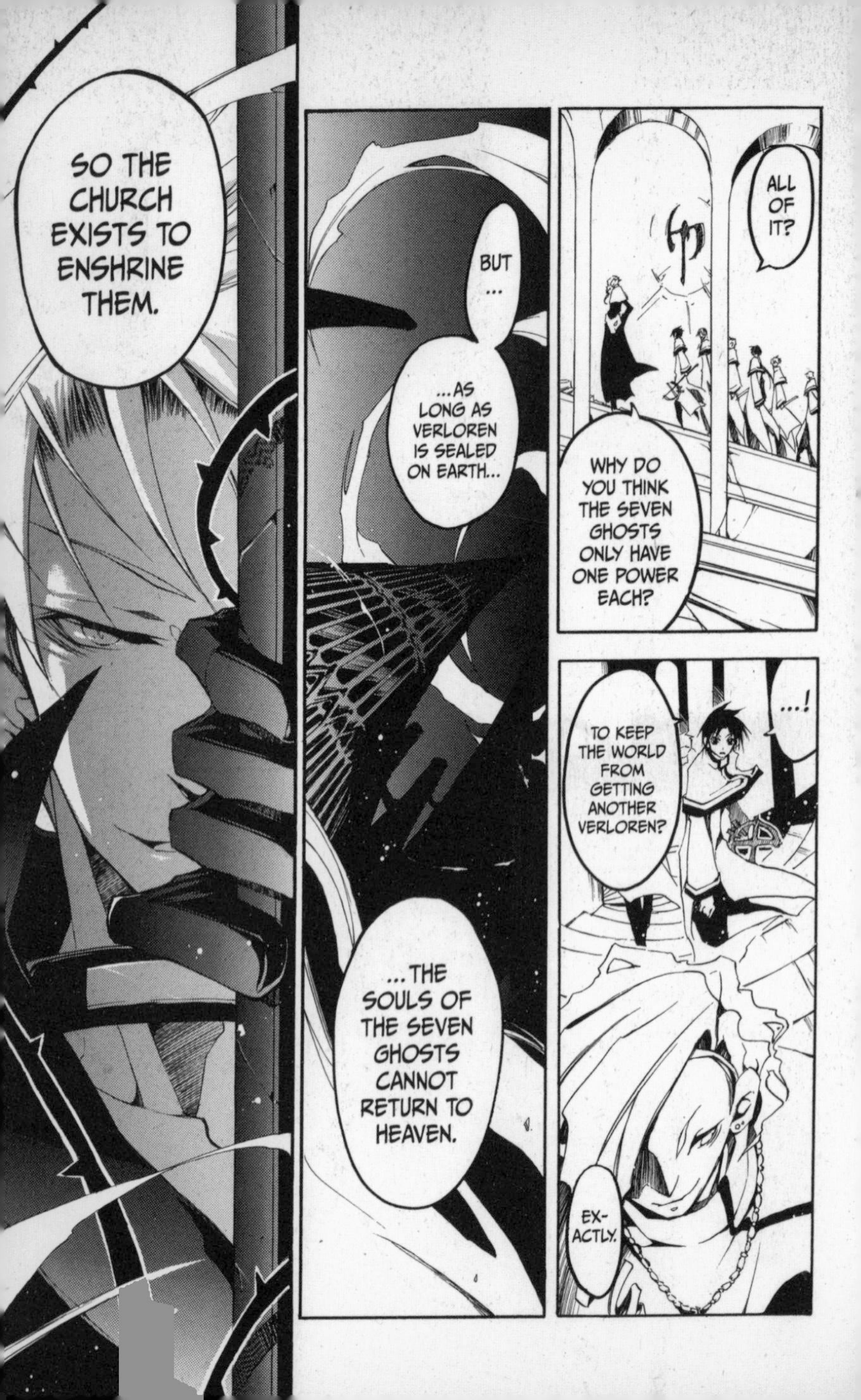
ALL OF IT?
WHY DO YOU THINK THE SEVEN GHOSTS ONLY HAVE ONE POWER EACH?
...!
TO KEEP THE WORLD FROM GETTING ANOTHER VERLOREN?
EX-ACTLY.
BUT ...
...AS LONG AS VERLOREN IS SEALED ON EARTH...
...THE SOULS OF THE SEVEN GHOSTS CANNOT RETURN TO HEAVEN.
SO THE CHURCH EXISTS TO ENSHRINE THEM.

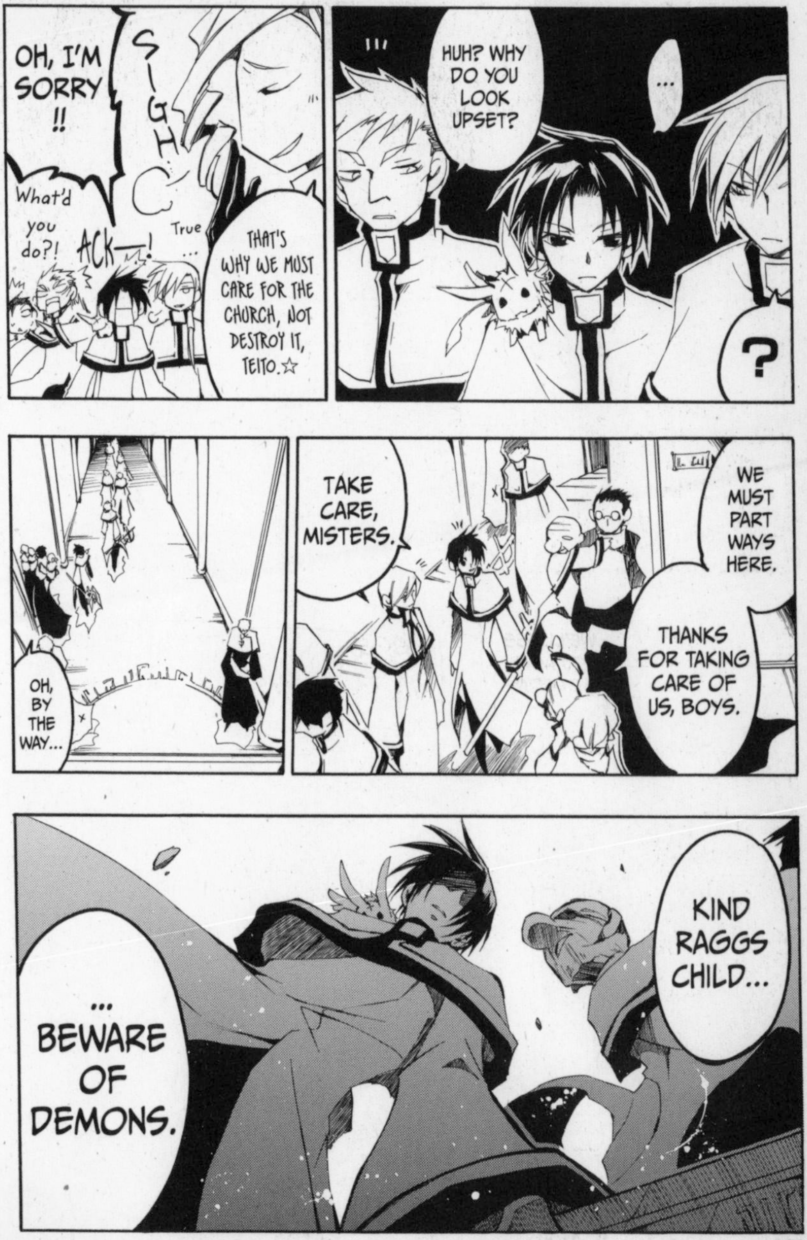
...
HUH? WHY DO YOU LOOK UPSET?
!!!
?
SIGH
OH, I'M SORRY!!
THAT'S WHY WE MUST CARE FOR THE CHURCH, NOT DESTROY IT, TEITO.☆
True ...
ACK—!
What'd you do?!
WE MUST PART WAYS HERE.
THANKS FOR TAKING CARE OF US, BOYS.
TAKE CARE, MISTERS.
OH, BY THE WAY...
KIND RAGGS CHILD...
... BEWARE OF DEMONS.

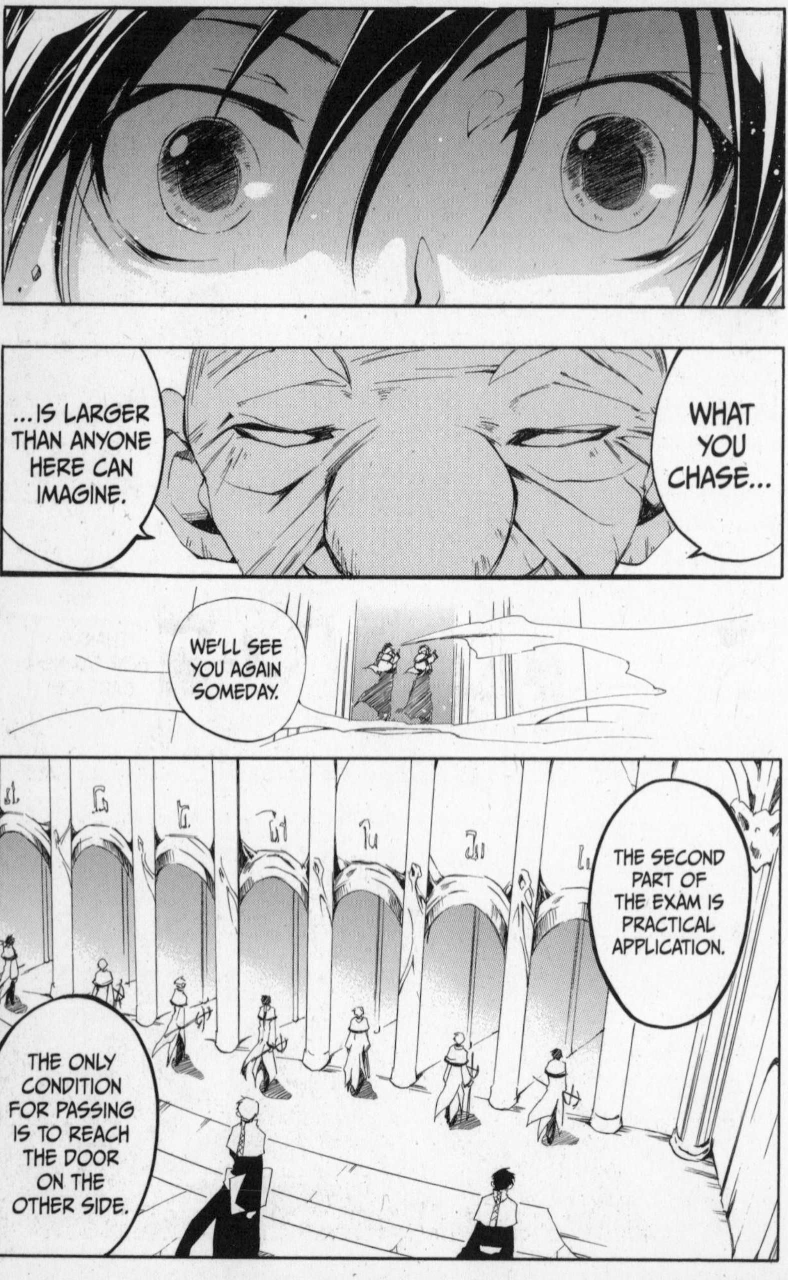
WHAT YOU CHASE...
...IS LARGER THAN ANYONE HERE CAN IMAGINE.
WE'LL SEE YOU AGAIN SOMEDAY.
THE SECOND PART OF THE EXAM IS PRACTICAL APPLICATION.
THE ONLY CONDITION FOR PASSING IS TO REACH THE DOOR ON THE OTHER SIDE.

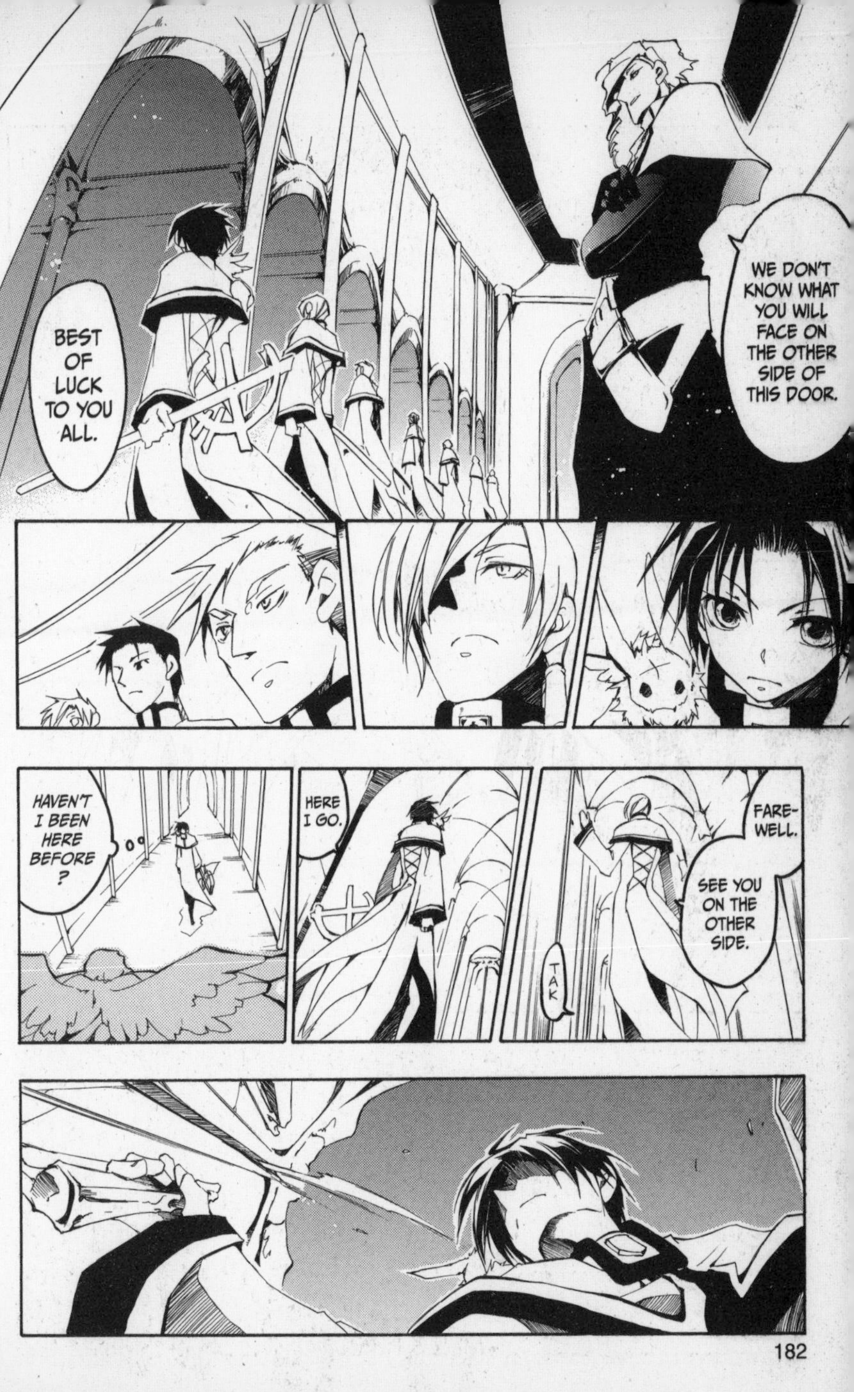
WE DON'T KNOW WHAT YOU WILL FACE ON THE OTHER SIDE OF THIS DOOR.
BEST OF LUCK TO YOU ALL.
FARE-WELL.
SEE YOU ON THE OTHER SIDE.
TAK
HERE I GO.
HAVEN'T I BEEN HERE BEFORE?

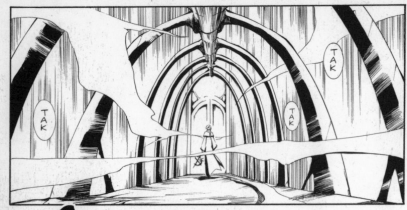

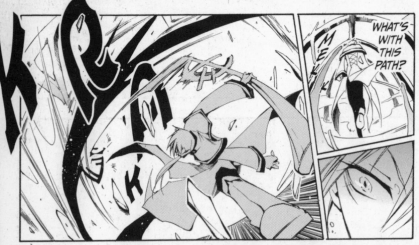

WHAT'S WITH THIS PATH?

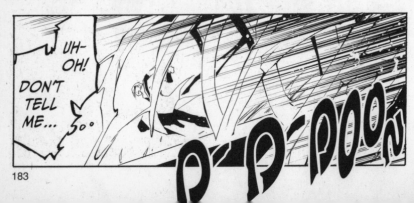

UH-OH!

DON'T TELL ME...

183

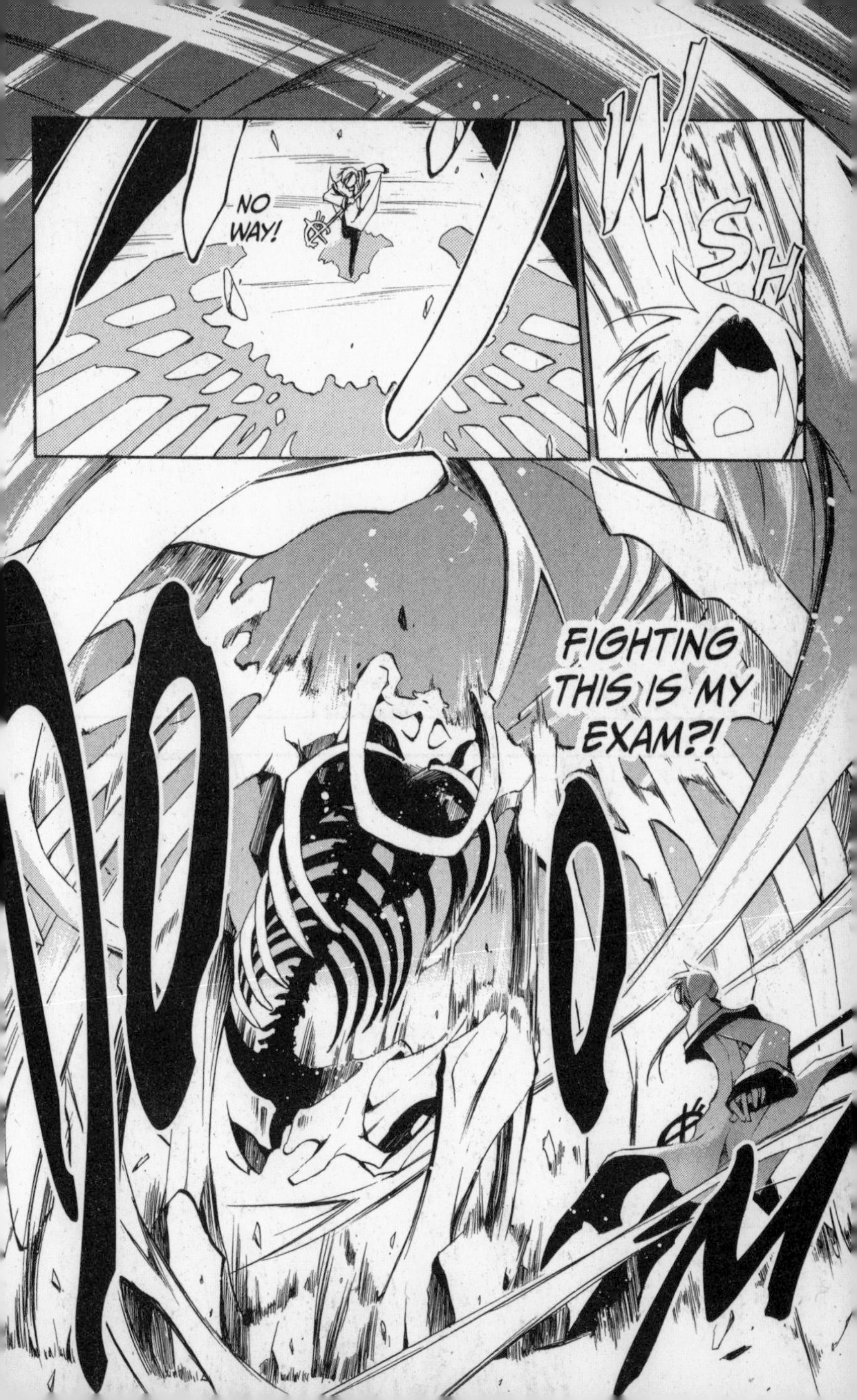
WSH
NO WAY!
FIGHTING THIS IS MY EXAM?!

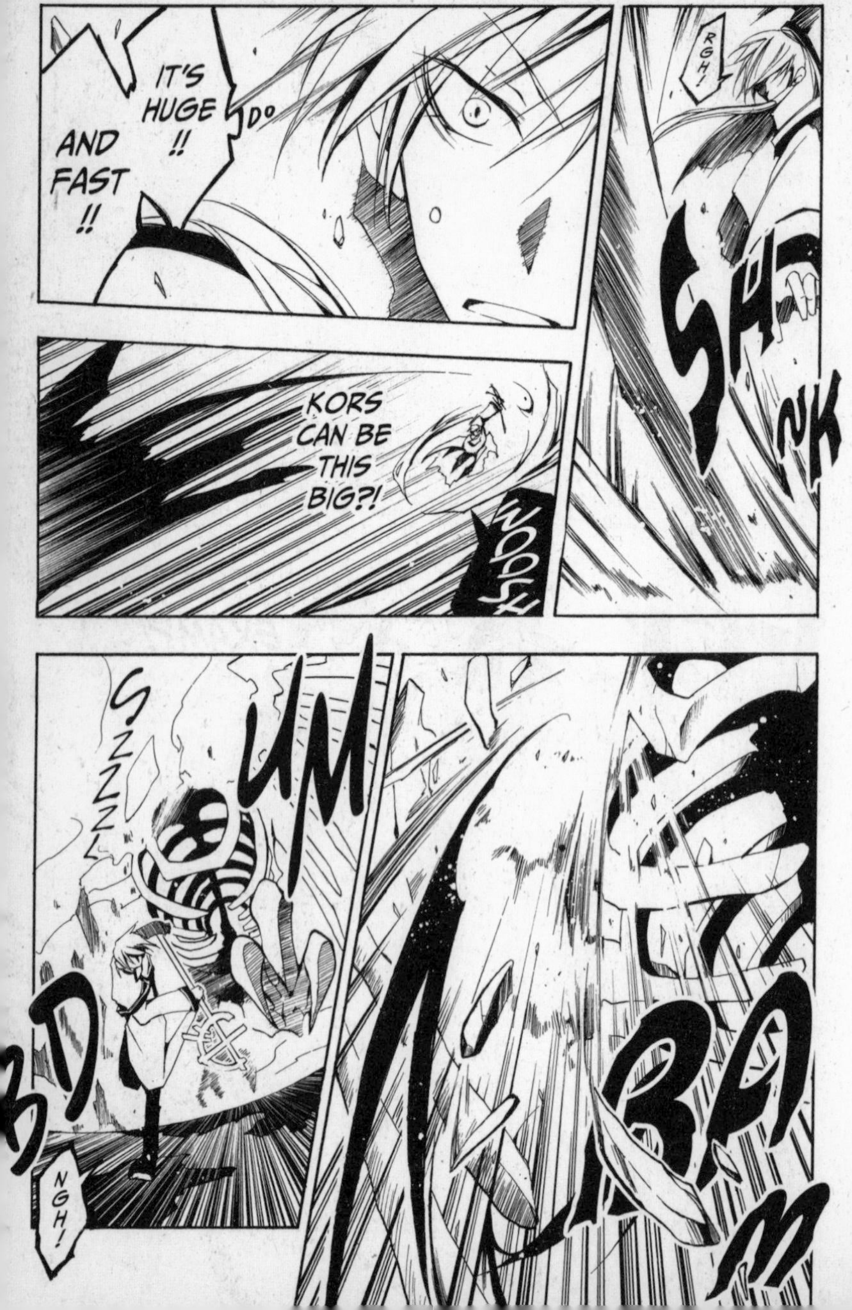
RGH!
SHUNK
DO
IT'S HUGE!!
AND FAST!!
KORS CAN BE THIS BIG?!
WOOSH
BAM
SZZZZL
BDUM
NGH!

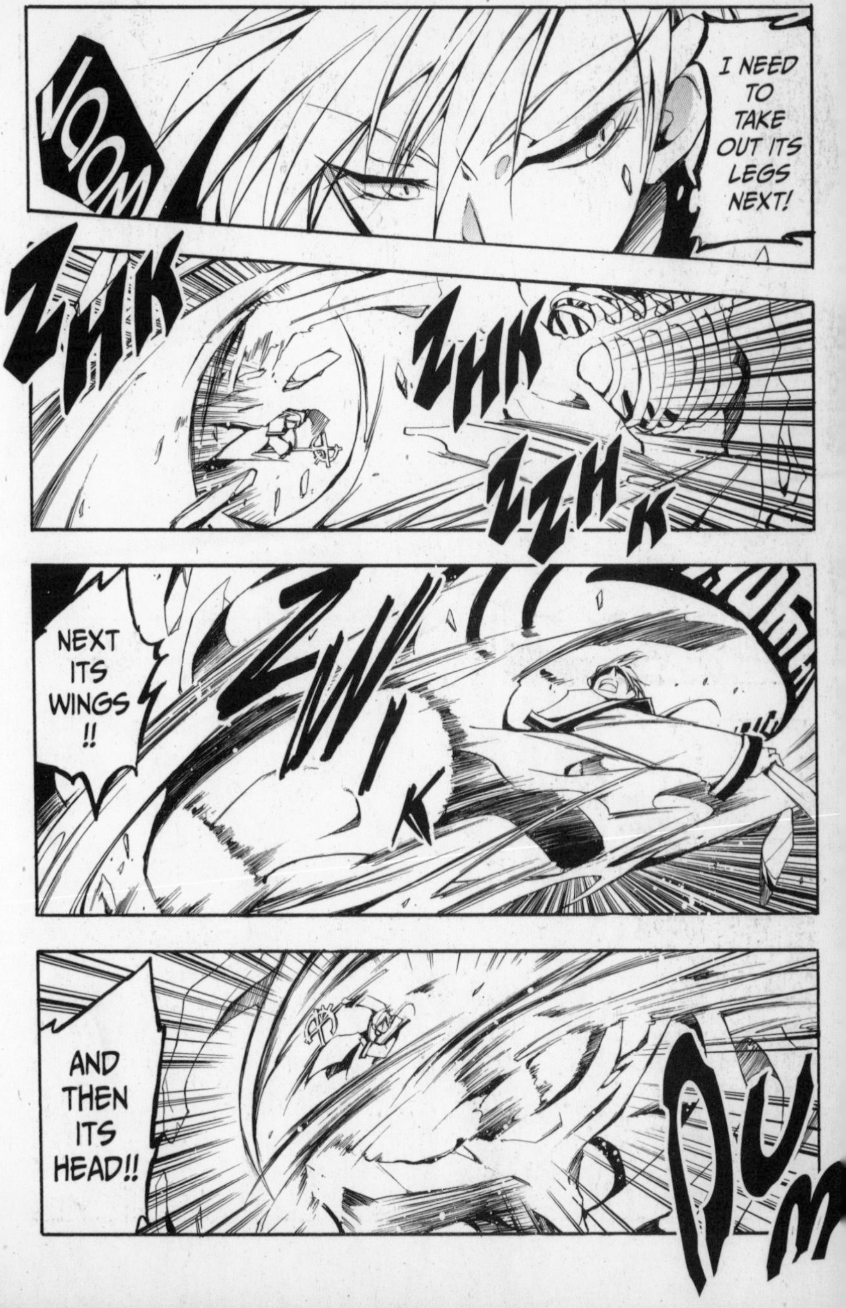
I NEED TO TAKE OUT ITS LEGS NEXT!
VOOM
ZHK
ZHK
ZZHK
NEXT ITS WINGS !!
ZWK
AND THEN ITS HEAD!!

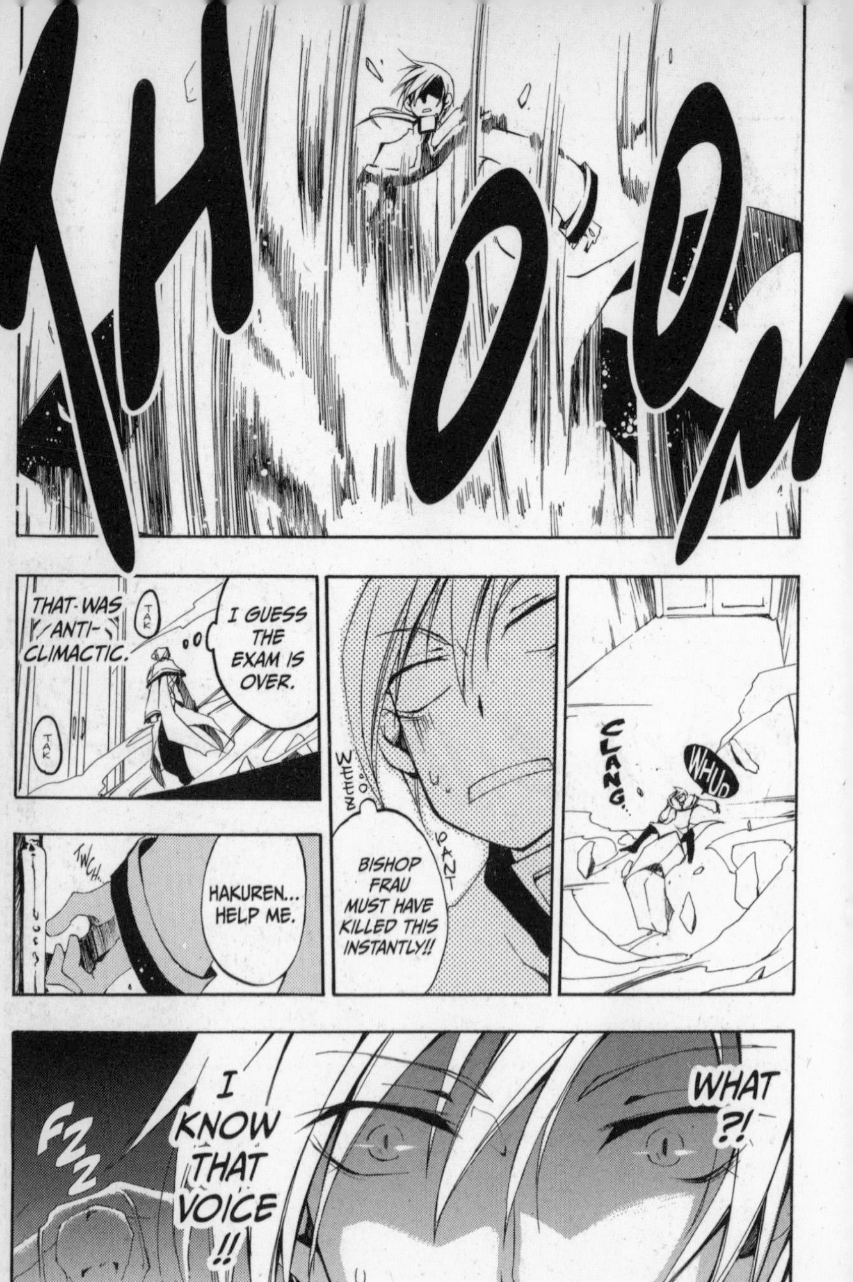
THOOM
CLANG...
WHUD
WEEZ
PANT
BISHOP FRAU MUST HAVE KILLED THIS INSTANTLY!!
I GUESS THE EXAM IS OVER.
THAT WAS ANTI-CLIMACTIC.
TAK
TAK
HAKUREN... HELP ME.
TWCH
WHAT?!
I KNOW THAT VOICE!!
FZZ

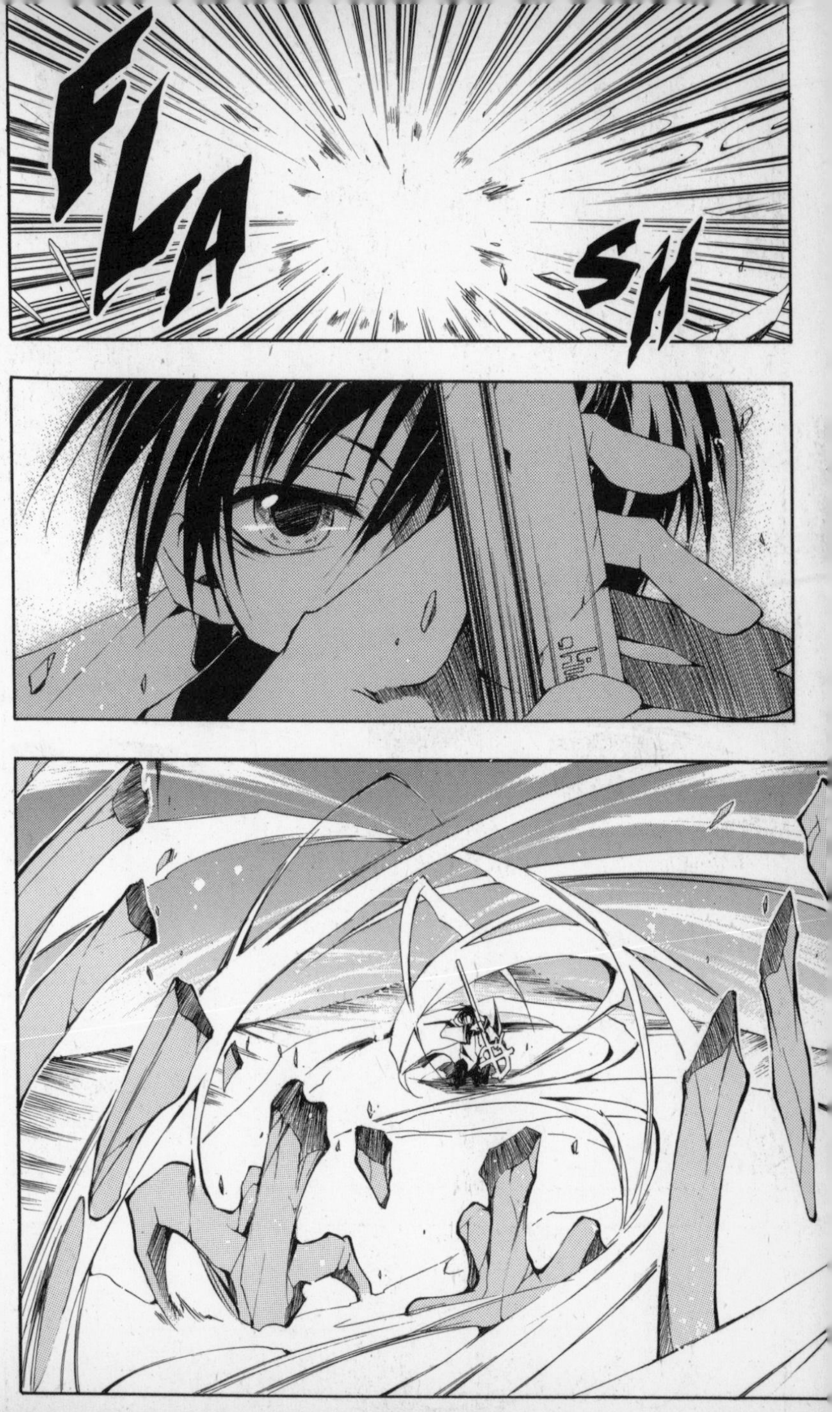
FLASH

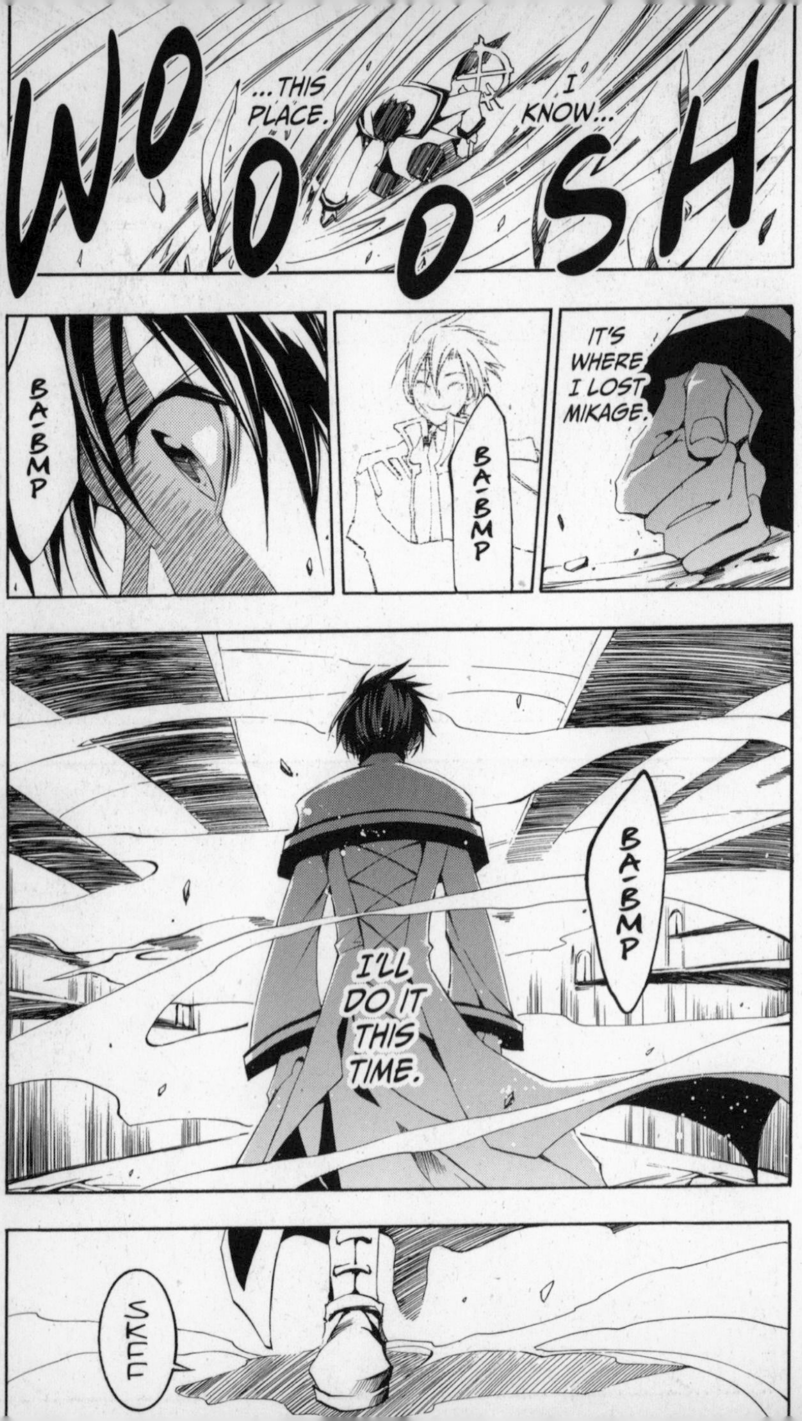
WOOOSH
I KNOW...
...THIS PLACE.
IT'S WHERE I LOST MIKAGE.
BA-BMP
BA-BMP
BA-BMP
I'LL DO IT THIS TIME.
SKFF

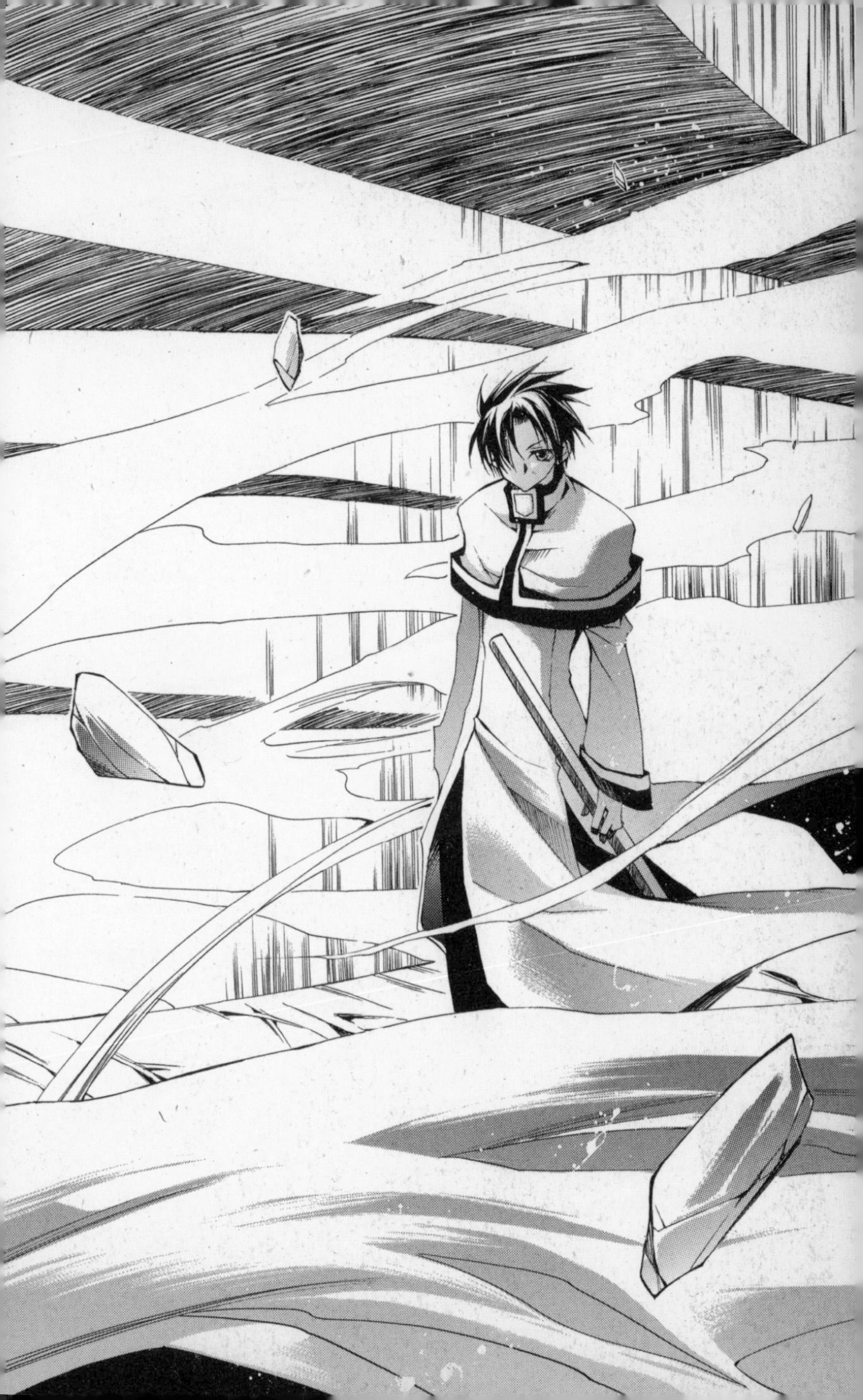

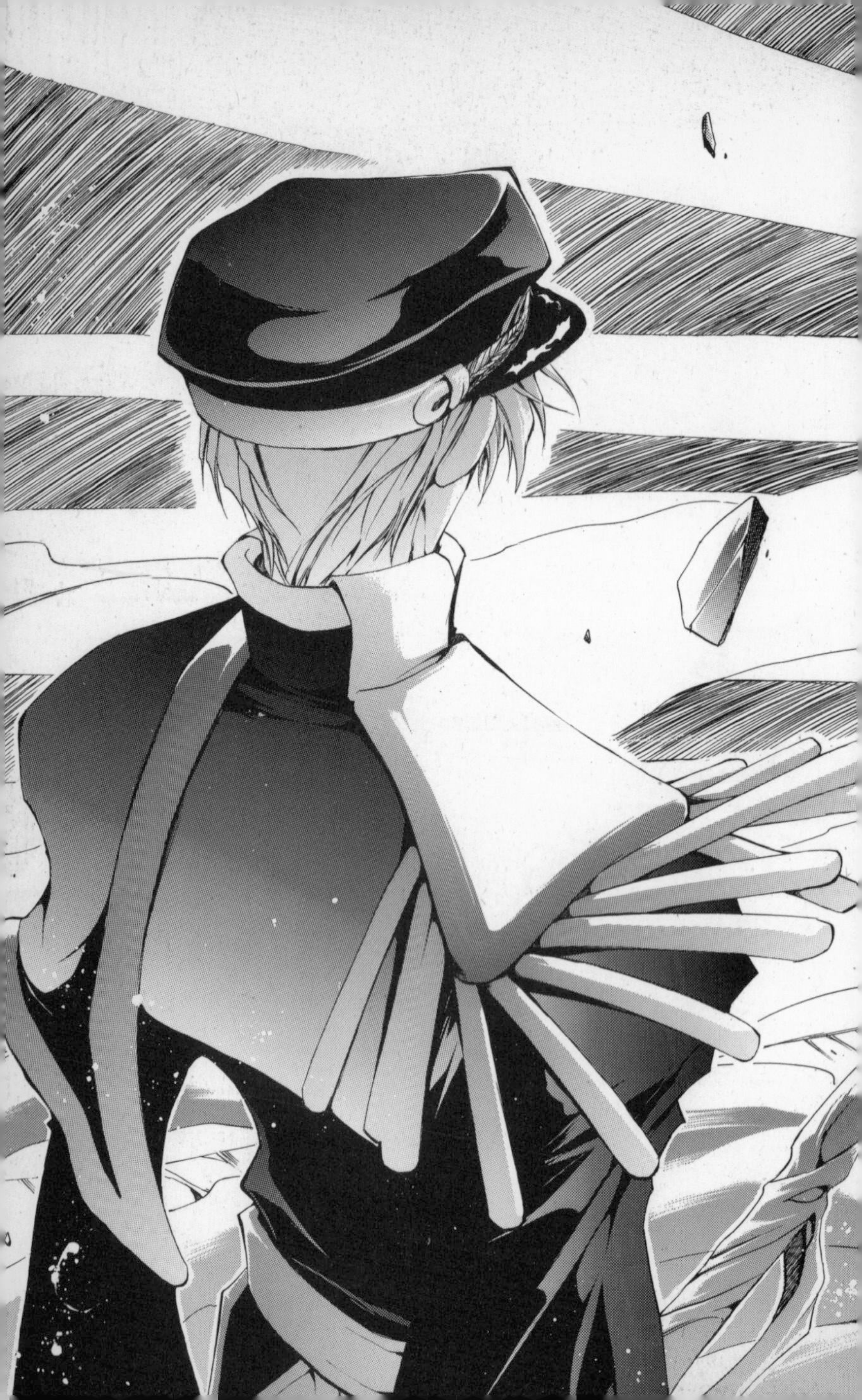

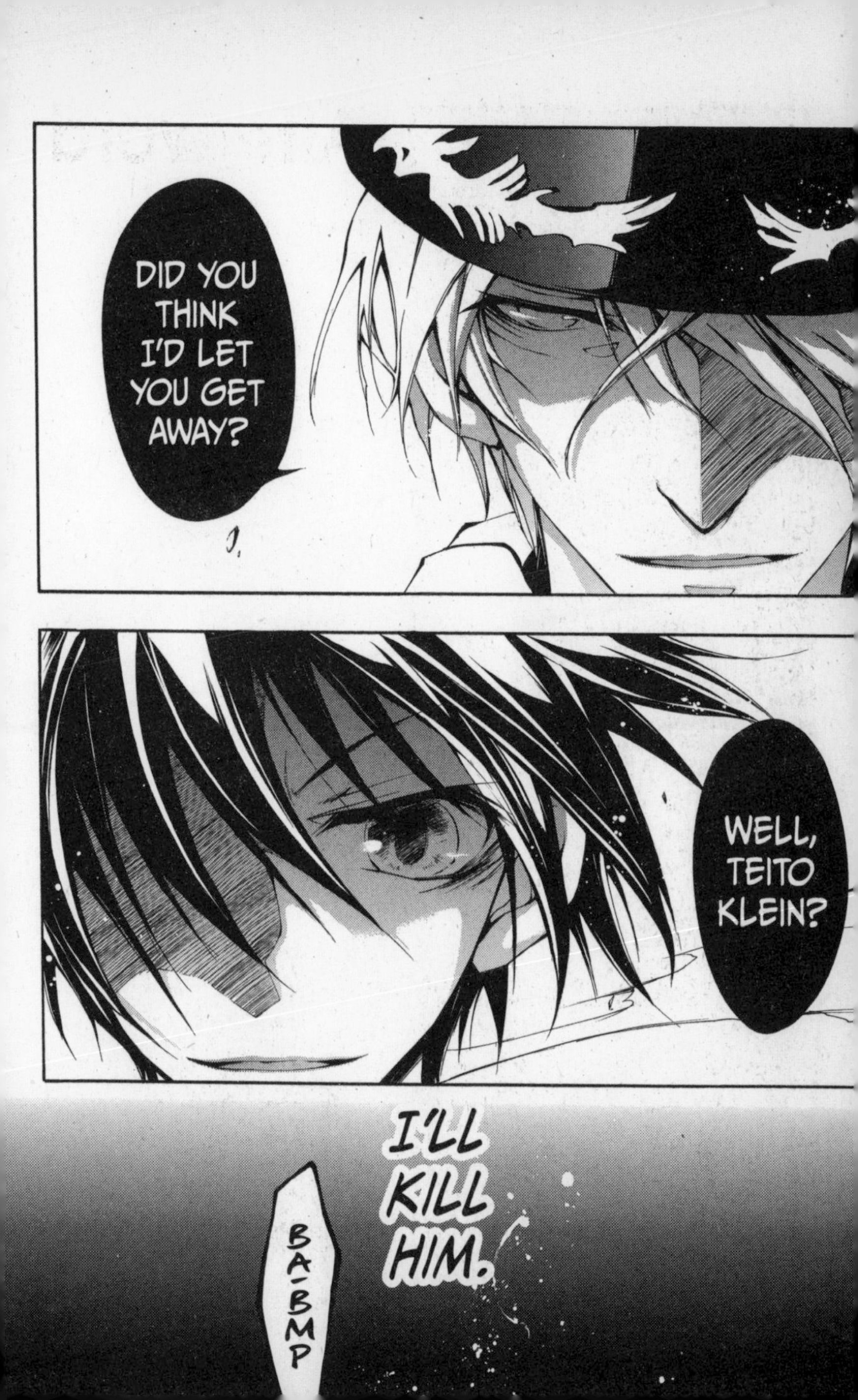
DID YOU THINK I'D LET YOU GET AWAY?
WELL, TEITO KLEIN?
I'LL KILL HIM.
BA-BMP

Afterword

Thanks to everyone, volume 4 is out!

Thank you for picking it up (*deep bow*).

The church arc is reaching its climax, and starting next volume the story will move into its middle stage.

Please continue to join Teito and the gang on their new journey.♥

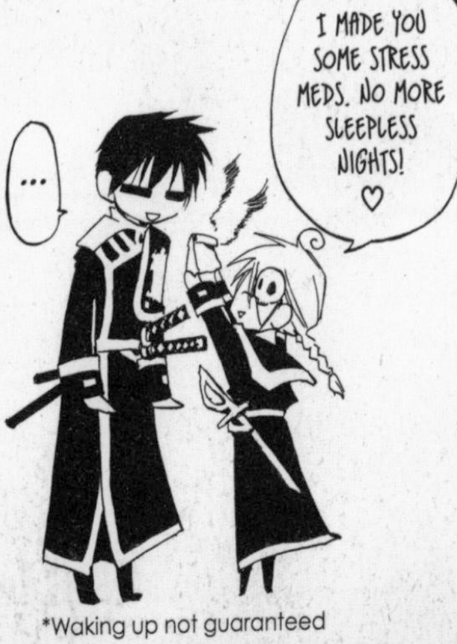

I MADE YOU SOME STRESS MEDS. NO MORE SLEEPLESS NIGHTS! ♡
...

*Waking up not guaranteed

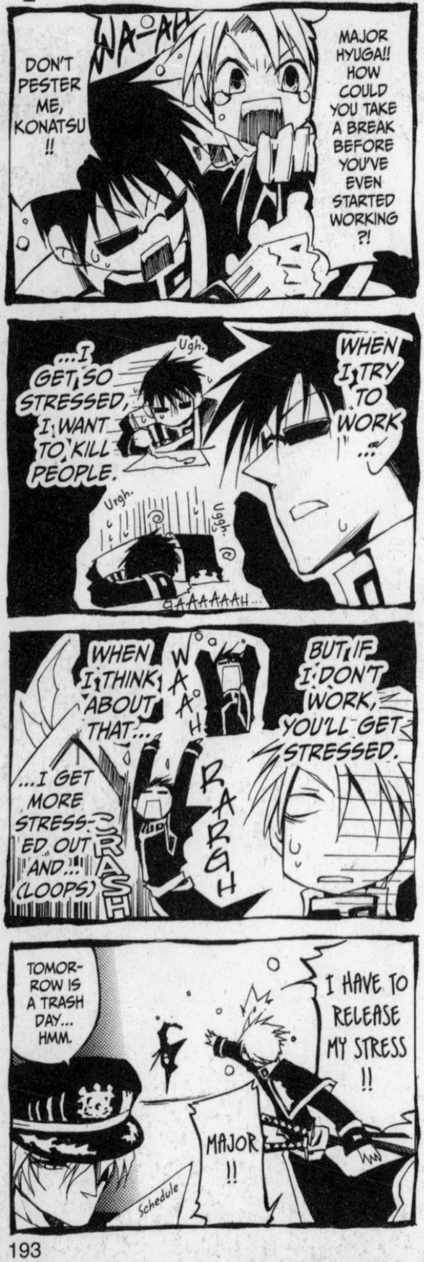

1
MAJOR HYUGA!! HOW COULD YOU TAKE A BREAK BEFORE YOU'VE EVEN STARTED WORKING?!
WA-AH
DON'T PESTER ME, KONATSU!!
WHEN I TRY TO WORK...
Ugh.
...I GET SO STRESSED, I WANT TO KILL PEOPLE.
Urgh.
Uggh.
GAAAAAAH...
BUT IF I DON'T WORK, YOU'LL GET STRESSED.
WHEN I THINK ABOUT THAT...
WAAAH
RARGH
...I GET MORE STRESS-ED OUT AND... (LOOPS)
CRASH
I HAVE TO RELEASE MY STRESS!!
MAJOR!!
TOMORROW IS A TRASH DAY... HMM.
Schedule

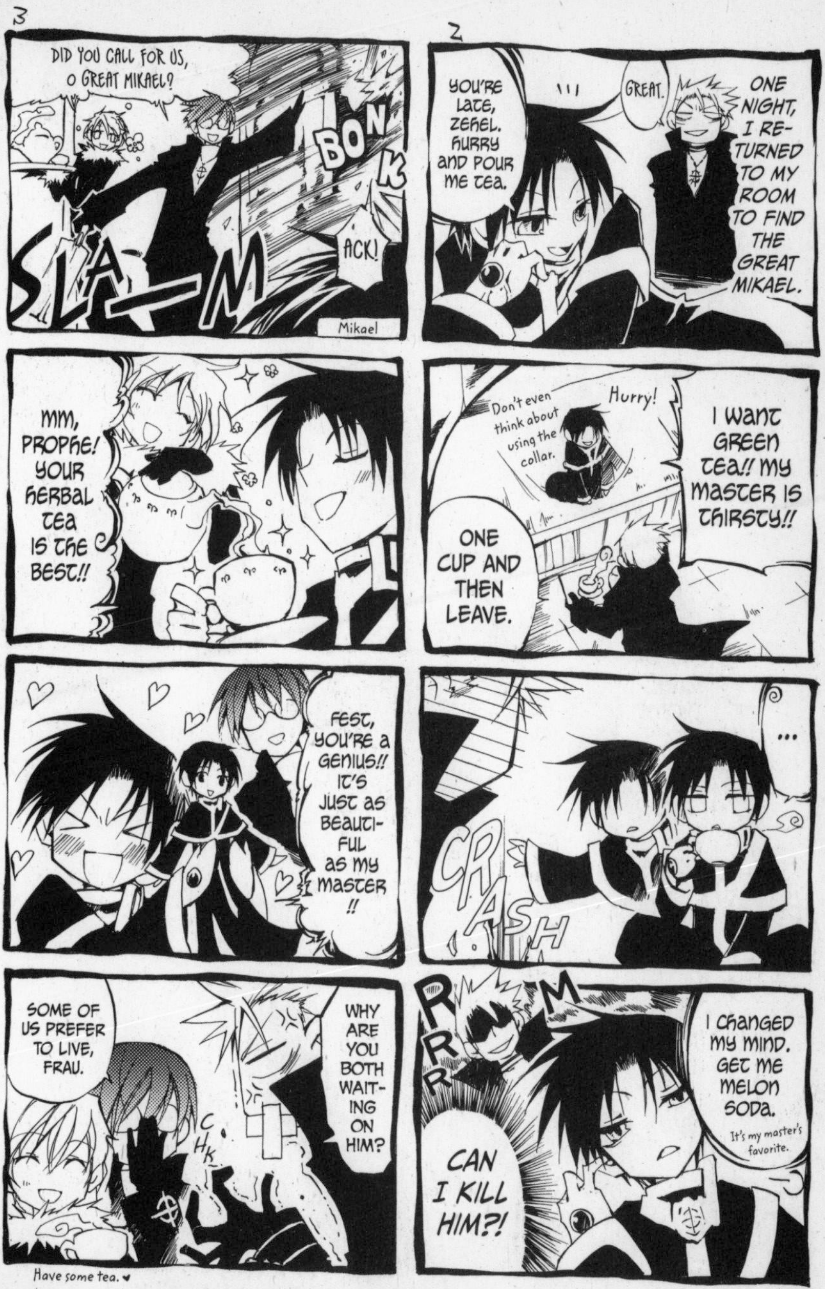
2
ONE NIGHT, I RETURNED TO MY ROOM TO FIND THE GREAT MIKAEL.
GREAT.
YOU'RE LATE, ZEHEL. HURRY AND POUR ME TEA.
I WANT GREEN TEA!! MY MASTER IS THIRSTY!!
Hurry!
Don't even think about using the collar.
ONE CUP AND THEN LEAVE.
...
CRASH
I CHANGED MY MIND. GET ME MELON SODA.
It's my master's favorite.
RRRM
CAN I KILL HIM?!
3
DID YOU CALL FOR US, O GREAT MIKAEL?
BONK
ACK!
SLA—M
Mikael
MM, PROPHE! YOUR HERBAL TEA IS THE BEST!!
FEST, YOU'RE A GENIUS!! IT'S JUST AS BEAUTIFUL AS MY MASTER!!
WHY ARE YOU BOTH WAITING ON HIM?
SOME OF US PREFER TO LIVE, FRAU.
CHK
Have some tea.♥

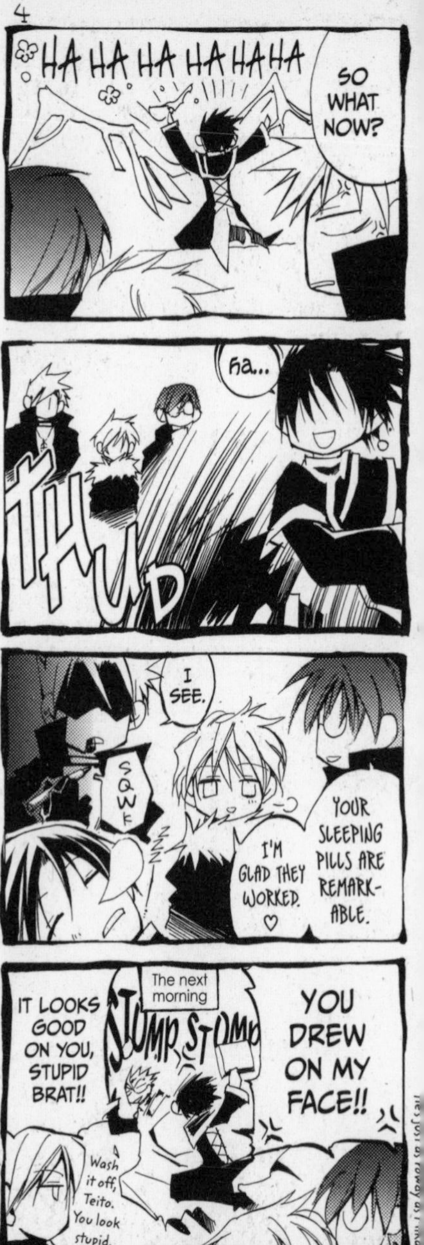
4
HA HA HA HA HA HA HA
SO WHAT NOW?
ha...
THUD
I SEE.
SQWK
YOUR SLEEPING PILLS ARE REMARKABLE.
I'M GLAD THEY WORKED. ♡
ZZZ
The next morning
YOU DREW ON MY FACE!!
STUMP STOMP
IT LOOKS GOOD ON YOU, STUPID BRAT!!
Wash it off, Teito. You look stupid.
↑ Scribbles on his face
He's just as rowdy as I made...

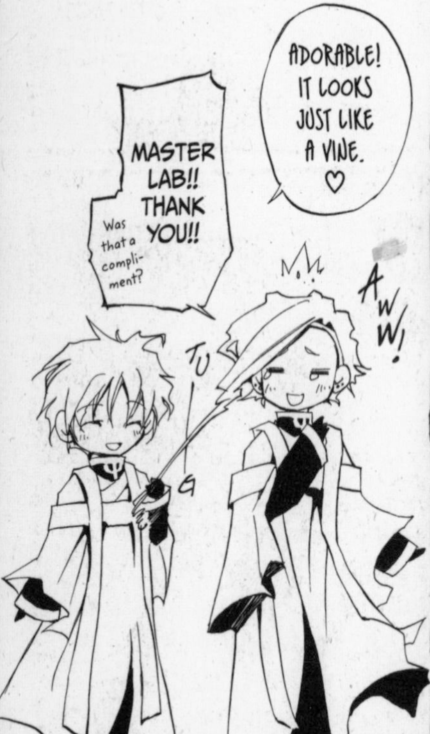
ADORABLE! IT LOOKS JUST LIKE A VINE. ♡
MASTER LAB!! THANK YOU!!
Was that a compliment?
AWW!
TUG

Thank you very much! ♪ Amemiya & Ichihara April 2007

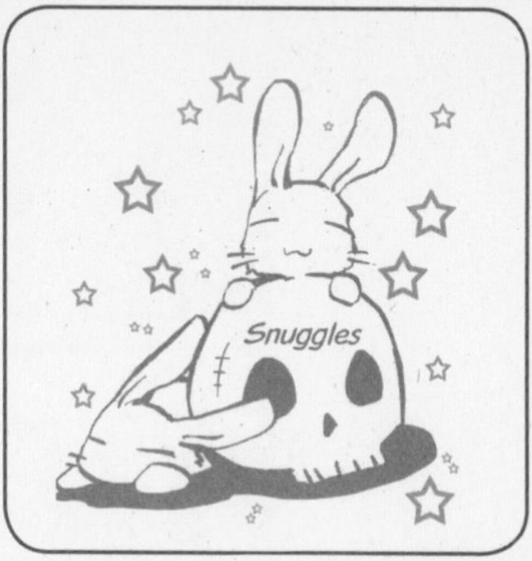
Snuggles

We keep flowers in our workspace to relax and comfort us. The flowers seem to wilt faster when we're having a hard time. According to a friend, plants absorb people's negative energy, which causes them to wilt. Oh my gosh! Thank you, flowers!

—Yuki Amemiya & Yukino Ichihara, 2007

Yuki Amemiya was born in Miyagi, Japan, on March 25. Yukino Ichihara was born in Fukushima, Japan, on November 24. Together they write and illustrate *07-Ghost*, the duo's first series. Since its debut in 2005, *07-Ghost* has been translated into a dozen languages, and in 2009 it was adapted into a TV anime series.

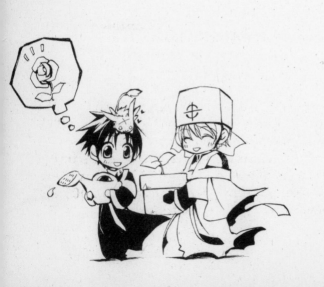

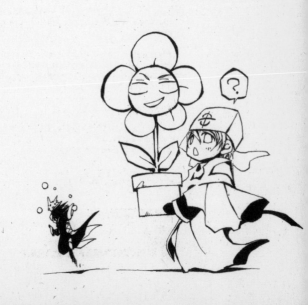

07-GHOST

Volume 4

STORY AND ART BY
YUKI AMEMIYA and
YUKINO ICHIHARA

Translation/Satsuki Yamashita
Touch-up Art & Lettering/Vanessa Satone
Design/Shawn Carrico
Editor/Hope Donovan

07-GHOST © 2007
by Yuki Amemiya/Yukino Ichihara
All rights reserved.
Original Japanese edition published by
ICHIJINSHA, INC., Tokyo.
English translation rights arranged with
ICHIJINSHA, INC.

Printed in Canada

Published by VIZ Media, LLC
P.O. Box 77010
San Francisco, CA 94107

10 9 8 7 6 5 4 3 2 1
First printing, May 2013

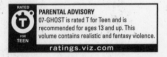

www.viz.com

Hey! You're Reading in the Wrong Direction!

This is the end of this graphic novel!

To properly enjoy this VIZ graphic novel, please turn it around and begin reading from right to left. Unlike English, Japanese is read right to left, so Japanese comics are read in reverse order from the way English comics are typically read.

This book has been printed in the original Japanese format in order to preserve the orientation of the original artwork. Have fun with it!

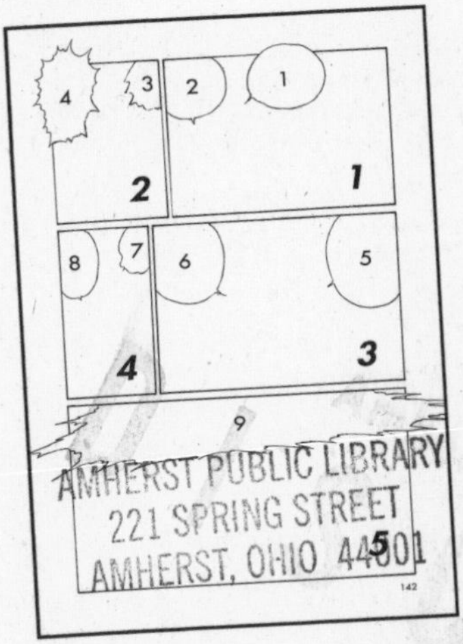
1
2
1
3
4
2
5
6
3
7
8
4
9
5
142

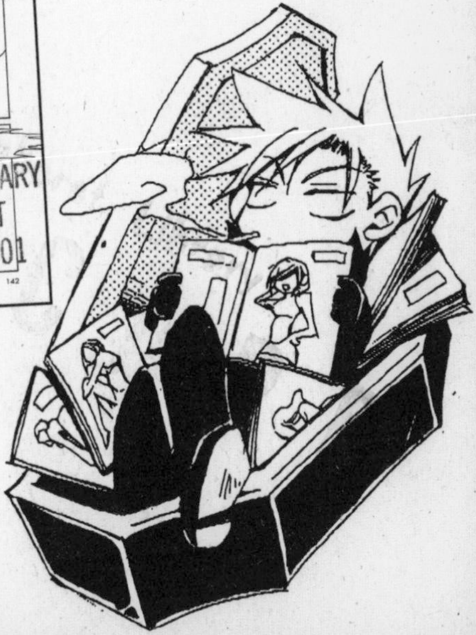

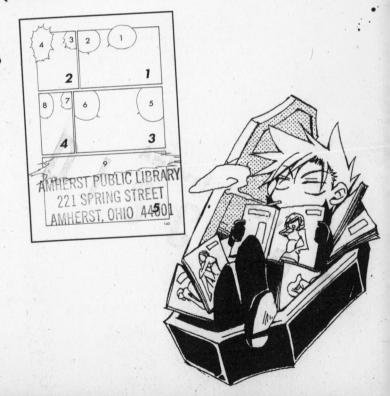